EDGE OF GLORY

The Inside Story of the Quest for Figure Skating's Olympic Gold Medals

CHRISTINE BRENNAN

A LISA DREW BOOK
SCRIBNER

A LISA DREW BOOK/SCRIBNER
1230 Avenue of the Americas
New York, NY 10020

Set in Sabon
Designed by Jennifer Dossin
and Colin Joh

Manufactured in the United States of America

1 2 3 4 5 6 7 8 9 10

Library of Congress Cataloging-in-Publication Data
Brennan, Christine.
Edge of glory : the inside story of the quest for figure
skating's Olympic gold medals / Christine Brennan.
p.   cm.
"A Lisa Drew Book"
Includes index.
1. Skating—Tournaments. 2. Skaters. 3. Winter Olympics. I. Title.
GV850.5.B74   1998
796.91'2—dc21   98-9519
CIP

ISBN 0-684-84128-2

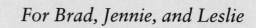

For Brad, Jennie, and Leslie

Contents

Prologue

SEVEN MINUTES

Seven minutes on the ice.

Give or take a few seconds, that's all a figure skater gets at the Olympic Games. After ten or fifteen years of training, after giving up school and families and any semblance of normalcy, it's all over in seven minutes.

"The test of life," Russian skater Ilia Kulik calls it.

Seven minutes to forever change the course of a life.

Or seven minutes for a dream to turn into a nightmare.

They came to figure skating for all the right reasons. Michelle Kwan fell in love with skating because she was thrilled with the sensation of flying. Tara Lipinski found the sport because she wanted to jump all day. Todd Eldredge loved competing in front of a crowd. Elvis Stojko was lured by the thrill of being on his own on the ice. Tonia Kwiatkowski came to the rink because it was "a place of freedom, where the wind was in your face and no one could bother you."

As they began to grow up in the sport, they found out there was more to figure skating than they ever could have realized. Behind its grace and beauty, figure skating was ruthless. It demanded much of its future stars. As children, Kwan, Lipinski, and Eldredge left home to find better coaches. Some skaters' lives became so one-dimensional that their tutors were the only people they knew who were not involved in the sport. Their parents risked the family's financial security to pay the skating bills, which reached $50,000 a year.

As some families slowly went broke, others encouraged their thirteen-year-olds to sign with agents. When the Tonya Harding–Nancy Kerrigan episode of 1994 turned one night of Olympic women's skating into the sixth-highest-rated television program in U.S. history, TV executives, promoters, and advertisers wanted more. Amateurs became millionaires before ever qualifying for the Olympic Games. Long gone were the days of Peggy Fleming and Dorothy Hamill, when no one made a cent before winning an Olympic gold medal.

With the money came pressure—and relentless physical demands. Triple jumps were in vogue; quadruples, even, for the men. Ever-younger girls and boys were forcing their developing bodies to the brink of serious injury. Teenagers were expendable. Retirement could come before high school graduation. When one skater quit, another little jumper quickly took the ice, and the sport moved on.

But even before 1994, figure skating had been an unforgiving sport. Skaters perform what amounts to a high-wire act. When a skater takes off for a jump, he or she might be the Olympic gold medal favorite. But, on the way down, if the skater slips off the edge of his or her skate—just a quarter-inch blade of steel—and falls, the gold medal most likely will go to someone else.

No sport has a more recognizable and final moment of decision. Skaters get no second serve, no third strike, no fourth down.

And even if they skate the best they ever have, they can lose. Skaters do not control the outcome of the competition. That's up to the nine international judges—most from other countries, many who speak a different language.

It's enough to drive a skater, a family, and a coach absolutely crazy.

So, after all that, why do skaters stay in the sport?

Throughout the year leading to the 1998 Winter Olympic Games in Nagano, Japan, when asked if winning the Olympic gold medal meant more to them than anything else, every top skater from around the world answered by saying, first of all, they wanted to skate well at the Olympics.

If they accomplished that goal, then yes, they said, they hoped it would be good enough to win the gold medal.

It turned out that the reason they stayed with the sport was the very same reason they originally came to it. Skating was about flying, about feeling the wind in their faces, about interpreting beautiful music, about skimming across the frictionless ice below their feet.

Winning was wonderful. But to thrive in figure skating, athletes had to dig deeper. They had to find pleasure in what they did, not in where they finished. Their dreams were simple: They wanted to skate the best they ever had at the most important time of their lives.

At the Olympic Games. For seven minutes.

The Lineup

Nicole Bobek, 1995 U.S. national champion and world bronze medalist known for her show-stopping talent, getting injured, and moving from coach to coach.

Surya Bonaly, three-time world silver medalist from France, a controversial jumper trying to ward off injury and her federation to reach her third Olympics.

Maria Butyrskaia, the grande dame of Russian women's skating; known for her exotic costumes and inability to break into the medals at the world championships.

Philippe Candeloro, the 1994 Olympic bronze medalist, a showman who can play "The Godfather" or "Napoleon" with equal aplomb.

Lu Chen, lyrical 1995 world champion who had a disastrous 1997 season because of a nagging foot injury and financial conflicts with the Chinese federation.

Scott Davis, two-time U.S. champion who has battled vertigo and a lack of competitive fire in a curious, up-and-down career.

Todd Eldredge, five-time U.S. champion and 1996 world champion, who has hoped his reliable, steady style would overcome the raw jumping talent of his opponents.

Vanessa Gusmeroli, 1997 world bronze medalist from the French Alps, a championship water-skier who now prefers performing when the water is frozen.

Laetitia Hubert, known as "The Human Zamboni" for falling at least five times—"or maybe it was six or seven," she said—at the 1992 Olympic Games; she upset Tara Lipinski in the autumn of 1997 in her native France.

Ilia Kulik, 1996 world silver medalist from Russia who has it all: boyish charm, balletic flair, and enviable jumping ability.

Michelle Kwan, 1996 U.S. and world champion, suffered through three consecutive losses in 1997, but was still the darling of the U.S. skating community, recapturing the national title in 1998.

Tonia Kwiatkowski, 1996 U.S. national silver medalist, a college graduate with Olympic dreams who watched her sport being taken over by teenagers.

Tara Lipinski, surprising 1997 U.S. and world champion, the youngest ever; a tiny spinning and jumping machine who is known as one of the great perfectionists in her sport.

Evgeni Plushenko, gangly world junior champion from Russia, who, at fifteen, was the up-and-coming skater in Coach Alexei Mishin's St. Petersburg rink.

Irina Slutskaia, 1996 world bronze medalist from Russia, who battled a changing body to try to stay near the top of her sport.

Elvis Stojko, three-time world champion from Canada, the greatest jumper in the history of men's figure skating, and one of the sport's most intense competitors.

Tanja Szewczenko, stunning 1994 world bronze medalist from Germany, nearly went broke after missing almost two years of skating with a foot injury, then two viruses, before a triumphant return in the autumn of 1997.

Alexei Urmanov, 1994 Olympic gold medalist from Russia in the gloves and flashy outfits, still searching for the respect of his peers as he tried to overcome a serious groin injury.

Michael Weiss, 1997 and 1998 U.S. national silver medalist, who became the first American to land a quad, then had it taken away by instant replay.

Alexei Yagudin, 1997 world bronze medalist, another promising Russian teenager trained by Alexei Mishin, Urmanov's coach in St. Petersburg.

Elena Berezhnaia and **Anton Sikharulidze,** Russian coach Tamara Moskvina's young pair who came together after Berezhnaia was hit in the head by a former partner's skate.

Marina Eltsova and **Andrei Bushkov,** conservative 1996 world champions from Russia, they train in the same rink as their rivals.

Kyoko Ina and **Jason Dungjen,** perennial understudies who became 1997 and 1998 U.S. champions; strong jumpers and "business partners" in a discipline where some of the participants are in love.

Oksana Kazakova and **Artur Dmitriev,** innovative Russian pair teamed together by Tamara Moskvina after Dmitriev won the 1992 Olympic gold medal and 1994 Olympic silver medal with another partner.

Jenni Meno and **Todd Sand,** husband-and-wife team with three U.S. titles, but plagued by injuries and miscues in 1997.

Mandy Woetzel and **Ingo Steuer,** Germans who bided their time to finally win a world title in 1997 after a jarring fall at the 1994 Olympic Games.

PART I

February 1997

NATIONALS

A Deer Caught in the
Headlights

"Oh my God! I'm on the ice! What am I doing down here?"

Seventy seconds into her long program at the U.S. national championships, it happened. Michelle Kwan was sprawled on the light blue ice, sliding momentarily out of control, having slipped off the edge of her skate blade after landing an extremely easy jump. This was not supposed to happen to Michelle Kwan. Not at the national championships. Not during what was certain to be her dazzling four-minute coronation as America's next great ice princess.

"I'm lying on the ice! What am I doing on the ice? I'm not supposed to be on the ice. What's happening to me? Get back up. Hurry. Hurry!"

It had been a year since Michelle Kwan, the reigning world and national champion, had fallen in a skating competition that mattered. She was invincible, unbeatable, the surest thing in all of figure skating. She was supposed to win nationals, win the world championships, then roll right along and win the 1998 Olympics. It was all set, wasn't it?

Every day at her mountaintop training site in southern California, Michelle Kwan practiced getting up after a bad fall and continuing to skate, as if her run-through that day was, in fact, the long program at nationals. That's what made Kwan so dependable in the big events. She never stopped during practice; her coach, Frank Carroll, told her it was as important to know how to recover from a fall as it was to be able to skate a clean program. Practice every eventuality, he told her, and nothing ever will surprise you when you're all dressed up and the nation is watching.

But even Frank Carroll thought it was unlikely that Kwan would have to prepare for falling at the end of a triple toe loop–double toe loop combination jump. They rarely thought about slipping on a double toe loop, because it was too easy. The triple lutz, triple flip, and triple loop: Those could be trouble. But a triple toe loop–double toe loop was the simplest triple combination of all.

Kwan landed the jump precariously on her right skate blade, but as she took a step and grabbed for the ice with her left skate, it gave way and she went sliding off the edge. Kwan slammed into the ice. It was a silly mistake, like an infielder taking his eye off the ball, or a receiver trying to run before catching a pass. She dashed to her feet, a few yards from Carroll, who was standing beside the boards in Nashville Arena. Carroll's eyes found Michelle's. He saw shock. His heart froze for a beat. Michelle was scared. And there were nearly three minutes left in the performance—with some tough jumps coming right up to meet her.

"What am I going to do?" Kwan frantically said to herself.

Without reaching for her legs as she glided across the ice, she tried to feel them working, to reassure herself they were doing what she had told them to do several hundred times before, from the summer through the fall to this moment in February 1997. Just to know they were working underneath her would let her know she was all right. Muscle memory would get her through this. And she knew the nine judges would understand one silly stumble. She had dominated her sport over the past year and a half; she won nine out of the ten national or international competitions she entered. Her only loss came when she had strep throat and a bad cold and could barely breathe. Michelle Kwan was America's heir to the Olympic crown, everyone's one and only pick to become the sixth American woman to join the most exclusive club in sports, that of the U.S. women who had won the coveted Olympic gold medal in figure skating. Tenley Albright, Carol Heiss, Peggy Fleming, Dorothy Hamill, Kristi Yamaguchi . . . and Michelle Kwan. Who else was there?

She was beloved by the skating community. Brian Boitano said she reminded him of himself. The work ethic, the intensity, the class: She was just like Boitano. And he was the most admired professional in skating. But Boitano wasn't the only one who loved her. Even cynical reporters found her irresistible. They had their reasons. Most skaters barely knew the names of the journalists covering them. Kwan knew their names and their addresses, and even sent them Christmas cards. She signed autographs for every child who walked up to her in a hotel lobby. "Wouldn't you want her to be your daughter?" asked an admiring Dick Button.

Kwan, sixteen, was a nice girl who kept finishing first. Realistically, who else could win the 1997 national title? College graduate Tonia Kwiatkowski, the living, breathing antithesis of skating's youth movement, was just a bit too old and predictable. At twenty-six, she was a lock in the short program, nearly always completing the required elements. She had done that again at these nationals. However, when she skated her long program minutes before Kwan came onto the ice, Kwiatkowski made numerous mistakes. In four short minutes, Kwiatkowski, a world team member in 1996, became an also-ran in 1997.

Nicole Bobek, the blonde bombshell who had been injured and usually did not train hard enough to keep herself together for more than a couple performances in a row, was too far behind to catch Kwan. Bobek, at nineteen, could have been the favorite for the 1997 nationals, and the 1998 Olympic Games, but she was too erratic. She withdrew from the 1996 nationals with a bad ankle, then missed several months of training leading up to the 1997 nationals due to a bad back. After winning the 1995 national title, she had changed coaches twice, and now was on the tenth coach of her peak-and-valley career. Bobek was trying to do the unthinkable at this event: leap from the second-to-last skating group into the top three to make the 1997 world championships. Sixth in the short program, she had improvised, skating a watered-down program with all the artistry a showgirl could muster, then had to hope three people in front of her made enough mistakes to let her sneak into third. After Kwiatkowski's performance, it was possible. But the spot in question for Bobek was third place, not first. Bobek could not win.

And then there was Tara Lipinski, the tiny fourteen-year-old who would skate last. She would close the show. But wasn't she too young? She was a pipsqueak, a rink rat who said she would practice on the ice all day if her coach allowed it. A reporter soon would name her "The Robotic Shrimp" for her uncanny ability to land her tiny jumps no matter how great the pressure or how high the stakes. But she had been fighting her nerves in Nashville. One day earlier, Lipinski had been scared to leave her hotel room for the short program, so she asked her parents if she could call someone who might help her. She wanted to talk to Bela Karolyi, the legendary gymnastics coach she had met through her agent. She had the number for his private line in Houston.

She called and he answered.

"I'm really nervous," Tara said into the phone. "I need help. Could you help me?"

"I've seen you skate," Karolyi replied. "I can see into the future. You will call me and tell me what you did, and it will be great. Now go skate."

Lipinski had been charging hard in the 1996–97 season, and had become a whirling dervish to be reckoned with. But there were some things skating judges would allow, and some they would not. This was the ladies event, not the juniors. Jumping beans were bobbing to the surface fast these days in the wake of the elimination of compulsory school figures, but this fast?

Lipinski had worked on her artistry with one of the masters, Sandra Bezic, who applied the finishing touches that transformed Brian Boitano from cumbersome athlete to graceful Olympic champion in 1988. But even so, there was only so much one could do with a four-foot-nine, seventy-five-pound skater. Lipinski made Kwan look positively ancient.

So as Kwan struggled back on the ice, there could be no doubt about it. The judges would tolerate one fall from her at least. Perhaps two.

But with the triple flip and triple loop approaching, Kwan knew she needed her legs.

She couldn't feel them.

It was as if they were not there.

"Oh no," Kwan muttered.

She was a canoeist heading for white water without a paddle. There was no stopping this. Coming up, out of a back sit spin, was a triple flip. She dreaded the flip. It occupied her thoughts for many seconds as she approached it.

"Don't bend forward," she admonished, knowing that only if she stayed upright, would she land the jump.

She reached back with her right foot to launch herself into the air.

She bent forward.

She stumbled coming back down. Arms flailing, body twirling, she reached for the ice with her left palm, then her right fingertips. The cold surged into her hands. Twenty-five seconds after the first fall, Kwan again was touching the ice.

One fall usually was Kwan's quota for an entire skating season. Now there had been two in less than half a minute. Once the mistakes started happening, she couldn't get them to stop. On a Saturday night in Tennessee, in front of a capacity crowd of 16,000 in the arena and millions more at home watching on live television, Michelle Kwan, the calm skating machine, was gone. A panicky teenager was skating in her place.

And the jumps kept coming. Next up, the tricky triple loop.

The triple loop can be difficult on good days, a jump that isn't launched with the help of a toe pick, but instead pops up off the back outside edge of the skate blade. You cross your feet and glide in and wait until you feel your least pessimistic, and then you propel yourself into the air for three revolutions, after which time you see if you're still standing.

"Oh no!"

Kwan was down again. It was an ugly fall, a jump that went sideways from the moment she took off, and ended with her sprawled on the ice, actually sitting for a moment, directly in front of the judges.

"What am I doing?" The voice inside her head was screaming. "Somebody hit me!"

Near the midpoint of a four-minute long program, the music usually softens and the skater slows down, easing into what is known, logically enough, as "the slow part." About a minute long, give or take a few seconds, it allows the skater to catch her breath and settle down before picking up the faster pace once again to the conclusion. Kwan's triple loop came in the middle of the slow part. She was supposed to have time to get ready for it, land the jump, then rest again for the next jump. But Kwan had lost track of her strategy. She was simply trying to survive.

When she pulled herself up after the triple loop and carried on to the soft strains of an exotic piece of music from Azerbaijan, the audience sighed, then began to applaud. There was a groundswell building for Kwan as she skated. The ice queen had melted before their eyes; a little girl was in trouble. They tried to revive her.

Kwan, who usually tried to shut out every noise, heard the applause. She let it wash over her.

"Okay, Michelle, wake up! This is a bad nightmare. The fans are trying to wake you up. Come back to life."

Kwan's next jump was a double axel. Once as flowing as the finest silk, Kwan's current version of the jump was an adventure. Perplexed about this development earlier in the season, Kwan had stopped former world champion Yuka Sato at a competition to ask her a question.

"Yuka, what are you thinking of as you go into the double axel?"

Sato pondered the question for a moment.

"Nothing," she replied.

"Okay," Kwan chirped. "I'll try that."

Kwan threw herself into the double axel. Somehow, she reined it in.

Then came the lutz, skating jargon for the triple lutz. There was no way this was going to come off well, Kwan knew. Two days earlier, in her second practice session in Nashville after flying in from California the night before, she had missed seven of nine of them. After using a gliding, long-line approach to the triple lutz for several seasons, she and Carroll changed her entry into the jump, making it shorter and quicker, shifting her weight from her right foot to her left and back to her right toe pick, giving her less time to think about it. The lutz scared Kwan most of all, and, in her inexorable procession of jumps, it was coming next.

She creeped toward it, tentatively, without the speed or force she knew was necessary to pull off the most difficult jump any of the women do. Kwan checked out in the air. She stopped spinning and came back to the ice early.

A double.

The unraveling was complete. Kwan was a skater undone. She had made four mistakes in two and a half minutes. She landed the two easiest triples, a salchow and a toe loop, in her program's final sixteen seconds. Her music blared its last, stunning beat, and as it gave out, so, too, did its skater.

"What did I do?" she asked herself breathlessly, hitting herself in the head with her hands, then touching both palms to her cheeks in dismay. "Why did I get scared?"

Carroll put his arm around Kwan as her scores, a low of 5.3 to nothing higher than 5.7 technically (on a 6.0 scale), jumped off the TV screen in front of them. They were sitting in "Kiss and Cry," the area where the skaters join their coaches, see their scores, and then kiss, cry, or both.

"You're all right," Carroll said softly. "You can't be perfect all the time."

Michelle had been holding back tears for several minutes, but she could do it no more. She began crying. ABC Sports wanted an interview. Not now, Carroll said. Give her some time.

Kwan went on TV a few minutes later, and quietly said she had panicked. There was no other answer. This was a total breakdown. And to think, just weeks earlier, she had watched a procession of newspaper sportswriters traipse to her door to interview her about her impending coronation at the national championships. She had told them what they wanted to hear, that being a skater was so much fun, she might skate forever. Laughing with TV commentators at a pro-am event in Tokyo in January, she had talked not just about the 1998 Olympic Games, but the 2002 Games.

And those in 2006 as well.

"Why not?" she said. "I'll only be twenty-five!"

Now, six weeks later, skating had turned into a nightmare. With just one tiny skater left, Kwan knew she was in big trouble. Even in her moment of complete collapse, she could find enough logic to realize that she did not deserve to win.

Who ever thought, she asked herself, that she would have been the one to panic? What was happening to her?

Her father had made a deal with a different skate boot company that season, and she had never grown comfortable with the new skates. Was that it?

Her body was beginning its inevitable changes. She was five-foot-two and 103 pounds, nearly 10 pounds heavier than two years earlier. Her bustline had begun to develop, as had her hips. Her center of gravity had changed. She was going through puberty on national television. Was that it?

She had been national champion and world champion for a year then, and even though she told herself to act like she was "the hunter, not the hunted," she couldn't make herself believe it. She had been skating like she was trying to protect her title, not win it again. Was that it?

Still wearing her skates, Michelle Kwan clomped down the hallway toward the locker room and cried some more.

As Kwan's scores rang out over the public-address system in the arena, the tiny skater wearing delicate white lace glided in circles on the ice, killing time. She was eager to start jumping. That was Tara Lipinski's way; the kid loved to jump. She wheeled back to the boards, still waiting for her turn, and came close to her coach, Richard Callaghan, who was standing where Frank Carroll had just been.

Callaghan tapped his seventy-five-pound jumping bean on the back as she sped away toward the middle of the ice to begin her program.

"Smile!" he reminded her.

Tara needed to remember the little things, like smiling. The jumping, that came naturally.

Callaghan and choreographer Sandra Bezic had made big gains with Tara in the year since she had come to train at the Detroit Skating Club. Tara, an only child, had tried out several coaches after her mother and her former coach had a screaming match at the world junior championships in Australia in 1995. That story quickly made the rounds in skating; everything involving little Tara was fast becoming big news. Love her or hate her, skating people couldn't stop gossiping about her. Tara and her mother settled in quickly with Callaghan (while Tara's father, an oil company executive, stayed behind at the family home in Houston), and even though Tara didn't grow much bigger, they made her look a bit older. First, the hair went up into a bun, just as Michelle Kwan's had the year before. Kwan jumped from fourth to first in the world that year. While it was true that Kwan had become a more graceful skater and a surer jumper during that time, the mature hairdo certainly hadn't hurt her in the eyes of the judges.

Even before she changed her hair, Tara had done some leaping of her own, from second in the country in juniors in 1995 to third in the seniors (Olympic division) in 1996. She went to the world championships in Edmonton, fell twice in her short program, skated perfectly to a standing ovation in the long program and finished fifteenth. It was a good beginning. But Tara, her parents, and Callaghan wanted more.

In addition to making her look older, they put Tara in ballet classes. They gave her grand soundtracks from *Little Women, Sense and Sensibility,* and *Much Ado About Nothing* to buttress her skating. They told her to extend her arms, to reach for the audience. She had been coltish. By Nashville, the awkwardness was gone, and she almost looked leggy. That was a feat; four-nine, no bigger than the flower girls who collected the gifts her fans threw on the ice . . . and leggy.

But a baby molar threatened the grand plan. Tara had lost a baby tooth the week before nationals, and Jo-Ann Barnas, the skating writer for the *Detroit Free Press,* had reported it as a note in her coverage from Nashville. Callaghan wasn't happy about that; he was worried that the story would remind the judges how young Tara really was. Frank Carroll was lucky with Kwan; he had a sixteen-year-old who could, with the right makeup and hairstyle, look twenty-one. Richard Callaghan knew he had a fourteen-year-old who looked ten. He needed everything to fall just right to pull this off. And newspaper dispatches about the tooth fairy visiting the Lipinski condominium were not going to help him.

It was no secret Tara didn't have the presence Michelle did on the ice, but after Kwan dissolved in her long program, presence didn't matter. If Tara landed her jumps, seven triples in all, she would win. And there was no reason to think she wouldn't. The child was a machine, having to be told by Callaghan back in Detroit to stop her incessant practicing of the same jump for fear that she might burrow a hole into the ice. Or, even worse, risk an injury that could keep her out for months. Jumping was her obsession; there was no one more meticulous a perfectionist in the sport than young Tara. Her mother and her former coach had even grown scared watching Tara make mistakes on a particular triple jump over and over on a certain day; her mother called them her daughter's "frenzies," and they could be devastating.

Sometimes, these "frenzies" would lead Tara and her mother to dash out of one of the rinks at the University of Delaware, her old training site, and into the parking lot, where they got into their van and left for a few minutes to regroup emotionally before going back to the ice.

Those parking lot scenes seemed far away as Tara took the ice in Nashville. Skating like a spinning top, hurtling into tiny jumps, blasting a double axel here, a triple lutz there, Lipinski didn't flinch. She landed the first triple loop–triple loop combination ever by a woman at nationals; what Kwan had such trouble with once, Lipinski blithely uncorked twice.

By the time her music reached its delightful conclusion, the crowd that had been in shock for Kwan was on its feet, roaring for Lipinski.

"Good grief," gushed Dick Button, ABC's longtime skating commentator. "What have we wrought on the world? Oh my. Oh my. Oh my. Oh my!"

"Oh, Tara," Callaghan said, grabbing her close to him as she stepped off the ice.

"Oh gosh," Tara panted, unable to catch her breath. "I'm so happy."

Her marks popped up, 5.8s and 5.9s across the board.

Lipinski squealed.

"Oh my God!"

Tara Lipinski was the winner, becoming the youngest U.S. ladies champion ever. Michelle Kwan dropped to second and Nicole Bobek leaped into third place to qualify for the final U.S. spot at the world championships. The only college graduate of the bunch, veteran Tonia Kwiatkowski, finished a devastating sixth.

Tara's skates barely scraped the floor as she sat in front of the television cameras, tossed her head back, and began laughing.

It was Saturday, February 15, 1997. Tara Lipinski was America's new ice princess; Michelle Kwan, its fallen champ. In exactly one year and three days, February 18, 1998, the ladies short program at the Olympic Games would be held at the pristine new White Ring arena in Nagano, Japan.

In White Ring on the day Tara beat Michelle half a world away, a man climbed onto the zamboni and drove the machine across the perfect white ice, smoothing it out, leaving it wet and glistening.

Six thousand miles and 368 days away, the Olympic ice already was ready and waiting for the teenagers from America.

2

THE QUAD

Nashville, Tennessee, was a strange place to hold the 1997 U.S. national figure skating championships. No one could name even one famous figure skater from Tennessee. Usually, the U.S. Figure Skating Association picked a place of some skating significance to hold its nationals; San Jose, the site the year before, was a logical spot. It was America's skating mecca. From the vast suburban sprawl south of San Francisco came Peggy Fleming, Brian Boitano, Kristi Yamaguchi, Debi Thomas, and Rudy Galindo. If there were such a thing as a fantasy figure skating league, the team from the Bay Area would have been tough to beat.

But there was no skating Dream Team from Nashville, unless Kenny Rogers and Dolly Parton had secretly begun working on side-by-side double axels. No, Nashville couldn't provide any skating history, but it had recently discovered an insatiable appetite for big-time sports, and it had a brand-new arena to unveil, a place so austere that skaters and coaches said it didn't even *feel* like the nationals when they went inside it. Where was the tension? Where was the gossip? The place was too big and impersonal for their tastes.

Nonetheless, figure skating had become so popular around the nation that it didn't matter which side of the Mason-Dixon line the USFSA found itself on; you could hold the nationals in a place where water barely froze, and people would still come. For tension and gossip, it was suggested, try the hotel bar—or wait for the news conferences.

As Todd Eldredge took his place at the long press conference table perched on a riser in front of about a hundred reporters, he sighed. He was glad his week was over. Even though he had just won his fourth national championships in the last eight years, he had not been perfect. On a couple of jumps, he flew sideways through the air, and kept from falling only because he always came to earth like a cat. Feet-first.

Feeling more relieved than victorious, he sat beside his coach, Richard Callaghan, fiddled with the microphone, and smiled shyly. For all his time in the limelight, Eldredge, twenty-five, often appeared sheepish in victory. It was an endearing quality; he was known as one of the most likable guys around. But he certainly was not the life of the party. Perseverance was his forte; Eldredge simply never gave up. He left his Cape Cod home at the age of ten to follow the strict and disciplined Callaghan around the country, and now, fifteen years later, after injuries, illness, and more than their share of setbacks, each man's loyalty to the other once again had been rewarded.

They sat side by side, waiting for the questions to begin.

Sitting next to Eldredge and Callaghan was Michael Weiss, a cocky kid by Eldredge's standards, only twenty years old. He was the runner-up. Weiss had been touted as America's Next Great Boitano, or Eldredge, or Whomever, but he never had delivered the goods—until that week. Attending a press conference was new for him, and for his coach, Audrey Weisiger, who tried to slip to the back of the room, behind the reporters, to allow Michael to have the spotlight all to himself up front. No, no, no, officials said. This was a serious break in figure skating press conference tradition. Unlike almost every other sport on the planet, figure skating all but required its coaches to sit beside their athletes in press conferences. It was as if the skaters needed their security blankets to face the media. Some coaches even answered for their skaters; Tonya Harding's various coaches got good at that. But Weisiger and Weiss were different. Even though she had trained Weiss's older sister and had known Michael since he began showing up to practice in Fairfax, Virginia, in a pair of his sister's skates when he was eight, Weisiger and Weiss did not shadow each other the way Callaghan and Eldredge did. Callaghan and Eldredge were almost always together at competitions; Weisiger and Weiss were not. Nonetheless, Weisiger was shooed up to the table with the others, and dutifully took her place beside Weiss.

At the other end of the table was Dan Hollander, the third-place finisher for the second consecutive year. His longtime coach, Diana Ronayne, sat beside him.

When everyone had settled in and pulled the microphones close to their faces, the press conference began.

"Mike, I just want to confirm, was that the first quad toe in nationals history?"

Weiss smiled and shrugged. "That's what everybody's saying."

"Michael, did you feel like you just had nothing to lose so you went for it today?"

"There was never really any doubt whether I was going to try it or not," Weiss said. "I've been doing it in practice for the last year now. I've been hitting it all week in practice."

Eldredge stared blankly toward the back of the room.

"Michael, what went through your mind when you landed it?"

"Yea!" Weiss broke into a smile. "I don't know," he continued, "I guess I just really wanted to maintain my composure and tell myself, 'Don't blow the rest of the program just because you're excited about one thing.'"

"Michael, you've been on the threshold of this for a couple of years. After the short program, did you wonder whether you'd ever get over that threshold?"

"I just really felt like I didn't want to be sitting on the sidelines again this year," Weiss replied.

Eldredge shifted in his seat. Callaghan stared into space.

"Michael, did you turn your double axel into another triple jump at the end?"

"Yes. If I do two triple-triple combinations, I have a double axel at the end. Since I did a triple salchow–double toe, I did a triple lutz."

"How long have you been practicing the quad and when was the first time you actually did it in practice?"

"I first started working on it two or three years ago," he said. "I attempted one at nationals in 1995 and missed it. Last year, I didn't try it. At some summer competitions this year, I tried it and landed it so that I could be getting ready for nationals this year."

A reporter asked Hollander about his season before someone finally, mercifully, asked Eldredge his first question.

It was about his performance.

"Obviously, it could have been better," he replied, "but to win the fourth title, that's great."

Eldredge's voice was flat.

The next question: "Todd, you're one of the best jumpers in the world. Did you see Michael's quad?"

"Yep."

"Have you ever seen one executed and landed that cleanly and that under control?"

"Yeah. Actually, [Alexei] Urmanov's done it and Elvis [Stojko] has done it a couple times, with triples afterwards. Obviously, it was great today—for Mike to do it."

As he clipped off his words, Eldredge's answer hung in the air. A few reporters snickered nervously. Audrey Weisiger's eyes grew wide. Weiss looked at the table. Weisiger and Weiss were surprised. Normally gracious and understated, Eldredge always had been a friend to Weiss. They thought Eldredge might slap Weiss on the back and congratulate him. They didn't expect him to sound jealous.

The questions kept coming, twenty-six in all, the last to Weiss.

"Was it important for you to be the first U.S. skater to do a quad?"

"Of course it's important to me," Weiss said. "To be the first to do anything is always very flattering. I feel like I've been capable of doing it the last two years and I've been practicing hard, so to actually go out and hit it when it counted definitely is very important to me. Especially to do it at a national championship, where nobody else has done it before."

The skaters stood up and scattered. A cluster of reporters cornered Weiss. He was particularly fascinating. Here was a body-building, hockey-playing, muscle-bound figure skater who was raised in a gym owned by his parents and whose father was a 1964 Olympic gymnast. His family joked that Michael spent most of his childhood upside-down, trying some flip or somersault. Weiss had been rising through the figure skating ranks the past few years, but this was his first foray onto the medal stand at the national senior level. While his overall performance had been superb, it was the quadruple toe loop, the four-revolution jump that no American man or woman had ever landed in a major competition, that was the reason reporters wanted to keep him in the room. Canada's Kurt Browning had been the first to receive credit for landing the quad in 1988. Russians Alexei Urmanov and Ilia Kulik had landed it, and so had Elvis Stojko of Canada. Brian Boitano had tried in the late 1980s, but no American man ever had successfully landed one. Until Weiss on that Saturday afternoon in Nashville.

History was hard to quantify in a subjective sport like skating, but it had just happened. And it was made all the more intriguing by the fact that a vibrant young star—not one of the older veterans—had been the one to pull it off.

Weiss had an agent, Jerry Solomon, Nancy Kerrigan's husband. This was the big breakthrough for which he and Solomon had been waiting. And the U.S. Figure Skating Association, the national governing body for the sport in America, could jump on the bandwagon too. The association was always looking for new, marketable faces. The quad was a good thing for many reasons. There was no telling where it would take all of them.

Little more than two hours later, however, something happened to change history once again. Another press conference was called in that same room. This time, a man hurriedly left his table at a downtown restaurant to dash over to the arena, climb onto the riser, sit at the long table and announce to those same reporters that Michael Weiss's quad wasn't a quad after all.

"I was in the audience watching the event," began Morry Stillwell, a veteran skating judge and president of the U.S. Figure Skating Association. "I did not see anything that looked strange to me. I was as excited as anyone else."

But after a reporter asked to see the videotape of the jump to make sure Weiss had made the required one-footed landing, questions began to surface. Stillwell, eating dinner, got a call and returned to the arena to take a look at the replay from ABC Sports, the network televising the event. When he saw the tape, he realized U.S. skating history was about to be unmade.

"He clearly two-footed the exit," Stillwell said. "The USFSA can't recognize it as a clean quadruple jump, as much as I would love to do it. It was a wonderful maneuver, I compliment Michael altogether for trying it, he kept his form and it was close."

Stillwell couldn't discern the two-footed landing at normal speed on the replay; he needed slow-motion to tell for sure. Only then did he see it clearly; Weiss's landing leg, his right foot, slammed down solidly at the end of the four revolutions of the quadruple toe loop.

But in a split second, as he brought his free foot, the left, around his landing leg and toward the back, the blade scuffed the ice, creating a two-footed landing. It happened so fast that if there had been no slow-motion replay, Stillwell said he was sure that the jump would have gone into the record book.

Ironically, organized figure skating had been adamant in its opposition to trying instant replay as an aid to its judges as they score competitions. And, in fact, the replay decision had no effect on Weiss's marks from the judges or his second-place finish. It only affected the record book. Where history was involved, the USFSA thought it was fine to look at the replay.

This was not a decision that the organization made on its own. It was caught flat-footed by Weiss. It wasn't prepared to have to sign off on a history-making jump. It wasn't ready to check the landing. It never anticipated a problem and never thought through how it would react to such a situation. That's why it took Weiss one second to land the jump and the USFSA three hours to take it away.

The jump was wiped from the book only because reporter Philip Hersh of the *Chicago Tribune* asked to check the replay after hearing that ABC's commentators and rival coaches, including Callaghan, were raising eyebrows about the landing. If Hersh had not gone into the TV truck to watch the replay, the USFSA likely would have done nothing and Weiss would have been credited with the jump.

After a couple hours of celebrating, Weiss was perturbed when reporters caught up to him on his way out of the arena to tell him his quad was gone.

"As far as I know, I landed it," he said. "As far as everyone else saw, I skated great. I don't know whether it's true or not. I don't know what they said."

Weisiger, who had found a seat in the arena to watch another event, also was chagrined.

"They shouldn't have given him credit in the first place if they were going to take it away," she said. "He still did it; he just did it with a slight two-footed landing."

Weisiger wasn't the only one who was upset. Some reporters already had filed stories about the history-making quad, and wire reports already were in print in Europe detailing Weiss's exploit.

"How do you expect to be taken seriously as a sport if you keep having public relations blunders like this," shot out Jere Longman of the *New York Times*.

"You can call it a PR nightmare," Stillwell replied, "but I'd venture to say a lot of people didn't see it."

One of the reasons the USFSA was adamant about reversing the decision so many hours after the jump was the fact that the event—and the jump—had yet to be televised nationwide. ABC taped the event Saturday afternoon to show Sunday afternoon. If the USFSA had said nothing and let the jump stand, it was worried ABC would come back a day later and point out the mistake.

But when Weiss's program was shown Sunday, ABC did no such thing. It did not go out of its way to call attention to the two-footed landing. On the contrary, as Weiss landed and pumped his arms into the air, Dick Button proclaimed, "Very good! I think there was a slight double-footing on the landing."

ABC sidekick Brian Boitano chimed in: "It was two-footed."

"But so what?" Button exclaimed. "Good . . . that's a really positive, positive move."

"Very easily done," Boitano added.

After the performance, ABC ran a slow-motion replay of the quad for its audience.

"There's a slight double-toe landing, but who cares?" Button said.

Unlike a home run in baseball, or a touchdown in football, a jump in figure skating requires narration to help the public understand its importance and meaning. Only a very few skating fans can identify the six jumps—toe loop, salchow, loop, flip, lutz, and axel, in order of difficulty from easiest to hardest—or notice if the landing is two-footed or not. Even the judges have trouble with the nuances. At the 1994 Olympic Games, eventual gold medalist Oksana Baiul badly two-footed her triple lutz in the short program, but at least one judge said she couldn't tell. Had a replay been used, or had the judge been able to see it clearly, the judge and some of her colleagues likely would have placed Baiul lower in the standings. If that had happened, Baiul might not have been able to catch Nancy Kerrigan two nights later in the long program and win the gold medal.

When Button said "So what?" and "Who cares?" on the air, he all but confirmed Weiss's jump as good. If the USFSA had said nothing, Button's call only would have reaffirmed the jump.

There was another reason Button didn't make a big deal about the two-footing. He knows figure skating's history is full of questionable landings. He knows this because he's responsible for at least one of them. Button himself is credited with being the sport's greatest athletic innovator. He is in the skating record book for having landed the sport's first double axel in 1948 and the first triple jump, the triple loop, in 1952. But slow-motion video replays never were available for those jumps.

"My triple loop was clean," Button said. "It's really very hard to cheat a triple loop. But my double axel had a little glitch at the end. It was not two-footed, but there was a fraction of a turn left on the ice."

Button chuckled slightly. Thankfully for him, no one could go to the videotape in 1948.

More recently, Kurt Browning was credited with landing the first quadruple jump nine years before Weiss's attempt. However, after seeing Weiss's jump on television, and hearing it had been disallowed, Browning had an interesting comment for USA Today's Debbie Becker:

"His was actually better than mine."

*   *   *

The quad/no quad controversy was the best thing that ever happened to Michael Weiss. He led the sports section of the *Washington Post* the next day. Most of Washington's television stations greeted him at the gate with camera crews as he arrived home to Dulles Airport Monday morning. The *New York Times* and *Chicago Tribune* prepared stories on the quad, with Weiss as the jump's poster boy.

Weiss knew how to handle the on-again/off-again news. He simply ignored the USFSA's pronouncement, and went on as if he had landed the jump.

"Everybody saw it," Weiss said. "It looked like a great quad. The excitement, exuberance, happiness, and energy it created in the crowd made it well worth it. The crowd was so responsive. Everybody saw me do it. It really doesn't matter what anybody said. It was a great jump for me."

The quadruple toe loop is a magical jump, an extremely difficult maneuver that is nearly impossible for the untrained observer to detect (Was it three revolutions? Was it four?). Most skaters who have tried it find that the height they reach on a quad is the same as a triple, so they have to spin much faster to get four revolutions into the same space as three.

"You have to have great technique and great strength," said Weisiger, Weiss's coach, "and you have to have guts. If you fall, you really smack the ice."

"Every time you add a revolution, it's not like it's just a little step up," Weiss said. "It's, like, eight times as hard to do a quad as it is to do a triple."

With his performance in Nashville, Weiss opened a window to a different side of figure skating, the masculine side that over the years had been overwhelmed by issues ranging from flowing costumes to effeminate men to the tragedy of AIDS. Dozens of skaters, coaches, and choreographers had died from complications related to the disease, including 1972 Olympic gold medalist Ondrej Nepela and 1976 Olympic gold medalist John Curry.

Weiss, skating's five-foot-eight, 160-pound heterosexual hunk, straddled the two worlds of male skating. While he lived on the straight side, and he and his parents made sure everyone knew he was "all boy," he well understood the homosexual side. For three years, his programs had been choreographed by Brian Wright, an openly gay man who walked Weiss through every step and every arm position of his short and long programs, the programs he used to win the silver medal at nationals.

Wright was dying of AIDS.

"Brian has had a lot of influence on me turning the corner in terms of skating more artistically," Weiss told reporters at nationals. "AIDS is something Brian lives with and deals with every day. He's been hanging on for so long already, I'm sure he's very happy with staying alive as long as he has, and so are we."

Weiss cared about Wright. He skated in exhibitions to help him pay his medical bills. He enjoyed the time they spent together on the ice. He loved learning from such a gifted choreographer.

But skating always was a balancing act for Michael Weiss.

Moments after talking tenderly about Wright, Weiss was back answering questions about himself.

"When I skate well," he said, "I don't want to look like a wimp."

There was little danger of that. Weiss wore black pants and tight, bicep-hugging, multicolored T-shirt tops when he skated. His long program that included the quad was strictly tie-dye and Santana. He wanted nothing fancier. He was known to come to a morning practice in the T-shirt in which he had slept. He wore baseball caps to hide his unkempt hair. He sometimes didn't shave. For a world that once had an unwritten rule that all men (and women) wear elaborate costumes to practice at competitions to impress the watching judges, Weiss was a renegade, a breath of fresh air.

There were other things about Weiss that distinguished him from the others. He was a hockey player, having played right wing as recently as two years earlier in a full-contact Capital Beltway league. And he was engaged to be married to his jazz dance teacher, a thirty-year-old blonde divorcée named Lisa Thornton.

When two cynical skating reporters heard Weiss was engaged, each immediately blurted out: "To a woman?"

Yes, they were told.

To a woman.

Going into the 1997 nationals, Weiss was one of the favorites for second place. There was no doubt who would be first. Todd Eldredge—the fisherman's son from Cape Cod, the man who had come back from devastating defeats three times in a row in the early 1990s to resurrect his career—was a lock to win.

But after the two-minute, forty-second short program, worth one-third of the overall score, Weiss was not second, or third, or fourth. He was fifth, behind Eldredge, Damon Allen, Scott Davis, and Dan Hollander. He had put both of his palms down on the ice as he landed his triple axel, the difficult three-and-a-half-revolution jump. Disgusted with himself, Weiss tried to leave the arena before reporters found him, but was spotted by a USFSA official who shepherded him to the waiting journalists.

"The triple axel–triple toe loop is a combination I can do in my sleep," Weiss said. His voice was a monotone. He managed a few more sentences before he slipped out a door and into the night.

"He's just got to get over this thing of not doing it," Weisiger said. Her mind was on the mistakes of previous nationals. Every year he came in with great expectations. And every year he screwed up. Could it be, she wondered, that he never would put it together when it counted?

But Weiss had allies in all the right places. Figure skating judges, the volunteers who ruled the sport, liked him a lot. For several years, they had marked him high, even a bit higher than he deserved, because of his potential. They had to deduct several tenths of a point for his mistakes, but they could prop him up on the second mark, the artistic one. And that they did.

The judges had their reasons. As a youngster, Weiss had performed well on the world stage. He was America's best international hope after Eldredge. He was the kind of skater they wanted to send to the world championships. He won the national junior title in 1993 and the world junior championship in 1994, and, as a fourteen-year-old, finished second in senior men's compulsory school figures in 1991. That meant he was a young man with not only the jumping ability to win the big championships, but the fundamentals to please the sport's purists.

Compulsory school figures, the painstaking tracings of figure eights, were officially eliminated in 1990, but, for old time's sake, a figures competition was held every year at the national championships. Weiss was enough of a throwback that he won the national novice figures title at thirteen and finished second in the top division the next year. This was important to veteran judges worried that the sport was turning into a jumping contest.

But after moving to the senior (Olympic) level at the 1994 nationals, Weiss showed that he also had the unnerving potential to keep making mistakes. He did not skate cleanly at the nationals of 1994, 1995, or 1996. And now he could add 1997 to the list.

Weiss was bitterly disappointed because he had come into the competition so certain that this year would be different. He had had a strong season up to the nationals. He finished third in two of the sport's new grand prix events, one in France, the other in Russia. He was a beneficiary of skating's new world order; because the Olympic, or amateur, division wanted to entice its skaters to not turn professional, it developed a tour of its own, called the Champions Series. Skaters could earn prize money with top-three finishes in series events; by season's end, the top performers accumulated more than $100,000.

This helped Weiss tremendously. Instead of arriving at nationals virtually unknown—as skaters like him did five years earlier—Weiss came in as America's second-ranked competitor. Overall, he ended the fall season ranked eighth in the world.

For Weiss, it was the season of the quad. Prior to 1997, he had been waiting for great things to happen to him. Sometimes, he became rather complacent. But he realized he had it all wrong. He would have to push himself. So, preparing for the 1996–97 season, he and Weisiger put in the quad as the second jump in the long program. (Quads were not allowed in the short program.)

Weisiger, a former national-level skater in the days of Dorothy Hamill, suggested that Weiss enter some minor summer competitions so he could get the feel of being on the ice. Twice, he landed the quad. And with each landing, Weiss gained confidence. They would take his show on the road soon, but Weisiger wanted him to begin to build a backlog of good performances so that when he got nervous, he could tell himself he had done it all before.

Even more important, the word was out. From the summer of 1996, the skating world knew, through phone calls and e-mail and talk at the rink: Weiss was landing his quad.

The morning after the men's short program at the 1997 nationals, Weiss arrived at the rink for a practice session. It was 7 A.M. It was time to focus completely on the long program a day and a half away. But his mind still was on the short program. He was disconsolate.

His father went with him to the rink.

"Michael," Greg Weiss, the ex-Olympian, told his only son, "we're here to skate."

Weiss's head was down.

"Whether you win nationals or not will all be determined by this program, right now, how you skate in this practice," Greg Weiss said.

"You should just rip off this program. Show 'em all, show everyone, that you're not here to be fifth."

As the Weisses talked, Weisiger tried to filter through the advice she was receiving from all her friends—and even some of her rivals—in the coaching ranks.

"Take out the quad," they told her. "Play it safe. He can make the top three without the quad. Top three and he goes to worlds. You want him on that world team, don't you?"

The quad was a risk. It was much more likely he would fall on it than he would successfully land it. All Weiss had to do to make the top three and earn a trip to the world championships was skate cleanly, Weisiger knew. If he did that, the strength of his program (even without the quad) and his classic line and edges would win out. Some of the other men ahead of him probably would fall. And even if they didn't, the judges could place Weiss ahead of them because they liked his skating, because they liked his masculine look, because of his terrific season internationally . . . because they just wanted to.

This was figure skating. Weiss was a favorite of the judges. He had a perfect image for the sport in the late 1990s. If he just stayed on his feet (skating slang for not falling) he would be heading to Lausanne, Switzerland, for the world championships in March.

But Weisiger would have none of this, nor would Greg or Michael Weiss. Taking out the quad was out of the question. Others might play it safe, people like Eldredge, for instance. He had been practicing the quad, but was reluctant to try it for real. Eldredge also knew he didn't need the jump, at least not on the national level, at least not in 1997. But not Weiss, who had been landing the jump in practice since he was eighteen. He hadn't been working on that jump for two years to shelve it when it mattered.

Weisiger and Weiss had had a conversation before they left the rink in Fairfax, Virginia, to travel to Nashville.

"Come hell or high water, this is your program," she said to him. "You're doing the quad."

This philosophy dated to his days as a junior, when she sent him out to compete with all sorts of risky commands.

At the 1994 world junior championships, Weiss was the last to skate in the long program, and both he and Weisiger had seen enough of his competitors to know he didn't have to do much technically to win. It would have been very easy for them to pull back and have him do, say, a triple lutz–double toe loop combination as his toughest move, play it safe, and go home with the gold medal.

But Weisiger told Weiss to do his triple axel–double toe loop. He looked long and hard into her eyes. She nodded her head, as if to say, "You're doing it." They both knew he never had landed the triple axel–double toe loop combination in a competition. They also knew that the one thing that could get in the way of his march to the world junior title was a bad fall on his combination, which might trigger more trouble later in the long program.

But that day Weiss understood. He nodded his head.

"Okay," he said.

He landed the combination cleanly and won the title.

At the '97 nationals, in that early morning practice session the day after his mistake in the short program, Weisiger said it again.

"You're going for broke. If you want to be Olympic champion, you can't ever be conservative. You're not going out there just to stay on your feet. You're going out there to win. You're going to do the quad, and you're going to land it."

"Okay," Weiss said. "Okay."

Nashville's new arena, hosting its first big sports event, attracted 9,392 spectators for the men's long program.

Scott Davis, a two-time national champion and the country's best spinner, had battled vertigo and was mired in a two-year slump. He skated first in the final group, which included all the top skaters after the short program. Davis had become the sport's poignant basket case, a man who was having such trouble he fell flat on his stomach trying to land a triple axel at Skate America the previous autumn. He had left his coach of nine years, Kathy Casey, and struck out on his own, eventually landing in Simsbury, Connecticut, with Ukrainian legend Galina Zmievskaia, the mentor of Olympic gold medalists Viktor Petrenko and Oksana Baiul.

Zmievskaia wasn't certain she wanted Davis when he showed up for a tryout in the spring of 1996.

"I have Viktor, I have Oksana, this is big responsibility," she told Bob Young, executive director of the International Skating Center of Connecticut.

Young watched them work together for a few hours.

"Well?" Young said.

"Bob," Zmievskaia said as she skated over to him, "this is good boy. I love this boy."

At first, Zmievskaia and Davis communicated mostly through hand signals. He became immersed in the old Soviet school of skating.

Unlike some top American coaches, Zmievskaia did not have a dozen pupils, so she began spending hours a day with Davis. They worked on tiny details Davis had barely thought of before, "down to the fingertips," he said. This kind of training worked for Oksana Baiul, who won the Olympic gold medal in 1994 not because of her jumps, but because of her mesmerizing arms and hands.

"You seduce," Zmievskaia said, "with the fingers."

Davis found himself surrounded by the great Russian and Ukrainian skaters in Simsbury, including Ekaterina Gordeeva, the two-time Olympic pairs gold medalist whose husband, Sergei Grinkov, had died the year before. Davis sometimes stopped his practices to watch her glide across the ice, marveling at how, when she skated, he couldn't hear a sound as her blades skimmed the ice. He wanted to skate like that.

But Davis did not get better by osmosis, and he suffered through an uncertain autumn. He dropped behind Eldredge and Weiss in the international standings. And he was beginning to get some worrisome warnings from the judges who came by to watch him—the official USFSA term for the judges' visits is *monitoring*—during his practice sessions. These judges came to Simsbury not out of curiosity, but because they were told by the USFSA to go there. One of the jobs of a top-flight skating judge is to occasionally drop in to watch a skater perform his or her programs. The judge, who never comes by unannounced, tells the skater and the coach what he or she thinks of the programs, which might include a warning that a spin is against that year's rules, or that two jumps are being performed in the same spot on the ice. The monitor also fills out a report that goes back to USFSA headquarters, detailing how the skater is progressing. This is not cheating; it's the way a skater receives feedback, and how the USFSA checks up on skaters prior to sending them to international competitions. It's all within the rules.

Figure skating—in the United States, and around the world—is a closed, tight-knit sport run by a few dozen key people. The judges are the bosses; most started as skaters, then began training to be a judge. Some moved up to a volunteer position running a national federation. Most hold down real jobs and judge on the side. But they all know each other, and they all know and talk to the coaches, who then relate their advice to their skaters. Skating is one big gossip session. There are no secrets. In life, there are the so-called "Six Degrees of Separation," which led to the book tying Hollywood figures to actor Kevin

Bacon. In figure skating, it's more like the "Three Degrees of Scott Hamilton." Everyone in skating has close ties to everyone else, and almost everyone can find a link to Hamilton.

Davis, for example, had been coached by Casey, who also coached Hamilton. But that was a different life for Davis. To the judges who showed up as monitors in Simsbury in 1996, Davis was looking entirely too much like Petrenko and Baiul, the Ukrainians who had taken gold medals from Americans Paul Wylie and Nancy Kerrigan at the 1992 and 1994 Olympic Games.

He was told he was posing in front of the judges rather than skating and spinning in the traditional American style. Cut out the preening, he was warned. At a made-for-TV event in Edmonton called "The Continents Cup," another U.S. judge pulled him aside and suggested he make some changes and skate the way he used to—an entertaining mixture of jumps and spins, including eye contact with the audience rather than the judges.

Davis said he and Zmievskaia heeded the advice and made some alterations—but it was hard to tell. This was an East-West tug-of-war. Judges from the former Eastern bloc were telling their pal Zmievskaia that they liked Davis's long program, skated to the upbeat soundtrack from Once Upon a Time in America. Ominously, the U.S. judges at international events were sending a very different signal. Janet Allen is a highly respected U.S. judge who sided with Brian Boitano at the 1988 Calgary Olympics in a controversial and ultimately wise decision. She certainly wouldn't sabotage an American skater. But at the grand prix stop in Japan, Allen gave Davis horrible marks. Davis made mistakes on most of his jumps in the long program, and she doled out a 4.6 and a 5.0 and placed him ninth. A majority of the other judges had him fifth.

Allen apologized to Davis when they bumped into each other at the post-competition dinner. But she was troubled by his penchant for stopping and posing, and even mentioned something to the referee at the competition in an attempt to explain her low scores.

This should have been a warning, but Davis and Zmievskaia didn't take the hint. Despite what the Americans told them, they listened to Zmievskaia's friends overseas and refused to eliminate most of his posturing.

"Representing the Broadmoor Skating Club in Colorado Springs, Colorado, here is Scott Davis!"

Sticking with his old club, even though he was training two thousand miles away, Davis got off to a fast start, blasting four strong triple jumps in less than two minutes.

But then the invasion of the Russian body snatchers began. Davis made eye contact with the nine judges sitting in a row along one side of the rink. He danced in front of them, looking very much like Petrenko, for *fifteen* seconds. He threw his arm out and nodded at them. There were times he couldn't take his eyes off them.

As his jumps faltered—a triple axel became a single, a triple lutz was turned into a double—he peeked at the judges. He swept by, and he nodded. Seven times in all, he either stopped in front of the judges, or gave them a look.

Meanwhile, his spins suffered. If Davis was known for anything in skating, it was for snapping off the best spins in the land. Todd Eldredge had such respect for Davis's spins that he forced himself to become a better spinner in order to keep up. Davis said his problems with vertigo were over; that could not be an excuse. Yet his spins were not nearly as tight or as lengthy as they once had been. Davis had given away one of his great advantages.

Davis should have known that changing his ways and trying to emulate the old Soviet school of skating never could be a winning strategy at the U.S. national championships. He was not demolished by the judges, but he wasn't warmly received by them either. He received marks of 5.6 and 5.7, predominantly.

After he skated, Davis yanked off his skates and his tuxedo-vest, shirt-and-tie costume in the locker room, put on sweats, and wandered over to a big television in the skaters' lounge. Davis knew his scores did not leave him in good shape with all the other top skaters yet to come. There was too much room for everyone else above marks of 5.6 and 5.7 on a 6.0 scale.

Eldredge was up next.

"I can't watch this," Davis said.

He walked down the long corridor to the empty interview room, where Eldredge and Weiss would end up in an hour, put on his headphones, and listened to rock music, alone.

He missed Eldredge's performance entirely, and while the reigning world champion wasn't as sharp as he had been much of the season, he was good enough. Skating to the soundtrack from *Independence Day,* Eldredge saved the two sideways jumps and doubled another jump. By playing it safe, he was in fine shape. First place was Eldredge's. It was not a contest.

Davis also missed seeing Dan Hollander, a jaunty "Barber of Seville" whose skating was better than Davis's. He moved ahead of Davis as well.

Davis pulled off his headset and wandered back to the lounge with the other skaters and coaches to see where he stood. He was third, on the bubble, with Michael Weiss up next.

"I know Michael's going to do it," Davis told Zmievskaia. "I'm not going to make it."

Weiss was the final skater. Strategically, it wasn't bad to be last. In 1996, skating last, Rudy Galindo brought his hometown crowd in San Jose to its feet with the finest performance of the year in his sport. Weiss hoped for nothing less. He landed a smooth triple lutz to open the program, then traveled down the ice and vaulted himself into the air for the quadruple toe loop. In flight, he spun and spun and spun and spun. Coming back to earth, the blade under his right foot grabbed the ice. Weiss was so certain he landed cleanly when he came down that he flexed his arms, bodybuilder style. Greg Weiss leaped from his seat. Reporters sitting in their seats in the arena looked around.

"Was that a quad?"

A few people nodded. "I think so." Others weren't sure.

They would ask later.

Weiss's only error, a slight one, was to put his hand down upon landing his triple loop, the difficult edge jump that sent Michelle Kwan sprawling in front of the judges when she tried it. The crowd groaned for Weiss. Otherwise, he was solid and strong, landing the only triple axel–triple toe loop combination of the competition. As Carlos Santana's "Abraxas" rolled along, Weiss hit every note, pumped his arms again and drew energy from the roaring crowd. As he spun into the final seconds of his performance, spectators stood and cheered loudly for a skater they hardly knew.

Weiss punched his right hand into the air.

"Yesssss!" he screamed.

Standing by the boards, Weisiger was sobbing. All those years . . . and now Michael was on the world team. She didn't have to wait for the scores. Weiss had taken over the building. He was certain to move into the top three. The standing ovation swelling around her told her all she needed to know.

At that moment, rubbing tears away as fast as her eyes were producing them, Weisiger took a small plastic pony from her purse and tossed it onto the ice. It was a strange thing to do, she knew, but it had been her mission, and she was pleased she remembered to do it.

The boys and girls who gather up the flowers and stuffed animals that are thrown onto the ice picked up the brown and black pony and handed it to Weiss among all the other gifts. Weisiger grabbed it out of the pile as she sat beside Michael in Kiss and Cry, waiting for ABC to come out of its commercial and the judges' scores to pop up.

Weiss looked at the pony.

"Oh no," he said. "You brought it?"

The toy had been known to show up as a prank almost anywhere at Fairfax Ice Arena, where Weisiger worked and Weiss trained. Audrey's daughter Kelly had left it in the coaches' room six years earlier, and when one of the coaches threw it away, another rescued it and began placing it in surprising spots. It showed up in the refrigerator at the rink. It left the rink for a night in the purse of an unsuspecting coach. It even appeared at that coach's wedding reception. In the wedding photo album, the toy is peeking out from the gifts in one shot, and floating with the assistance of helium balloons in another.

This time, the pony made the trip to Nashville so Weisiger could surprise the coaches back in Virginia with the toy's debut on national television.

"Well," said Weiss, still smiling broadly a minute after his performance, "at least wait until after the commercial so you're sure you're on TV."

Weisiger nodded. At the right time, she held the toy high for the camera, prancing it through the air and onto TV screens across the land.

Weiss smiled at his coach, but he really didn't care what she was doing. It was, he thought later, the happiest moment of his skating career. And it was so typical of Weisiger to use their mutual stage to play a practical joke. Weiss figured if the silly pony was there to share the stage with him, and if it made Audrey happy, so much the better.

When Scott Davis saw Weiss's scores on the TV monitor, it was official. He'd dropped to fourth. There would be no world team for him for a second year in a row. His season was over.

Nonetheless, Davis was oddly encouraged by the turn of events. He had skated better that night than he had the whole year, and even though he had been far from perfect, he felt he was progressing.

"I probably would have done a clean program at worlds," he told Zmievskaia. "If I just could have been skating for one more month, I could have gotten it. If they had only given me that one more month . . ."

The final standings were Eldredge, Weiss, Hollander, and Davis. Although Hollander took the third spot from him, it was Weiss who actually bumped Davis off the world team, because he had been fifth after the short and had leaped over Davis, who had been third, at the very end. But Davis could muster no bitterness toward Weiss. He liked Michael and trusted Weisiger. For several years, he and Michael shared Brian Wright as a choreographer. In a sport where few rivals spoke or got along, Davis and Weiss were friends, and Weisiger always had a soft spot for Davis and his troubles.

There was one moment that no one in the Weiss camp ever would forget. The 1994 world junior championships were held in Colorado Springs, and Weiss was one of three skaters in the men's competition representing the United States.

Instead of feeling like a crowd favorite in his home country, though, Weiss felt like the enemy. One of his U.S. teammates, Jere Michael, trained in Colorado Springs, and drew loud applause during practice sessions when he landed the simplest triple jump.

Weiss, on the other hand, landed his jumps in deafening silence. He may have been an American, but he was a member of a rival camp at that event.

During one practice session, Weiss gracefully landed a triple axel, the toughest triple. Out of the stillness, he heard the sound of applause. It was only one person, he could tell that. A single pair of hands, clapping for him.

Weiss looked into the stands. He saw a skater, a member of the Colorado Springs group, applauding all alone. Weiss recognized him as the reigning national champion at the time: Scott Davis.

The Weiss family usually gathered at Michael's competitions, even if everyone had to pack into one car and drive all night to get there. For the 1997 nationals, however, Margie Weiss, his mother, remained at home. The family had just bought its second Gold's Gym, and she decided to stay behind to work at the facility in Gaithersburg, Maryland.

After Michael finished, his sister Genna dashed to a pay phone in the arena to call their mother. She couldn't find her at either gym. So she paged her. But instead of punching in a telephone number, she pushed only one number: 2.

She figured her mother would know that meant Michael was second.

Margie Weiss's pager went off as she was driving on the Capital Beltway, crossing the Potomac River from Maryland back toward the family home in Virginia.

She looked at the message. She saw the 2. She knew exactly what it meant. By herself in her car, Margie Weiss screamed in delight. After a dozen years of training and more than half a million dollars of expenses, her only son had finally hit it big.

Word of Weiss's performance had to travel one other place, Audrey Weisiger knew. Because ABC was not showing the event live, but by tape-delay the next day, Brian Wright had no idea how Michael had done. He was too sick and disheartened by his battle with AIDS to fly from his home in Seattle to attend nationals. He knew where Weiss stood coming into the long program. He knew that this, of all years, was Weiss's to shine. "If not now, when?" Wright had said to himself. It was time for Weiss to make the world team. Wright had been waiting too long and working too hard with Weiss and Weisiger to believe anything less.

That day, Wright filled in for a friend (who was near death) on a shift answering the phones at the Seattle AIDS Support Group. He knew that the men's long program was going on at the same time, 2,500 miles away. He had no way to find out the results, so he waited.

"Seattle AIDS Support Group, this is Brian."

Every time the phone rang, he wondered if it would be Audrey, his skating confidante and best friend. Instead, it was someone who needed to get to the hospital, or had a problem with his medicine, or just wanted someone to talk to as AIDS slowly killed him.

Brian knew that whatever Audrey had to say would relieve him of the tremendous weight of the disease he shared with these callers, if only for a few wonderful minutes. His own problems—that he had only part of a stomach, that everything he ate had to be flushed out through a plastic bag, that his medical bills were approaching $6,000 a month—would flutter away when she was on the other end of the phone, talking about Michael's skating.

But Audrey didn't call during his shift. "Perhaps the event isn't over yet," Brian told himself. He went home, anxious and edgy.

He had not been there long when the phone rang.

"Brian, he's second!"

"Audrey?"

"Brian, Mike's second! He's going to worlds!"

Wright punched the air. "Awright! Who was first? Who was third?"

"Who cares?" Weisiger chastised him. "Ah, Todd and Dan Hollander. He landed the quad, Brian. Isn't this great?"

Wright could barely believe what he was hearing.

"Brian, I wish you were here with us. I feel kind of guilty that you aren't here right now, that we aren't doing this together."

"I know," Wright replied. "That's okay."

A few minutes later, they hung up. Audrey was calling from the hotel lobby in Nashville, and had to go. But her words rang inside his head. She sounded happy, but not ecstatic, he thought. He knew she felt bad that he was not with them. He knew he was missed. He wished that made him happy, but it did not.

Wright stood up. He suddenly felt very sad. Michael had done it. He had nearly won the long program; he had stolen the show and he was going to the world championships. Brian had played a huge part in Michael's development. He had created the programs Weiss skated in Nashville. And yet he had played no role in his week at nationals.

Wright walked through his sister's home, where he had been living for several months.

"We planned this for years, Audrey and I," he said to himself. "This is absurd. I should be so happy, yet I feel so distant."

Wearing gray sweats and a blue denim jacket, Wright opened the back door and walked into the backyard. The Seattle afternoon was partly cloudy and mild. The backyard was streaked with reluctant sunshine. He breathed in cool, fresh air.

"God, I wish I could have been there," Wright said out loud, to no one.

He walked toward a bench, shaded by willows and a large fir tree. All alone in that backyard in Seattle, as far away as someone could possibly be from Nashville and still be in the continental United States, Brian Wright sat down and began to cry.

PART II

February and March 1997

TO WORLDS

3

THE MAKING OF
A CHAMPION

A boom microphone reached out to record a little girl's tender good-bye to her father in the crowded lobby of Nashville's Renaissance Hotel. The father was headed to Houston where he lives and works, the daughter to New York to appear on ABC's *Good Morning America* and CBS's *This Morning*, then to Detroit, where she and her mother reside so that she can skate. The father wouldn't see his wife and only child for two weeks.

They hugged. The camera rolled. The father waited until the camera moved and got into position again, then walked out the glass doors of the lobby and into the cool night air. The girl and her mother waved, then turned and walked away. The camera caught it.

A scene from the movies?

No. Just another typical farewell in the hectic life of America's fourteen-year-old national champion, Tara Lipinski.

Earlier, the network camera crew had visited the Lipinskis' hotel room, filming the family packing its suitcases. Almost nothing was off-limits for the Lipinskis. Publicity was becoming their constant companion, and they couldn't get enough of it.

"It's hard to say 'no' to the media," Pat Lipinski had lamented two years earlier.

So she and her husband rarely did.

At her news conference immediately following her victory at the national championships, Tara was asked if she knew what was about to hit her.

"I think everything will be just . . . normal," she said.

Richard Callaghan, her coach, smiled wryly as he sat beside her.

"We'll talk later," he told her.

But Tara was right. Everything would be normal for her. There would be national television cameras recording her every move. She had always enjoyed that. It had been going on, to the family's delight, since she was twelve. There would be agents buzzing around, morning shows calling, expectations to be met—and, on the ice, nothing but practice, practice, practice.

None of this was new to Tara Lipinski. It was exactly what Jack and Pat Lipinski had hoped would happen. It was why they willingly lived 1,300 miles apart. It was the very reason they hired an agent, the frenetic Mike Burg, when Tara was only thirteen. She had not yet won any important figure skating titles at that time, but Burg had been courting the family for a year, and he told them that he could make her a star. He was right. Tara had become the best little skater in America. And she, her parents, and her agent were going to take it and run with it—for all that it was worth.

Within an hour of her triumph on Saturday night at the nationals, a stack of paper appeared in the press room at Nashville Arena. It was a new press release.

MEDIA ALERT was the headline.

"Online with Lipinski," it continued.

"Visit America's hottest skating sensation at 'www.TaraLipinski.com,'" read the news release from Edge Marketing, Burg's company. "Visitors can dive inside Tara's life by checking out her biography, family life stories, and other fun facts about Tara (i.e., Which of Tara's talents might pose a threat to Martha Stewart?)."

The answer, the Website reported, was her penchant for designing customized pillows and stuffed animals.

Within one month, www.TaraLipinski.com would receive nearly 60,000 hits by people on the World Wide Web. The Lipinskis were more than willing to share many things with strangers who signed on to computers, including biographical anecdotes about Jack and Pat Lipinski.

"Although they'll never know for sure, Patricia and Jack Lipinski might have exchanged passing glances long before meeting in high school," the Website announced. "Jack was born in a Jersey City, N.J., hospital in 1951—the same hospital where Pat would greet the world a mere three days later."

The Lipinskis thrived on life in the public eye. The adoration and attention was a significant reward for them, especially because of what they were giving up for the sport. The financial cost was overwhelming: $58,000 in 1994 alone for Tara's skating, including living expenses in Delaware, her former training site, travel, coaches' fees, ice time, skates, and costumes. That was why they needed an agent. It didn't take the Lipinskis long to realize that some of their costs could be defrayed by a very welcome addition to the family revenues: Tara Lipinski.

But there were other costs that even Tara's earnings could not cover. Tara, a ninth-grader in the 1996–97 school year, stopped going to school in sixth grade and was in her third year of being tutored full-time. Meanwhile, the family was together only on occasional weekends, for a couple weeks during summer and the holidays, and at competitions and ice shows. Otherwise, Tara wished her father good night by telephone.

Their lives were marked by a one-dimensional quality rarely found in families of active, bright American teenagers, Pat Lipinski acknowledged sadly in extensive interviews in 1995 and 1996. Mother and daughter spent their entire day at the rink, from nine in the morning until three or so every afternoon, give or take a few hours. Tara would skate as much as four hours during the day, and Pat would be there in the stands for every single minute of practice. Even though her daughter loved skating to the exclusion of almost everything else, both she and Pat found that the ice often wasn't the escape they had hoped it would be. Quite the contrary, it became Tara's workplace, and there were times when the pressure built to the breaking point for both mother and daughter.

"I would see this face," Pat Lipinski said, describing her daughter as she practiced on the ice. "It'd be this frozen look. I already knew, we're not going to land anything [triple jumps] now, we're in a frenzy. I call it our 'frenzy.' Some people throw things on the ice, some people curse, some people give up and just go home, my daughter stays and tackles it, but sometimes she can't come out of it."

Tara's frenzies occurred three times a week in practice, Pat Lipinski said, when Tara skated at the two-rink facility at the University of Delaware in Newark, from 1993 to late 1995. They also happened occasionally during her first few months at the Detroit Skating Club in early 1996, her mother said. They usually occurred after she attempted a triple jump, fell, got up, tried again, and fell again. A terrified look would come over her daughter's face, Pat Lipinski said.

"She would go around and I would come out of the stands [in one of the two Delaware arenas] and come to the glass and say, 'Calm down, you're in a frenzy, calm down,' and then the tears would come," Pat said.

"I want to do my five [repetitions of one triple jump]," Tara said during a frenzy, according to her mother.

"Get off the ice," Pat Lipinski said she replied.

"No, I want to do my five."

"I want you off the ice now, Tara," Pat Lipinski said.

"No, Mommy, no, Mommy," Tara said.

"Tara," her mother admonished, "they're watching."

Pat Lipinski, a heavyset blonde with a forlorn smile, said there was nothing the mothers of rival Delaware skaters enjoyed more than to see Tara Lipinski in a frenzy. The mothers in Delaware were given a nickname: "Birds on a Wire," because of the way they sat in a row in the stands and watched their children take skating lessons all day long. The "birds" knew all about the Lipinskis, how the father lived in their dream house in Houston, alone, and the mother shared a rented apartment with Tara, living the life of a devoted, subservient skating mom. They had watched *PrimeTime Live* cameras film a feature on Tara in 1995; they had seen her on network television in exhibitions arranged by Mike Burg even before he became her agent. The daughters of the other Delaware mothers weren't receiving this kind of attention; among twelve- and thirteen-year-olds, tiny Tara was the most publicized skater in the land.

"If there's anything I can't stand," Pat Lipinski said, "it's for my daughter to put on a show for those coaches or for the mothers there, because the mothers just love it. You know, anybody that's doing better, they love to see that, especially if their daughters are competing with mine. So I had to talk like this [softly] because these people were watching."

"I'd say, 'Off the ice now. Come get your things.' I'd hold her arm while she'd put her skate guards on."

By that point in her frenzy, Tara had stopped her practice session and was standing beside the boards with her mother.

"'Now Tara,' I'd say, 'we've got two choices. We can either go to the bathroom and get this settled real quick and you can get back on the ice and be okay, or if you're in that big of a frenzy, let's take it to the car, calm down, go get Taco Bell, whatever, and we'll talk this thing out. But you are not going to do this in front of these people because you look like you've gone nuts.'"

Pat Lipinski said that on some occasions, while watching her daughter go through a frenzy, she would tell her that if she didn't calm down and skate better, she would take her back home to Houston, where Jack Lipinski works as vice president–refining for The Coastal Corporation, an oil firm.

"I would tell Tara, 'You're going to go to Texas if you're not practicing the way you're supposed to,'" Pat Lipinski said. "I have four dogs at home. It's killing me. I haven't seen them in three years. My husband, the house—our house is beautiful. Everything I could want there, my husband belongs to a country club because of his job. I could have that, I could have cars. I could have anything I want. But I love her [Tara] and I would give my life for her. We don't need the sport of ice-skating. We don't. We're not sports-minded people. I don't need it for the money. We could go home and have the best life ever, she could be in the best schools, we could be going on vacations, I could go buy a new car, she could go to all the parties and be with all the kids that she wants to be with. She could have all that.

"We are giving up a lot for ice-skating," Pat Lipinski continued. "Some people use ice-skating as a way to maybe get a better life because they don't have a good life; it hasn't been like that for us. We can have anything we want to have. If anything, skating is draining us. It's taking away the good life that we could have. But then you look at her, she works so hard. She knows one thing, though; she'll go back to Texas if she doesn't work hard. That's my thing."

"The biggest threat was to take her back to Texas," said Jeff DiGregorio, Tara's coach for nearly six years at the University of Delaware. "If she didn't skate perfectly, or hit five jumps in a row, she was going home. The mother would leave the rink and Tara would run off the lesson, put on her skate guards and go out after her. It was a nightmare for me to try to keep the kid stable."

DiGregorio, who quit teaching Tara during a shouting match with Pat Lipinski at the world junior championships in December 1995 in Australia, said he occasionally watched from the doorway as mother and daughter dashed from the University of Delaware's Blue or Gold Arena into the parking lot. He said he saw them walk or run to their van and sometimes go inside it and drive away. DiGregorio said this happened "almost every day" from the summer of 1994 until the Lipinskis left after the fight in Australia.

One day in August 1995, a University of Delaware skating coach was sitting outside the university's main rink—the Blue Arena—on a bench, enjoying the fresh air before going indoors to give a lesson. All of a sudden, Pat Lipinski "stormed out the door with an angry look on her face," said the coach, who requested anonymity, and went to her van in the parking lot.

"A few seconds later, Tara came out with a happy-go-lucky look of hope on her face," the coach said. "She said something like, 'Wait, Mom,' and went hopping behind her mother."

The coach said she watched Pat Lipinski and Tara get into the van. "[Pat] sat there screaming at her for ten minutes," she said. "The mother's arms were flailing. Then they drove off."

Tara said sometimes her mother would leave the rink first, sometimes she would.

"If I was throwing a scene, [my mother] would come down from the bleachers and sit on the lower level and I would sometimes just walk off the ice and run into the parking lot, because I knew my mom didn't want scenes," Tara said. "Sometimes my mom would go out first, and then I would follow, because she never wanted me crying in the middle of the rink, so she would walk out and we would sit in the car for a while and calm me down and then I would come back in."

DiGregorio and the other coach were not the only people who watched Pat and Tara Lipinski's unscheduled departures from Tara's practice sessions.

"We got oblivious to it," said Gloria Tyson, who works as a rink monitor at the University of Delaware. "It was a normal, everyday thing that happened. Tara's here; Tara's not here."

One of the Delaware parents said many of the mothers knew what was going to happen when Pat and Tara dashed to the parking lot.

"Well," they said to one another cynically, "Tara's taking another ride."

TV cameras and sportswriters never saw Tara's frenzies. They never occurred at competitions. And when journalists began streaming to the rinks in Delaware, and later, to the Detroit Skating Club, no one ever saw anything but a dedicated and focused little girl landing jump after jump after jump, working harder than anyone else in the rink.

Tara said that her crying was "not a big deal. It's not like I'm totally depressed. It's frustration. Most people get frustrated or kick the ice, but I don't do that. I usually just cry. It doesn't feel like something's really, really wrong. It's just how I get mad at myself."

DiGregorio felt differently. He was concerned Tara was not in "control of her own body" during her frenzies.

"She would sort of self-destruct," DiGregorio said. "She would be so obsessed with a jump being perfect. Every jump has a feeling to it. Tara would go crazy if a jump didn't feel perfect."

Megan Faulkner, who coached Tara in Houston before she moved to Delaware in 1993 and still occasionally joins her at major competitions, also saw the frenzies.

"She can really work herself up in a state, and can't get anything done," Faulkner said. "It got to the point where it was detrimental. I remember a time with the triple loop after the Olympic Festival [a junior event Tara won in 1994]. She must have done thirty in fifteen minutes, all the same way, and fell on each one or at least they were a little cheated [not perfect] on the landing. Finally, Pat said for her to get off the ice and she settled down and then was fine."

The Lipinskis are not the first skating family to become so obsessed by the sport. Figure skating—especially women's skating, where the money and fame is the greatest—is filled with uprooted parents and children crisscrossing the country searching for skating nirvana. Unlike most other children's sports that can be played in school, figure skating is taught at rinks off school grounds. The hours available for practice time at the rink often conflict with the hours classes are taught in school. For that reason, elite skaters nowadays usually end up being tutored so that they can travel to the shows and competitions that can make them millionaires before they learn to drive. Kristi Yamaguchi and Brian Boitano could well be the last of a vanishing breed: U.S. Olympic gold medalists in figure skating who graduated from a high school they actually attended, rather than one to which they mailed their assignments.

Elite figure skaters usually end up gathering at one of about fifteen to twenty rinks in the United States, those that have the reputation of churning out champions. If parents have a child who wants to figure skate, if they want their child to get excellent instruction from a national-caliber coach, they most likely will have to travel to find it.

Two of the best training centers in the world are the University of Delaware in Newark, and the Detroit Skating Club, where Richard Callaghan works, in the suburbs north of Detroit. Tara ended up at both.

It was clear early on that Tara was headed for greatness in some sport. The question was: Which one would it be?

Growing up in New Jersey, Tara tried horseback riding, tennis, gymnastics, and even baton classes (she quit when the baton hit her in the head), but she was drawn to two particular sports, roller skating and figure skating. She started roller skating first, at age three. By the time she was nine, Tara was national primary girls champion. Roller skating was good for her, the Lipinskis thought. She was learning how to win at a young age, and jumping in those heavy boots made her legs extremely strong. When she took up figure skating at six and a half, she felt as if she was light as a feather.

For three years Tara split time between roller skating and ice-skating. But one day, Pat Lipinski decided it was time for Tara to devote herself to only one sport. And that sport, Pat concluded, would be figure skating.

It was the day before Thanksgiving 1991, and Tara was at roller skating practice.

"I said, 'Come on, get off,'" Pat Lipinski said. Tara left the roller rink with her mother, assuming she was just in a hurry and they would be back the day after Thanksgiving for practice.

But Tara never went back.

"That was it," Pat said. "It was as if I made a decision to not buy soap anymore, or something like that. I made the decision and we never went there again."

"It was okay," Tara said. "I got used to it."

The family had been transferred from New Jersey to Houston that year, and Tara was ice-skating at the Galleria Mall. Conditions there were less than ideal. Private ice time was available only at 4:30 A.M. A Christmas tree went up in the rink at Thanksgiving and came down in January, and it sat right in the middle of the ice.

"Tara's not going to make it here," Pat Lipinski said she was told. "Everybody knows you don't get better in Houston."

During the summer, Pat and Tara went back north to train at the University of Delaware, where she had taken some lessons, then returned to Houston. But that didn't last long. Tired of the "awful" predawn practice sessions, mother and daughter moved back to Delaware full-time in June 1993, around Tara's eleventh birthday.

Jack Lipinski stayed behind.

"That is not a decision made very lightly," said Jack Lipinski.

All three of them knew that it would hit Pat hardest because her life would be disrupted most.

"Is it difficult? Yes," said Jack Lipinski. "Would I recommend to anyone to do this? No. Sometimes you step into something and then want to change it, but both Pat and I want to support Tara."

"When I had Tara, my idea of a child, of a daughter, was a piano, a private school, the best education I could give her, ballet, I love gardening, those are my things I love in life," Pat Lipinski said. "Not sports. I'm not a sportsperson, I'm not athletic. I've never done a sport in my life. In high school, those people I didn't take to, I just thought they felt they were better than me, and it bothered me. And the last thing I wanted was for my daughter to be like that."

But the little girl Pat named for the plantation in her favorite movie, *Gone With the Wind,* became exactly like that. Of all the sports she tried, Tara adored ice-skating most of all.

"I love it and I love to compete and I like the feeling out there," Tara said. "I like to be out there by myself. Millions of people are watching and you're the only one out there and you can show them what you can do and they applaud. . . . They're all there just for me, you know?"

Upon moving to Delaware, Tara's love for figure skating soon superseded even the most basic family requirement—spending the 1994 Christmas holiday together.

"I made her come home for Christmas Eve and Christmas Day," Pat Lipinski said. "She was supposed to stay that week, until New Year's, but she flew out, came to Delaware for five days to train, and then flew back to Houston New Year's Eve.

"I told her, 'Well, that's what you want to do, fine, that's your Christmas gift. The extra flight, that's the money for your gift.'"

Mother and daughter flew back to Delaware a few days later.

"Is this child driven, or what?" Pat Lipinski asked.

At the time, the Lipinskis marveled at their devoted little girl and expressed nothing but admiration for DiGregorio, to whom Tara had become quite attached. DiGregorio, who was thirty at the time, was thrilled to be coaching such a talented skater. He had trained good skaters before, but only Tara was eliciting calls from the likes of the *New York Times*. When *PrimeTime Live* was scheduled to pay a visit, DiGregorio made sure to wear a tie to work that day.

He was caught up in the media feeding frenzy. "Maybe I can't see past her," he said.

Even so, he suggested the Lipinskis leave for a week so Tara could take a few lessons from another coach. He was interested in having someone else take a look at her tiny jumps, and perhaps suggest changes. It's not unusual for a skater to see another coach; a different viewpoint is considered to be a help for jumps, spins, or footwork.

Pat Lipinski, however, disputed DiGregorio's claim that he was the one to suggest the trip; she said it was the family's idea, and that she had to keep it a secret from him.

In April 1995, the Lipinskis arranged a visit to Toronto to work for several days with Doug Leigh, who coaches Elvis Stojko.

But Tara did not want to go, her mother said.

"She cried all the way to the airport, cried on the plane, cried when we got off the plane," Pat Lipinski said.

The reason? She was worried about leaving DiGregorio, even for a couple of days, Pat Lipinski said.

"I get her to the rink, Doug Leigh comes in, and if you took a stone and put the stone on the ice, that was my daughter. And I'm looking at her, and I'm going, 'This isn't happening.' So she's standing there and I'm going, 'Don't do this to me.' That's why I couldn't take her to a U.S. coach. I had to take her out of the country, because I knew she was going to do this."

Pat went to a phone at the rink and called Jack at his office in Houston.

"I'm on the phone and I'm hysterical," Pat said. "I'm going, 'Jack, it's just like I told you. Thank God we didn't take her to a U.S. coach. What do I do now?'"

As Pat Lipinski talked to her husband, Tara left the ice and put on her coat.

"She's leaving, she's at the door," Pat said. "We've been there twenty minutes."

Pat hung up, grabbed her coat, and they walked out the door.

The next morning, they were back at the rink in Delaware.

"I felt like a fool," Pat Lipinski said.

Tara joyfully returned to DiGregorio and began preparing for what would be her final few months in Delaware. They had made such a delightful picture at the nationals in February 1995, the anxious young figure skating coach standing behind his little starlet, his reassuring hands securely resting on her tiny shoulders, awaiting the judges' marks. She was figure skating's Shirley Temple, a darling prodigy who snapped off her tiny triple jumps without a care in the world. Older girls carried the baggage of a developing body, with hips, thighs, and breasts that made rotating a triple jump so much harder. Not Tara. At least not yet. She and DiGregorio were all the rage in Providence, R.I., site of those nationals. The front page of the paper, the sports highlights on the TV news; you couldn't miss them.

Everyone was caught up in Tara-mania. Claire Ferguson, the U.S. Figure Skating Association president at the time, introduced readers of the *Providence Sunday Journal* to Tara by including her with some very impressive company: "Dorothy Hamill was an unknown twenty years ago. Michelle Kwan is here and Todd Eldredge. And there's a twelve-year-old named Tara Lipinski who is going to be something else."

As sportswriters from around the nation took the bait and wrote incessantly about Tara, something interesting happened: She didn't win. Sydne Vogel, a strong jumper out of Alaska, quietly and methodically ruined dozens of reporters' stories by easily defeating Tara in both the short and long programs of the junior ladies competition.

No matter, the journalists figuratively replied. *USA Today, Sports Illustrated* and *Good Morning America* all decided to go ahead and feature the runner-up. Tara-mania was in full throttle. Mike Burg, who was yet to become Tara's agent, joked that he would make T-shirts emblazoned with the slogan: Tara-mania.

Tara moved up to the senior (Olympic) division for the 1995–96 skating season. After her short visit to Toronto, she and DiGregorio got down to the business of preparing for the next nationals. And her parents got down to the business of making skating pay off, officially signing Burg in June as Tara turned thirteen.

Asked why she needed an agent, Tara said, "I don't know. It was my parents' decision, and Jeff's."

Jack Lipinski defended the decision to sign Burg, saying it was only to perform in five shows.

"I don't think you've seen her on a box of Wheaties," he said. "She will do a handful of shows which help defray the cost of skating."

Pat Lipinski said it simply enough: "This is an expensive sport."

"While it would be real nice to do it the old-fashioned way," Jack Lipinski said, "we're not riding around on horses anymore, we're driving cars."

Asked if signing an agent would put more pressure on his daughter to keep skating even if her body changed or she grew tired of the sport, Jack Lipinski said, "If she's no longer competitive, she'll go on to something else. She did real well in roller skating. Now it's ice-skating. What's to say she won't do tennis?

"There's a lot of people in this sport who live through their kids," he said. "We'll never do that."

The variety sounded nice, but Tara could not have been more focused on one thing: figure skating. Tara did not have a school locker; she did not have a homeroom. She had a full-time job. She said she loved it and wanted to skate more than anything in the world, and that was all that mattered to her parents. It was Tara's dream, they said. But to pursue it, she was living the same kind of one-dimensional life Americans had decried when the dream was state-supported and came from an enemy land. When East Germany or the Soviet Union plucked children from their families at an early age—three, six, nine—and sent them to sports camps, Americans thought it was awful.

But, increasingly, little-girl figure skaters in the United States were living a life that seemed eerily similar. The government didn't tell them to do it, and perhaps their parents didn't either. Jack Lipinski often said he and Pat simply were following Tara's wishes. What were they to do? Hold her back? Tell her she couldn't try to achieve the highest goals in her sport? Let her skate around that Christmas tree in Houston?

These were difficult questions. But the fact was, Tara Lipinski's life was governed completely by a sport. For Tara and girls like her, everything else—school, even living with a parent—became secondary.

The Lipinskis had high hopes for Tara heading into the 1995–96 season. Before the nationals that year, they traveled to Brisbane, Australia, for the world junior championships. It was a prestigious event, and one they thought Tara could win. However, those lofty dreams quickly dissolved into a nightmare.

It's not uncommon for a parent and a coach to have a disagreement over strategy at a major competition; it is quite rare, however, when they shout at one another in front of judges, skaters, officials, and reporters from around the world.

DiGregorio and Pat Lipinski certainly had had their troubles. DiGregorio didn't like what he perceived to be Pat Lipinski's nitpicking of his coaching decisions, and found all the emotional outbursts between mother and daughter to be extremely distracting. Pat wanted DiGregorio to devote much of his coaching time to Tara even though he had other skaters to coach. It was a constant tug-of-war between the two of them, with little Tara stuck in the middle.

In Brisbane, Tara came in seventh in the short program, a disappointing placement for a skater who had performed perfectly. As the competitors gathered to draw their skating positions for the long program, DiGregorio and Pat Lipinski saw each other for the first time after the competition.

Pat Lipinski was angry. She was convinced DiGregorio had made a crucial strategic mistake by not allowing Tara to try her hardest triple jump in the program. Tara had attempted and landed a triple loop, not the more difficult triple lutz. The judges didn't give her as much credit for the loop as they would have for the lutz. That, Pat Lipinski said, was why her daughter was seventh.

DiGregorio replied that he had been told by the judges before the event that Tara should not try her triple lutz because it was a flawed jump. The judges told him that Tara's triple lutz was "cheated on the takeoff." It was what skating people called a "flutz"—coming off the easier inside edge of the blade like a triple flip, not the outside edge as the triple lutz should be performed. Because of that, DiGregorio said he was advised to replace that jump with the triple loop, one of Tara's steadiest jumps, and be done with it.

"Are you insinuating I made the wrong decision?" DiGregorio asked Pat Lipinski.

She rolled her eyes.

"I am the coach and I call the shots," DiGregorio retorted.

"And it's probably your last one," Pat Lipinski replied.

"That's it," DiGregorio said. "I've had it. I'm done."

Tara was standing beside them, wide-eyed. She screamed and ran into the bathroom, leaving reporters standing there with no one to interview.

"It was like the worst night of my life," Tara said later.

DiGregorio walked out of the room. On his way out of the arena, he passed Jack Lipinski.

"That's it," DiGregorio said. "I can't take it anymore."

"You can't abandon her like that," Jack Lipinski said.

DiGregorio kept walking.

The Lipinskis returned home and immediately embarked on a nation-wide search to find a new coach. They visited Galina Zmievskaia in Connecticut, Kathy Casey in Colorado Springs, Carol Heiss Jenkins in Cleveland, and Richard Callaghan in Detroit. They were some of the best coaches in the land. The touring tryout camp was called "the Lipinski circus" in one of the rinks.

But the coaches were intrigued. "How could you not be?" asked Heiss, the 1960 Olympic gold medalist.

In the end, the Lipinskis chose Callaghan, whose no-nonsense discipline was renowned. He had taken notorious underachiever Nicole Bobek to the national title in 1995—"surprised the hell out of people," he said with pride—and he and Todd Eldredge had risen to the top of the sport together. Callaghan never was seen in public without a tie; even in practice, wearing his skates and a parka, he wore one. He was all steely-eyed business on the ice. Jack Lipinski and Mike Burg liked the fact that Callaghan would take charge of Tara and her practice sessions. They wanted to see the frenzies disappear. They wanted Pat Lipinski to find something else to do all day besides sit in the rink; Burg kept mentioning volunteer work, once they got settled. The northern suburbs of Detroit would be the place for Tara, they all decided.

Leaving DiGregorio proved costly. The Lipinskis had to get rid of their apartment back in Elkton, Maryland, just over the Delaware line, and find a new place in Detroit. They ended up leasing a condominium near a golf course in Bloomfield Hills, Michigan. Again, it was just mother and daughter. Dad would remain in Houston.

To help pay for the move, the Lipinskis sought financial assistance from the U.S. Figure Skating Association. They requested about $2,000 from a fund that is reserved for special circumstances for skaters and their families. Usually, the fund gives financial assistance to skaters in need; it has helped a skater whose mother died of cancer, and another whose house burned down.

The USFSA turned down the Lipinskis' request. A move based on a screaming match with a coach was not the kind of situation the fund was designed to help. Furthermore, when the Lipinskis filled out the form requesting the money, they were required to list their salary. It was an eye-popping six figures.

The Lipinskis also made bold moves trying to seek publicity for their daughter. Dan Cunningham, the sports editor of the *Houston Chronicle,* said he had received five or six calls from Jack and Pat Lipinski, or a friend or representative of the family, since Tara was ten. The callers wanted to know either why the paper wasn't writing more about Tara, why it wasn't reporting on one of her competitions, or why it wasn't covering her return home to the airport after an event. Cunningham said his reporters were in fact writing stories about Tara, but whatever the paper did, it didn't seem to satisfy the Lipinski camp.

Jack Lipinski flexed his muscles when a column in the *Providence Journal* questioned during the 1995 nationals how the Lipinskis had allowed Tara to make decisions that split up their family.

"We are told, confidently, that this twelve-year-old is doing what she wants to do," wrote columnist Jim Donaldson. "How, I wonder, does a twelve-year-old know exactly what she wants to do? Especially a twelve-year-old who has spent most of her life in skating?"

Incensed, Jack Lipinski and then-USFSA President Claire Ferguson wanted to hold a press conference to rebut Donaldson's column. The USFSA's public relations staff quietly talked them both out of it.

"I just couldn't believe what I was reading," Pat Lipinski said. "So we went nuts from it, I mean, me and Jack, by ourselves."

Despite the upheaval of moving to a new coach a month earlier, Tara Lipinski skated very well at the 1996 nationals in San Jose, coming in third after two top skaters—Nicole Bobek and Kyoko Ina—withdrew due to injuries. Ina, a world team member in pairs with partner Jason Dungjen, might not have beaten Lipinski, but Bobek almost certainly would have.

Bobek, the reigning U.S. champion and world bronze medalist, warmed up for the long program in San Jose, but a sore right ankle, injured in the autumn, swelled during the warm-up. Midway through eventual winner Michelle Kwan's long program, Bobek withdrew from the competition. Normally, this would mean no world team berth. But Team Bobek—agent, manager, public relations man, and mother—wasn't worried; it was counting on a gift from the U.S. Figure Skating Association to send her to the world championships. Immediately after the competition, the USFSA's international committee met to determine which three women would attend the 1996 world championships in Edmonton, Alberta. The Bobek camp expected that the committee would bump Lipinski, the third-place finisher, and place Bobek on the team with Kwan and Tonia Kwiatkowski.

For one hour and twenty minutes, the twenty-five members of the international committee debated furiously. Judges and officials spoke one after another about an issue much bigger than Bobek's swollen ankle. They were arguing about control of their sport.

Bobek had not injured her ankle while training at home for the nationals. She hurt it skating with Nutcracker on Ice, a monthlong tour that paid her about $90,000. After getting injured, instead of leaving the tour completely, or resting for a few days, Bobek kept on performing. When the tour ended in late December, she was left with a throbbing ankle and two weeks to get ready for the nationals.

Her behavior angered most of the members of the international committee. They looked at her decision as a slap in the face of the

USFSA, which ran the nationals and considered them the most important week in a skater's competitive season.

Most of those in the room felt that it was time for the USFSA to take charge of Olympic-style figure skating, to issue a warning to its skaters. The association looked at the flood of agents, promoters, and managers entering the sport in the wake of the Tonya Harding–Nancy Kerrigan incident in 1994—and felt powerless. It couldn't stop the professional side from scheduling meaningless, made-for-TV pseudo-competitions ("Rock and Roll on Ice" or "Battle of the Sexes") that diluted the overall product. But it did have a way to control Olympic hopefuls like Bobek, and that was to dash her hopes and not send her to the world championships.

Some in the room also were worried that if they replaced Lipinski with Bobek, Bobek might skate in other moneymaking ventures in February, not heal properly and then withdraw from the world championships in March, further embarrassing the USFSA. Bobek was known to go for the money. The Bobek gang left one coach—the highly respected Evy Scotvold, who coaches Paul Wylie and Nancy Kerrigan—simply because Nicole wanted to make a few thousand dollars skating at the Goodwill Games in Russia, while Scotvold urged her to stay home and practice.

On the other side of the Bobek argument were those in the USFSA who wanted to stick with precedence. Top skaters such as Christopher Bowman, Todd Eldredge, and Kerrigan had been placed on world or Olympic teams after not participating at nationals because of injuries. Bobek was a polished, energetic beauty who had won a bronze medal at the previous year's worlds. If she was healthy in Edmonton, she could become world champion. Tara could not. She was too new to be embraced by the judges. Why not send someone who could win the event?

In the end, the vote was 13–12 to send Tara Lipinski to worlds instead of Nicole Bobek. As one committee member said, "We wanted Nicole to know she cannot take nationals lightly." Left unsaid was the real message of the committee's decision: "We're in charge here."

Bobek publicly said she accepted the decision, even though it came as a total shock. She quickly realized what a miscalculation it had been not to skate in the long program that evening at nationals. Had she toughed it out and skated a watered-down long program, even with a stumble or a fall, the judges would have admired her effort, given her wonderful marks for her artistic presence and put her in third place, according to one prominent judge.

The big winner that night was Richard Callaghan. He had coached Bobek for more than a year before she abruptly left him during the Nutcracker tour and returned to one of her old coaches, Barbara Roles Williams. As Bobek departed, the Lipinskis came calling. By a one-vote margin of the international committee, Callaghan was headed to the world championships with Lipinski, whom he had been coaching for one month, while a chastened Bobek was going home to look for another new coach.

At the 1996 world championships, the old and the new of women's figure skating were on display within minutes of one another at Edmonton Coliseum. The skating order in the short program had Tara Lipinski, thirteen, following twenty-six-year-old Midori Ito. Ito, who at the time was planning to return to the 1998 Olympic Games after winning the silver medal in 1992, had been hospitalized with anemia earlier in the week. She was nervous as she took the ice, holding her side before she skated. She tried to land her trademark triple axel, the most difficult jump any woman ever has attempted, and she fell. As Ito's marks for technical merit were being read over the public-address—scores as low as 5.2 and 5.3—Lipinski stepped onto the ice to prepare for her short program.

Tara couldn't help but hear the marks, and she couldn't believe her ears. Ito was one of her heroes. Skaters try not to watch the competitor before them; they usually are holed up in a room or hallway backstage, spending time with their coach or listening to music on headphones. Tara had not seen Ito's performance, but she knew by the marks that something must have gone very wrong.

In the few moments before she began, Tara started to think that she might actually beat Midori Ito. Here she was, a rookie at the worlds, and she might leap ahead of the 1989 world champion and 1992 Olympic silver medalist. Lipinski couldn't shake the idea from her head: She could beat Ito.

In her program, Lipinski hung on to a shaky triple lutz landing, but unexpectedly fell on the second part of the jump combination, her double loop. She slipped and fell again on her next jump, her triple flip. As she got up, Tara glanced plaintively at Callaghan, standing beside the boards close to where she had fallen. She looked as if she wanted to leave the ice. She kept on going, but she was devastated. Two judges dished out technical marks in the 3s—3.8 and 3.9. She barely made the cut to the long program; twenty-four out of the thirty skaters moved on. Lipinski was twenty-third.

But Tara Lipinski was not yet finished. As she and Pat talked before the long program, Tara said, "Mom, I'm gonna show 'em I can skate."

Spectators were still arriving for the long night of competition when Tara skated her four-minute long program, landed seven triple jumps, earned a standing ovation, and leaped to fifteenth place overall. A few hours later, at the end of the competition, Michelle Kwan and Lu Chen staged an epic battle for first place that was won by Kwan. But Lipinski served notice; she, too, could unleash a perfect program, even if that year it came hours too early, and meant almost nothing.

Being the parents of a prodigy never has been easy for Jack and Pat Lipinski.

"Excuse me if I walk by in a trance at nationals," Pat once kindly warned a reporter. Pat said she spent most of her time at a major competition in her hotel room. It was too nerve-racking to go out except for meals and the competition itself.

The pressure on figure skating parents always has been unbearable. Some mothers cannot watch their children compete. Jan Gardner, the mother of former world-pairs champion Randy Gardner, would hide in the bathroom until Randy and Tai Babilonia finished their program. She would, however, listen for applause.

Other mothers can't stand even that. One in Ohio used to go to the women's bathroom and continually flush the toilet during her daughter's program. She had her reasons. She knew exactly where her daughter's jumps came in relation to the music, and if she didn't hear any applause, she knew her daughter had fallen. So she drowned out the music with the toilet until her daughter's program was over.

There are dozens of things for a parent to worry about, and, by 1997, Pat Lipinski had considered all of them. Injuries, distractions, Mother Nature; Pat knew anything was possible. She had given up so much for Tara's skating that she was hoping against hope that her daughter would keep winning. Tara's body appeared to be cooperating. Doctors told Pat that her daughter wasn't expected to reach five feet. Most mothers would find this news disheartening. Not Pat Lipinski. For a skating mom, the information was strangely comforting. Her daughter's body would stay small. All the better to land the triple jumps.

"The slightest little growth spurt can throw off all her jumps," Pat said.

Pat knew that puberty was the enemy. Jack, on the other hand, seemed to think his daughter could do something no other girl could—control what happened to her body.

He was asked what would happen if Tara's body changed, if a pound or two on her hips or a developing bustline might force her out of the sport. It had happened to hundreds of girls over the years in figure skating; hips and thighs come, triple jumps go. It certainly could happen to his daughter.

"If she wants to leave the sport, that would be fine with us," Jack Lipinski said.

But what if it were not her choice? What if it just happened?

Jack Lipinski was relentless.

"If she wants to leave skating, that's fine."

Not all of the girls who left skating wanted to leave.

For some, their bodies made them do it.

Tara and Richard Callaghan had a slightly different take on the puberty question. They both thought Tara could train right through it. But that wasn't a concern in 1997. So far, Tara didn't have a thing to worry about. As she became a teenager, her body kept its tiny shape. No hips, no thighs, no breasts, no problems.

But Pat knew better. She knew there was so much to fear. She was living with Tara, and also living through Tara. Two people were living one life. Pat and Tara had been on their own, just the two of them, for so long that they acted more like sisters than mother and daughter. They often finished each other's sentences. Pat found herself saying "we" to refer to what Tara had done, or to how Tara was preparing for the season. "We always do our slow climb," Pat said.

They worried about each other in unusual ways. Pat encouraged Jack to come to Detroit to visit more often because Tara was "really pulling away," and spending more and more time with her friends. Jack's visits became more regular, usually every other weekend.

But Tara would never ignore her mother.

When Pat Lipinski left their condominium to drive to the mall, Tara always yelled out, "Mom, call me when you get there, okay? Drive safely, and call me."

And Pat Lipinski always dutifully called to check in with her daughter when she got there.

By 1997 they had arrived, Pat and Tara. The forty-six-year-old mother was becoming a fixture backstage in the skating world. Her daughter was national champion, and heading for greatness. Pat was proud. And Pat was scared.

She had said it in 1995, but it was true every day her tiny daughter laced up her white skates and went onto the ice:

"An injury, a bad day, thinking about something else, maybe wanting to go out with her girlfriends," Pat Lipinski said. "Anything can mess up her day. That's the stuff you hope people understand. If you just keep telling yourself it's not a for-sure thing, you'll be okay, you'll survive it. But I'm more scared of it now than I was before. It's easier to strive for it than to have it, and then you have to hold on to it."

THE PERFECT PACKAGE

Three days after she returned home from the devastating 1997 nationals, Michelle Kwan received a phone call at her training site in Lake Arrowhead, California.

"I was just calling to see if you're okay," Brian Boitano said.

Boitano worried about Kwan the way a big brother would be concerned about his kid sister. Over the past two years on the Campbell's Soups Tour of World Figure Skating Champions, they spent hours on the ice together in dark, empty arenas, well before the spectators arrived, practicing their jumps. Boitano relished the time he spent with Michelle, helping her with her triples. He and Elvis Stojko joined forces to work on Kwan's triple axel; she wouldn't try it in competition because it was too risky and unnecessary, but she could always say she knew how to land it because two of the best in the business had taught her how.

Boitano, the 1988 Olympic gold medalist, also respected the way Michelle Kwan prepared for competition: "Michelle closes her eyes and looks down and relaxes her shoulders right before she goes onto the ice. I do the same thing."

By the 1996 world championships in Edmonton, Alberta, Boitano had developed a proprietary interest in Kwan. At thirty-two, his Olympic career was long over, yet he continued to skate in professional shows and add his considerable athletic talents to the multitude of made-for-TV competitions. He also signed with ABC Sports to commentate on men's Olympic division skating, becoming the heir-apparent to Dick Button, who would be sixty-eight by the 1998 Olympic Games.

At the '96 worlds, the men finished before the women began, but

Boitano, his assignment over, didn't immediately fly home to San Francisco. He stayed in town for one reason. Wearing blue jeans, a T-shirt, and a baseball cap, he walked into the ABC booth by the ice at Edmonton Coliseum and stood perfectly still to watch Michelle compete in the short program.

Kwan and her coach, Frank Carroll, were standing face-to-face, holding each other's hands—she on the ice, he on the other side of the boards—for his last words of advice to her before she began. Suddenly, Kwan's eyes darted up and to her right, where they found Boitano's eyes focused like a laser on her, one hundred feet away. Kwan's face immediately brightened. She began to break into a large, warm smile. She wanted to wave hello to her friend.

But Boitano, without saying a word, wouldn't let her. His face never cracked. Refusing to take his eyes off hers, he solemnly and slowly nodded his head once, driving his chin into his chest to accentuate his seriousness. "Concentrate," he was telling her. "Don't pay attention to me. Don't even look at me. Get ready to skate."

Michelle Kwan got the message. Her eyes returned to Carroll's eyes. Her face darkened as quickly as it had brightened. It was as if she pulled down a shade over her emotions. She focused in on Carroll, nodded at him, then charged away to take her starting position.

For the next two minutes and forty seconds, Kwan took over the ice as no other young woman in the world would in 1996. She was impeccable. She finished first in the short program and first in the long program to become, at fifteen, the second-youngest women's world champion in history, to fourteen-year-old Sonja Henie in 1927.

Boitano wasn't in Edmonton to see the awards ceremony. After watching Kwan skate her meticulous short program, he left for California and watched the finale on television.

"You weren't there for the long," Kwan teased him over and over in the year that followed. "I looked up. You weren't there."

Boitano vowed he would not miss any of Kwan's national or world performances again.

Michelle Kwan called Brian Boitano on Christmas Day 1996. She had admired Boitano from the moment she first saw him, as a seven-year-old watching the Calgary Olympics on television. Seeing Boitano win the gold medal, Michelle decided at that moment that she wanted to try to win one too.

Boitano called back a few days later, but Michelle was off to Japan to skate in a pro-am event. The next time they saw each other was

Nashville, but Kwan was in no mood to talk about her disastrous long program, so Boitano told her he would get in touch in a few days.

He called Kwan from his cellular phone as he drove toward his home in San Francisco. He soon pulled into his driveway and sat there for the rest of the conversation. He did not want to drive his Jeep Grand Cherokee into the garage and lose the signal.

"I didn't want you to be killing yourself," Boitano said.

"I'm doing okay," Kwan said.

"What was going on out there?" he asked.

"I worried," Kwan said. "I missed the double toe and I began to worry, 'Oh no, I don't want to miss the next thing.'"

"It looked like you started to panic," he said.

"That's exactly what I did."

"It looked like it took you by surprise that you fell on the triple combination and that's what started the whole thing."

"Yeah, yeah, that's exactly how I was feeling."

"Then you did the back sit spin and then when you stepped out of it, you looked like a deer caught in the headlights," Boitano said.

Kwan laughed.

"Then you started doubting yourself, then each time you went into a jump, it's 'Oh man, I missed the combination, then the triple flip, now I have to hit this triple loop,' and then it goes past the technique and it's like worrying about staying alive."

"That's exactly how I felt."

"It's a natural thing for figure skaters," Boitano told Kwan. "That's why skating is so volatile, because in one second, you can change a performance from going in a good way to going in a horrible way and sabotage yourself. The thing you have to work on is that, even though you're surprised, forget about it. Just think of what you need to do technically to make the next thing good. When you start putting a mental checklist together in your mind, 'I missed the double toe and if I miss the triple flip, then I don't trust the triple loop enough,' then you get into trouble.

"So, Michelle, you've got to stop the mental checklist and literally forget about it, pretend like it didn't happen."

"Pretend like I landed the jump?"

"No, no, no, you can't do that. Pretend like it just didn't exist. You just have to start anew."

Kwan told Boitano that going into jumps, she was thinking negatively. "Don't do this . . ." or "Don't do that . . ."

"You need to think of positive things," he said.

He had a story to tell her. At the nationals in 1984 in Salt Lake City, which were the U.S. Olympic trials for the Winter Games in Sarajevo, Boitano was the last skater of the evening. Scott Hamilton, the reigning world and national champion and an Olympic gold medal favorite, had skated beautifully. Boitano didn't think he was going to defeat Hamilton (upsets in skating, rare in the 1990s, were unheard of in the 1980s), but he certainly wanted to skate well and qualify for his first Olympics. He began to feel unbearable pressure.

"I kept thinking, 'What if I miss the triple lutz! What if I miss the triple axel!' And guess what? I put my hand down on the triple lutz and I popped the triple axel. What I thought of ended up happening. I said, 'I'm never ever going to think of the negative side of jumping again.' If I'm worried about a triple axel, I'm going to say, 'All I need to do is kick the knee through and it will be okay.' And if I'm worried about a triple lutz, all I have to do is get over the toe pick and it will be okay.

"Michelle, don't think, 'What happens if I don't do something? What happens if I don't get over the toe pick?' Think of positive things, and it will happen."

Boitano added something else before they hung up.

"Remember, Michelle, I've been through it all. I can help you. Call me anytime. I'll be there."

Not long after the call, Boitano ran into a friend at a skating event who suggested Kwan might need a sports psychologist.

"No she doesn't," Boitano replied. "She'll be fine."

Laughing, he added, "She has me."

The skating gurus didn't know what to make of Michelle Kwan's humiliating performance in Nashville. Peggy Fleming stood in the lobby of the Renaissance Hotel the day after Kwan made all her mistakes and talked about Kwan's long program in the softest, saddest tones imaginable, the way one would speak of death. She said quietly that nothing like that ever had happened to her, even though Fleming wasn't trying triple jumps when she won the Olympic gold medal in 1968. Still, this was an unspeakable skating horror, and Fleming felt nothing but empathy for Kwan. Few great skaters fell apart that badly on the national stage. And there was no doubt that Kwan still was a great skater.

The irony was that Kwan had self-destructed at the exact moment that the skating world felt she would anoint herself as the undisputed women's gold medal favorite heading into the 1998 Olympic year. Journalists were so certain that she would win the 1997 U.S. national title that they were focusing mostly on the Michael Weiss quad controversy and Todd Eldredge's fourth national title in their stories for the Sunday paper. They would save room for Kwan's victory, but it would require a few paragraphs, nothing more. Kwan's second consecutive national title hardly would be big news; this teenager was steamrolling right to the Nagano Games. National title, world title, Olympic gold medal, ho-hum.

Kwan had skated perfectly in the short program and even with her practice troubles with the triple lutz, there was no reason to expect that she would fall even once in the long program. Kwan was a gamer; no matter how ugly her practices, she always rose above them when it came time to perform. At the Japan pro-am in January, she had fallen three times on the triple lutz in her warm-up. When she skated for real, she nailed it.

She had been on a nearly perfect roll for two full skating seasons, since the 1995 U.S. nationals in Providence, the last time she had been predicted to win an important event and had failed to do so. The '95 nationals sat perched at the beginning of the four-year Olympic cycle leading to 1998, and with the retirement of Nancy Kerrigan to the professional ranks and Tonya Harding to community service, Kwan was next in line to lead American ladies skating. She had been the alternate at the Norway Games in 1994, and it was etched in ice, so to speak, that she would be the next great one, with four years to build to Nagano.

But Michelle Kwan's career wasn't going to unfold quite so neatly. A fall on her second triple lutz in the long program doomed her to finish second at the nationals that year in Providence. Eight of the nine judges gave Nicole Bobek first place. The other had Kwan first.

One month later, the two American teenagers departed for Birmingham, England, site of the 1995 world championships. Their reputations preceded them. Bobek had been arrested for home invasion, a felony burglary charge, at a fellow skater's home near Detroit the previous autumn, and the news had only recently swept like wildfire through papers in the United States. Her arrival in Great Britain was met by saucy tabloid headlines: "Brass Knuckle Dust-Up," read one, referring to a nickname used once by Richard Callaghan, Bobek's coach at the time, describing Bobek's old habit of wearing a ring on every finger and both thumbs. The Brits were in heaven: One year after the Tonya-Nancy affair, America had produced another blonde skater with an attorney, a court record, and an uncanny ability to land triple jumps.

While flashbulbs popped in Bobek's face, Kwan slipped into the country quietly. She was skating's sweet and innocent wallflower. On the day that Bobek had to face the rabid British press concerning the arrest, Kwan and her father took the train to London to see "the Big Ben," to use Michelle's words. There was a delightful innocence about Michelle that appealed to almost everyone in skating—almost everyone except the judges. With her long black ponytail bobbing, her simple, pink, little-girl dress, no earrings and only a touch of lipstick, Kwan skated and looked like the shy fourteen-year-old she was. Her vulnerability was as obvious as her jumping ability as she stood alone on the ice.

Once the world competition began, Kwan skated the most difficult and best-executed short program of any female skater—and ended up in fifth place, behind four women who either had easier jumps or made mistakes.

What went wrong?

"She still skates like a junior skater," French team director Didier Gailhaguet chided. "Small jumps, slow skating, beautiful style, beautiful technique, excellent, very good hope for the future, but not there yet."

Frank Carroll was well aware that the other skaters, including Bobek, France's Surya Bonaly and China's Lu Chen, were older and better known by the judges. He knew skating well enough to know Michelle could not win. Figure skating wasn't like other sports, where someone easily could come out of the blue and win the title. In skating, that happened once or twice a decade. Kwan could have jumped through the roof in the long program and still not have won. The deck was stacked against her at the 1995 worlds. The "junior skater" was not going to be allowed to win the world title. That would go to someone who looked like a lady, not a schoolgirl.

Not that Kwan really cared. U.S. skating officials were furious, but the little kid was having the time of her life. "I skated like it's a sport, went for everything and just gave it my best shot," she said. "It turned out great. I had nothing to lose. You might be the best in your heart, but not in other people's sight."

Kwan charged into the long program the next day and outdid herself. As she finished, she began to cry with the realization that she had landed seven triple jumps and skated perfectly. In the middle of the ice, as a standing ovation roared down upon her, she put her face into her hands and sobbed. Her body shook. Carroll, skating's renowned pillar of coaching strength, bit his lip because he, too, felt tears welling in his eyes. Michelle had done the absolute best she could do on the grandest stage of her career. Two judges gave her first place, but because she had been fifth coming into the long program, she managed to move up only to fourth overall. She was out of the medals by one spot, and there was only one reason why. She looked too young. Michelle Kwan needed to grow older—and fast.

Coincidentally, Lori Nichol, Michelle's choreographer, was ready with some mature, exotic music that she thought would take Kwan to the next artistic level. Figure skating without the painstaking compulsory school figures, eliminated in 1990, had become a sport in which it was better to look twenty-one than be twenty-one. Nichol and Frank Carroll knew that, but they also knew that a skater had to be ready to embrace artistic development. And they believed that, after Birmingham, Kwan was.

As Kwan joined the skating tour in the spring of 1995, Carroll went home to Lake Arrowhead, California, to ponder his skater's future. Lake Arrowhead, a mountaintop retreat of tall green pines, lingering snow, and sun-streaked beauty, was the perfect place to reflect on the intricacies of a figure skating career. "There's nothing here but skating," Carroll once warned Christopher Bowman, his temperamental skating star who preferred the nightlife of nearby Los Angeles. "If you come up here, you live and breathe skating."

That suited Carroll just fine. While Michelle was traveling to a different city every night on tour, he and Nichol buckled down to plot her future success.

Two years earlier, Carroll had hired Nichol, a coach and former skater living near Toronto, to be Michelle's choreographer. Carroll and Nichol became soulmates in their quest to ensure Michelle's skating excellence, often playing obscure compact disks for one another over the phone long-distance as they envisioned the next year's short and long programs. For the 1996 nationals and worlds, they planned Spanish music for the short program and for the long program, a real shocker—Michelle would portray the biblical temptress Salome, who wins the head of John the Baptist with an enticing dance.

While music was the driving force behind the transformation of Michelle Kwan from "junior skater" to mature young lady, it wasn't the only thing. Carroll approached Danny and Estella Kwan, Michelle's parents, and suggested a makeover for their daughter. It was time, Carroll implored. She was going to play a new role on the ice and she had to look the part. Michelle, who turned fifteen that July, finally was ready for makeup, he said, even though she joked that she was afraid to jump with mascara on, for fear that she would not be able to see.

But there was even more, Carroll told them.

"I think Michelle's beautiful," he said. "She has a beautiful face. But her ponytail hanging down doesn't do anything to enhance that. It's an unsophisticated look. We need to make some changes."

"No! No! No!" Danny Kwan replied. "You put makeup on, what is the purpose of makeup? You really take away something from the child."

The Kwans were traditionalists, raising their two daughters and one son true to their strict Chinese heritage. Danny was born in China in 1948 and grew up poor. Life had been so difficult for his ancestors that when Danny's father was a boy, he was sold to a wealthy farmer and told to stand guard over one of the man's cows. Several years later, a family member found the money to buy back the boy who would become Michelle Kwan's grandfather.

Estella was born in Hong Kong in 1950. They got married and moved to Los Angeles in 1974. They were a modest family: Danny worked as a manager for Pacific Bell and helped run the family's Chinese restaurant, Golden Pheasant, at night. There was nothing particularly special about them, or the way they were raising their children.

Until the girls began skating.

Money soon became scarce with two girls, Michelle and her older sister Karen, taking lessons. Even at the lowest levels, it costs several thousand dollars a year to keep one girl on the ice. And the Kwans had two. One year Danny Kwan told the family they wouldn't be able to have a Christmas tree, but Michelle entered a contest at school and won one.

They ran out of money for skating lessons for nine months, so the girls practiced on their own. The family sold its home in Rancho Palos Verdes and moved to a house owned by Danny's parents in Torrance, in a neighborhood of modest tract homes behind the restaurant.

With skating draining the family budget, the pressure began building. Leaving the rink in Torrance where Karen and Michelle skated, Danny Kwan once got so angry that he flung their skates into the parking lot.

But the girls were talented, and, as is the case with most skaters on the rise, the Kwans decided it was time for them to train in a place that could make them even better. Ice Castle International Training Center in Lake Arrowhead was that place. There would be sponsors and scholarships; the Kwans would be able to make ends meet. In December 1991, Michelle and Karen moved up to Lake Arrowhead, two hours east of Los Angeles in the San Bernardino Mountains, to work with Carroll. For three years, Danny Kwan drove "up the hill," as they called it, every night to sleep in his daughters' cramped, one-bedroom cabin. Estella moved into the tiny cabin in 1994 to live with her daughters. At first, Michelle attended a local school, but when she began traveling, she turned to tutors. Her life, like Tara Lipinski's, was centered around skating.

Skating became intoxicating. One weekend in the spring of 1992, when Carroll was out of town, Danny drove not-yet-twelve-year-old Michelle to Los Angeles to take the skating test that would allow her to move from the junior level to the senior (Olympic) level. Michelle had mumbled to her father something about Carroll giving the okay for the move to the highest rank of skating, even though Carroll had done no such thing. When Carroll returned home, he found out he was coaching a senior skater. He was furious he had not been consulted. He didn't think Michelle was ready for the big time. He thought she needed more seasoning.

Danny Kwan, traditionalist, became Danny Kwan, skating dad. He took charge of his daughter's weekend practices. He got involved in skating decisions and business decisions. He began directing his daughter's career. A friendly, chain-smoking, worrywart who always has a piece of philosophical wisdom to share with a stranger, Danny Kwan demanded a lot from Michelle. If she ducked out of signing autographs on the skating tour (she tried it once), he made sure she went back and gave her signature to every single person waiting in line. He asked Michelle to write a thank-you note to the instructor who failed her on her first attempt to get a driver's license.

He harped on the basics: "Remember, it's a sport," he told her. When she made a mistake on the ice, he would ask: "What have you learned from this?" He wanted her to work hard. Defeat, he told her, was not the enemy. Regret was.

Danny Kwan even hired an agent for his daughter in the midst of the Tonya-Nancy saga. Michelle was the Olympic alternate going into the 1994 Games, and when TV satellite trucks parked at the rink every day, the Kwans decided they needed help. They hired Shep Goldberg, who represented only one other athlete: Mary Lou Retton.

That was just about all the mild-mannered Goldberg needed to earn a very comfortable living: the multimillionaire gymnast, and the future millionaire skater.

Danny Kwan was a contradiction to some in the skating world. He and Estella were so conscientious that the U.S. Figure Skating Association sent other parents to them for advice on how to survive with a child in skating. But he also was making sure Michelle and the family made all the right moves in the sport. Fame and fortune were there for the taking. The rules were changing quickly in skating. The Boitanos never hired an agent before the 1988 Olympics; there was no money in the sport then. The Yamaguchis signed with International Management Group only in the weeks before Kristi's 1992 Olympic triumph. What would the Boitanos and Yamaguchis be doing if their child were training for the Olympics now? Could they have held out? Could anyone anymore?

By the spring of 1995, when Frank Carroll was telling Danny and Estella Kwan about the physical changes Michelle needed to make, he was talking to parents who were in a quandary. They wanted to remain true to their Chinese roots. But they also trusted Frank Carroll, and, of course, they wanted their child to do well on the international skating stage.

"She's not going to the schoolyard here," Carroll told the Kwans. "She's appearing before 18,000 people and millions on television. This would not be extraordinary if she were in the ballet. It's okay for a girl her age to wear makeup. It's part of the shtick. She's not performing a school exam. She's performing before thousands. You want her to look the part."

Danny and Estella Kwan sat down with Michelle. She said she was willing to try whatever was necessary to succeed on the ice. In 1992, after failing miserably as a junior at the national championships, she told Carroll she would train like crazy to get better. In 1995, she was willing to put on makeup, fix her hair, and attempt to play an exotic, mature role on the ice. She wanted to push herself artistically. Whatever was necessary.

Danny Kwan gave Carroll the go-ahead. He rationalized the change by telling Michelle she needed to look better on television.

"If you go to a funeral," he said, "you don't wear blue jeans. You wear what you have to wear to skate. You dress for respect."

But off the ice, his daughter would not wear much makeup. And on the ice, she absolutely would not wear earrings, Danny Kwan said. Some things would not change.

The transformation of Michelle Kwan came from July through October 1995, in the skating off-season. It's a time when journalists and television cameras aren't around, when the skater discards the previous season's programs and starts anew for the season to come. After skating on the springtime tour, Kwan came home to find Carroll and Lori Nichol, who flew in from Toronto for a few weeks, ready to go to work.

The role of Salome required Michelle to undergo a complete makeover. Carroll wanted Michelle's jet black hair pulled tightly into a bun. At first, Michelle braided the hair and tried to hold it in place with bobby pins. But one jarring landing on the triple lutz and the bobby pins went flying.

Carroll wouldn't leave anything to chance, not even bobby pins.

"You can kill yourself if you step on one of those things," he told Michelle.

The bobby pins were history. Michelle's hair would be sewn into a bun with yarn, a project that would take half an hour on the days she was competing.

Carroll was a stickler for this detail. One day at a competition, Michelle arrived for practice with her hair down and in the old ponytail. Judges come to practice to carefully watch the skaters go through their routines and begin to make decisions about how they will rank the skaters. Carroll didn't want to give them even the slightest chance to remember Kwan as a "junior skater."

"You don't get the point," Carroll said to Kwan, steaming. "Never appear again at an important practice with a ponytail! You have to look the part. Your grooming shows you care about this. You want to do everything to be the best!"

This was a message often given to skating stars. Peggy Fleming once took Kristi Yamaguchi aside after seeing a rather unflattering practice photo of her in the paper. Like a big sister, Fleming suggested to Yamaguchi that she always wear makeup when she skated in public.

The costume for Salome reflected Carroll's insistence on Michelle's emerging maturity. The cotton candy–colored dresses of her early childhood, the ones with the long sleeves and high necklines, were gone. In their place came an open-at-the-midriff, purple costume with short sleeves.

Observers barely recognized Kwan when she unveiled the new look publicly at the 1995 Skate America competition in October, which she won. Most had grown accustomed to the new Michelle by the nationals, which she also won. But reporters still wondered if there wasn't something devious about Carroll's grand plan. Was he trying to make a little girl look older simply to try to win a skating competition?

"I don't think it's vulgar," he said. "I'd be concerned about it if I thought it was vulgar. I think I'm a person with taste, and her parents have taste. I don't think I'd do something that was not tasteful. She looks marvelous. She loves this look now, and she's also reaching the age where she suddenly realizes she's an attractive girl. I think she feels pretty."

"I'm definitely a lot more confident now," Kwan said, obviously delighted. "I think having the new look helps me. I've worked really hard on the artistry, every finger, every movement."

If Frank Carroll was the brains of the operation to turn Kwan from international also-ran to world champion in fifty-two weeks, Lori Nichol was its heart. A former national-level skater from Philadelphia and Colorado Springs with sophisticated, girl-next-door looks, Nichol had been touring with John Curry's skating company when she took a break to visit relatives in Toronto. One day they went to a Mexican restaurant, where she took one look at their waiter and announced that she had just found the man she was going to marry. She was right. She ended up eventually moving to the Toronto area, where she became a skating coach and choreographer.

Nichol had been in awe of Carroll since he taught a seminar she attended as a teenager in the late 1970s. For more than a decade, she had no contact with Carroll, except to watch from afar as he coached Linda Fratianne to two world titles and the Olympic silver medal in 1980; then Tiffany Chin for several years before her emergence as an Olympian in 1984; then the erratic Christopher Bowman to the 1988 Olympic Games and the 1989 national title and world silver medal, among other achievements.

In the summer of 1992, Nichol took ten of the skaters she coached in Canada to Lake Arrowhead to take lessons from Carroll for a few weeks. She remembered seeing a "spitfire" landing triple jumps around her skaters. That little girl was Michelle Kwan.

While Nichol was watching Kwan, Carroll was admiring the way Nichol's skaters carried themselves on the ice. Six months later, he picked up the phone and called Nichol.

"I noticed when you were here," Carroll said, "that I was drawn to watching your skaters. Would you come and choreograph for Michelle?"

Nichol began working with Michelle heading into the 1994 Olympic year. Michelle turned thirteen the summer before the Norway Games, and while she was landing all her triple jumps, she was not yet much of an artist. There was an awkwardness to Michelle's skating at that time, but it alarmed absolutely no one. Girls who look perfect at thirteen rarely make it in skating. It's the gangly ones with room to grow into their bodies who have a chance.

But Nichol noticed there was something different about Michelle. She understood when Nichol talked about artistry. She couldn't pull it off on the ice yet. But she understood.

Nichol purposely inched along with her young skater. That first summer, as they prepared her programs for the 1994 nationals in Detroit, which also were the Olympic trials, Nichol gave Michelle one word to think about as she skated:

Ooze.

"I want you to ooze across the ice," Nichol said. "Think of how toothpaste comes out of a tube. I want you to ooooooze."

Kwan giggled.

Michelle began to skate more smoothly, from the edge of her skate blade all the way up to her arms and hands. Nichol was pleased. *Ooze,* it turned out, was the perfect word to tell Michelle Kwan.

That season, Kwan finished second behind Tonya Harding at the nationals and was bumped into the alternate spot when Nancy Kerrigan was placed on the Olympic team.

Heading into the next year, the 1994–95 skating season, Nichol made more progress with Kwan.

"Just once," Nichol said with a smile to Kwan, "point your toe for me. Just point your toe once. Show me a pointed toe!"

They both dissolved into laughter.

Nichol demonstrated intricate hand and arm positions—not that Michelle would be able to imitate them, but so that she would be introduced to them. She showed her how a sharp turn of the head could be extremely effective. Nichol even talked with Michelle about how her head sat on top of her shoulders and back. Nichol was doing the most basic skating choreography; she was introducing Michelle Kwan to her own body.

"This is your canvas, this is your brush, this is your paint," Nichol told her.

Nichol didn't go to Birmingham, England, for the 1995 world championships, but instead watched Michelle perform on television. Unlike the critics, Nichol didn't see a "junior skater." She saw a work in progress.

She noticed immediately that Kwan was "always off the music," meaning she was a beat or two ahead or behind the way they had practiced.

But as Nichol watched, she began to smile.

She found herself talking to Michelle through the television set:

"You know how to think your way through a program, don't you? You're beginning to understand the little tiny ideas of how to be an artist. You're ready to begin making a difference."

A year later, months after Kwan's makeover, Frank Carroll stood in the empty stands in Edmonton the day of the ladies qualifying round for the 1996 worlds. Kwan didn't have to qualify; she had already made the cut. But even if his girl wasn't on the ice at that moment, Carroll could find reason to worry.

Midori Ito of Japan, the 1992 Olympic silver medalist and the greatest jumper in the history of women's skating, was back, having reinstated from the professional ranks for a run at the Olympics in Nagano. Lu Chen, the defending world champion, was there. Irina Slutskaia, a Russian teenager with rosy cheeks and aggressive jumps, was also in the event.

It was enough to give Carroll an ulcer.

"My ace in the hole, if I have one, is Michelle's artistic mark," said Carroll, dressed in a wool tweed sports jacket, ever the proper skating gentleman. "Michelle should get 5.9s. Slutskaia, for instance, should get 5.7s. That's probably my biggest advantage—the look. I think Michelle has class. What I'm seeing Michelle evolve into, and I'm delighted about it, is she's become an artist. Two years ago people would say, 'Gee, she really jumps.' Now, people don't mention her jumps and spins anymore. They say, 'That was gorgeous, that was beautiful.'"

Carroll brought up the name of Janet Lynn, the 1972 Olympic bronze medalist from Illinois who still is considered the skater's skater, the most beautiful performer of all time.

"Janet was artistry in motion. I don't want Michelle to be Midori Ito or Tonya Harding with the jumps. I don't want people to say, 'Michelle Kwan, the girl who does the triple axel.' I want her to do the triple axel, but I don't want her to be known for that. I want her to be known as a real artist, like Janet Lynn."

But for all his talk of aesthetics, Carroll knew he was about to embark on an incredibly fierce competition.

"By the end of the week," he said sardonically, "you'll either find me floating in the bathtub in blood or celebrating at the bar."

Everyone in skating knew that if there was one man you wanted worrying for you, it was Frank Carroll. When other coaches were asked to name the prototypical skating coach, they invariably mentioned Carroll. Those coaches absolutely wanted Michelle Kwan to win the 1998 Olympic gold medal, but not necessarily because they felt so strongly about Michelle Kwan. Their affection was reserved for Carroll; they wanted Frank Carroll's skater to win the gold.

As a boy, Carroll learned to skate outdoors on a pond in Worcester, Massachusetts. "I would go to the movies and there would be newsreels on people skating and I would get so excited, I would almost wet my pants. I would break into a sweat, I would get so excited about it."

Carroll's father, a school official, considered skating frivolous. "He thought it was a waste of my mind," Carroll said.

But that didn't stop his son.

"To me, figure skating is a divine sport," he said. "It's a sport made by the gods. It's frictionless, there are beautiful, flowing costumes done by a costume designer, there is musical interpretation, there is emotion, there is athleticism and tremendous physical strength involved. It inspires people to cry, it inspires people to cheer, it pulls the emotions out of people."

And Carroll was one of its most inspired, emotional students. In the 1950s, he was trained by a skating legend, Maribel Vinson Owen, at various rinks around the Boston area. He once watched Owen slap the leg of world champion and future Olympic gold medalist Tenley Albright when Albright made a mistake while practicing compulsory school figures.

"Tenley Albright was the goddess of all time, and Maribel slapped her on the leg," Carroll remembered. "'My God,' I told myself, 'she touched the divine Tenley.'"

Owen, a nine-time national ladies champion in the '20s and '30s and the 1932 Olympic bronze medalist, used the same boot camp techniques to mold Carroll into a strong national-level skater. But she wanted more from him.

After graduating from Holy Cross with a degree in education, Carroll joined Ice Follies for $250 a week in 1960. Owen soon told him to quit skating and go to law school.

"Now, remember," she told him, "this is your last year in the show. You get yourself out of the show. And if you're not out of it, I'm going to call and have you fired!"

In 1961, however, Owen was killed in a plane crash that wiped out the entire U.S. delegation heading to the world figure skating championships in Prague. Her two daughters, one of whom had just been crowned the U.S. ladies champion, were also on the flight. In all, thirty-four skaters, coaches, judges, officials, and family members were killed in the crash near Brussels.

Frank Carroll never went to law school.

After four and a half years in the ice show, he became an actor in Los Angeles doing "terrible B movies," he said, and teaching skating in the afternoon. His part-time distraction, however, soon became his life's work, and Southern California—with its wealth, dense population and numerous rinks—proved to be a fertile skating training ground.

Carroll was a natural. He had strong ties to the Boston skating establishment, and, in time, some of his childhood friends became big-time judges and skating officials. This would be helpful in the years ahead, especially when one of his skaters needed a little advice, or even a little nudge, to qualify for, say, the national championships. Some coaches and skaters had little patience for judges who barged into their lives like a meddlesome great-aunt, but Carroll didn't mind. He loved to play that game. He knew when to take the advice, and when to nod his head and ignore it. Carroll also was a master technician, having been taught by the best. No one coached skating any better than he did. Even his language reflected his skating heritage. Skaters were "boys" or "girls" even if they were in their twenties. "I like her girl," Carroll would say of a female coach's skater.

Carroll had several strong skaters—some "girls," some "boys"— who emerged on the national scene before his first true star appeared. That was Linda Fratianne, who succeeded Dorothy Hamill as U.S. champion from 1977 through 1980. Heading into the 1980 Olympic Games in Lake Placid, New York, as a two-time world champion and gold medal favorite, Fratianne lost a close decision to East German Anett Poetzsch. It's a loss that still breaks Carroll's heart.

Carroll believes Fratianne was robbed of the gold in one of figure skating's most wicked political decisions. Those were the glory days of compulsory school figures, in which coaches and judges often negotiated behind the scenes to ensure the final placement of skaters well before the competition ended. Because it was nearly impossible to objectively judge the skaters' tracings of the figures on the ice, the judges could do whatever they wanted, and no one could argue.

One of Carroll's rivals was Carlo Fassi, an accomplished Italian skater and coach who came to America to find work after the top U.S. coaches were killed in the 1961 plane crash. After coaching Peggy Fleming, John Curry, and Dorothy Hamill to Olympic gold medals, Fassi took Great Britain's Robin Cousins into the 1980 Olympics.

Although Fassi consistently denied it, some within U.S. skating believed he worked a deal with the communist bloc judges in Lake Placid that made Fratianne a sacrificial lamb in order to give East Germany a gold medal. If Cousins defeated East Germany's Jan Hoffman for the men's gold medal, the agreement was that the judges would give East Germany the women's gold medal by putting Poetzsch over Fratianne.

That's exactly what happened.

"It was a setup job from day one," Carroll said. "Linda wasn't going to win. They kept her down in figures and she couldn't pull up in the short program and the free skate [long program]."

Carroll never was certain Fassi worked the East German switch, but he was sure about one thing: Fassi did not go out of his way to lobby for Fratianne in Lake Placid. This was galling to Carroll because he had sent Fratianne to Fassi for help on her school figures prior to the Olympics. Fassi, therefore, had been one of Fratianne's coaches. Why, Carroll wondered, would he not help her when she needed him most? But Carroll figured he knew the answer, that Fassi wanted Fratianne to stay with him and become his full-time pupil. When Fratianne did not stay and instead returned to Carroll, the theory goes, Fassi must have decided he owed Fratianne no loyalty.

After Fratianne lost, the two coaches bumped into each other in the Olympic arena. They screamed and yelled. Carroll was beside himself with anger. For years, they barely spoke.

But in 1993, Fassi showed up to coach at Lake Arrowhead, where Carroll already was ensconced as skating director and Kwan's coach. Although they didn't become best friends, they were civil. Fassi even tried to crack jokes about what had happened thirteen years earlier.

"You were really mad at me in the Olympic year," Fassi said jauntily to Carroll at the rink.

Before Carroll could say anything, Christa Fassi, Carlo's wife and coaching partner, stared at her husband and made sure he didn't say another word.

Carroll was pleasantly surprised that he could share the ice—and even the tight quarters of the coaches' room—with his old enemy.

"I didn't think we could work together, but we could," he said. "We talked and wound up telling stories about the old times and even laughing with each other."

Even so, Carroll never has gotten over Fratianne's defeat, and has vowed never to throw himself so completely into the career of one skater.

"I will never feel the same way about anyone else as I did about Linda Fratianne," he said. "Linda was the little girl I never had. She was my first world champion, and she was the special one."

On his left hand, Carroll wears a Viennese coin that the Fratiannes made into a ring for him. Linda's late mother, Virginia, was one of Carroll's best friends. He was so close to Linda and her family that coaching her almost became too much for him.

"It was horrible," he said. "It was agony to watch Linda compete. I had the feeling of a knife in my stomach. I literally had chest pains when she skated. And I wore gloves all the time because I could never shake anybody's hand because my hand was all sweaty."

After Linda left the amateur ranks, Carroll coached two more skaters who were among the best in the world: Tiffany Chin and Christopher Bowman. Those were stormy times for Carroll; both of those relationships ended with the skater leaving in an intensely emotional breakup. Carroll sometimes sat at home at his weekend retreat in Palm Springs wondering why he had been saddled with skaters whose immense talent was accompanied by such distressing psychological baggage, either the skater's or the family's. Would he ever get the chance to coach someone with talent but without the baggage? Would he ever again have another Linda Fratianne, a skater he loved with all his heart?

Then, one day in 1991, something wonderful happened to Frank Carroll. A tiny Chinese girl from Torrance, California, walked into his rink with her mother and big sister. Within days, Carroll realized that if he hung on to Michelle Kwan and gave it a few years, he would have one more chance to coach greatness.

On Saturday night, March 23, 1996, Frank Carroll and Michelle Kwan were holed up in the flower girls' room as Lu Chen's marks for the long program were being read over the public-address system in Edmonton Coliseum. First came the technical scores.

Then the artistic: "5.8, 5.8, 5.9, 5.9, 5.8, 5.9, 6.0, 6.0, 5.8."

"Two 6.0s!" Michelle Kwan gasped.

"Yes, Michelle," Carroll replied, "there were two 6.0s, but she got a lot of 5.8s too. You've got to believe in yourself. You can do this."

"I'm going to have to do a quadruple loop," Kwan said. She was nearly breathless imagining what it would take to beat Chen.

Quickly, she got herself back on track.

"No, no," she said. "Okay, what the heck, I'll have to do everything. Well, why not?"

Lori Nichol was sitting in the crowded stands. After Chen came two more skaters, then Kwan, who was next to last. There was an agonizing fifteen-minute wait for Michelle and Carroll backstage. Nichol fidgeted in her seat. She was a nervous wreck. She couldn't imagine how the other two were holding up with such a long wait, knowing Chen had skated so beautifully.

Nichol soothed her nerves with one thought: "Michelle can't be in better hands."

Carroll always looked for a quiet, off-the-beaten-path spot to wait with Michelle before it was her time to go out and skate. Sometimes, they sneaked into the men's dressing room, figuring no one would be there during the women's event. This time, it was the flower girls' cubbyhole, but there was one problem with that spot. It was not soundproof. Carroll's idea in hiding out, espoused by most coaches and skaters, was to find a spot where he and Michelle would not hear the scores of any other skaters before she performed. There was no point in a skater hearing other scores because there was nothing they could do to change them and it usually made them even more nervous than usual. This was all the more imperative for Michelle Kwan in the long program at the '96 worlds because Chen was the defending world champion. She also was as graceful as Kwan, if not more so, and stood in second place behind Kwan after the short program—a position from which she could leap to first overall simply by winning the long program.

But because the P.A. announcer's voice leaked into the flower girls' room, Carroll and Kwan knew more than they wanted to know. It would be the ultimate test for Michelle Kwan. Could she push what she knew of Lu Chen out of her head?

As Kwan took the ice and began skating, Nichol thought she looked a little tight. "But only I knew," Nichol said. "I could see her mind working furiously, thinking through everything."

Kwan's rendition of "Salome" that evening was to become a classic, as revered in some skating circles as Katarina Witt's "Carmen" in

1988 and Oksana Baiul's "Black Swan" in 1994. In four minutes, Kwan became a skater who ensured she never would be forgotten. She *became* Salome, portraying the role with great passion and exotic drama, but never losing sight of the program's athletic challenges.

As beautiful as she was artistic, it was Kwan's athleticism that won her the title. Ironically enough, all the talk of lipstick and mascara and sewn-in hair was forgotten as Kwan made the most important decision of her career to that point. Because she had to knock out the defending champion, Kwan knew before she began that she needed to land all seven of her planned triple jumps. But she pulled back on one of them early in the program, landing only a double on the end of her triple toe loop combination. Her mind began working quickly. She needed to add another triple to her program.

At the very end, in the final two seconds, she was scheduled to perform a double axel, a stunning finishing move at the end of four furious minutes of exertion. That would be where she would make the switch to the triple toe loop. She and Carroll had gone over that strategy from the moment they ran through the program for the first time the previous summer.

"If you don't do triple–triple here," Carroll would tell her over and over, "you add the triple in place of the double axel at the end, okay?"

Instead of taking off forward, off the edge of her skate blade into an axel, Carroll had said, she should come in backwards and pick in for a toe loop. As her energy waned and her body was about to give out, she would have to turn a double—the most difficult double, the double axel—into a triple toe loop, the easiest triple. Coach's orders.

Kwan knew she had no choice. She launched herself with her toe pick into the air for the triple toe loop, and landed perfectly, throwing an arm to the rafters as the music abruptly stopped and applause overtook the arena.

Kwan had done it. She had landed seven triples. Chen had landed six. Six of the nine judges awarded Kwan the higher technical mark. It looked good for Kwan when those first set of scores were announced. But Chen was reigning world champion. She was older. Her artistry was superb. If a majority of the judges picked her as the superior artist, she would repeat as world champion.

The announcer's voice rang out with Kwan's presentation marks: "5.9, 5.9, 6.0, 5.9, 6.0, 5.9, 5.9, 5.9, 5.9."

Quickly, in their heads, Kwan and Carroll compared Kwan's artistic marks with what they remembered of Chen's. It looked good for them. Moments later, the placements popped up on the TV screen.

Kwan had done it. She had beaten Chen on the second mark as well. Combining both marks, six judges went for Kwan, three for Chen.

"Oh my God, this is the world championships," Kwan said, catching her breath, "and I just skated the best in my life."

Michelle Kwan soon was a millionaire. She made a good portion of her money on the Campbell's Soups tour, where she commanded at least $5,000 a night for seventy-five shows in the spring of 1996. She skated an exhibition in China and joined Elvis Stojko's Canadian tour. Everything she did brought in big bucks. With the pace of her sport quickening as the 1998 Olympic Games drew closer, Kwan's calendar was packed.

Her family's life was changing too. Danny Kwan took early retirement from Pacific Bell in September 1995. "I wasn't putting my heart and soul into my job," he said. "I was putting my heart and soul into my child."

The family bought a home in Lake Arrowhead. Karen went off to Boston University. Michelle, who had been tutored since eighth grade, had moved into eleventh grade by the fall of 1996. Increasingly, she was doing her homework on airplanes.

Lori Nichol and Frank Carroll had been planning Michelle's short and long programs for the upcoming 1996–97 season even before they all got together at Lake Arrowhead in the summer of 1996 to teach them to Michelle. Brainstorming sessions had occurred in Carroll's Edmonton hotel room between practice sessions at the world championships. CDs once again had been played long-distance over the telephone. Nichol asked a music consultant in Canada to look for particularly obscure selections for her; it had come to the point where Michelle had to skate to something no one else ever had skated to. They had set a standard with "Salome," and they could not go back.

By the time summer came around, they began working on the programs. They had the music for the four-minute long program—from Azerbaijan, of all places—but they didn't yet have a theme. Nichol spent weeks researching mythology, goddesses, and exotic buildings, but had come up with nothing.

One day, Frank Carroll asked, "What about the Taj Mahal?"

To Nichol, it sounded perfect.

As a child, she used to collect and draw pictures of the Taj Mahal. The building fascinated her. If she could transfer her feelings to Michelle, she thought it would work. She would have Michelle represent the Taj Mahal from sunrise to sunset, in the form of the empress who lived in the palace. For a second consecutive year, Kwan would be playing a mature female role.

Nichol and Kwan put on their skates and went out to try some moves on the smooth ice surface at Lake Arrowhead as the music played over the loudspeaker.

"What could we do here, do you think?" Nichol asked Kwan.

Michelle played around for a few minutes as Nichol watched. Eventually, the theme developed. Hours were spent on intricate moves. To begin the program, Kwan struck a pose with her arms raised, and looked down at the ice. When she heard the first note of her music, she intuitively lifted her eyes. The eyes were Kwan's idea, not Nichol's, and they were a big hit. There wasn't a TV director in the world who would miss that opening shot.

For the short program, they picked "Dream of Desdemona," a dramatic score about Othello's slain wife. Nichol loved the two-minute, forty-second short program. She loved seeing how artistic she could make a technical program. She enjoyed editing the music to highlight the eight required elements: two jumps; one jump combination (two jumps in a row); three spins; and two fast step sequences or footwork. Omitting any one of those can result in a deduction of half a point off the first mark—the technical mark—by the judges.

But while the plans for Kwan were moving along, something was not right.

Nichol noticed a difference in Kwan in the summer of 1996. She had more demands on her time. And Nichol herself was anxious about having to live up to heightened expectations as the choreographer of the reigning world champion.

She was concerned that their work was not clicking as it had the year before. "Everything," Nichol said, "was a real struggle."

Michelle Kwan's problems all began with B:

Boots.

Body.

Brain.

Like most skaters, Kwan began breaking in a new pair of boots in the spring after wearing out her old pair. And, like most skaters, she complained long and loud about them. But, unlike most skaters, Kwan never got comfortable in them. Throughout the summer, her boots, made by SP-Teri, were a nagging concern. She tried different pairs. Nothing felt right. She wasn't skating well, and her feet felt awful.

Weeks before the autumn competitive season was to begin, Danny

Kwan had had enough. "It was driving me nuts," he said. He engineered a deal to switch from SP-Teri to Riedell, another American boot company. Riedell offered Michelle Kwan something she had never had: custom-made boots. Just like a beginning skater, Kwan got her boots off the shelf. She had been doing it for years, and never gave it a second thought. She then had those boots—the SP-Teris—fitted to her specifications. Riedell's offer of specially-made boots was understandably appealing.

So was word that Riedell boots were not as heavy as other companies' skating boots. They were made differently in the sole, which made them feel a bit lighter on a skater's feet.

Riedell also planned to feature Michelle in avant-garde, Nike-style advertising in various skating magazines. And the deal was lucrative: more than $100,000 over three years.

Traditionally, there was little money to be made in boots. Skating boots are not like sneakers; most Americans wear sneakers, but very few people ever buy a pair of skates. Riedell, however, wanted Michelle, and was willing to pay to get her.

As good as the agreement sounded, there were problems. The biggest was that no one had consulted Frank Carroll. When he found out, he was shocked. Why change companies so close to the new season? Why change companies at all? It was eerily similar to the time he found out Michelle had taken the test to move from juniors to seniors when he went away for the weekend. Every now and then, these things happened with the Kwans, but this one was particularly confounding. Why would the family of the new world champion change something so vital as the boots on her feet—even if it was for a six-figure deal?

At first, Kwan liked the Riedell boots. They were lighter and easier to break in. But Michelle soon started complaining that she felt uncomfortable on the ice. Something was wrong. Was it the boots? Speculation in the Kwan camp was that she was leaning back too far, as if her heels were riding too low inside the boots. They began to adjust the mountings of her blades. Her toes began to hurt. Nothing felt quite right. And that included, most critically, her triple jumps.

"Is it a boot problem?" Danny Kwan asked himself. "Is it her problem? We might never know."

Boots are finicky things. When they are custom-made, every pair is different. In 1993, Brian Boitano was having trouble landing his triple axel. Trying to figure out what was wrong, his coach, Linda Leaver, checked old videotapes of his jumping technique and even measured the angle of the blades mounted on the boots. For three months, they were confounded—until Boitano and Leaver compared the heels of his new boots with the heels of his old boots, both made by the same company, and found that the new boots had heels that were one-quarter inch lower.

He switched back to the old ones and within one week his jump was back.

But Kwan had to stick it out with the Riedells. The ads were going to be running soon—beautiful, trendy, full-page ads:

"You've spent long hours in a lonely rink. You've worked while others slept and practiced while others played. You're reaching for the future and it calls your name. We understand. Welcome to Riedell."

Then there was Kwan's body. That had changed too. She had gained almost ten pounds in two years to reach five-foot-two and 103 pounds. While she still was petite (her clothes size was 0, or, at most, 2), she was growing in a way that didn't necessarily enhance her jumping. She had developed a bustline. Her hips were filling out. This was significant. Although Kwan was nine years younger than Kristi Yamaguchi, the last U.S. Olympic gold medalist, Kwan already had a more substantial figure. It was a simple law of physics: Spinning and jumping became more difficult when the object doing the spinning and jumping became bigger.

"Even if it's a little bit of weight, it throws you off," Kwan said. "If you gain one pound, it makes the jump lopsided. Some days, oh my God, I can't get off the ice. And other days, I'm floating. It's harder to run through the long program now than it was before. When I was thirteen, it was like, 'Let's do another one.' Now I'm winded."

Finally, there was Michelle's brain. It was racing one hundred miles an hour. A bright, inquisitive child, she began to do something that world-class athletes—especially figure skaters—shouldn't do very often: think.

"I practice every day and some days I'll be a little off and I'll be wondering, 'What's wrong with me that I can't do this? Is it me? Am I thinking too much?' I just have to adjust to what I have and if my body does something wacko, I have to adjust to that."

At home in Lake Arrowhead, Kwan watched the 1996 Summer Olympic Games from Atlanta every night on television. She started to get nervous, as if seeing the Summer Olympics made her think of her role as the favorite at the upcoming Winter Games in 1998.

"She enjoyed watching the U.S. gymnasts," Lori Nichol said. "She

Tara Lipinski rejoices after a perfect performance at nationals. (*Copyright Leah Adams, 1997*)

Michelle Kwan falls at the 1997 national championships. (*Copyright AP/Wide World Photos/Cliff Schiappa*)

Lu Chen tries to make a comeback at the 1997 world championships. (*Copyright Leah Adams, 1997*)

Scraping the ice with his left foot, Michael Weiss lands his controversial quadruple toe loop. (*Copyright Associated Press/Mark Humphrey, 1997*)

Canadian superstar Elvis Stojko
stops, stands, and points.
(*Copyright Leah Adams, 1997*)

Nicole Bobek performs her trademark
spiral. (*Copyright Leah Adams, 1997*)

The Weiss family at the 1997
world championships: Margie, Greg,
Michael and Lisa Thornton.
(*Author's collection*)

Tara Lipinski answers questions
at the 1997 world championships.
(*Author's collection*)

Shep Goldberg joins client Michelle Kwan backstage at the 1997 Champions Series final in Canada. (*Author's collection*)

Brian Boitano hugs Michelle Kwan as Peggy Fleming (far left) and Dick Button wait their turn at the 1997 worlds. (*Copyright Leah Adams, 1997*)

Michael Rosenberg with two of his popular clients, Tai Babilonia and Randy Gardner. (*Courtesy of Michael Rosenberg*)

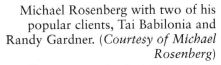

Mike Burg, Tara Lipinski's agent, is surrounded by reporters at the 1997 worlds. (*Author's collection*)

Oksana Baiul had a difficult time on tour in the spring and summer of 1997. (*Copyright Leah Adams, 1997*)

Nancy Kerrigan donates one of her skating dresses to Planet Hollywood, June 1997. (*Author's collection*)

Tonia Kwiatkowski and Carol Heiss Jenkins at a pro-am competition in 1996. (*Courtesy of Tonia Kwiatkowski*)

Tonia Kwiatkowski was eight years old when she began taking lessons from Carol Heiss Jenkins in 1979. (*Courtesy of Tonia Kwiatkowski*)

Audrey Weisiger helps choreographer Brian Wright at the 1996 AIDS walk in Washington, D.C. (*Author's collection*)

Veterans Tonia Kwiatkowski and Rudy Galindo backstage on tour, 1996. (*Copyright Leah Adams, 1996*)

Brian Wright and Audrey Weisiger work on the music for Michael Weiss's short program in a recording studio in April 1997. (*Author's collection*)

Coach Galina Zmievskaia with Scott Davis during practice in Simsbury, Connecticut, August 1997. (*Author's collection*)

Ilia Kulik heads to practice in Marlboro,
Massachusetts, August 1997.
(*Author's collection*)

Todd Eldredge and Tara Lipinski meet
the press in Detroit, August 1997.
(*Author's collection*)

Lori Nichol, Frank Carroll, and
Michelle Kwan plan Kwan's
Olympic programs at Lake
Arrowhead, California, April 1997.
(*Copyright Cindy Lang, 1997*)

Lori Nichol, Michelle Kwan, and Frank
Carroll—the perfect skating package—
at a 1996 competition.
(*Copyright Cindy Lang, 1996*)

Richard Callaghan listens
as Tara Lipinski talks to reporters
at Skate America, October 1997.
(*Author's collection*)

Tara Lipinski and Michelle Kwan
share a ride on a golf cart at
Skate America, October 1997.
(*Author's collection*)

Surya Bonaly, in the stands in
Russia, hoping for another Olympic
berth. (*Author's collection*)

Tamara Moskvina and Alexei Mishin (middle)
defeated the Protopopovs (left) and
Irina Rodnina and Alexei Ulanov (right) to win
the pairs title at the 1969 Russian nationals.
(*Courtesy of Tamara Moskvina*)

Artur Dmitriev seeks the advice of Tamara Moskvina and Igor Moskvin at practice in St. Petersburg, Russia, November 1997. (*Author's collection*)

Alexei Urmanov, complete with gloves, performs in Springfield, Massachusetts, 1996. (*Copyright Leah Adams, 1996*)

Alexei Mishin walks and talks as injured star Alexei Urmanov listens during practice in St. Petersburg, Russia, November 1997. (*Author's collection*)

Elena Berezhnaia and Anton Sikharulidze, Tamara Moskvina's new pairs skaters, captured the attention of the skating world in 1997. (*Copyright Leah Adams, 1997*)

was happy when they performed well and sad when they didn't do so well a few days later. I think she started thinking about the Olympics, her Olympics, in 1998. She was already facing the demons, already putting the wheels in motion."

Kwan had Olympics-on-the-brain. She couldn't help it. Everyone reminded her about it. Some nights she had trouble going to sleep. "Oh my gosh, there's next year," she would say over and over, "and then the Olympic year. You know it could be one horrible day . . . a little mistake can cost you the gold."

Skating had become much too complicated for the little girl who first went to the rink because she loved the feeling of flying on the ice.

It was more chaotic than usual at Lake Arrowhead in the summer of 1996. Flashy Nicole Bobek, one of Kwan's strongest rivals, had shown up to begin taking lessons from one of her former coaches, Carlo Fassi. She had left Coach No. 9, Barbara Roles Williams, and, running out of coaches whom she and her family had not alienated, she settled on Fassi, one of the few former Bobek mentors who would take her back. This didn't upset Michelle, but Frank Carroll fumed. He too had coached Bobek. It was a competitive coach's worst nightmare; you wake up in the morning and go to the rink and find out Nicole Bobek has shown up to share the ice with your skater.

Carroll and Fassi, the old warriors from the 1980 Olympics, soon found themselves visiting with Carol Probst, the owner of the rink at Lake Arrowhead.

Fassi wanted Bobek allowed in; Carroll did not.

"My concerns were for Michelle, not with what Nicole was doing," Carroll said. "This is Michelle's backyard, this is her rink. I wanted no interference in anything Michelle was doing. My reaction was, 'Why do I need this? Why do we have to have her here? Why should we have this situation?'"

Carroll and Fassi shook hands and waited for Probst's decision, which, upholding tradition, went Fassi's way.

But Bobek injured her back and could barely train throughout the fall, so it was as if she wasn't there after all.

Despite her problems with her skates and her changing body, Michelle Kwan rolled through the 1996 fall schedule. She won three events in three different countries, but Carroll was not entirely happy.

"She's okay, but she hasn't been in her top form," he said. "I think she would rather feel that she skated really well, came off the ice and did a good job, than win and get off the ice feeling that she did a crappy job. There's not great joy in winning that way."

Carroll also happened to mention that Kwan was having trouble adjusting to new boots.

"It's like having bum equipment," he said. That was as much as Carroll would say. The Kwan camp didn't want to advertise the fact that the new boot deal wasn't going exactly as planned.

One week before Christmas, Kwan competed in the U.S. Figure Skating Association's pro-am in Philadelphia, a made-for-TV extravaganza noteworthy for only one reason: Kwan fell in a short program for the first time in ten months.

It was not a real event; everyone seemed to get 6.0s. The fall didn't count and never was mentioned in her statistics. But the embarrassingly inflated scoring system obscured a very important development for Michelle Kwan on her way to the 1997 nationals, and, indirectly, the 1998 Olympics: She bombed in the short program. If she had done the same thing at a nationals, worlds, or Olympics, she almost certainly would have been out of the running for the gold medal.

That night in Philadelphia, after falling on the triple lutz, she went up for her planned double axel and came right back down, turning it into nothing in mid-air.

"I'm okay, I'm alive," Michelle said, exasperated. "I decided to drop the whole situation from my mind, because I never do that [fall]."

Four days later, she went to Boston to compete against Kristi Yamaguchi in another made-for-TV event. Yamaguchi, the professional skater most likely to be able to keep up with the Olympic division jumping beans, was taking the battle with Kwan very seriously. She wanted to win it. But she fell and Kwan did not, and Kwan won another event.

Kwan spent Christmas at home, then flew to Tokyo for another pro-am, the Japan Honda Cup. She and her parents celebrated New Year's Eve, California time, on the two-hour shuttle bus ride from Narita Airport into the city. She arrived two days ahead of some of her competitors to get acclimated to the time change; the Kwans and Frank Carroll and Shep Goldberg wanted her ready even for the most insignificant of events.

Kwan was the youngest skater in Japan and soon found herself surrounded on the practice ice by Katarina Witt, Yuka Sato, Nicole Bobek, Irina Slutskaia, and Surya Bonaly. Both Witt and Bobek were skating to music from *Evita,* while Sato was performing to Debussy's exquisite "Prelude to 'The Afternoon of a Faun,' " music made famous twenty-five years earlier by Janet Lynn.

Kwan was skating to music from *Pocahontas,* an exhibition-style number.

She skated over to the boards where Carroll was sitting in the stands, all alone.

"I hate this," she pouted. "Everyone else is Evita or some other grown-up character, and who am I? I'm Pocahontas!" Kwan put her hands on her hips and threw her head back petulantly.

Carroll laughed out loud.

"Well, let's see how you *do* as Pocahontas before we worry about changing the program," he replied.

She did just fine. The youngest was the best, once again. As her competitors made mistakes or skated less difficult programs, Michelle hung in again, overcoming the three practice falls on her triple lutz to skate well and win another title.

Douglas Haw, who runs a rink in Toronto where Michelle skates when she works with Lori Nichol on the East Coast, had come to the Japan event and was watching Kwan from the stands.

"She's the best-packaged skater in the world," he said. "Think about it. The three perfect people—Michelle, Frank Carroll, and Lori Nichol—got together at just the right time to produce the perfect package. You don't see that happen very often in this sport."

Kwan looked so dominant on the ice that it was natural for everyone, even the television reporters covering the event in Japan for Turner Sports, to wonder if after winning the Olympic gold medal all but conceded to her in 1998, she would stick around for the 2002 Games in Salt Lake City.

Danny Kwan was nearby as a nighttime practice session ended.

"Hey, Danny," they shouted, "if Michelle . . ."

"Nooooo," Danny Kwan said, realizing what was coming and backing away with a nervous smile.

The reporters continued.

"If Michelle wins in 1998, will she go on to 2002?"

Danny Kwan nodded his head confidently.

"It's a sport," he said. "Of course she'd be back."

"She'd be twenty . . ." one of the commentators said, quickly searching for Michelle's age.

Danny Kwan held up one finger.

"Twenty-one," he said.

"Not that you've thought about this, eh, Danny?" the reporters shot back amid laughter.

Just then, Shep Goldberg, Michelle's doting agent, came by.

"Would she come back in 2002?" Goldberg was asked.

"Yes," he said quickly.

"2006?"

"You bet," Goldberg said. "That's why we wanted Lillehammer, so we could have had four [Olympics]."

Goldberg was referring to Michelle's alternate status in 1994 as the Tonya–Nancy saga unfolded.

The TV reporters chuckled. On their way out of the practice rink, they bumped into Michelle, rubbing her aching toes as she took off her skates in front of a row of lockers.

"Okay, Michelle," they said, "we were just talking to your dad and Shep about this. If you win the Olympic gold medal in Nagano, will you stick around 'til 2002?"

"Yes."

"And 2006?"

"Why not? I'll only be twenty-five," she shot back without hesitation.

The commentators laughed and walked out of the building.

"That's all fine," said one of them, 1984 Olympic pairs silver medalist Peter Carruthers, "but let's see her win the first one."

Before and after her trip to Japan, Michelle Kwan welcomed a procession of journalists to Lake Arrowhead, each of whom wrote glowingly about her upcoming coronation as national champion and Olympic gold-medalist-to-be. The name Tara never came up. This was a one-woman show.

"I want to be a legend, like Dorothy Hamill and Peggy Fleming," she told the *New York Times*. She said these things so politely, so reverently, that she never came off as boastful.

Kwan flew to Nashville, where, for the first time in a competition in the 1996–97 skating season, she would be on display for the national media. Only a handful of American reporters showed up for the autumn skating events. But the nationals drew a crowd. When the journalists gathered at a dingy practice arena on a rainy Thursday and watched Kwan miss lutz after lutz, seven of nine in all, they started to realize that the Michelle Kwan of 1997 wasn't the infallible

Salome they remembered from the year before. But even so, they knew that Kwan always pulled herself together in time for competitions. She was a self-correcting machine, a performer who thrived in the spotlight.

And, anyway, who else was there?

Carroll dismissed the problems as "lutzitis," and helped Michelle change her entry into the jump, a switch akin to a golfer with the yips suddenly changing to a different putting grip the week of the U.S. Open.

But sometimes when a skater is having trouble, change can be a good thing. That's what Carroll hoped. Instead of running across half of the length of the ice on the outside edge of her left skate, then picking in with her right toe to launch herself into the air, Kwan approached the jump on her right skate. She quickly shifted her weight to the left skate for less than a second, then picked into the ice with her right toe. She went up. She came down. Often, she landed not on her feet, but on her seat.

Carroll kept it a secret, but he was pretty sure he knew why Kwan had "lutzitis."

The boots.

She simply could not stay perfectly balanced—the skating term was "hold an edge"—as she glided across the ice on the outside edge of her left skate. What she could do a year earlier in the SP-Teris, she could not do as well in the Riedells. Even her spiral, the beautiful maneuver in which she puts one leg in the air and glides on the edge of her other skate, had become scary. Carroll actually held his breath when she performed her spiral. When Kwan wobbled inside her boots, who knew what would happen?

But boots and all, Carroll still figured Kwan was good enough to win her second consecutive national title. He was banking on her reputation to come through when it mattered most.

"All I have is our track record to go by," he said, as he was cornered by twenty writers at the conclusion of the dreadful practice session. "She's a really cool competitor and right on when the time comes. Then again, this is a really different scenario. You're now talking about the national champion and world champion defending her title. It's very different defending a title than struggling to win one. Our job is to be cool and calm and appear totally in control."

But that only went so far.

"It's fine talking, but until you get into a situation, you don't really know what it's like," Carroll said. "So, here we are."

*   *   *

Kwan survived the short program by gritting her teeth and landing the triple lutz, and was in first place heading into Saturday night's long program.

At her home in Canada, Lori Nichol turned on her television set, as she always did when Michelle was skating and she couldn't be there. When she saw Michelle slip off the edge of her blade after landing the triple toe loop–double toe loop combination, she knew it was a fluke. The jump had been fine. Those things happened. But, almost immediately, Nichol noticed Michelle was not fine. She saw her hesitate. Michelle was tensing up. She was thinking too much.

Nichol knew Kwan was in big trouble.

The amazing thing to Nichol was not that Kwan fell apart in the next few minutes on the ice, but that she had held off having that kind of disastrous performance as long as she did. What a season it had been for the little sixteen-year-old. It was one thing to try to repeat as a U.S. or world champion in the volatile 1990s. It was quite another for Kwan to try to keep her titles as her body developed and her feet wobbled beneath her.

When *Sports Illustrated* hit the newsstands less than a week after Nashville, it featured not one, not two, not three, but four pictures of Michelle falling, all in living color.

"All they're saying is the truth," Kwan said with a chuckle about the magazine photos. Life went on. Brian Boitano called. She laughed with him. CBS came by on February 18, one year to the day before the women's short program at the Olympics, for an on-camera interview. The network of the Olympics didn't visit Tara that day. It wanted only Michelle. She smiled some more.

Nine days after the nationals long program, she was talking on a conference call with reporters preparing to cover the Champions Series final in Hamilton, Ontario, at the end of February and beginning of March. It was the first time she had been asked extensively about nationals. It was as if she were talking from a shrink's couch. She had a lot to say.

"I think it was good this happened," Michelle said. "I was going through a weird time, not thinking the right way. Going into nationals, I was thinking, 'I can't miss a thing. Will I miss the combination in the short?' I felt I had more to lose than gain. I thought I had to be perfect . . . I skated like a scared chicken . . . After my performance, I said, 'Hit me, Dad. Wake me up.'

"It was like someone else took over my body. My evil twin skated for me. But I threw her away. She doesn't live anymore."

She was a little girl looking for answers anywhere she could find them. Carroll suggested she "erase the names of the competitions," so she wouldn't be heading to the Champions Series final, or to worlds. She would simply be going to different countries to skate.

The problem was, Michelle Kwan was too smart for that. She was searching, trying to grab ahold of anything to make things right. Within a twenty-minute conference call, she listed half a dozen antidotes. The only thing she didn't touch on were her boots. No one asked about them.

"I just heard Michael Jordan shot only fourteen shoots," Kwan said, laughing at herself for her awkward misstatement. "People would say, 'Michael Jordan only had fourteen points?' Well that's what they are all saying about me. 'Can you believe Michelle Kwan skated so bad?' "

Michael Jordan, however, plays a sport that gives him eighty-one other regular season games and the entire playoffs to make up for it. And he has a team to help him win when he is not playing well.

Michelle Kwan's sport rarely gives an athlete a second chance, but this time, it would. The national title was gone, but Kwan was thrilled to have the Champions Series final in Canada just two weeks later. Tara Lipinski would be there, and so would the international judges who had low-balled Kwan as a fourteen-year-old at the 1995 world championships. Now fourteen-year-old Tara would get to face the music, and sixteen-year-old Michelle could return to her rightful place at the top of the sport.

It all set up so perfectly. It was what soothed her in the most frightful moments immediately after the long program in Nashville, when she went to the dressing room and cried and cried.

"It's okay," she told herself, "I still have the grand prix [Champions Series] final. I still have worlds."

But if there was one thing Michelle Kwan was beginning to understand about her career, it was that things that looked so certain were not quite what they appeared to be.

THE ATHLETE
AND THE ARTIST

There are two scores in figure skating, one for technical merit, the other for presentation. In the mid-to-late 1990s, one man in the Olympic division personified the first mark. Another man who lingered in the Olympic world, then turned professional, embodied the second mark.

Elvis Stojko and Rudy Galindo are their names.

The gray clouds never lifted over Hamilton, Ontario, the week the skaters came to town. The city looked forbidding; the skyline was etched against the low clouds, with Lake Ontario sitting quietly nearby. In the middle of this town was the ice arena. There, the people of Canada came in from the cold and found Elvis.

In the last days of February and the first days of March, Elvis Stojko was under siege. If his competitors weren't after him, the press was. There was criticism of his blunt, no-nonsense skating style. His jumps were monumental, the best in his sport. But his artistry, to some, was nonexistent. His skating had grown slow, his footwork dull.

Sensing trouble, Canadians came out in droves to support their countryman. If Elvis was in the building, they wanted to be there too. Even the practice sessions turned into Elvis support groups. Some skaters train in silence. Elvis practiced to standing ovations.

The best skaters in the world came to Hamilton, to a town just an hour drive from the Toronto area where Elvis was born and raised, to take on the king of skating. This was one of the newer competitions on the Olympic division landscape, the Champions Series final. It came at a strange time, three weeks before the world championships. Although it had no effect on Olympic qualifying, it was a preview of sorts of the 1998 Games, because it was likely that the future men's gold, silver, and bronze medalists were in Hamilton on that ice. Todd Eldredge and the Russians Alexei Urmanov and Ilia Kulik had come to take on Elvis. So had another Russian Alexei, the not-quite-seventeen-year-old Alexei Yagudin, already carrying the promise of the next generation of Russian skating.

Urmanov, the virtually unknown 1994 Olympic gold medalist, and Kulik, the baby-faced assassin regarded as the sport's most talented athlete, came extra-prepared. They had a quadruple jump in their skating repertoire.

So did Elvis. The quad was his jump most of all. No one did it better.

Elvis knew what his competitors were doing, and he relished it. If some of the others had a quad, he would go one step further. He would develop a quad combination—a quad and another jump, done back-to-back. The art of competition drove him. The art of artistry did not. "I want to show that it's not a ballet recital, it's not a dance recital," he said. "It's a sport."

Athleticism was one part of the equation. But what about presentation? According to some experts, Elvis didn't have any presentation. He maintained, of course, that he did, that his martial arts style—with black leather accoutrements and jumps that reached the rafters—was artistry in the '90s in men's figure skating.

Elvis was on one side of the argument. On the other side were people who said his skating reminded them of a man with his feet stuck in drying cement.

"Tedious, two-footed approaches . . . an utter lack of artistry," was the way the *Chicago Tribune*'s Philip Hersh analyzed Stojko. Banter in the press room did not spare him. After watching Elvis stretch his arms to the audience and to the rafters, point toward imaginary targets and generally flail away for four and a half minutes, Jere Longman of the *New York Times* said, "I don't know if he skated well, but two planes landed during his performance."

Previous generations of male skaters also criticized the two-time world champion and 1994 Olympic silver medalist. They were concerned that Stojko, once quite refreshing, had changed, that he had moved into a universe all his own, creating a world-be-damned, Elvis-style choreography that appealed artistically to almost no one but Elvis himself.

"I think he has got much more talent and ability than what he's presenting," 1984 Olympic gold medalist Scott Hamilton said days after the Champions Series final. "I hope for anyone in skating that they present the best of themselves at the biggest time of their life. It's kind of the ' Here-I-am time.' I think Elvis has got a lot more in there. I see moments where I think he's absolutely brilliant, then I'd see other moments where I'd go, 'Why did you do that? You're better than that. Challenge yourself.'"

Fellow Canadian Kurt Browning, a four-time world champion, told CBS Sports that Stojko "is so geared towards being a warrior that he might miss the boat on how to win. Sometimes I worry about Elvis not . . . playing smart and going ahead and, for the Olympic Games, maybe giving the audience and the people what they want and . . . allowing himself to win. He insists on standing on his own ground, which I totally respect, but there's nothing against listening too. Sometimes he shuts out."

Coaches chimed in as well. "He's slow," said Evy Scotvold, known for guiding Paul Wylie and Nancy Kerrigan to Olympic silver medals. "All he does is stand around. You never see that hard stroke, that acceleration, like a hockey player going around the corner, doing crossovers."

"The program is blank," said Joe Inman, a highly regarded world judge from Virginia. "From a musical point of view, you'll find a lot of blank areas that don't fit. There are areas that don't make sense with the music."

As the criticism rang in his ears, Stojko thrived. If Browning was correct—that Stojko was a warrior—this, then, was Elvis's ultimate battleground. Deep inside, Stojko knew he was right. Stojko had a recklessness that he learned from his parents, Steven and Irene, both of whom fled from their communist homeland in 1956. Steven escaped from Yugoslavia (the current Slovenia) at the age of twenty-one, crossing the Yugoslav-Austrian border with seven others one night. Irene darted between bales of hay to avoid searchlights as she and twenty others fled Hungary for Austria. They both settled in Canada, where they met and married.

Years later, Steven Stojko was in a musical group when Irene was pregnant with Elvis. They sang ballads, including Elvis Presley's "Love Me Tender." When their son was born in 1972, it seemed only logical to name him after Presley.

Elvis Stojko was not born to be a skater. God gave him a short, squat body with stubby arms. It was more of a wrestler's body, a good build for his other pursuits, dirt bike racing and martial arts, in which he has a black belt in karate. If he wore short sleeves, his arms looked even shorter and less artistic. At five-foot-seven and 157 pounds, he was not a pretty skater.

But that was what appealed to his fans. He was different. He had become every bit the rebel in skating that his namesake had been as a performer.

Elvis wanted to rip the ruffles right off male skating. If he wasn't the most handsome or fastest out there, so be it. He often would talk of where he wanted "to take the sport," as if he were its one and only savior. Elvis fashioned himself as a skating action hero. He was certain that his efforts were taking skating in the right direction, that, in the late '90s, men's skating needed Elvis more than Elvis needed men's skating.

"I've been put down for the fact that I looked different, that I had a more masculine style," he said. "A guy that's masculine and wants to skate like a man should not be ridiculed for being a man. There's going to be criticism anyway: 'If he jumps well, let's see what else you can hack down.'"

He didn't play by skating's rules. He defied the judges, he defied tradition. When a gaggle of teenyboppers squealed his way, he beamed. That told him he was a success. He skated for the audience, and he skated for himself. He did not skate for the judges, the people who ultimately controlled his career.

This wasn't a new philosophy for Elvis Stojko. From the moment he stepped onto the international stage, Stojko was a controversial figure. In 1992, the first of his two Olympic Games as Kurt Browning's understudy, Stojko was lowballed by the judges who were definitely in a wait-your-turn, Kurt's-the-one-we-care-about-now mode. This happens when a country has two good skaters of different skating generations in the same major competition. Brian Boitano waited in the wings for Scott Hamilton, Janet Lynn for Peggy Fleming. Rarely will international judges give one country two medals at an Olympics or world championships.

In Albertville, Stojko skated a nearly flawless long program and actually dropped a place from sixth in the short program to seventh overall.

"That was really weird," he said. "I knocked on the door, I've put in my time, I've skated cleanly so many years, why aren't I recognized? But I said, 'I'm not going to let them affect the way I think about my skating or the way I think about myself. I'm going to put it down again [Elvis-speak for skating cleanly] and they're going to have to deal with me again because I'm going to be there, I'm going to be there all the time.'"

A few weeks later, Stojko went to the 1992 world championships. "I came back, I put it down again. . . . Third place."

At the 1994 Winter Games, he once again went in as a backup to Browning, the reigning world champion. But as Browning, Brian Boitano, and Viktor Petrenko, the pre-Olympic favorites, fell and took themselves out of the running, the gold medal came down to a clear choice between the frilly, Dutch Masters style of lyrical Alexei Urmanov, and the kung-fu, black-on-black, Bruce Lee–look of Elvis Stojko.

"I have seen the future of figure skating, and it is Elvis," wrote C. W. Nevius in the *San Francisco Chronicle*. "Tonight in the men's free program, Canadian Elvis Stojko will not be doing an interpretation of the unfolding of a tulip. He will not pretend he is a fluffy cloud, a jolly snowman or a sad little bumblebee. He is doing martial arts."

Urmanov and Stojko each made one mistake on a jump, but otherwise performed spectacularly. Stojko, who skated before Urmanov, did not go backstage and hide in a bathroom or closet when his competitor took the ice, as other Olympians had over the years. He settled in beside Browning near the Canadian television booth to watch Urmanov skate. This was a sport, Stojko knew, and if he was going to lose, he certainly wanted to watch the man who beat him.

After Urmanov finished an exhausting four and a half minutes of beautiful if a bit uncertain skating, Stojko knew it would be up to the judges to decide. This was not good news for him. A tie almost always goes to the Russians. Nine-judge figure skating panels often are made up of a majority of Europeans; so it was at the Olympics. When the jumps were about equal, it came down to a matter of taste. And European judges, unlike North Americans, rather liked their male skaters in ruffles.

As Urmanov's scores popped up, Stojko leaned over Browning's shoulder to see the Canadian broadcasters' TV monitor, where the ordinals, or placements, would immediately appear and the standings would be determined. To see the screen, Stojko also had to look over the shoulder of another man, one of the announcers from Canada. The man was wearing a suit and headset in 1994, but, in 1988, he had known the agony of waiting to find out his own Olympic fate. As Elvis Stojko stared over the shoulders of Kurt Browning and Brian Orser, they all saw what none of them wanted to see again—another Canadian second-place finish. Orser had lost the "Battle of the Brians" to American Brian Boitano in 1988; Stojko had lost the battle for male skating's soul to a man dressed as the Jack of Spades.

Within minutes, Elvis was standing on a platform wearing a silver medal around his neck and a polite smile on his lips. He turned around to look at his friends in the crowd in the tiny arena in Hamar, Norway. He raised his eyebrows. He took a deep breath.

This wasn't what he had come to the Olympics to do—finish second.

Stojko knew what he had to do. Right then, he knew there could be no other choice. This was not right. He wanted the gold. It was obvious he had to stay in the Olympic side of his sport—not turn professional—for another four years.

"It's not so much striving for a gold medal but striving to push yourself as an athlete, and pushing yourself to your limits," Stojko said. "Amateur skating is where it's at, to be able to push those limits athletically and artistically, and I find that I still have so much more to give, rather than cash it all in. I would not be satisfied with myself if I just sort of turned pro and rested on my laurels. I'm not like that. I would not be fulfilled. It would bother me if I had turned pro."

Onward Elvis went. As an Olympic division skater, Stojko powered his way to two consecutive world titles before thudding to earth in the most unthinkable spot: Canada. In his short program at the 1996 world championships in Edmonton, Alberta, Stojko leaped for his triple axel, and, coming back to the ice, slipped and fell.

A capacity crowd in Edmonton Coliseum gasped in horror.

The headline ELVIS IS DEAD blared the next day, and that was correct. Elvis *was* dead, for that competition. Mired in seventh, skating only for himself, he landed a quad in a monstrous jumping clinic in his long program. But when the skaters took the medal stand in his homeland, he was not on it. He could manage only fourth place.

It was an omen, Stojko told himself. He would enter the pre-Olympic year with something new gnawing at him, with something more to prove. He never would have chosen to fall, but it turned out just fine. He had to fight some more. The warrior was back in business.

*   *   *

The men were sneaking glances at one another in practice at Copps Coliseum, the arena in the center of town, the week of the 1997 Champions Series final, skating's grand prix finale. They were watching each other. They were checking to see who had a quad, and who did not. Todd Eldredge landed one a time or two in practice, just to keep up, but he hedged in his interviews: "We might not put it in here [in Canada], we'll see what happens at worlds . . . We might want to have one extra week with it in practice before I decide to put it in at worlds."

Quads don't just happen, Stojko said.

"The quad can be a finicky jump. It takes quite a bit of toll on your body. It does take a lot to do it in a program. I've had experience with it since 1991. I've had it on and off, it's a tough, very difficult thing to do, so we'll have to see. . . . It just doesn't happen one day."

Ironically, had Eldredge wanted to try one, that would have been the week to do it. Stung by the publicity Michael Weiss had received for his near-quad in Nashville, Eldredge had nothing to lose if he went for the big jump in Hamilton and fell. Winning or losing the Champions Series final meant nothing in his career. The nationals and worlds were places to guard your reputation, not a two-year-old event that was receiving a mere paragraph or two in most U.S. sports sections.

Weiss was not in Hamilton; he finished eighth in the standings in the international competitions the previous autumn, and only the top six made it to the final. Eldredge was the lone American, Stojko the only Canadian. The other four were all from the former Soviet Union: Urmanov, Kulik, and Yagudin from Russia, and Dmitri Dmitrenko from the Ukraine.

The first skater in the long program was Alexei Yagudin, the newest star in the ever-expanding Russian constellation of top male skaters. Russians used to rule just pairs and ice dancing. Now, they were cornering the market in men's skating as well.

Yagudin is coached by Alexei Mishin, the same man who puts Urmanov onto the ice in flashy, elaborate costumes. The more Americans recoil in horror, the more Mishin loves it.

One of Urmanov's most memorable outfits was his "Swan Lake" getup two years earlier. Urmanov skated as the white swan, traditionally a woman's role. He wore hip-hugging white tights and a blousy white, collarless top with wide, winglike black-and-white sleeves. His skates were covered with white cloth.

"He did a small part of the ladies' role, not because he's gay; he's very masculine," Mishin said. "I just had him thinking about the lady. Everybody criticized me for that."

"Alexei Urmanov can certainly come out in the widest range of costumes I've ever seen," Dick Button once exclaimed on ABC.

"If people talk, it's our plus," Mishin said. "At least we have a question asked of us. When someone skates and no one asks a question, then no one wonders. We are not afraid."

The three Alexeis are alone against the world in many ways, not only in fashion. The two skating Alexeis (Urmanov and Yagudin) still train with the coaching Alexei (Mishin) in Russia, while many of their countrymen and women have fled to America for fame, fortune, and glistening new practice facilities. While a top-level coach might make $300 a month in Russia, he or she can earn that in three hours in the United States. It's not uncommon for the best U.S. coaches to make $100,000 or more a year.

Mishin and his skaters, however, chose to remain in St. Petersburg, where Urmanov sleeps in the living room of a two-room apartment he shares with his mother, and Yagudin's family shares an apartment with another family, and where they all put up with a training facility that sometimes is overtaken by horse shows and other times can't keep its rutted ice from melting.

There are some things more important than money, said Mishin, who is quite well off by Russian standards. He has a stable of five male skaters, including Evgeni Plushenko, who won the 1997 world junior title at fourteen, and the two Alexeis. "They all do triple axel–triple toe, all of them," Mishin said. "I am able to compete versus any country."

The competitive spirit Mishin encourages in his St. Petersburg practice sessions would be lost in a beautiful new American rink.

"In the West, kids have everything," he said. "They have computers, they take vacations. They are not stimulated for high results. They can be lazy. We have a saying that hunting dogs with a full stomach never run fast. Or, in sweet, warm milk, nobody swims fast. You understand? If kids in the beginning of life have everything, sometimes it's not good."

Mishin isn't a big fan of the old Soviet system either. From 1975 to 1978, including the 1976 Innsbruck Olympics, he was not allowed to leave the Soviet Union to travel with his skaters. "The government said, 'He speaks English, he's a good coach, he would leave,'" he said. "If they gave Mishin permission to leave the country, it would have been a one-way ticket to the moon."

* * *

Yagudin, so unknown that no one in the West knew what syllable to emphasize in his last name (it's the second), was sluggish in his performance in Hamilton, and finished fifth, ahead of only Dmitrenko. If someone came into the arena not knowing who coached him, one look at his costume would have made it obvious.

Mishin!

The teenager was dressed in black with a short-waisted jacket encrusted with gaudy gold trim. The outfit looked heavy. Even worse, Yagudin hadn't yet developed a style to go along with a demonstrative jumping ability, but under the devilishly intuitive Mishin, there was no doubt he would.

In Russia, nothing was "Mishin impossible."

"Nobody," Mishin said, "knows the possibilities of this skater."

In the procession of Olympic contenders on display eleven months early, Ilia Kulik came next.

"He jumps like a god," Brian Boitano gushed a year earlier, when Kulik nearly defeated Eldredge for the world title in Edmonton. "It's as if there are strings from the rafters pulling him up."

Kulik, who came from Moscow and was not coached by Mishin, is the envy of the skating world. Tall and thin, he jumps effortlessly. He uncorks triple axels from a standing position in his sneakers on the floor. On the ice, he looks like he isn't trying. He performs the most beautiful triple axel in all of skating, one that flows out of a magnificent spread eagle. It requires him to switch from grace to power in a split second, to throw himself into the air for the toughest triple jump without any pause or planning. Peggy Fleming was renowned for performing a spread eagle into a beautiful double axel; Kulik has taken the delightful maneuver to a new level.

"I live vicariously through him," Boitano said.

Kulik also has an appearance rarely seen in men's skating. Kulik is the perfect boy skater, beautiful and rough-and-tumble all in one picture. He has the best hair in skating since Janet Lynn's pixie look of the 1970s; blond, straw-like hair flowing in the wind, askew and wispy, then quickly falling back into place, hanging into his eyes and reaching over his collar. His cheeks flare with the slightest effort on the ice and become rosy and bright. And when Kulik speaks, a deep, mischievous voice lingers long after he has made a quick exit from another press conference.

Just two months before turning twenty, Kulik was a favorite to beat Stojko in Canada. He can jump as well as Stojko. He can perform as well as Urmanov. If he's on, skating experts know, he should win.

"He can blow people away," said Paul Wylie, an accomplished pro and 1992 Olympic silver medalist. "If he lands all the triples in his program, he wins."

But, since winning his silver medal at the 1996 worlds, Kulik rarely was on. He left Moscow and moved to Marlboro, Massachusetts, west of Boston, where he is coached by Tatiana Tarasova, a famous Russian ice-dancing coach. His choreography is terrific, Russian ballet on ice. But he has become showy, and his jumping technique has become sloppy.

"Busy and meaningless," was the term floating around the hotel lobby in Canada to describe Kulik.

Tarasova and Kulik were trying too hard. His moves were wondrous and exquisite, but there were too many of them. He was throwing himself all over the ice, arms going this way, legs going that way, wearing himself out, and finally wearing down in the final minutes of his long program.

Triple jumps turned into doubles or singles. He was having trouble keeping up a pace that, for four and a half minutes, had become overwhelming.

"It's an ice-dancing program—but with all the triples added in," Paul Wylie said. "I appreciate what he's doing and I'm glad to see he's trying it, but he needs to take his time on the ice and let the audience see his face. If he looked straight ahead and he put his head up and his arms out and did a spiral, he'd have you.

"Less is more, but the Russians don't get that or understand that."

On the ice in Canada, skating to *Romeo and Juliet,* stunning in all-white with black trim, Kulik nailed his quadruple toe loop twenty seconds after he began his program, but soon was making those dreadful little mistakes all over again. He was unable to complete three of his triple jumps and ended up in fourth place, a mighty disappointment for the man with so much potential.

Kulik shrugged as he left the ice. There would be another chance in three weeks, at the worlds. But when was he going to get his act together?

Dressed in black, Stojko was next. He is a movie guy. Some men skate to Beethoven. Elvis skates to movie themes, as does his rival south of the border, Todd Eldredge. In the skating world, Stojko had become identified with his characters. In 1995 and 1996, it was Christopher Columbus from *1492*.

When Elvis began plotting his pre-Olympic season, he chose *Dragonheart*.

"The whole concept of it, the way the dragon was the symbol of honor, integrity, strength, power. That's what I base my skating upon and when I saw the movie and heard the music, I'm thinking, this is me. This is what I believe in. Always doing the best you can, always doing it with pride and honor and integrity and with passion. The way the dragon was portrayed in the movie was striking for me. That's the mental process I'm going through when I'm out there. It's the all-out attack with honor and pride and dignity and the push towards your limits."

Eldredge happened to be seated next to Stojko at a press conference as Stojko prattled on about the movie. Sensing the media's growing amazement at Stojko's soliloquy, Eldredge chimed in:

"I give it two thumbs up!"

Stojko smiled and playfully grabbed Eldredge by the shoulder.

Whether it's a jump or a philosophy, Stojko usually takes himself very seriously. People who listen to him meander from cliché to cliché often wonder aloud, "Is this guy for real?" Then, quickly, they realize he is.

Stojko actually uttered this masterpiece at a 1997 press conference: "We've got some great skating and we're all in the same boat. Anything goes each day and we're up and down and we push through and make the best we can. It feels great to be able to put it together. It's been an up-and-down season last year and trying to pull it through this season and it feels great to be on top and have a good skate. All I wanted here was a good skate and whatever happens happens."

Stojko is so true to his beliefs that he sometimes wonders how honest his competitors are when they skate. Are they faking it, he asked, for the sake of the judges?

"Is the arm movement that's stuck out there just stuck out for the sake of choreography? Or just thrown in there because it's supposed to be busy? Or is it put there for an idea or a concept or an emotion or a thought? That's what takes it to another level."

With Elvis, what you see is what you get. He is a fighter. He has a scar slicing through his left eyebrow. He picked it up in 1993.

"I was doing backflips and I missed one," he said. "I went up sideways, I stretched out and landed on my face. I almost broke my neck."

The very next day, he went back to the rink and did another back-flip.

"Everyone else was more nervous than I was. I did it for a few days, then stopped, just so I knew I could do it."

Now he was back on Canadian ice, in Hamilton, in 1997. As the music for his long program began, Stojko stood perfectly still and stared into space for an interminable twenty seconds before moving a muscle. The music had been running for nearly one minute before he attempted his first triple jump. And much of his time between his massive triples was spent setting them up. But all the waiting was rewarded when Stojko tore down the ice, stuck his left toe pick into the crusty surface, and vaulted himself into the air. One, two, three, four revolutions. The quad toe loop! As he came back to earth, his body lurched forward, but he had enough strength to land and grab the ice with the quarter-inch blade of steel under his right foot. It wasn't pretty, it wasn't completely upright, but he had done it. He had landed cleanly, on one foot.

Immediately, there was more. Back went his left foot again, searching for a spot to quickly pick in once more. In went the teeth at the front of his left blade. Up, up, up he went. One, two, three revolutions. A triple toe loop! He came down hard again. His arms quickly shot into the air in triumph. So close to the crowd that the fans leaping out of their seats almost could reach out and touch him, Stojko celebrated for just a moment. He pumped his fists. And why not? He had just become the first skater in history to land a quad-triple. Seven revolutions in the air in two seconds. It had happened, and Elvis had done it.

The crowd cheered madly for twenty seconds, then quieted quickly. Stojko moved on. He was far from perfect the rest of the way, dearly holding on to the landing of a triple loop and slipping like a hook-sliding baseball player on his second triple axel. He also skated much slower than he had in major competitions in previous years; the snappy, upbeat style that nearly won him the Olympic gold medal in 1994 had dissolved into a lugubrious, plodding performance that left skating experts shaking their heads. Stojko was slow because he wasn't prepared, some thought. He wasn't spending enough time training his competitive programs. He was too busy reaping the rewards of being Elvis. He had stretched himself to his limits by touring around the United States on the Campbell's Soups tour all spring, then putting together his own show—the eight-city Elvis Tour across Canada—in the fall. And there also was the occasional Elvis TV special.

It was time-consuming being Elvis.

Nonetheless, Stojko left the ice in Hamilton on the night of March 1 feeling overjoyed. That was the magnitude of the quad-triple; it glossed over everything else. Stojko received a 6.0 from the Canadian judge for technical merit, although four judges gave him only a 5.7 or 5.8 for artistry, leaving room for the final two contenders, Eldredge and Urmanov. If either man received scores of 5.9, 5.9 from four of the seven judges, they would defeat Stojko. But that meant they had to skate perfectly.

Urmanov, wearing white gloves, black velvet, and ruffled cuffs, wasn't up to the task. Skating last, he landed a quad, the third of a spectacular night of jumping, all of which were checked quickly on videotape to prevent snafus like the one the U.S. Figure Skating Association experienced with Michael Weiss at the U.S. nationals.

But Urmanov took himself out of contention midway through his program when he ran out of gas and doubled two triple jumps. There was no room for those kinds of mistakes that day. Urmanov may have been the crown prince of the ice in Norway in 1994, but he was going nowhere in Hamilton in 1997.

Unlike Urmanov, Eldredge rose to the occasion. He skated immediately after Stojko, which meant before he skated, he had flower duty. A raucous standing ovation by the crowd of 11,000 had turned into a national flower-throwing celebration as dozens of cellophane-wrapped bouquets flew out of the stands like wounded missiles and dropped safely onto the ice. Flower petals were everywhere. As the flower girls picked up the debris, Eldredge, who was skating in circles to get warmed up, leaned down several times to help. A tiny piece of a flower can ruin the takeoff on any triple jump, or abruptly alter any spin. Eldredge had a vested interest in cleaning up the place.

Skating to his music from *Independence Day,* Eldredge was artistically superior to Stojko, and nearly perfect athletically on all he attempted—everything except for the quad, which he didn't try. He landed seven triples and slightly two-footed the eighth. He was crisp and energetic. He didn't stand motionless at the beginning of his program; he tore off after five seconds. His footwork was more intricate and faster than Stojko's. His spins were better than Stojko's, which was one way to tell the difference between the two. Eldredge would never be confused with John Curry, the late artistic genius of skating, but he had matured into a confident, controlled performer. As a younger man, when he won consecutive U.S. titles in 1990 and 1991,

Eldredge looked like an awkward kid trying to be artistic. At twenty-five, he looked like a skater who was comfortable with the role he was playing. He was pleasing to the eye, which was not easily said about Stojko. While Stojko had a program packed with more difficulty due to the quad-triple, Eldredge clearly was the master in artistic ability.

But the judges were thunderstruck by the quad-triple. John Curry could have returned from the dead and skated, and they still probably would have given first place to Stojko. The judges were caught up in the moment, and only one—the U.S. judge, John LeFevre—gave Eldredge a higher artistic score than Stojko. The other six (there were seven judges at the Champions Series final, not the nine found at nationals or worlds) either tied the two skaters on the artistic mark or went with Stojko. Quad fever was catching. Artistry was dead. Long live Elvis.

And long live the Elvis debate.

"It was so obvious to me," said LeFevre, a veteran skating judge who was a Federal Trade Commission attorney in Washington, D.C. "The second mark [artistic] clearly was the differentiation between the two skaters. The obvious question is, Does everyone who does a quad automatically win? Sure it's an accomplishment, but it's not the only accomplishment."

Combining the technical and artistic marks, Stojko carried six of the seven judges' first-place ordinals (LeFevre put Eldredge first overall as well) to win the gold medal, while Eldredge took the silver and Urmanov the bronze.

One grand moment—Stojko's quad–triple—outranked a complete skating package—Eldredge's long program. This was troubling to some in the skating establishment.

"Instead of coming up with a performance, coming up with an entire thing that really packages yourself in a unique way, that is really innovative, you . . . have a checklist of things you have to put in your program," Scott Hamilton said, referring not to Stojko specifically, but a skating trend he found disturbing. "The programs just become connect-the-dots, and the dots are jumps."

"I hope the quad isn't needed," Brian Boitano told USA Today. "Skating needs to be more complete. By doing quads, you don't have time to do an interesting program."

"There's an incredible sensitivity to the jump in skating these days," Paul Wylie said. "You're not seeing artistic programs. You're seeing the results of the way the rules are written. A four-and-a-half-

minute program with eight triples gives you very little time to do anything else. This breeds a certain type of skater."

It was clear that the balance in men's skating had swung to jumps
at the expense of artistry. Quad-mania had taken hold and was not
letting go. Perhaps it was time for a new description of the sport. This
wasn't exactly figure skating. It was more like skate jumping. It was
as if the game of baseball had turned into simply a home run–hitting
contest. Something was missing in skating. The jumping was sublime,
but where was figure skating's heart? What had become of the artist?
Where had he gone?

Months later, Rudy Galindo still could hear the roar. More than
10,000 people, many with tears streaming down their cheeks, stood
and cheered for him as he skated the final few seconds of his long program at the 1996 nationals in San Jose, California. It was his hometown, and this was, he said to himself as the noise rained down on
him, an unbelievable dream come true. So poor he had to ride a bicy-
cle to practice, so old by skating standards that people wondered if he
was retired, so forgotten that his picture and biography were not
included in the USFSA media guide, Galindo achieved the impossible
in figure skating. He came out of a trailer park—the sports equivalent
of nowhere—to win the 1996 U.S. men's figure skating title. He won
the championship wearing velvet, an earring, and a goatee. He didn't
make any attempt to hide his homosexuality, or his Mexican-American
heritage, even as he faced nine judges who never before had anointed
someone like him a U.S. skating champion.

When people call it the greatest upset in the history of skating, they
are not exaggerating.

Had Rudy Galindo stayed in the Olympic side of his sport, he might
have been in Hamilton. He might have been on his way to the 1997
world championships. But no one could say for sure, because Rudy
Galindo left the Olympic world and turned professional in September
1996.

One thing you could say was that he would not have been landing
a quad. Galindo was a terrific jumper and a great athlete, but, at
twenty-seven, it was his artistry that set him apart from the others.
That was where he was breaking new ground, not with his jumps.
Like Stojko, Galindo didn't mind doing exactly as he pleased on the
ice. He ignored the judges too. But unlike Stojko, he did it with such
grace and style that, when he skated flawlessly, people actually stood
in the aisles and cried.

That's what happened on January 20, 1996, the day figure skating finally embraced Rudy Galindo. Men's figure skating changed forever that day. It turned out that the jumping wasn't the only thing that made men's skating a real sport. A victory by the first openly gay man to win the U.S. national title showed that even in the most prim and proper and historically biased sport on earth, anything was possible.

In practice that week at the 1996 nationals, the coaches noticed something about Galindo. He was skating beautifully, jumping flawlessly, and showing up the other skaters who shared the ice with him. Practice is part of the competition at a skating event because the judges sit and watch to get an idea of who is doing what—and how well they are doing it. If someone is skating particularly well, a buzz develops about him or her. Word spills from that practice session into the concourse of the arena and eventually into the lobby of the skaters' hotel. Skaters and their coaches want to get people talking. They want the buzz to be about them. Galindo had it that week at nationals. The talk in skating was about Rudy, which was absolutely stunning, because Galindo was the last person who was expected to do anything at nationals. Or even to be there, for that matter.

After a disappointing eighth-place finish at the 1995 nationals, Galindo retired for eight months. He started teaching children how to skate so he could pay his bills. Then twenty-six, with nothing to do and nowhere to turn, he decided to give the nationals one more try. His sister Laura would be his coach; she worked for free. The event was coming to his hometown; this, he told himself even before the competition began, would be his farewell to his sport.

Rudy Galindo's career, to that point, had been remarkable for two things: its bad timing, and its unspeakable sadness. Galindo had been a pairs skater, and a great one, both flamboyant and athletic, teaming with Kristi Yamaguchi to win the 1989 and 1990 national titles. Running herself ragged competing in both singles and pairs, Yamaguchi left Galindo after the 1990 season to devote herself entirely to singles skating. It was a wise decision. Yamaguchi won the Olympic gold medal in 1992, something she and Galindo almost certainly would not have won together. They would have been fortunate to win the bronze.

Galindo took several years to get over Yamaguchi's decision. At the same time, he was battered by the AIDS-related deaths of those closest to him: two of his coaches and his only brother. His father, a truck driver, died in 1993 after suffering three strokes and, finally, a massive heart attack. It was an awful time for Galindo, going to one funeral after another.

At the 1996 nationals, after finishing third in the short program, Galindo drew the last skating spot in the long program. Being third meant he could win the national championships by winning the long program—not that the judges would ever let that happen.

Rudy? National men's champion? Over Todd Eldredge and Scott Davis? No way. Perhaps the silver medal. But the gold? Never.

The judges felt that way not because they were biased against a gay man; some of the judges *are* gay men. There are dozens of gay men in skating, coaching, and judging. No, the judges just knew Rudy would make a mistake and ruin another nationals, because Rudy always made mistakes. The judges were not the only ones who believed this. The other skaters felt that way; the officials and reporters and fans felt that way. Rudy could not win. This was skating, not tennis. Upsets of that magnitude didn't happen in figure skating.

Standing beside the boards that Saturday afternoon for the long program, all dressed up, was Laura Galindo. After toiling in obscurity with her younger brother, she had watched him skate well enough to make the final group, and there they both were on live national television. Laura knew her younger brother was talented enough to win. Talent by itself wasn't enough, however. Rudy had to train, and hard work never had been his strong suit. But this time, he had been disciplined. He had worked hard. He was in shape. He wasn't staying out late as he had in the past. He was giving it everything he had for one last chance.

"Come on, Rudy, just do it," Laura said softly to herself. "Get all those demons out of your head and do it."

Swan Lake, his long-program music, came on, and the triples began. The eighth triple jump, it turned out, was as lyrical and lilting as the first. Each one was perfect. Galindo didn't skate as fast as some of the others, but no one touched the audience as he did that afternoon in northern California. Long and lithe, he was a dancer on skates, unafraid to experiment, executing flowing moves with his arms and legs that the others simply could not do.

Eldredge had been very shaky, landing only five clean triple jumps. Davis had been a disaster; he made five mistakes in four and a half minutes.

But Galindo was magical. And whimsical. A kind man, Galindo spotted a skating student of his and Laura's in the stands, and waved to her as he skated by during his long program.

No one ever waved to a child as they performed their long program at nationals!

Soon, Galindo finished. The crowd already was standing and cheering. Fellow skaters wiped tears from their cheeks as they watched. Galindo screamed to the rafters: "Thank you, Dad! Thank you, George, Jim, Rick!" They were the men who tragically had left Rudy behind—his father, his brother George, and coaches Jim Hulick and Rick Inglesi.

Skating always is a two-act play; first someone performs, then the judges render their verdict. Galindo had brought down the house, but that didn't mean he was going to win. Eldredge was defending national champion and 1995 world silver medalist; anything was possible when Galindo's marks flashed on the scoreboard.

The first set of scores came up, the ones that rank the skaters technically, by how they jump, spin and move athletically:

5.8, 5.9, 5.7, 5.9, 5.9, 5.9, 5.9, 5.9, 5.9.

Except for two judges, they were better than Eldredge's first set of scores.

The artistic marks almost always made the difference. Galindo's popped onto the scoreboard:

5.8, 5.9, 6.0, 5.9, 5.9, 5.9, 5.8, 5.8, 6.0.

Galindo gasped in delight and leaped to his feet, clapping his hands. He couldn't believe his eyes. Two 6.0s!

One was deceptive. Judge No. 3, Jim Disbrow, gave Galindo 5.7 and 6.0. He gave Eldredge 5.9 and 5.9. Added together, Eldredge's total of 11.8 from Disbrow beat Galindo's 11.7. Disbrow put Eldredge first, Galindo second.

Galindo ended up with seven first-place marks from the judges to Eldredge's two. Galindo was the national champion.

The other judge to go for Eldredge was Joan Gruber of Wyomissing, Pennsylvania.

Gruber, a venerable judge who adores Rudy and his sister, was Judge No. 1. She gave Galindo 5.8 and 5.8; Eldredge, 5.8, 5.9. Gruber penalized Galindo for technical flaws: the fact that he stood at center ice not moving midway through the program for "a prolonged period of time," she said (a few seconds, which allowed him to catch his breath), and that, in her opinion, his triple lutz was a "flutz," taken off on the wrong edge of the skate blade.

"Even though I felt he skated the performance of his life and Todd missed the combination [his triple-triple], I felt Rudy made technical errors as well. I deducted for those. I'm not sorry I did it, but I'm thrilled with how it turned out for him."

Gruber did not know what the other judges would do and realized she was in the minority, seven to two, only when the marks came onto the scoreboard.

"It was a great moment for him, but I still had to do what I had to do," she said. "I thought it was the right thing to do, but it turned out I was not in the majority. But that's okay. That's why there are nine of us."

The skating world cried with Galindo, but some in that world also cringed at what had just been unleashed. Never before had the sport crowned an openly gay man as national champion. Who knew what to say? Who knew where this would take the sport?

Surrounded by three reporters, wiping away his own tears of happiness, U.S. Figure Skating Association President Morry Stillwell made a clumsy effort to put it into perspective, "There are a lot more weird people in this sport than Rudy, and you all know that."

In seven minutes and ten seconds on the ice in San Jose Arena in January 1996 (the combined length of the men's short and long programs), Rudy Galindo forever changed his life. The people in skating who used to laugh and make fun of his costumes and his effeminate ways not only had to respect him immediately—some even had to hire him. "We've got Rudy" became a sentence every promoter wanted to be able to utter.

The man who wore the huge red AIDS ribbon around his neck as he skated his exhibition number the day after winning nationals was the hottest skater on the planet.

Within months, a millionaire would be living in the Foothill Mobilodge trailer park in San Jose, California.

It was intoxicating. It was overwhelming.

"It was H-E-L-L," Galindo said. "I didn't have an agent, Laura was taking the calls, the phone was ringing every five minutes, the machine was full."

A week after his triumph not only over Todd Eldredge but also over the decades of blue-blooded principles for which American skating stood, Galindo found himself running out of a San Jose restaurant in tears.

His future brother-in-law, Andy Black, chased after him and caught him in the middle of the street.

"It's too much," Galindo sobbed. "It's too much."

Soon Galindo was getting help. He signed Michael Rosenberg, the perennially tanned, Palm-Springs-agent-to-all-the-skating-stars, including, at one time or another, Dorothy Hamill, Tai Babilonia and Randy Gardner, and Tonya Harding.

"I remember Michael Rosenberg, even when I was in eighth place, always was so nice to me. He always took the time to say hello. He always told me he loved my skating," Galindo said.

Rosenberg signed Galindo with the Campbell's Soups tour for more than $400,000 for four months' work. Other deals would push his total earnings to the $1 million mark. There would be a book. There was talk of a made-for-TV movie. He appeared on the cover of a gay magazine and on the front page of the sports section of *USA Today*. He could have all the work he ever wanted.

But first, he had to go to the world championships in Edmonton and prove he wasn't a fluke.

Conventional wisdom said Rudy would fold at the worlds and order would be restored to his sport. He told friends he was hoping for nothing more than a top-ten finish. But when Elvis Stojko crashed to the ice on his triple axel in the short program, Galindo had the opening he needed. Skating on a sore ankle, he landed every jump, and while he wasn't quite as stirring as he had been in San Jose, he was good enough to win the bronze medal. Todd Eldredge, still smarting from losing at nationals, took the gold and Ilia Kulik, the silver.

Galindo was gaining new stature in his sport every time he took the ice.

"He now has . . . a class about him that does not have a parallel in figure skating," Dick Button said on ABC's world championships broadcast.

Galindo also was taking his sport to a new level in a very important medium: television. If skating officials weren't crazy about his image, they loved what he was doing for TV ratings. The night he skated in the long program in Edmonton, ABC Sports' live broadcast received a 10.1 rating (a rating point equalled 956,000 households). Going head-to-head with the skating was the highly publicized NCAA men's basketball tournament on CBS. The basketball earned only an 8.8.

Before the competition began at the world championships, Joan Gruber pulled Laura Galindo aside to talk. They had spoken before; one of a judge's roles is to advise skaters and their coaches after watching practice. This is especially true at international events. Judges, coaches, and skaters from the same nation see themselves as part of the same team. At worlds, Gruber mentioned her concern with Galindo's stationary position in the middle of his program, where his hands are moving but his feet remain still.

"Could he just rotate?" Gruber asked.

Laura said no, she would leave it as is. The last thing Laura Galindo wanted to do was change her brother's program the week of worlds.

But Laura Galindo thanked Joan Gruber, and Gruber felt she had done her job.

"If there's something you can correct and you have the ability to point it out to them, why wouldn't you?" Gruber said.

Over the years, judges had had other suggestions for Galindo. Judges had a lot of complaints about Rudy. One of the most common was that he was skating too slowly across the ice.

"They've always said that," Laura said, "that his footwork is not intricate or fast enough. Some judges at nationals said to make sure he speeds it up. What are you going to do? Tell him right before he skates? You've been practicing for months, and now you're going to change? I didn't tell him."

At the world championships, Gruber also told Laura Galindo the technical reasons why she had given Rudy the marks she did at nationals.

"I thought that was so great," Laura said, "that she had the nerve to come up to me and say, 'I think Rudy is a wonderful person and this is why I placed him second.'"

Heading into the 1996 nationals, Rudy Galindo hoped to finish fifth or sixth, turn professional, get himself invited to the occasional professional event as a last-minute fill-in or low-priced warm-up act, and teach children how to skate. How strange it was to him, then, that throughout the spring and summer of 1996 he was checking into the finest hotels in America, walking onto the tour bus beside Brian Boitano and Oksana Baiul, and living a life that he never thought could belong to someone like him.

"The year before, I'm sitting at home, watching them on TV," he said. "Now here I am, joining them on the bus."

After the tour, he went back to northern California and got into trouble. In August 1996, Galindo was arrested in Los Gatos, California, when he drove his BMW over a curb after leaving a bar. Later, he failed a breathalizer test, according to police. He was booked on one count of misdemeanor drunken driving. Two months later, he was fined $1,576, ordered to enroll in a counseling program, and sentenced to nine days on a weekend work program, which required him to help clean up a police shooting range.

"It was a major mistake," Galindo said of his arrest. "I was going out with my friends, celebrating someone's birthday. That taught me a lesson. Now I'm boring but happy."

Less than a month after his arrest, on September 11, 1996, Galindo made more news. He announced in his hometown that he was quitting Olympic division skating and becoming a professional. With the 1998 Nagano Games less than a year and a half away, he was doing to himself what Yamaguchi had done to him six years earlier, leading to the Albertville Olympics—he was knocking himself out of a chance to be an Olympian.

"My dreams as an amateur skater have been more than fulfilled," he told a news conference in the elaborate lobby of San Jose's Fairmont Hotel. "Now I have new challenges to undertake and goals to strive for as a professional."

Left unsaid that day, but very much on Galindo's mind, was the fact that he was hurt over what he perceived as one final snub from the USFSA. According to a story that appeared that morning by Jody Meacham in the *San Jose Mercury News,* the USFSA had decided not to send Galindo to Skate America, the Olympic-style competition that is the most prestigious for an American skater, but decided instead to ship him off to Russia and Germany for similar competitions there. The reigning U.S. national champ was being sent practically to Siberia. It was an unusual move. The USFSA told the Galindos it wanted Todd Eldredge, the reigning world champion, at Skate America. That was understandable. But there would be two other U.S. male skaters at Skate America, Scott Davis and Dan Hollander. Galindo believed his exclusion showed once again how little respect the USFSA had for him—and how little control he had over his career.

"They were doing another trick, another number on him," Laura Galindo said. "I didn't want to be a part of it and Rudy didn't want to be a part of it anymore. We also felt that with Rudy's DWI, if he made any slight mistakes, [the judges] would slaughter him."

Galindo was tired of playing the games he and his sister felt were required to compete in the Olympic side of the sport. If he wanted to wear effeminate, flashy outfits, he didn't want to have to explain himself to even one more judge.

"What I like about skating is the artistic side and playing a role," he said. "I don't want to have to worry if they like my costume or not."

Then there was the money. Lots of it was waiting for him on the other side—the professional side. "For the first time in his life, Rudy could take care of his mother and his sister," Rosenberg said. Galindo could have made a very good living staying in the so-called amateur world, but not as much as he could by turning pro. USFSA rules prevented any Olympic-eligible skater from competing in unsanctioned professional events, and even if Galindo packed his schedule with sanctioned shows and tours, he would have needed to make time for USFSA competitions and the intense practice required of any Olympic-level skater.

Galindo had other reasons for leaving the Olympic world. He knew he never could re-create the 1996 nationals, not only in his ability to perform, but also in the drama of the moment.

"I feel like San Jose was my Olympic Games," he said.

And he knew he was getting too old; he would be twenty-eight at the time of the 1998 Olympics. "All the young ones are coming up," he said. He didn't want to have to work quite as hard as an Olympic division skater would have to work to prepare for Nagano. Why knock himself out, he wondered privately, when a slight stumble in the short program at the 1998 Olympic trials could put him out of the Games? What would he have then? He would have ruined some of the "magic of San Jose," as he called it, if he went to another nationals and failed to perform the way he had in 1996. This way, he was leaving on top. Baseball's Ted Williams homered in his final at-bat. In his own way, Rudy Galindo did too. He stepped off the ice at his hometown nationals at the pinnacle of his career to deafening cheers—and he never returned.

How did the USFSA and the Olympic side of the sport react to his departure?

There was no reaction.

"No one called or wrote," Laura Galindo said.

Except, she said quickly, one judge.

Joan Gruber.

Gruber's note came a few weeks after the announcement. She told Galindo he was going to be missed in the Olympic world but that he had accomplished so much, she understood why he would move on. Gruber wished him well as he embarked on his new life in the professional ranks.

"I was just wishing him the best," she said later, explaining why she wrote. "I had no idea I was the only one. I just wanted him to know how happy I was for him."

Galindo's professional debut came in Albany, New York, at the end of October 1996. Accompanied by his sister Laura and Andy Black, whom she had married in August, Rudy Galindo sat in the stands at Knickerbocker Arena watching the women practice. He hadn't yet competed as a pro, but he already felt quite at home.

With the innocence and candor of a child, Galindo watched two-time Olympic pairs gold medalist Ekaterina Gordeeva, whose husband Sergei Grinkov died of a heart attack nearly a year earlier, skate on her own for one of the very first times.

"I wonder if she misses being tossed in the air," he asked. "She was up there pretty high. There's a freedom up there. I wonder if she misses it."

Dorothy Hamill, the 1976 Olympic gold medalist, was another competitor swirling around the ice.

"Do you think she ever gets tired of her hairstyle and wants to have a new one?" Galindo wondered.

Everyone smiled. Anyone might have thought it, but no one else would have said it.

"He's so honest," Laura Galindo said. "Sometimes I get a little worried, like, 'What are you going to say?' That's why people love Rudy, because he is so open and so honest. There are no barriers."

Said agent Michael Rosenberg, "There are no restrictions anymore in his life. He's so happy. You see it when you talk to him. You see it when he laughs. A troubled, frustrated kid has become a happy, fulfilled person."

Galindo didn't waste any time making a fashion statement as a pro, wearing a tight black velvet unitard with blue and white "wings" symbolizing the water in the movie *On Golden Pond*. His avant-garde costume didn't get him into trouble in that event, but his jumping did. Galindo fell twice during the competition in Albany, the U.S. Pro Figure Skating Championships. He finished fourth out of five men, behind Kurt Browning, Paul Wylie, and Viktor Petrenko.

"He was really off," his sister said quietly. "That was unlike him. The nerves really got to him."

"I was trying so hard," Galindo said.

By the middle of December, Galindo was skating to "Babalu," at the World Professional event in Landover, Maryland, and making fewer mistakes. He still finished fourth behind Browning, Brian Boitano, and Petrenko, but he was gaining on the seasoned veterans.

"I've gone from Pacific Coasts [a sectional qualifying event] to competing with Olympic gold medalists," Galindo said. "Isn't that amazing?"

The next week, he was off to Europe to skate some more. He went to Innsbruck, Austria, to the Challenge of Champions, and won the men's event, defeating Petrenko. In the coming months, there would be more tours, more shows, more four-star hotels.

"I want to make a name for myself in my professional life," Galindo said. "I don't have to worry about going home to take care of my brother or take him to the hospital, or worry about my dad being sick. There's nothing to be depressed about anymore."

For Rudy Galindo, two skating performances at the right moment forever changed his life.

"I sometimes think about what his life would be like if he didn't win in San Jose," said Joan Gruber, the skating judge who placed him second that day. "And then I think of that performance."

Gruber stopped for a moment.

"Good for him!" she said. "Good for him!"

6

COMPULSORY FIGURES

Carlo Fassi looked tired the day of the women's qualifying at the world figure skating championships, March 17, 1997, in Lausanne, Switzerland. At sixty-seven, he refused to slow down, and it was beginning to show. He thought nothing of this latest trip, flying from California to Europe. He had come to the continent where he began skating more than half a century earlier as a boy in Milan, Italy, to accompany Nicole Bobek to her third world championships. Bobek, the nineteen-year-old skating nomad, thought of Fassi as the father she never had. (Her father had left her mother, Jana, when Nicole was a baby.) They had had two tours of duty together, Bobek and Fassi. He had coached her as she rose through the junior ranks in 1990, and she had come back to him in 1996—after working with five other coaches—to try to get herself on track for the 1997 season and, ultimately, the 1998 Olympic Games.

Already, Fassi had worked his unique brand of magic with Bobek at their training site in Lake Arrowhead, California. After she had missed the entire fall season of 1996 with a back injury, and was mired in sixth place following the short program at the 1997 U.S. nationals, Fassi watered down her long program so she could get through it.

"What are you going to do in the last minute of your program?" Fassi had asked Bobek in Nashville.

"I'll figure it out when I get there," Bobek replied, flashing a mischievous smile.

She did just enough to move to third, a spot that the U.S. judges joyfully gave her. (The top three qualified for worlds.) They wanted Bobek at the world championships; nearly everyone in U.S. skating wanted Bobek representing the United States at major competitions, because, when she was on the ice, anything could happen. Sometimes it was good; oftentimes the past two seasons it had been bad, as Bobek battled injuries, a chronic lack of training, and her advancing age in the land of the teenyboppers.

But there was something about working with Fassi that made Bobek's spirit soar. He instilled confidence in her. He understood her. He knew her and he loved her, moving vans and all. Bobek never stayed in one place very long. She left coaches often, three in 1994 alone. She had worked with almost every top coach in the sport by the time she came back to Fassi, Coach No. 4 and Coach No. 10. At the world championships every year, it was always possible to call to order a meeting of the "Bobek Alumni Club," which counted among its members Frank Carroll, Evy Scotvold, Christy Ness, Richard Callaghan, and Kathy Casey. Say this about Bobek, she had good taste. Those were some of the best coaches in the history of the sport. Most skaters would love to have any of those coaches give them a lesson; Bobek had taken lessons from them all, and dumped every one of them. Sometimes she and her mother and her mother's companion, Joyce Barron, got angry when the coaches didn't drop everything to devote all their time to Nicole. Other times they didn't like what the coach was telling them, even if it happened to be the truth.

Bobek, for all her promise, also was quite a handful growing up. She often loafed at practice the moment the coach's head turned, she liked to smoke, she rarely went to school, and she got herself into more than her share of teen trouble. She once was with a group of Estonian skaters when they emptied a minibar on a skating trip in Seoul, South Korea. When they tried to finger her as the one who should pay the bill, she slipped away and was missing for an hour before wandering back to the hotel.

Bobek rejoined Carlo Fassi in late summer 1996, and soon injured herself trying to get into shape. Not wanting to reinjure the right ankle that had caused such trouble at the 1996 nationals, she got on a rowing machine—and strained her back. She underwent an MRI and bone scan that revealed an inflammation of the nerves near the spinal column, as well as a sciatic nerve condition and degeneration of two discs in her lower back. For several days, she had to walk with a cane, and could not seriously skate for a month.

She eased back slowly in a couple of made-for-TV events. Although she didn't do well, she never lost her sense of humor. At a pro-am in

Philadelphia, she said, "I'm afraid that if I do a really bad fall, I won't be able to get up."

She went to Nashville, then, as the great wildcard. There, she and Fassi pulled off the miracle finish and happily snapped up their tickets to the world championships. As Tara Lipinski and Michelle Kwan grabbed the headlines, Fassi and Bobek knew that if Bobek could land her jumps at worlds, she just might sneak into third place and ensure an American sweep of the medals. And if one of the other two U.S. skaters stumbled, who knew what the possibilities could be?

It was enough to make an old pro like Fassi superstitious.

"My back's not bothering me," Bobek proclaimed under a white tent set up for interviews at the Malley Sport Centre, site of the world championships.

Fassi rapped his fist against a wood table in front of him. He knew what he had in Bobek when she was healthy, happy, and hardworking. Fassi knew everything; he had seen it all in more than thirty years of coaching skating in the United States. Coming to America after the devastating 1961 plane crash, he led Peggy Fleming to the Olympic gold medal in 1968, and Dorothy Hamill to the gold at the 1976 Games. He took on pupils from all over the world, including Great Britain's John Curry and Robin Cousins, the 1976 and 1980 Olympic gold medalists. Going to Carlo Fassi was like going to finishing school.

He knew talent, and he knew Bobek. She had the goods, he thought, if she ever put her mind to it, to win an Olympic medal in 1998. He enjoyed being along for the ride.

But something was troubling him about what was happening to the women's side of his sport. He loved playing the politics of the old days of skating, when compulsory school figures ruled the day and a coach could make backroom deals with judges to help his skaters win. He admitted to speaking three languages, but others said he actually spoke five—"sometimes all together," said Lynn Plage, a skating publicist and long-time Fassi acquaintance—which meant he could chat with a judge in his or her own language. He denied ever making any shady deals, but there was no doubt that with his intimate knowledge of the sport and its power brokers, Fassi was a formidable ally for any skater, especially on the world stage.

The disappearance of figures after the 1990 season not only deprived Fassi and others like him of the chance to maneuver behind the scenes. It also meant that the sport had changed—and not for the better, he thought.

In 1987, three years before the compulsory school figures were eliminated, Fassi had predicted a dramatic change for his sport if it got rid of the time-consuming tracings of figure eights.

"If we cancel figures, it will be like gymnastics, with young girls who can do all the jumps at age thirteen and quit at age fifteen," he told the *Chicago Tribune*. "I don't like gymnastics anymore. It's little muppets just tumbling around. Where is the beauty of that?"

Fassi's prediction had been perfect. Ten years later, women's figure skating had become almost exactly what he said it would be. School figures required hours of daily practice; in the 1980s, Nancy Kerrigan said she spent five hours on the ice every day, and three of those hours were devoted entirely to figures. When they were eliminated, her practices changed dramatically; she trained for four hours, all on freestyle skating, which included all those triple jumps.

"When you have something that takes that long to perfect," Scott Hamilton said about school figures, "you have champions who wait their turn and really learn their craft. Now, if you've got a triple jump, you can win tomorrow."

The little jumping beans were bobbing to the surface faster than ever. There was nothing to slow their progress. Fundamentals were out; quick, snappy revolutions in the air were in.

The only way to stop the little girls would be for the judges to dole out horrid artistic marks. Figure skating judges were the gatekeepers of the sport; there were expectations that they would become the ones to draw the line, that they would tell the little girls to wait a while by giving, say, a 5.8 for their athleticism, then, say, a 5.3 for their presentation and sending them back to their home rinks to work on their artistry and grow a year or two older.

But the judges were shocking everyone; most of them were not sending that kind of message. They were acting just like the johnny-come-lately sportswriters who had no idea what they were watching, but knew a fall when they saw one. Sportswriters and judges were doing the same thing; they had resorted to simply counting jumps. That made skating a bit more understandable to the average fan. And it made crowd-pleasing upsets more likely. But as long as the sport had two distinct marks, it didn't necessarily make it right.

Leaders within the international skating federation were confounded. At precompetition meetings, the referee would spell out to the judges the importance of artistry, then watch time and again as judges rewarded athleticism with a high first mark and did not sufficiently lower their second mark for a skater's inherent lack of artistry.

Could it be that the judges were aware that they were being watched on network television and in magazines and newspapers as never before? And that they found themselves avoiding controversy by emphasizing the easily quantifiable elements—the jumps, the falls, the stumbles—while ignoring the fuzzier artistic and presentation elements they were supposed to be including in their overall evaluation of a skater, male or female?

Were they taking the easy way out, saying, quite simply: You jump the best, you win?

Some judges admitted that the answer was yes. Part of an international judge's motivation was self-preservation; any judge too far out of line with the other eight on the judging panel has a lot of explaining to do. On rare occasions, a judge can be suspended for doing a bad job. So, to avoid trouble, a judge—who has all of five to ten seconds to punch in a skater's marks—can make decisions based on jumps. Then if he or she gets called in for questioning, the defense is easy: Just count the jumps. If a decision is based on artistry, it can be more subjective and open to criticism.

Skating was undergoing an identity crisis. Coaches who had been told for years by judges and skating officials that artistry mattered were becoming extremely confused. What should they tell their skaters now? Forget the fancy footwork and jump, jump, jump? Others wondered about the legacy of the new breed of skater. Two decades after her Olympic victory, forty-one-year-old Dorothy Hamill still was a big draw in shows. Would the jumping beans have that kind of staying power? And all one had to do was look at Michelle Kwan's swollen, tear-streaked face at nationals to wonder if too much was happening too soon for some of these young girls. What kind of immense pressure was being placed on their tiny, quivering shoulders? How could this be a good thing? What in the world was happening to the beautiful, graceful sport of women's figure skating?

It also was obvious that a bustline had become a detriment in skating. Talk about a compulsory figure: A girl almost had to be sans hips, thighs, and breasts to win. This was the era of "The Young and the Breastless," exclaimed Philip Hersh of the *Chicago Tribune.*

It was humorous—to a point. What had all this jumping wrought? Fassi worried not only about the sport's loss of artistry, but also about the pounding girls and women were taking to try to learn and keep the almighty triple jumps. A mighty-mite like Tara Lipinski, who had the figure of a seven-year-old girl, could jump all day and not feel the pain the next day. In a few years and a few more pounds, that probably would not be the case. In 1997, however, Lipinski was invincible.

But Fassi often thought of the older girls (women, actually) who were fighting skating-related injuries—world championships medalists Lu Chen, Surya Bonaly, and Bobek, among others. He said he was certain it was because of all the jumping they were doing, and the pounding their growing bodies had to endure. Skaters like Fleming in the 1960s and Hamill in the 1970s never were required to do triple jumps, so they never faced such problems.

Fassi of course knew how to solve the problem. He had a solution for everything. He didn't want to raise the age limit for senior (Olympic) level competitors. "No," he said, with Bobek by his side that day in Lausanne. "If that happens, in five years, the juniors will be better than the seniors."

Fassi wanted to limit the number of triple jumps a woman could do during a long program, ensuring that spins and footwork and other forms of artistry would keep their place in the sport.

He did not at all welcome the rise of Lipinski. She was fourteen, which meant she did not meet the minimum age requirement of fifteen for the 1997 worlds. But Lipinski was "grandfathered" into the event because she had participated in the world championships in 1996 at the age of thirteen, before the age rule was put into effect.

"We have a young girl, who, according to some nations, shouldn't be here, and she's leading [the qualifying round]," Fassi said. "It's crazy."

Things were spinning completely out of control in women's figure skating. Comparisons with previous figure skating heroines were astounding. When Nancy Kerrigan was fourteen, which was 1984, she was a novice-level skater who not only failed to qualify for the nationals, she didn't even make it out of her regional competition in New England. Kerrigan would take seven more years to grow and make her mistakes out of the public eye before qualifying for her first world championships in 1991. To Fassi, that sounded like a measured and reasonable way to advance in the sport.

After his short tirade against the new ways of figure skating, Fassi and Bobek settled back into a delightful recitation of how they had worked together to get her back to the worlds, where she had won the bronze medal two years earlier with Richard Callaghan as her coach. (She left him nine months later.)

Bobek was Fassi's kind of female skater, someone who had been hanging around the top of the sport for much of the decade, not just a few months. She was a skater who could never be dismissed. She had the ability to come out of the blue to win any event she entered. She loved to perform before a crowd. The more people, the better. Plus, she looked great. In figure skating, looking great was a wonderful thing. The blonde hair and the French braid and the makeup laid on thick made her look like the next great American ice princess.

"Nicole has a sparkle that's incredible," Fassi had once said. "She's a natural, she's exciting. It's nothing studied. Some have it, some don't. She has it."

Bobek relished the new role she was playing, that of skating's grown-up girl.

"When I was younger, I just would go out and skate," she said. "I appreciate it more now."

Soon, Bobek and Fassi looked at one another, nodded to the reporters, left the tent and burst into the bright sunshine of a gorgeous Alpine afternoon. There was no reason for either of them to be anything but ecstatic. Bobek had skated well enough to qualify easily for the short and long programs later in the week. Things were going exactly as planned.

For three days the skating world basked in balmy sunshine at the world championships. The gaudy, swishy skating establishment could not have been happier; if it didn't feel at home in Lausanne, the headquarters of the International Olympic Committee and one of Europe's most beautiful, snow-capped playgrounds, where did it belong?

Skaters, coaches and judges milled outside the Malley Sport Centre between skating sessions and couldn't help but look up to see the Swiss Alps on their right and the French Alps across Lake Geneva on their left. It seemed like good days would go on forever.

But, in the middle of the week, the weather turned, and by Thursday, March 20, it had become cold and gray.

The skaters and coaches and others who came to the world championships awoke that Thursday morning in Switzerland to hear disheartening news that had broken overnight from the United States:

Scott Hamilton had announced that he had testicular cancer, and that it had spread into his lower abdomen. Hamilton, a four-time world champion, the 1984 Olympic champion and, at thirty-eight, still one of the most popular skaters on the planet, was immediately leaving the "Stars on Ice" tour to check into the Cleveland Clinic to begin chemotherapy. Doctors were cautiously optimistic about his chances for a full recovery.

That morning, at the Malley Sport Centre, everyone was talking about Scott Hamilton. Carlo Fassi was there, visiting with other coaches in the skaters' lounge before attending the first of Bobek's two practice sessions that day. Fassi told his friends that he didn't feel good. He said he was dizzy.

It was just before noon. Fassi's wife, Christa, who also is a coach, and Diana Ronayne, Dan Hollander's coach, helped him walk to the medical room in the main arena. Ed Reisman, the U.S. team doctor who had been watching a practice session, rushed to the room. Fassi was alert and able to talk and answer questions, but he was light-headed and sweating. Concerned that Fassi could be having a heart attack, Reisman and the medical personnel at the rink called an ambulance to take Fassi to the hospital. When the ambulance arrived, Fassi was placed on a stretcher, given oxygen and taken to the front gate of the skating complex. Reisman and Christa Fassi followed.

Several of Christa Fassi's fellow U.S. coaches who had been told that Fassi was ill were standing by the gate.

"Will somebody please be with Nicole on her practice?" Christa Fassi asked them.

They assured her they would.

Christa turned back to look at them.

"Don't worry," she said. "We'll be all right."

At the hospital, Carlo Fassi's condition worsened. He was having a severe heart attack. His blood pressure was weakening. Reisman joined Christa in the waiting room as doctors worked to save her husband's life.

Soon, Christa walked into the room where her husband was being treated.

"I love you," she told him.

"Go and see Nicole practice," he said, so softly she could barely understand him.

"Okay," Christa replied.

At 2:30 P.M., Carlo Fassi died.

For the second time in less than eight hours, horrible news traveled like wildfire through the byways and corridors at the Malley Sport Centre. Coaches and judges wept and embraced in the same open-air gathering place that Fassi had walked through that morning on his way to the skaters' lounge. It was hard to believe; the news that Scott Hamilton was fighting cancer was awful, but to lose Carlo Fassi, one of the most beloved and respected men in the sport, was much more devastating because it was so final.

Peggy Fleming, announcing the world championships for ABC Sports, was in her hotel room when she heard the news.

"He really knew how to draw out the best in his students so they had their own identity," she said sadly a few hours later, after visiting with Christa Fassi. "He was a very special individual to be able to handle all the different personalities he did and bring out such high quality again and again and again.

"I'm certainly very grateful to have had him in my life," said Fleming. "And he forever changed it."

She came to Fassi in Colorado Springs, Colorado, as an unpolished California teenager in 1965. Three years later, she was the Olympic gold medalist and headed toward the most wondrous of public lives.

Bobek practiced in the early afternoon without knowing the seriousness of Fassi's condition. After being told that Fassi had died, she went to her evening practice session, where Robin Cousins, a skating commentator for British TV, stood by the boards to act as her coach. She skated halfheartedly for twenty minutes before leaving the ice and hugging Cousins as she departed.

A short while later, Bobek, wearing dark glasses to hide her tears, met with reporters to talk about Fassi. "He was always here for me and he always cared. He took the place of being a father for me. . . . From what I heard, one of Carlo's last words were to Christa, asking her to please be with me for my competition. We all love him and we will miss him."

As she spoke, her voice cracking, Bobek stood under the same white tent where she and Fassi had been speaking after the qualifying round three days earlier. Only this time, she was alone.

The very next day, at 3:30 in the afternoon, Bobek was standing on the ice to begin her short program, while Christa Fassi, in a black leather jacket, was standing beside the boards, exactly where her husband wanted her to be. In the small arena, there was an air of expectation. What if Bobek skated so well that the judges had to put her in first place? Wouldn't that be something? If anyone could pull it off, Bobek was the one.

But it was not to be. Emotionally spent and physically drained, skating with tears in her eyes, Bobek stumbled badly in the middle of her triple lutz combination, then leaned forward on the landing of her triple toe loop and braced herself from falling by putting both her palms on the ice.

Her first set of marks, for required elements, reflected the mistakes: a low of 4.6 to a high of 5.0. Her presentation marks shot up to 5.4 through 5.7. She was eighth after the short program. Christa Fassi sat beside Bobek as they watched the marks come up in the arena. Their faces showed little emotion as the terrible scores were read. The victory for them was in being there at all.

The next afternoon was the long program, and Bobek, all but out of the running for a medal, could muster none of her customary energy. She was trying to skate well for Carlo Fassi, but she had nothing left to give. She planned to try five triple jumps; she was unable to cleanly land even one of them. As she finished, she dropped to her knees, clasped her hands in prayer and sobbed silently, then looked toward the ceiling before skating off into the arms of Christa Fassi and Robin Cousins. She said later that she didn't want to get off the ice, that all she wanted to do was try again.

Bobek dropped to thirteenth place.

"I tried," she said, "but it was just too hard."

The other two American teenagers—Tara Lipinski and Michelle Kwan—were the ones who would rule the ice in Lausanne. Theirs was a strange battle. It kicked up quite unexpectedly in Nashville, and had two more stops before the end of the 1996–97 season: the Champions Series final, and the world championships.

Or was it so unexpected?

On December 20, 1994, Frank Carroll sat in the living room of the home he built around a mountain bend from the rink at Lake Arrowhead, and mused about future competition for Kwan.

"I think there will come a time when there will be a young one, somewhere on the horizon, who is going to come up and give Michelle a run for her money," Carroll said. "Now I don't know who that little person is. It might be this little girl who's skating in Delaware, who's so cute, but that will happen, and Michelle has got to understand that."

The cute little girl in Delaware was Tara Lipinski.

It took two years and two months for her to prove Frank Carroll correct.

Midway between the disaster in Nashville and the world championships in Lausanne, Kwan went to Hamilton, Ontario, for the

Champions Series final. There, she laughed in the face of danger. Before the competition, she joined Carroll in the pressroom to chat with a few reporters about her problems. She was so brutally honest, those listening to her believed she had figured out whatever it was that had gone wrong.

"I was a scared chicken out there at nationals," she said.

Someone asked if the "scared chicken" was gone.

"Yeah, hopefully, I killed it already," Kwan replied. "I think I just have to go for everything, not hold back at all. The worst thing you could do is hold back, because it's not your best."

"If that scared chicken happens again," Carroll jauntily chimed in, "she's going to be chicken soup!"

Introspection was in vogue in the Kwan camp.

"People don't think of figure skating as a sport, but it's a damn hard sport," Carroll said. "And if it is a sport, there are going to be tennis players that win, there are going to be golfers that win, there are going to be teams that win, and lose. If it really is a sport that's judged fairly, if the skater goes out there with courage on the day, puts it out and does it, then they're going to win. In the past, we had school figures to manipulate the results, and the true artiste was the winner. Well, the artiste, at this point, better damn well skate."

"Okay!" Kwan said with a huge smile.

"We have a tendency in figure skating," Carroll continued, "to put these girls on these pedestals, like Michelle's the Venus de Milo in the Louvre or something, but she's not, she's an athlete."

They had come up with a new game plan for the Champions Series final, where the top six women in the world would compete.

"What we've tried to do," Carroll said, "is just talk about Michelle Kwan going out and doing Michelle Kwan's best for herself, and forget whether it's nationals, worlds, grand prix, or anything. Just feeling good about the way you skate, feeling good about what you did for you, not for the public, not for television, not for mummy, not for daddy, not for Frankie."

"Frankie?" Kwan laughed.

"You know who used to call me Frankie?" Carroll said. "Nicole Bobek. She gave me a coffee cup once for my birthday and it said, 'Frankie Baby,' on it. She's the only one who would dare."

There was a public honesty in Kwan and in Carroll that caught everyone by surprise. Figure skaters usually were so guarded. But not those two. Their refreshing psychobabble delighted everyone; no one had to read their minds, because they willingly told everyone exactly what was in them. Even in the midst of defeat and uncertainty, they seemed to have no fear.

"Maybe I expected too much of myself," Kwan said at one point.

"I don't know, I'm not in your head," Carroll said back, looking earnestly into her eyes.

What Carroll did know was that Kwan was once again having trouble in practice with her triple lutz. The boot problems, which continued, had led to a crisis in confidence. The lutz was the most difficult jump in her arsenal, and it was a mess. She practiced it over and over, the way Tara Lipinski trained her jumps, but could find absolutely no consistency.

Soon, Kwan was skating her short program. As she prepared to launch herself for her opening triple lutz–double toe loop, she knew she was in trouble. Using the new entry into the jump that Carroll had concocted in Nashville, she hesitated, waiting for "that perfect take-off," and she missed it. Her right toe slammed back into the ice before she could complete three counterclockwise revolutions in the air. Off-balance, with legs and arms askew, Kwan crashed to the ice.

A fall in the short program usually is figure skating death. Mistakes in the short program doomed Brian Boitano, Viktor Petrenko, and Kurt Browning at the 1994 Winter Olympics, and Tonya Harding and Midori Ito at the 1992 Winter Games. Skaters knew if there were mistakes to be made, they should save them for the long program, where there was more of a chance they could be tolerated.

But Kwan got lucky. The seven international judges were in a generous mood that night and placed her third out of the six skaters in the event. Third place meant she could win the title simply by winning the long program.

"What did I do to deserve this?" Kwan asked.

The answer: You won the world championships a year earlier, and everyone behind you made a mistake too.

Skating was becoming more and more of a sport, but every now and then, it gave a skater—especially a deserving one—a delightful, unexpected gift.

First place after the short program belonged to that little American sprite who was beginning to act as if she belonged at the top of the sport. Tara Lipinski nailed everything in her short program. The kid was unstoppable. She just wouldn't miss.

Lipinski completed her end of the bargain. Then it was the judges' turn. Richard Callaghan was concerned that they would lowball

Tara, just as Kwan was penalized for being too young at the 1995 world championships.

"It doesn't matter what they do to you," he told Lipinski as they waited for her marks. "You walk away feeling good about yourself."

The marks went up, and they weren't bad. Most were 5.6s or 5.7s, although the judges from Azerbaijan and Russia hardly were impressed, giving out 5.4 and 5.5, and 5.4 and 5.6, respectively. Those two saved their best marks for Maria Butyrskaia, the twenty-four-year-old femme fatale of the event. A year before, she had been a blonde. In 1997, she appeared as a shocking redhead. No judge deducted points for the dye-job.

Butyrskaia won the first-place marks of the two Eastern European judges because she skated cleanly, actually was an adult and, shock of all shocks, was from Russia. Imagine that, the old Soviet republics actually sticking together in figure skating! One year, the Soviet judges' behavior was so bad that the entire judging corps—every single Soviet judge—was suspended for a year.

Going into the long program the next evening, Lipinski was first, Butyrskaia was second, and Kwan was third.

In the long program, everyone else skated before Lipinski and Kwan, with the only shift of fortunes being the fact that Russia's Irina Slutskaia, who also was having trouble with her changing body, overtook Butyrskaia and finished third.

As all skaters do at the big winter competitions, Tara wore the same clothes and skated to the same music as she had at nationals. She was a vision in white lace—except that she was almost impossible to see at times because she blended in with the ice.

Uncharacteristically, she made a big mistake on her first jump, a double axel. The double axel was not a particularly sound jump for Lipinski; technically, she took off wrong, spinning off the ice on the edge of her skate rather than kicking her right leg through the air to throw herself into the jump. Without that lift, she never got very far off the ice.

Lipinski's axel is called a "roller-axel" because it's the technique used by a former roller skater. Roller skates are so heavy that a child who learns to jump in them, as Tara did, does not learn the proper technique for a figure skating axel. Tara wills herself into the air; it's a scary proposition, especially if her nerves ever get to her.

That night, Lipinski didn't get more than several inches off the ice and came out of the two-and-one-half revolution jump too soon. Her right foot thudded to the ice. A split-second later, her left foot hit. She stayed upright and never fell, but she barely missed smacking into the hockey boards as she whipped by.

"Don't let the rest of the program go downhill," she told herself. "Just pretend that everything is okay."

And everything was. She landed her unique triple loop–triple loop again and didn't make another error, earning better scores than she had in the short program: all 5.8s, except for one 5.7 and one 5.9. The 5.9 came from the Azerbaijan judge, who clearly was coming around to Tara's side.

However, the scores weren't fabulous. There definitely was room for Kwan to win. With 5.8s, there was, in fact, a gaping hole. But could Kwan come through two weeks to the day after she fell apart at the nationals?

She began as if she would. She landed two perfect combination jumps—including the pesky triple lutz and her first triple toe loop–triple toe loop of the season—and was breezing along until she reached the triple flip a minute and a half into the program. She had to put her right hand to the ice to steady herself. Thirty-five seconds later, she nearly fell on her triple loop, spinning around like a child playing the game Twister. She also two-footed a double axel. Kwan rallied in the final minute to complete two more triple jumps, but the damage was done.

Three of the seven judges gave her first place. But four went for Lipinski, and she was the winner for the second time in two weeks, with Kwan second.

"I felt good, but that middle section again . . ." Kwan said, referring to the triple flip and triple loop, which had been devastating in Nashville, and were yet again in Hamilton.

The Champions Series offered prize money. The final paid $50,000 for first place, plus a $10,000 bonus for reaching the final.

"What are you going to do with the sixty thousand dollars?" Lipinski was asked backstage.

She looked surprised. "I don't know," she said.

As she bebopped off, the first thing she said to Callaghan was, "Are they right? Is it really sixty thousand dollars?"

It wasn't a bad payday for a fourteen-year-old. For the entire autumn series, Lipinski earned $106,000, counting the final.

Mike Burg, Lipinski's agent, said he had a game plan for Lipinski that projected all the way to the 2002 Olympics, with nary a mention of 1998.

"Throw that plan out the window," Burg said, laughing.

Shep Goldberg, Kwan's agent, smiled bravely, but just as Burg had a plan, he did too, and this was not it.

Kwan took home $30,000 that night plus the $10,000 bonus to run her total for the series to an even $100,000, but all she really wanted were her jumps back.

In trying to assess blame, she looked to her body. "It's a lot harder," she said. "I remember when it was just jump and jump and jump."

A reporter offered that it was better to go through the changes in 1997 than in 1998, the Olympic year.

"Definitely," Kwan replied.

"But I'd rather not have to go through it at all," she added with a chagrined smile.

One person she would not blame was Lipinski. Asked earlier in the week if they were friends, Kwan replied, "We're not enemies," and left it at that.

Kwan and Lipinski didn't hate each other, but they didn't necessarily like each other either. They had no relationship; they barely knew each other. If she thought of her at all, Kwan considered Lipinski an understudy. There was no disrespect involved; Tara just was too new to know.

Their personalities are completely different. Tara is a detailed perfectionist; Michelle, a sensitive artist. Tara has tunnel vision when she is trying to complete a task; there is nothing that gets in her way. Michelle's mind is always on the move; Frank Carroll said he sometimes bumped into her away from the rink at Lake Arrowhead and tried to strike up a conversation, only to have Michelle wave him off because she was busy conjugating French verbs in her head.

But when she was asked during an interview with Canadian television what she thought of Lipinski, Kwan energetically praised her rival.

"Tara's having a great year. I can learn a lot from her, her speed on the ice, the way she goes into her jumps, her jumping ability."

Kwan knew it was her fault that Lipinski was the national champion and now, the Champions Series winner. Twice in two weeks, Kwan had opened a bottle and let a genie out. Somewhere, sometime, Kwan would have to get that genie back into the bottle. With her mistakes, Kwan created Lipinski, who otherwise would have been the happy-go-lucky silver medalist. Kwan knew she would have to stop making those mistakes. She would have to take charge once again.

* * *

Mike Burg was understandably ecstatic heading into the world championships. He had struck gold with his little skater. There were so many things running through his head: a Tara doll, a Tara tour, a Tara clothing line. Tara, Tara, Tara! What if she won the world championships? She then would have to be considered at least a co-favorite with Kwan heading into the Olympics! Oh, the endorsement possibilities!

And to think he had completely lucked into this little girl less than three years earlier.

One night in the summer of 1994, he was having dinner at the Washington, D.C., home of a friend, Dr. Caroline Silby, a sports psychologist and former skater. Silby was the figure skating team leader for the upcoming Olympic Festival in St. Louis, and had collected videotapes of all the skaters on the team. Burg had been asking Silby—and everyone else he knew—about the hot young prospects coming up in the sport. He represented Katarina Witt from 1991 to 1993, working with her on endorsements and made-for-TV skating specials. That simply whetted his appetite for more skaters; he was an executive with Jefferson-Pilot sports television, and he knew how successful skating broadcasts were. The ratings consistently made it the second-most-popular televised sport in the United States, behind only the National Football League. This was the sport for him. It was a new frontier, and there were no rules. That suited Burg just fine.

He signed Oksana Baiul, the 1994 Olympic gold medalist, to a ten-event, $1.5 million professional package. He was making deals with Nancy Kerrigan, Brian Boitano, Kristi Yamaguchi, and Paul Wylie to skate in made-for-TV events he was producing. And he was about to watch a videotape Silby suggested he see.

"This skater," Silby said, "is something special."

Silby popped in a tape of twelve-year-old Tara Lipinski.

Burg was hooked.

Lipinski ended up winning the Olympic Festival, a competition of junior skaters. That autumn, quickly making his move, Burg invited Lipinski to skate an exhibition at "Ice Wars," one of his prime-time TV extravaganzas. He paid Tara more than $5,000 for the performance, even though she was practically unknown and had won nothing in the sport except for the festival. Burg didn't care. He saw greatness in tiny packages. He already was representing Dominique Dawes, an Olympic gymnast, and had his eyes on another tumbling pixie, thirteen-year-old Dominique Moceanu. If it worked in gymnastics, why wouldn't it be the same with figure skating? To that end, he was becoming quite chummy with Jeff DiGregorio, Tara's coach at the time in Delaware, and with Jack and Pat Lipinski. He was making major-league agent moves.

"You're going for a kid who's still a junior?" veteran skating officials asked.

"She has a big-time future," Burg replied.

Burg giddily monitored Tara's progress all fall, but he was jolted when she was upset by a better, more mature skater for the U.S. junior ladies title in February 1995. He began to wonder if he might not want to represent that skater—Sydne Vogel of Alaska—as well as Lipinski. He flew to Alaska to visit the Vogel family. Burg wanted to make sure he picked the right girl—and if he signed them both, he knew he would be covered. But the Vogels decided to take things more slowly, and rejected Burg's advances.

It came as no surprise, then, that for her thirteenth birthday in the summer of 1995, Tara Lipinski got an agent. Burg guaranteed Tara a certain number of appearances in his events for a certain sum of money, as much as $100,000, and the Lipinskis readily signed up. In a flash, the $58,000 a year that they were paying in expenses for skating and living apart didn't seem quite so overwhelming.

Burg also began doing something that never had been done before in the Olympic division of skating: promoting his client openly and vociferously. He looked ahead to the 1996 national championships and proclaimed, "That third spot is wide open," meaning a place on the U.S. world championship team. DiGregorio knew enough about skating to know one should never be so bold, at least in public. He said he just wanted Tara to qualify for nationals in 1996. The coach was preaching caution; the agent was floating outrageous propaganda.

Six months later, that third spot at the 1996 nationals went to Tara Lipinski.

By March 1997, Burg was playing two roles as Lipinski's agent.

He was an arsonist.

He was a firefighter.

Burg loved creating problems that he could solve, or that would solve themselves. He wanted to be in the middle of everything. He was a magnet for controversy. He thought nothing of calling a newspaper editor or a network executive to complain about their coverage of Lipinski. He did so often and he did so proudly. He liked to rock the boat. That way, one person was in total control. Thirty-nine-year-old Michael Burg.

At the world championships on Wednesday morning, March 19, 1997, two days before the women's short program, Burg outdid himself. He juggled two controversies at once.

Incensed that an ABC producer had asked three questions of Tara Lipinski for an ESPN report on figure skating's image as "gymnastics on ice," Burg told ABC Sports executives that Lipinski might never again speak to the network. It was common practice for a TV producer to ask questions of an athlete for several different pieces in one sitting, especially in this case, because ABC and ESPN are owned by the same company. Burg knew the routine; he works in television. But he suspected this was an ambush of his young client, and told ABC exactly that.

ABC personnel replied by telling Burg it was nothing of the sort, then shook their heads and carried on. The ESPN report aired the next day as planned, Burg calmed down, and Tara Lipinski continued to be available to ABC's reporters.

At the same time, a battle had broken out in the ranks of the Lipinski camp over who was going to appear at a late-morning press conference. The three U.S. women—Lipinski, Kwan, and Bobek—were scheduled to talk to reporters at 11:30 A.M. Their coaches were expected to be by their sides, as is skating protocol.

But Richard Callaghan had a conflict. Todd Eldredge was to compete in the men's short program at 1:35 P.M. Callaghan and Eldredge had been together for fifteen years, and no matter how important Tara Lipinski was becoming, Callaghan's first priority was, and always would be, Todd Eldredge. Callaghan wouldn't apologize for his loyalty. The Bobeks had complained of Callaghan's devotion to Eldredge during the year and a half they spent in Detroit, even though Callaghan guided Nicole to her one and only national title during that time. When he lost Bobek, Callaghan barely batted an eye. He still had Eldredge. That was what mattered most to him.

At 11:30, according to Burg, Callaghan wanted to be with Eldredge, helping him get prepared for his short program. Megan Faulkner, Lipinski's coach in Houston, was in Lausanne, and she could sit with Tara at the news conference. It seemed like an easy solution.

Except that one person was not happy.

Pat Lipinski.

She wanted Callaghan beside her daughter. How would it look if the other top coaches were there, and their coach was not?

Pat Lipinski asked Burg to make sure Callaghan was there. Although it was a relatively meaningless press event, Burg sided with Pat Lipinski and strongly suggested to Callaghan that he make time in his schedule for Tara.

Lo and behold, when Tara walked in, Callaghan was with her.

The short program was two days later. As Tara Lipinski stood with Callaghan, receiving her last words of advice, the scores for France's Vanessa Gusmeroli were announced. Gusmeroli, a virtual unknown who wore her blonde hair in a wild Tonya Harding–style ponytail, had skated very well, and her scores were quite strong. There were many 5.7s, and even three 5.8s.

Callaghan held on to Lipinski's waist and looked straight into her eyes.

"Don't pay attention to those marks!" he said. "Focus, focus, focus!"

Callaghan was remembering a year earlier in the short program in Edmonton, when Lipinski got caught up listening to the bad marks for Midori Ito and fell on two jumps.

Although he was pacing back and forth during her program, Callaghan need not have worried. In her dark green velvet short program dress, Lipinski was perfect as usual, doing everything she had planned to do. Nearly two minutes into her program at the Malley Sport Centre, a butterfly fluttered over the ice, far over Tara's head. It was there for just a moment, as wistful and unencumbered as Tara herself was on the ice below, and then it was gone.

As Lipinski joined Callaghan and Megan Faulkner in Kiss and Cry to wait for her scores, she looked anxious. The judges had been kind at the Champions Series, but the worlds could be different. Lipinski craned her neck to see a scoreboard high in the corner of the arena.

The public-address announcer read the marks for required elements.

"5.8, 5.5, 5.5, 5.8, 5.7, 5.7, 5.6, 5.8, 5.8."

Lipinski stared at the scores of the second and third judges.

"5.5," she muttered.

She turned back toward Faulkner.

"5.5," she said again.

Lipinski had been saying she was hoping for a fifth-place finish at the worlds, but few were fooled. She was a competitor, and she wanted more. Her parents wanted more. Burg wanted more. The two 5.5s, from the Bulgarian and Polish judges, got their attention.

Her presentation marks went up, including 5.8s from Bulgaria and Poland. She moved ahead of Gusmeroli. But she had been the victim of some bizarre judging. The jumps she did were the most difficult in the event. If anything, it was her artistry that was suspect. But only three of the nine judges gave her a lower artistic mark. It was a small thing, but another example that the best judges in the world didn't know what to do with a fourteen-year-old.

Skating's age gap was accentuated by the next competitor, the veteran Maria Butyrskaia, who all but screamed out, "I'm old and proud of it," as she appeared on the ice. The exotic Russian wore a strange green outfit with gold trim that encircled each breast. She, too, skated cleanly, and was put right into the mix, in third place behind Lipinski and Gusmeroli.

The judges had not given out a 5.9 yet. Not a one. They were waiting for the next skater, the defending champion, Michelle Kwan. It would rain 5.9s if she skated well. Kwan arrived on the ice in glittering black, and the judges began watching.

Fifty seconds into the short program, she launched into the pesky triple lutz. Collapsing on the landing, leaning back too far in those boots of hers, she twirled around and took two extra steps before picking in with her left toe for her double toe loop, which completed the combination. She was supposed to go directly up off the left toe pick, not take the two steps to recover. The crowd groaned. It was a major mistake, necessitating a deduction of three-tenths of a point.

Kwan had done it again; another error at an awful time. And, unlike the Champions Series final, there already were three clean short programs.

She finished the program without any more trouble, then stood at the center of the ice, and, in a brief rage, tossed her head back and threw her hands down. Her first set of marks were low by necessity, because of the deduction due to her mistake, but two 5.9s popped up among her nine presentation marks.

After Irina Slutskaia crashed into the ice on her triple lutz, the final order was complete. Lipinski was first, Gusmeroli was second, Butyrskaia was third, and Kwan was fourth. (Slutskaia, the two-time

European champion and 1996 world bronze medalist, dropped to sixth.) Kwan's placement was significant. The skater in fourth place after the short program (one-third of the overall score) could not control her fate. To retain her title, Kwan would have to win the long program, and Lipinski would have to finish no better than third. If Kwan won and Lipinski finished second in the long program, Lipinski would win the championship.

Kwan soon met with American reporters under the white interview tent outside the arena door. Explaining a mistake had become an all-too-familiar ritual for the shell-shocked sixteen-year-old.

"I waited a little too long, like I did last time [in Hamilton], and I just couldn't get out of it quick enough, so I flipped out of it," Kwan said. "I'm in shock . . . It was like, 'What happened? Is it my timing? Was I nervous?'"

As she spoke, Kwan crossed her legs and mindlessly began fiddling with the skate lace from one of her boots. She didn't realize that she had untied the lace and was nervously retying it tightly around one of her legs. Sitting beside her, Carroll saw what was happening. He took a white tissue from his pocket and nonchalantly placed it over Kwan's knee to shield the scene from reporters.

Someone asked Carroll what went wrong.

"What can I say? You want an answer to something I probably don't even understand myself," Carroll said in quiet disgust. "She's been skating great in practice and I think that mentally she was very ready to do this. So you want an answer I can't give you."

"I don't know, it just makes me mad," Kwan continued, "because it's just one thing out of so many that I missed and that one was the one that counted the most."

Just one thing.

A very interesting situation was developing. The sport was in a quandary because Kwan kept making mistakes. She was skating's finest artist and one of its best, most polished jumpers. Even with a stumble, she still was the best pure skater on the ice.

"I must say, for me, this was clearly and far away the most mature and beautiful skating that we have seen tonight," Dick Button said while commentating on Kwan's short program.

And it was fourth.

No one was saying mistakes on the jumps should be discounted. It was instead a question of how much they should weigh against an otherwise tremendous effort. Put another way, Kwan beat the field on everything else she did: her spins, footwork, expression, maturity. Her second triple jump—the toe loop—was not as difficult as the three leaders' second triple, but otherwise, Kwan was better than all of them.

But she was behind them all because she took two steps between jumps.

It was all the more confusing because skating judges were not being consistent. At the 1994 Winter Olympics, they rewarded artistry over athleticism by giving Oksana Baiul the gold medal over Nancy Kerrigan. If they had counted jumps, Kerrigan would have won in a landslide.

Another inconsistency went back two years and involved a skater named Kwan. At the 1995 Birmingham worlds, Michelle flawlessly executed the most difficult short program in the competition. She was 1995's Tara Lipinski, without the makeup, swept-up hair, and packaging. She was that year's little jumping machine. And she was not first. She was fifth.

Nothing seemed quite right for Michelle Kwan. She broke into tears when U.S. skating officials gave her a hug in the interview room, where she went to draw her skating place for the long program.

After the draw, an announcer said, "The ladies placing one-two-three, please stay for a short press conference."

Kwan threw her bag over her shoulder and left the room.

Lipinski remained. She had leaped from twenty-third after the previous year's short program to first.

"Are you ready for this?" a reporter asked Lipinski. One more strong performance and she would be world champion.

"It never feels fast," Tara replied. "It may look that way to other people, but when you're actually in it, when you do your work, and it comes out that way, it feels normal."

Kwan was going through a difficult time, but she hardly was alone. Three women with resumés every bit as impressive as hers were enduring troubles far worse.

Little more than a year earlier, it would not have been far-fetched to envision these three skaters atop the medal stand at the 1998 Winter Olympic Games: Lu Chen, Midori Ito and Surya Bonaly.

None of them, however, even made it to the long program at Lausanne.

Ito quit; Bonaly was forced to stay home by her federation; and Chen could barely jump anymore.

They had been as reliable as any trio of female skaters in the 1990s. At least one of them had won a medal at every world championships since 1992. Ito had a world title (1989), Chen had a world title (1995), and Bonaly had three second-place world championships finishes (1993–95). At least one of them had competed in the long program at every world championships since 1986.

By 1997, Ito was twenty-seven; Bonaly, twenty-three; Chen, twenty. All seemed a bit young to be having a career crisis. But the fact was that in women's figure skating, at their age, it probably was time.

Ito, the greatest female jumper in history and the first woman to land a triple axel in competition, left the Olympic world in 1992, came back in 1995, and left again in 1996.

After skating professionally for three years, she announced on April 1, 1995, that she would be reinstating as an Olympic-eligible skater for the 1998 Winter Games. Those close to Ito had not heard her mention the idea, but it immediately made sense. The Games were in Japan, her homeland. If she could land a triple axel, she could win a medal. She just might be the story of the Games.

But those who knew her also realized the pressure would be unbearable. Followed by hundreds of photographers throughout the 1992 Olympics, which were held in the French Alps, Ito fell in the short program, settled for the silver medal and issued an apology to her country. Her friends in the sport were scared for her; 1998, they knew, would only be worse.

As it turned out, Ito would never reach Nagano as a competitor. Early in the week of the 1996 worlds in Edmonton, she ended up in the hospital. The official word was that she was anemic, but it turned out to be something more.

"She wasn't eating due to the mental stress," said Katsuichiro Hisanaga, vice president of the Japanese Skating Federation.

Skating in pain, holding her side during practice, Ito fell on her triple axel in the short program and finished the competition in seventh place. She was miserable.

"When the competition day was coming close, she got nervous and didn't eat," Hisanaga said. "It's too bad."

It turned out that Ito's decision to try a comeback was not her own. Her sponsor, Prince Hotel, which was paying her a six-figure salary, wanted her to compete in Japan's Olympic Games, Hisanaga said.

While the comeback ended in failure for Ito, it was not entirely bad for the hotel.

"They did get one year of great publicity," Hisanaga said.

For Bonaly, it was just the opposite. She wanted to keep competing, but her federation told her to stay home. After recovering from surgery on her right Achilles tendon in 1996, Bonaly won the French nationals and assumed she was headed to the world championships. But the French federation demanded she pass a skating test to prove her worth. They scheduled it for February 20, a day after she had flown home from skating an exhibition in the United States.

At the test, Bonaly wore one of her skating costumes, but refused to perform any jumps. Although jumping always had been her forte, Bonaly said she didn't want to risk an injury that day. The French federation's judging panel decided, however, that because she didn't try any jumps, it wouldn't be sending her to the world championships, and it sent two other women, Vanessa Gusmeroli and Laetitia Hubert.

Bonaly said she felt as if a brick had fallen on her head.

Bonaly and the federation had had a hate-hate relationship for quite a while. Three years earlier, it had threatened Bonaly with expulsion if she turned professional for a year after the 1994 Olympics. A seven-figure contract awaited her that year, with the agreement that she would reinstate on April 1, 1995, as Ito did, and represent the French at the next few world championships and the '98 Olympics. But the French federation, worried about its television ratings in the year without her, said it would not let her back if she turned professional. Scared about her future, Bonaly backed out of the $1 million contract, settling instead for about $200,000 a year from the federation and its television partner, TF1.

As strange as her dealings with the federation were, they were hardly the most bizarre element of Bonaly's life. Early on, Bonaly was known as the child who had been born on an exotic island in the Indian Ocean, then adopted by a French couple; whose hair had never been cut; who ate birdseed; who wore one company's skate on the foot she jumped with and another company's skate on her landing foot. She had a skating coach, but her mother, Suzanne, was never far away from the ice.

Surya is short, muscular, almost always made-up, and black. Suzanne is lean, stern, plain, and white. They became two of the most recognizable people in their sport.

Surya's skating never was very pretty, but she had been a gymnast, so she knew how to jump. She even tried quadruple jumps in practice, one of the only women ever to do so. At the 1992 Olympics, she did a backflip in front of Midori Ito during a practice session, a move that rattled Ito, and was widely believed to have been intended for just that purpose. The Bonalys were reprimanded; Suzanne claimed the referee was trying to "unnerve" her daughter.

Eventually, the Bonalys admitted that Surya was not born on an island, but in southern France. She got her hair cut and received some coaching help in America. But no matter what she and her mother tried to do, she never won a world title or an Olympic medal.

Although the French were giving her a strong signal that it was time to move on, Surya said after the failed skating test that she would try once more in 1998.

That's what Chen planned to do, too, give it one more try for 1998. Unlike Ito and Bonaly, she was in Lausanne, and she came for just one reason: to finish in the top twenty-four and assure China of having one woman in the field in Nagano.

She did not make it. Two years after winning the world championships and one year after earning two perfect 6.0s in finishing second to Kwan, she managed just twenty-fifth place in the short program and failed to make the cut for the long program.

Chen, like Bonaly, was in a fight with her federation, and she, also like Bonaly, had been injured. She missed four months of training due to a stress fracture in her right foot and resumed practicing only one month before the worlds. When she arrived in Lausanne, she came as a mystery. Not only had she not competed all season, she also had been asked to return to China in the autumn of 1996 from her training base in Los Angeles to resolve problems with her Chinese coach, Li Mingzhu, and the Chinese skating federation. The troubles centered around the money she was making skating and touring in the United States. The Chinese federation, following in the grand tradition of the former Soviet skating machine, wanted more of her earnings than she had been handing over. Chen could have ignored the federation, stayed in America, and kept her money, but such a move likely would have ruined her hopes to compete at the Olympics because she, like any athlete, needed her country's blessing to compete in the Games.

So Chen—who has an American agent, Canadian choreographer, American publicist, and American dressmaker—had to play by China's rules. Her injured foot was treated not with modern medical techniques, but, she said, with "Chinese methods, Chinese medicine, the traditional way."

Yuki Saegusa, Chen's agent at International Management Group, said when IMG asked about the treatment, it was told, "This is the Chinese way. Stay out."

The Chinese way even included forcing Chen to speak Chinese at a news conference at the world championships, although she is fluent in English.

During her recovery from the injury, Chen gained twenty pounds, then lost about half that as she hurriedly tried to get ready for Lausanne. New costumes had to be made in a week, overnighted to Saegusa in New York, delivered by the agent to Switzerland, and given to Chen just four hours before she skated in the qualifying round.

Her performance that afternoon was a disaster. She landed only one triple, fell on another, and turned three more planned triples into single jumps. Nonetheless, Chen qualified for the short program four days later, where her troubles continued. She turned two of her four jumps into singles, and received one technical score as low as 3.0. She went from a 6.0 to a 3.0 in a year. Chen left Lausanne knowing she would have one more chance to make the Olympics in a qualifying competition in Vienna in October.

"Her face is not as it was," Saegusa said. "The joy has come out of it."

Sadder still was that Chen looked absolutely beautiful as she fell apart on the ice. She wore a stylish black dress with pink trim and a pink hair bow, and drew cheers and even some encouraging whistles as she began skating to the provocative "Take Five." At five-foot-four and 115 pounds, Chen was positively statuesque, a tall and elegant lady who was seven inches taller and forty pounds heavier than Tara Lipinski. Her only problem was she couldn't jump like she could when she won the Olympic bronze medal in 1994, or the world gold and silver medals in 1995 and 1996, respectively.

"I can't think I'm a champion anymore," she said. "I just need to start over. I'm a beginner. Right now, all the skaters are so young. Their bodies are different. But I can use my body to understand the music more than a younger skater can. I know I can do my jumps again and I know I will be back. I will come back and show people my beautiful side."

After the short program, in the car on the drive back to her hotel in the center of Lausanne, Michelle Kwan was furious with herself. She was crying, and she was angry.

Frank Carroll was listening when, all of a sudden, there was silence.

Kwan spoke a few seconds later.

"What am I doing?" she asked. "Look at Carlo Fassi. He's not here anymore. Scott Hamilton's struggling for his life, and we're here just competing. This is nothing. I need to realize that."

The other skaters and coaches in the U.S. delegation noticed Kwan's face when she arrived for the long program on Saturday afternoon, March 22. She looked different than she had the past five weeks. She didn't look nervous. She looked remarkably intense.

Drawing the next-to-last skating slot, she had to wait through the final skating group's first four competitors. First was Gusmeroli, the eighteen-year-old from the nearby Alpine town of Annecy, France. She made an early mistake, then recovered for a nearly flawless performance with a circus motif, complete with canned laughter.

Lipinski came next and was delightfully precise once again, her fifth flawless effort out of six performances over little more than a month. Given every opportunity to fail, to let the events of the previous five weeks get to her, she did not. She smiled from start to finish as she landed seven triple jumps, the most in the competition. The crowd of 4,000 leaped to its feet when she ended. U.S. flags waved joyously throughout the stands. Her marks were strong—no 5.5s this time—mostly 5.8s, with a few 5.9s sprinkled in. She easily passed Gusmeroli, but there was plenty of room above her marks for Kwan to beat her.

But was there enough room for Kwan and one other skater? That was the issue that would decide the world title. Kwan could beat Lipinski in the long program but Lipinski could still win the championship. In order to win a second consecutive world championships, Kwan needed to win the long program, then have one other skater fit between her and Lipinski, dropping Tara to third.

But the sport's attention was not focused entirely on Kwan anymore. Lipinski's remarkable performances were endearing her to some of the judges, including Joe Inman from Virginia, who did not work the ladies event.

"She exudes energy," he said. "You can tell the girl loves skating. She lives and breathes skating. It comes out in everything she does."

After Butyrskaia made a mistake to knock herself out of the medals, Kwan was up.

Brian Boitano, finished with his ABC Sports duties as a commentator on the men's event, was talking to a reporter in the press section of the stands moments before Kwan took the ice.

"Gotta go," Boitano told him. Although he and Kwan had not talked on the phone since right after the nationals, she had seen him outside the arena earlier in the week and had once again expressed her doubts about her skating.

"I tell myself not to bend forward as I go into the triple flip," she told him.

"No!" Boitano said. "Think positive. Switch it around. Can you say the opposite thing, like 'Get over the toe, get over the toe.' Think of one positive thing, and tell yourself, 'When I land the flip . . .' and if you say that, then you'll land it."

"Yeah," Kwan said, laughing nervously. "When I land the flip . . ."

"I'll be in the booth watching," Boitano said as he hugged Kwan. He adored Michelle. He called her "a sponge." Said Boitano: "She just soaks things up."

He dashed to the ABC booth beside the ice in time for Kwan's long program.

By the boards, Frank Carroll was giving his final instructions. "Attack," he said as he sent her out.

And that she did. It was as if Nashville and Hamilton had never happened. She was the Kwan of old—old being a year earlier for a sixteen-year-old skater. Triple lutz–double toe loop: no problem. Triple toe loop–triple toe loop. No sliding off the edge on the landing. Positive vibes into the triple flip. Thoughts of Boitano. No leaning, no falling. Perfect. The slow part went as planned. Her mind kept telling her to "fly" on the ice. And that's what she did.

Her only error, a slight one, was on her second triple lutz, which came with thirty seconds left in the program. Feeling uncertain, Kwan doubled the jump. Still, she landed six clean triples, one less than Lipinski, but that was not a major difference to the judges. As Kwan came off the ice, Boitano pumped his right fist into the air from the TV booth, and she pumped her fist back at him.

She sat with Carroll to wait for her all-important marks, but she barely cared when they came up. They were good, better than Lipinski's overall, including seven 5.9s for presentation. But Kwan already had what she wanted. The performance was the thing. As the marks were announced, she tossed her hand in the air as if to say "Who cares?"

She beat Lipinski, six judges to three, with Slutskaia still left to skate.

Slutskaia was an interesting case. The world bronze medalist in

1996, she had had a mediocre year in 1996–97, and came into Lausanne as an unreliable spoiler. The judges didn't expect much from her, and she proved them right when she fell in the short program and brushed away a tear as her low marks popped onto the scoreboard.

In practice four hours before her long program, the Russian teenager lowered expectations even further when she slammed back-first into the boards and underwent forty-five minutes of physical therapy in order to compete.

But Slutskaia caught the judges completely by surprise when she skated brilliantly in the long program, with six clean triples. Her performance might have been good enough to push Lipinski into third place, but the judges were in a bind. By the last skater in a three and a half hour event, the judges had left very little room on their scorecards for a big surprise, especially from the skater who was in sixth place. All those 5.7s and 5.8s create a logjam; the judges have no place to maneuver.

Had Slutskaia had a better year, or a better short program, she likely would have earned more respect from the judges, who might have saved room at the top of their marks for her.

The German judge, 1980 Olympic men's silver medalist Jan Hoffman, gave Kwan 5.8, 5.9, and Lipinski, 5.9, 5.8. He did in 1997 almost exactly what he had done three years earlier at the Olympics, when he gave Baiul 5.7, 5.9, and Kerrigan, 5.8, 5.8. In both cases, his totals tied the two competitors, and he broke the tie with his second mark, the artistic one, choosing Kwan and Baiul. (In the short program, the first mark breaks the tie. In the long program, the tiebreaker is the second mark.) Hoffman knows firsthand the pain of a close loss; at the Lake Placid Olympics, he narrowly lost the gold medal to Robin Cousins.

In giving Kwan and Lipinski the same total of 11.7 before Slutskaia skated, Hoffman ensured that he could not place the Russian between the two Americans, that he would have either Slutskaia ahead of both of them, or behind both of them. And that meant bad news for Kwan, who, if she were to win overall, needed a majority of judges to place Slutskaia behind her and ahead of Lipinski in the long program.

Slutskaia won the first-place marks of three judges, but the third-place marks of the other six, and was third in the long program and fourth overall. (Gusmeroli hung on to third and the bronze medal.) Kwan won three judges' first-place votes and the second-place marks of the other six. And Lipinski won the other three judges' first-place marks, three second-place votes, and three third-place votes.

Put all together, Kwan won the long program because she had a majority of second-place votes. When no one gets five first-place votes, first is decided by the total of first- and second-place marks. Only in figure skating do you win first place by having the most second-place scores.

Lipinski finished second in the long program, but held on to win the world title and the $50,000 first-place prize money. Had two judges flip-flopped Lipinski and Slutskaia, Kwan would have regained the world title. It was that close. Kwan settled for the silver medal and $30,000.

Lipinski became the youngest women's world champion in history, replacing the legendary Sonja Henie, who was one month older than Tara when she won the first of her ten consecutive world titles in 1927.

Frank Carroll knew Henie. "First of all, she was an egotistical woman," he said. "I don't think she would have liked anyone who could skate as well as she could. She's probably rolling over in her grave."

Carroll wasn't exactly doing cartwheels himself. Kwan appeared to be back on track, but what a disaster the previous five weeks had been. This skating business in the 1990s was no piece of cake; it was not easy being the coach of the girl at the top of the heap.

As Lipinski, Kwan, and Gusmeroli were answering questions at the front of the interview room after the competition, Mike Burg and Jack and Pat Lipinski were working the back. Burg had a cellular phone pressed to his ear, while Jack and Pat were available for interviews. Soon, reporters began leaving their seats and meandering back to the Lipinskis, where Pat was sitting alone, with a knot of journalists encircling her.

She startled a few of them by saying that the primary reason they left Delaware was that the rinks were too crowded and that she was concerned about Tara's well-being. Tara, she said, often had to look over her shoulder to make sure the pairs and dance teams with whom she shared the ice were not in her way.

Reporters who knew the Lipinski story were certain the family had left because of the screaming match with the former coach.

Whether Burg heard the interview or not, he soon was directing traffic.

He leaned toward Jack Lipinski, who was standing beside him.

"Jack, go squeeze in there somewhere," Burg whispered, and Lipinski was by his wife's side within moments.

Someone asked Jack Lipinski about the coming Olympic year and the pressure Tara would face as world champion.

"It shouldn't be any different," Jack said. "It's only if the media makes it different."

A few moments later, Jack Lipinski again looked into the faces of reporters from around America and mentioned the media as the "only" thing that would put undue pressure on his daughter.

Jere Longman of the *New York Times* turned his head toward another journalist. "Yeah," he whispered. "As if the media created www.TaraLipinski.com. . . ."

The Website had been announced within an hour after Lipinski won the national title in February.

The Lipinskis were jumpy about their new position atop the world of skating. Anything could create a controversy.

Even Tupperware bowls.

During an interview, Tara told Longman and Philip Hersh that when she was a little girl watching the Olympic Games on TV, she stood on boxes in front of the television as an athlete's national anthem was played. Longman thought the story was delightful and wanted to make sure he got the details right.

"Jack," Longman said, "can you give us the story, there are different versions of it, when she was five and standing on those boxes?"

Jack Lipinski glared at Longman. "Let me tell you, that got blown out of proportion—"

Pat Lipinski interrupted. "Can we clear that up—"

Longman: "Was it cardboard boxes or shoe boxes?"

Pat: "She was two—"

Jack: "and she was playing with Tupperware bowls. . . . I think it was the Summer Games in 1984. She liked to play with all that stuff, and every time some anthem would play, she'd stand on them."

Later, Jack Lipinski said he made a fuss over the Tupperware story because "It made it sound like I was sitting there pushing her up there."

A half hour earlier, Tara and Michelle had been on the ice, receiving their medals and their flowers, climbing a real medal stand with Tara at the very top, listening to the "Star-Spangled Banner," then circling the ice for photos and accolades. It was the first time U.S. skaters finished 1–2 at the worlds since Kristi Yamaguchi and Nancy Kerrigan in 1992.

As Lipinski remained for more pictures, Kwan made her way to the boards to leave.

Waiting for her at the rinkside ABC booth were three of the most celebrated names in her sport: Peggy Fleming, Dick Button, and Brian Boitano.

Kwan skated to them.

She was swallowed up in a commentator group hug.

"She was so open about her insecurities," Fleming said later, admiringly. "At nationals, she was devastated. Then we watched her pull it together at worlds, and she was quite proud of herself. It was an important lesson to learn, but of all the times to have that lesson, the year before the Olympics."

Kwan handed her bouquet of flowers to Boitano.

"These are for you," she said.

Boitano complimented her on her performance.

"But the second lutz . . ." Kwan said.

"Who cares?" Boitano said. "You did great. It's a perfect situation. You won the long program, but you finished second. It makes you hungrier."

Boitano lost the 1987 world title before winning the 1988 Olympic gold medal.

The ABC gang's admiration for Kwan was audible on network TV; when she landed a jump, there was joy in their voices. Kwan had been the chosen one since the 1994 Olympics. She could jump *and* she could skate; she was the athlete *and* the artist—if she didn't fall.

Kwan flattered Fleming, Button, and Boitano with her genuine interest in their skating careers, and they honored her with their answers. Kwan already was one of them, even if she didn't yet have what they had—an Olympic gold medal.

One U.S. Olympic gold medalist was conspicuously absent from the Kwan welcoming party. Dorothy Hamill wasn't there to hug Kwan in Lausanne, but she had done her part at the Champions Series final in Canada earlier in the month as an announcer for Fox television.

Hamill announced on the air that she had given Kwan a kiss and wished her luck before the long program. Then, after Michelle made mistakes on three consecutive jumps, Hamill leaped to her defense, pointing out that Kwan had "such poise . . . such maturity . . . she's light on her feet . . . she skates with emotion."

And when the camera showed Lipinski blithely waiting to find out if she or Kwan had won, Hamill warned, "Tara has nothing to lose. Let's see what's happening next year at this time."

Hamill. Button. Boitano. Fleming. It was quite a support group. Kwan engendered that kind of attention because they all saw her as one of them, as the woman most likely to become the next American Olympic champion, even with all her troubles in early 1997.

Lipinski, on the other hand, did not receive a group hug at the ABC booth. It wasn't because they didn't like her; it was because they didn't know her. Tara had just crashed the party. She was too young and too new for them to know and love.

Even though Tara did everything she could on the ice, even though she was the second-most-polished skater in the competition, even though it wasn't her fault that Kwan stepped out of the triple lutz in the short program and the judges gave her first place, she became a target of criticism for all who despised the jumping trend in the sport. Tara was the poster child for skating in the late 1990s. She was an easy target.

Early in the week, a Swiss newspaper called Lipinski "the flea who melts the ice."

The morning of the women's long program, the *London Times* arrived in Lausanne with a scathing column by sports columnist Simon Barnes.

"Lipinski is very talented, and, quite obviously, a massively strong-minded person," he wrote. "And it is horrible to watch her: really quite disturbing. . . . Women's ice skating finds itself in the absurd position in which puberty is a disadvantage. This is clearly silly. Michelle Kwan . . . is struggling. What was easy last year is hard today."

On the Monday after the competition, Barnes unloaded again:

"The Frenchwoman chose the circus as her theme, and skated the big top with all she possessed. But the American skated the freak show from the fairground next door and stole the judge's hearts. The name of the geek is Tara Lipinski, fourteen going on ten. On Saturday, they crowned a prepubescent little girl as women's world champion figure skater.

". . . The anomaly of it all was the extraordinarily high marks that Lipinski received for artistic impression. It was as if the judges believed that someone so technically gifted *must* be an artist. And it is not true at all. It is as if they thought the Venus de Milo was much the same thing as a Barbie doll. The judges acceded to the wishes of the American corporate hunger for teeny heroines.

"Thus they have brought discredit upon their sport, and insulted its participants. Why have marks for artistic impression in the first place, if you don't use them to discriminate between artist and freak?"

It wasn't just a Brit who went after Tara and the judges for anointing her.

"With all the really young skaters that are coming onto the scene," said twenty-two-year-old French skater Laetitia Hubert, "it seems that we are going back to the days of baby gymnasts, and yet skaters of my age can do triples but with the advantage of added experience and femininity."

She finished sixth overall at the world championships.

"If this keeps going, sixteen- and seventeen-year-olds are going to feel like matrons," said coach Evy Scotvold.

"A lot of the artistry and the beauty of the skating is gone," said Frank Carroll. "It's really how many turns you can do in the air that counts and the difficulty of the jumping only. The difficulty of the edges and spirals and spread eagles and the beautiful spins don't seem to count for much. I like to see the difficult jumps, but I'd like to see the other things given more credit too, so that it's a complete package."

Boitano wasn't planning to join the Tara Lipinski fan club either.

"It was nice," he said of her skating. "It was pleasing to the eye. But it was a little girl's program."

"I have not heard that criticism," Richard Callaghan told Terry Foster of the *Detroit News*. "Were you hearing it from people who know skating? It is their personal opinion. I think the majority of judges disproved some of what those people were saying."

The discussion, ultimately, was all about growing up. The little body that made it so easy for Tara Lipinski to jump would, inevitably, change. Lipinski's parents had those tests that showed Tara would not grow more than another inch or so. But if she didn't grow up, she would, eventually, have to grow out. Something was going to happen to her, just as it happened to every other fourteen-year-old girl on earth.

"I've been growing since I was young and it hasn't affected me," Tara said nonchalantly. "If you keep training every day, you're not going to lose it."

Perhaps that was true. But, more likely, Tara was about to enter a race that would shape the rest of her life.

What would she reach first?

Puberty?

Or the Olympic Games?

THE RUSSIANS ARE COMING

The man in the stands was figure skating's first true agent. The woman beside the ice was Russia's first true capitalist. They had come to the Malley Sport Centre to watch the pairs competition at the world championships, and they could not take their eyes off the two skaters in the center of the ice.

Michael Rosenberg, the American skating agent, and Tamara Moskvina, the diminutive Russian pairs coach, are two of the shrewdest people in their sport. Moskvina told Rosenberg that she had a new pair of skaters for him to see, and he made sure he didn't miss them. When Moskvina touted a new pair, Rosenberg listened. He had known Moskvina for years. She was the first Russian in skating to have a fax machine, then the first with an e-mail address. She also is the most innovative pairs coach in the world. If a man and a woman were intertwined like a pretzel on the ice, or swinging here and there like a trapeze act, you could be certain that Moskvina had something to do with it. The world pairs silver medalist in 1969 with Russian men's coach Alexei Mishin—"He was very reliable," she said, "he never dropped me once"—Moskvina had produced two of the previous four Olympic pairs gold medalists and the last three Olympic pairs silver medalists. As her homeland fell apart around her, as money ran out and fellow coaches and skaters bailed out to America, she, like Mishin, stayed in St. Petersburg and prospered. Her reputation didn't diminish. It grew.

After the competition, Rosenberg and Moskvina met for dinner.

"My God," he exclaimed. "That's the next Gordeeva and Grinkov!"

Moskvina nodded without smiling.

"You have good eye," she replied in English dripping with a deep Russian accent. "They will win the Olympics, if not in Japan, then the next. They are the next stars."

Elena Berezhnaia and Anton Sikharulidze thought the press conference was over. They had just finished their classical short program without a mistake, and were in third place heading into the long program. But as they got up to leave, they were swarmed by a dozen journalists wanting to hear the story. Again.

Berezhnaia remembered only that she had been spinning too close to her pairs partner at the time, Oleg Sliakhov, as they practiced side-by-side camel spins in a rink in Riga, Latvia, fourteen months earlier, in January 1996. Berezhnaia didn't remember the toe pick of Sliakhov's skate catching her on the left side of her head. Nor did she remember the blade carving a one-and-a-half-inch gash through her hairline, or penetrating her skull.

She never lost consciousness as she was taken to the hospital, where doctors, fearing bleeding in her brain, performed emergency surgery to open her skull and clean out bone debris.

Moskvina arrived in Riga from St. Petersburg five days after the accident—it took that long to obtain a visa—to find her beautiful little skater in a hospital bed, unable to talk and move.

"Let's not speak about her future as a skater," the doctors told Moskvina. "Let's speak about her health."

"Okay," Moskvina said, "let's speak about her health."

For one month, Berezhnaia stayed in the hospital. Gradually, she was able to walk, but her speech was severely impaired. She left the hospital not with Sliakhov, with whom she had had a stormy relationship prior to the accident, but with Sikharulidze, who knew Berezhnaia and was hoping to begin skating with her. He took a train from St. Petersburg to Riga, checked her out of the hospital and brought her to St. Petersburg with him.

Berezhnaia attended an international skating competition in St. Petersburg in February 1996, the month she returned to Russia. People were surprised to see her; she wore a scarf to cover her shaved head.

She began speech therapy and soon was talking slowly, with "a foreign accent," Moskvina said. She was told she was talking like an American, and she laughed.

By March, she was standing on the ice with Sikharulidze. Two months later, they began to skate together. Berezhnaia said she was scared just "a little bit, at the beginning," when she returned to the ice.

"But I was sure I would be able to skate," she said.

Moskvina was uncertain exactly how to begin teaching the two to become a pair. She told Sikharulidze to "please stay away, far away," from Berezhnaia as they practiced their side-by-side camel spins. She approached them cautiously, and she gave Sikharulidze a special piece of advice: "This is your crystal vase. It was already broken and it's very easy to break again a thing that has been broken once, so be careful."

Sikharulidze took such good care of Berezhnaia, he became her boyfriend.

Even as she struggled to regain her speech, Berezhnaia worked with Sikharulidze through the summer and fall, getting ready for the Russian national championships. They came in second. At the 1997 European championships in January, they finished third. They skated beautifully, with an elegance and grace reminiscent of Ekaterina Gordeeva and her late husband, Sergei Grinkov.

Gordeeva and Grinkov had been the chief rivals of Moskvina's top pairs for a decade. They defeated Elena Valova and Oleg Vassiliev in 1988 for the Olympic gold medal, then Natalia Mishkutenok and Artur Dmitriev for the gold medal in 1994. (No tears should be shed for Moskvina, however. Valova and Vassiliev won the 1984 Olympic gold medal and Mishkutenok and Dmitriev won the 1992 gold.) Moskvina's pairs were the innovative risk-takers; G and G, as Gordeeva and Grinkov were called, were the classical stylists.

Although Berezhnaia, nineteen, and Sikharulidze, twenty, still had a long way to go to reach greatness, their size differential (he is tall, she is tiny); their light, classical line; and their remarkable resemblance to Gordeeva and Grinkov—Berezhnaia is as softly beautiful as Gordeeva; Sikharulidze's handsome face and muscular build are as pleasing as Grinkov's were—made Moskvina pause.

"People are nostalgic for such a style," she said.

As they skated their short program, Moskvina stood by the boards, where she always is for her pairs, watching. She stood in the same place for her other pair, the husky Dmitriev and his new partner, Oksana Kazakova, as he doubled a triple jump, dropped to sixth place and incurred her subtle scorn.

"It's not the place to do double jumps," she said dismissively. In another day and age, Dmitriev might have been dispatched to Siberia. Now, he faced the wrath of Moskvina, his coach of thirteen years. It was debatable which was worse.

But when Moskvina watched the young ones skate perfectly and move into third place, she nearly wept.

"I am rather emotional, but I won't cry," she said. "But if I will be her mother, I would cry."

In the interview room, her story completely told, Berezhnaia was about to leave with her coach, but Moskvina doubled back and poked her head into a cluster of mostly American reporters. Moskvina knew their faces, and knew she was most welcome there. She made their lives easy; she was a quote machine with an accent. Few skating people were more accessible, more honest, or more wickedly humorous. Although she was not even five feet tall, Moskvina always was easy to find. She was constantly underfoot, and always up to something. At the 1994 Winter Olympics, she said she personally hypnotized Dmitriev and then-partner Natalia Mishkutenok after a fall in practice—and a few days later, they won the silver medal. She was the perfect match for a handful of playful U.S. journalists who already had boiled the long, cumbersome Russian names of Moskvina's hot skaters into something more cynical and descriptive. The lovely and fragile Berezhnaia would be known, crudely, as "Skate in the Head." Sikharulidze would be "Anton," or "Skate in the Head's partner." The reporters laughed at how preposterous it sounded, but it did make life simpler.

Moskvina didn't mind at all. She didn't care if they spelled the names right—or if they spelled them at all—as long as they got the story straight.

"I am now open to discussion," she said in the midst of the reporters, "for the sale of the rights."

She chuckled, and the reporters laughed with her.

Moskvina then scampered off, signaling the end of the evening's entertainment. But she would be back tomorrow. Today, Tamara, the next day . . . Moskvina always returned for more.

The next night was the pairs long program, and Berezhnaia and Sikharulidze skated last, right after Jenni Meno and Todd Sand of the United States.

Meno and Sand had come into the 1996–97 season with uncharacteristically high hopes for an American pairs team. U.S. pairs hardly ever won anything. They had never won an Olympic gold medal, and had won only two world championships, one in 1950, the other in 1979. U.S. skating is dominated by the singles; an individualistic country produces solitary skaters. When coaches put two American skaters together as a pair, they often perform like singles skaters who just happened to wander onto the ice surface at the same time. They tend to be remote, unemotional, and downright boring. U.S. pairs are like U.S. marriages; about half of them work, and even the couples who don't separate occasionally have problems.

Prior to the emergence of Meno and Sand, for instance, there was the tumultuous "Waitress and Truck Driver" pairing of Calla Urbanski and Rocky Marval. They argued, they fought, they split up three different times. Indeed, it was rocky. In her long career, Urbanski had skated with six partners, Marval included.

But Meno and Sand brought something different to U.S. pairs skating. From 1994 through 1996, when they won three national titles, they gave the United States its first husband-and-wife national champions since Nancy and Ron Ludington won four straight titles from 1957 to 1960. From the beginning of the U.S. national championships in 1914 through the 1997 nationals, this was the complete list of married pairs who became U.S. national champions: the Ludingtons, who later divorced, and Meno and Sand.

If it worked for the old Soviet Union, Meno and Sand figured, it could work for America. Finally there was a U.S. pair that was in love and not threatening to break up. They had begun to grow on everyone, even if Sand reminded some of a Ken doll on ice. Meno and Sand were the essence of quiet, romantic simplicity, something that had been sorely lacking in American pairs skating. In the previous few decades, the top U.S. pairs had been, by and large, brothers and sisters (such as 1984 Olympic silver medalists Kitty and Peter Carruthers), or young kids (Kristi Yamaguchi and Rudy Galindo), and, before them, the 1979 world champions and five-time national champions, Tai Babilonia and Randy Gardner.

While the former Soviet Union gave the world long-time partners who grew to love one another and spend their lives together, America presented the kids next door.

"Ours was very much like a platonic marriage," said Gardner of his relationship with Babilonia. Very often, the lack of romance on the ice from an American pair translated into a rout for the Soviets. For nine consecutive Olympic Games, from 1964 to 1994, a pair from the Soviet Union or Russia won the gold medal. During that time, U.S. pairs managed two bronze medals and one silver.

"The Russians got along, stayed together, and got married," said Ron Ludington, who has been coaching for more than thirty-five years. "In the United States, if a pair didn't skate well together after one year, they split up and found new partners. The reason the Russians have been so successful is that the two right people are put together to skate together. The communication and organization of the marriage can help them on the ice."

Babilonia and Gardner—"Tai and Randy" to millions of fans even today—looked as if they might be the Americans who would end the Soviet domination at the Olympics in 1980. They entered the Lake Placid Games as the reigning world champions. American hopes were high. But Gardner suffered a groin pull prior to the competition and was so badly injured he could not skate. When he and Babilonia left the ice after trying to practice minutes before the competition, ABC's Dick Button choked back tears. Announcing their withdrawal, he sounded as if someone had died.

Gardner went on to make a career out of skating, becoming a respected choreographer and part-time professional skater with Babilonia, one of his dearest friends. But as much as his life is centered around the sport, he never has watched a videotape of the events of that night in Lake Placid.

"Can't do it," he said.

If someone ever tried to show it to him, he said he would leave the room.

Life went on in U.S. pairs skating. John Nicks, who coached Tai and Randy, moved on to teaching other pairs at his training base in Southern California, and by the 1990s was coaching Meno and Sand. Two things were happening in 1997 to make Meno and Sand bonafide contenders for the Olympic gold medal in Nagano. After winning two consecutive world bronze medals, they had become a pair in every sense of the word, not simply two good skaters sharing the ice. Nicks joked that he sometimes felt as if he were an "intruder" at their practice sessions.

Even more important, heading into the 1996–97 season, no Russian pair—no pair around the world, for that matter—was dominant. Meno and Sand saw a void waiting to be filled. After overcoming wrist injuries, they won the Champions Series stop in Japan in 1996. Then they skated exquisitely to defeat the reigning world champions, Russia's Marina Eltsova and Andrei Bushkov, at a pro-am event back in Japan in January 1997, a competition that placed a premium on artistry. They believed they could go to Lausanne and contend for the gold medal.

But first, they had to win the U.S. national championships.

And they did not.

They made a huge mistake. "We did something we should never do," Meno said glumly. "We took it for granted."

Sand lost his concentration on a lift in the short program and Meno stumbled coming back to the ice. That glitch slowed them down and put them a beat or two behind their music. Trying to catch up to end at exactly the right moment, they went into their final move, a death spiral. In this maneuver, the woman is stretched out, nearly lying on the ice, revolving around the man, who is holding her by the hand as he crouches down and picks into the ice with the toe of his skate.

But Sand's left skate—the one that was supposed to give him the toe hold in the ice—slipped out from underneath him, and he lost his balance and went sprawling. Meno dropped several inches to the ice. That's how their short program ended, with Sand scrambling to get up and Meno literally lying on her back on the ice. The crowd in Nashville sat in stunned silence. It certainly was a memorable conclusion—only not exactly what Meno and Sand had in mind.

As Meno waited for the scores in Kiss and Cry, she stared into space, unhurt but stunned. She had been dropped on the back of her head by her husband. This didn't happen every day to a pair that was being touted for potential Olympic greatness.

They followed that effort with another lackluster performance in the long program two nights later. Three-time U.S. silver medalists Kyoko Ina and Jason Dungjen—"business partners," Ina said, not lovers—skated a program loaded with triple jumps, and easily defeated Meno and Sand for their first national title.

What a predicament this was for Meno and Sand. Beaten in their own country, their lofty international goals suffered a jolt. They went on to the Champions Series final, but a back injury to Sand, who at the ripe old skating age of thirty-three had done a lot of lifting in his career, forced them to withdraw.

A few weeks later at the world championships, Meno and Sand got a break. With mistakes by Ina and Dungjen, Kazakova and Dmitriev, and Eltsova and Bushkov in the long program, Meno and Sand had a rare and delightful opportunity. Sitting in fourth place after the short program, if they skated a smashing performance, and if Moskvina's new pair faltered, Meno and Sand might win the world title.

Sometimes in skating, this kind of rich opportunity turns into total disaster. That happened for Debi Thomas the night she faced Katarina Witt in the "Battle of the Carmens" at the 1988 Olympics. Given every chance to win when Witt skated a less-than-stunning performance, Thomas blew it. It was all there for the taking, a lifetime of fame and fortune, just four minutes away. But instead of rising to the occasion, Thomas made a mistake on her opening combination, and fell apart from there. She came off the ice apologizing and shaking her head. It was a skater's worst nightmare come true.

Although the moment in Lausanne was not nearly as riveting, Meno and Sand endured the same fate. Sand doubled an opening side-by-side triple jump, Meno landed awkwardly on a twist in the air, and they turned double axels into singles. Instead of rising to the medal stand again, they dropped to fifth place, and trudged off to try to pick up the pieces of a once-promising season.

The demise of Meno and Sand, to go along with the flaws of the others, set the stage for a story that seemed destined to go straight to Hollywood. Fourteen months after being hit in the head by a skate, a lovable teenager was on the verge of going to the top of her sport. All Berezhnaia and Sikharulidze had to do was skate cleanly, and they would be world champions.

Tamara Moskvina made sure her skaters were a pleasing package, gift-wrapped in pink: she in a pink dress, he in black pants and a pink shirt. Early in their program, they prepared for their side-by-side triple toe loops. Up they went. Down they came. Berezhnaia landed safely. Sikharulidze crashed to the ice. Moskvina watched stoically, but inside, she knew they were in trouble.

On their side-by-side double axels, which came next, he hit the ice again.

Bad turned to awful when she fell on one throw, then went sliding to the ice on another. Getting up, she wanted to skate off and hide. After four dreadful errors, they went through the motions for the rest of their program. As soon as they got off the ice, he split for the arena door and disappeared. Who could blame him? No one wanted to see the scores that were about to come onto the scoreboard. They were dreadful, from a low of 4.4 to nothing higher than 5.4.

Berezhnaia and Sikharulidze plummeted in the standings, from third to ninth overall.

"They heard everybody talking about them," Moskvina said, "but they are not ready for it yet."

There was no sadness in Moskvina's camp. The 1997 season was a bonus year; 1998 would come quickly enough. Moskvina knew that the endless possibilities of another year, an Olympic year, were about to unfold.

She also knew that her other pair, Kazakova and Dmitriev, would have been world champions had he not doubled a planned triple jump in each of the short and long programs. They settled for the bronze medal, but they were the most polished and innovative pair in the competition. If only the twenty-nine-year-old Dmitriev—husband, father, and pack-a-day smoker—could stay in better shape. He was the key to their success. He was the one who flew through the air as if he were in the Kirov Ballet, which, not coincidentally, he watched as a young man. (The Kirov is a fifteen-minute drive from the rink in St. Petersburg.) His performance was the one that counted. Kazakova was rock solid; it was Dmitriev who was the variable. His mistakes doomed them in Lausanne; if he cut out the errors, Moskvina knew she just might have both the pairs gold and silver medalists in Nagano.

The gold medalists at the 1997 world championships, however, were Mandy Woetzel and Ingo Steuer, the solid, athletic Germans from the former East German city of Chemnitz, Katarina Witt's hometown. They made two mistakes in their long program but still held on to win. After five years of climbing through the ranks, they were rewarded for their patience. But Woetzel and Steuer knew nothing was certain heading into the most important year of their careers. They knew a horrid fall always was lurking in pairs skating.

They will be known forever for one of the all-time spectacular falls in the history of their sport, a highlight-film crash if ever there was one. At the 1994 Winter Olympics, as Steuer held Woetzel's arms behind her during a tricky maneuver, she slipped and hit the ice chest-first, then bounced on her chin. As their music played on, Steuer picked up Woetzel and carried her off the ice.

Three years later, they were on top of the world. But it wouldn't be easy to stay there heading into the Olympics, mainly because the Russians were coming, with tiny General Moskvina leading the way.

When the men arrived at the world championships, Todd Eldredge, the defending champion, was haunted by the Q-word.

Eight triple jumps had been enough to win for Eldredge in 1996. But, a year later, he was being treated as some kind of skating novice because he did not have a quad. He was battered in interviews by questions about the four-revolution jump; often, nearly everything he was asked was about the quad. Eldredge finally waved the white flag of surrender. Yes, he would put in a quad for worlds if it was going well in practice. "No doubt," he said at the Champions Series final in Canada.

But five days after that event, in a practice back home at the Detroit Skating Club, Eldredge landed badly on a triple axel and sprained his right ankle. His right foot was the one that launched him into the air for a quadruple toe loop. With his ankle feeling tender to the touch, Eldredge informed reporters on a conference call that he "didn't see the quad happening" at the world championships.

So the questions began anew for Eldredge: "Can you win without the quad?"

And, once again, Eldredge said he could. He noted that in Canada, he defeated two skaters—Alexei Urmanov and Ilia Kulik—who landed the quad.

"It doesn't come down to just that one jump," Eldredge said for the hundredth time.

And, for the hundredth time, he hoped he was right.

It was ironic that Eldredge was being portrayed as The Man Without the Quad, for he had never given up on anything in his career.

"He knew what he wanted when he was six," said his mother Ruth. "And he was right."

At six, Todd Eldredge began taking skating lessons. He was so little his parents couldn't see him over the boards.

When he was nine, he brought a notebook to skating practice to write down what his coach told him. Things began to click; after falling dozens of times, he began landing a double axel. "I said, 'I'm improving. I'm nine or ten years old, and I can see myself improving. This is working for me. Let's stay with this.'"

When he was ten, he left home.

"The decision was totally made by Todd," Ruth Eldredge said. "I had said, 'I'm not going to do this. I'm not going to split my family up for this.' But he was so self-motivated. He knew what he wanted to do, and we just had to take that and assume it was the right thing to do."

To follow his skating dream, Todd Eldredge moved from Cape Cod to Philadelphia, where his summertime coach, Richard Callaghan, had taken a job. Eldredge lived in the home of Callaghan's stepmother-in-law, who happened to be a good friend of Ruth Eldredge's. Several other skaters lived in her house.

"At first, I was homesick all the time," Eldredge said. He flew home when he could, and the family got together on holidays, but for five years, until he turned fifteen, he didn't live full-time with any member of his family.

"I don't know if I ever had a kid if I'd want them to do that," Eldredge said.

But Eldredge did it, and thrived. By 1985, at thirteen, he had become national novice champion.

Back home in Chatham, Massachusetts, on the Cape, John Eldredge, Todd's father, was not thriving. A fisherman who caught squid, mackeral, tuna, and cod, John Eldredge was about to have to call his son to tell him to come home. He already had remortgaged the house three times. Business was not going well. Skating was draining the family.

"As much money as we needed for ourselves, we needed that again for Todd's skating," John Eldredge said. "It was a question of how far into debt we could go. I was two weeks away from telling him he would have to get out of skating."

Ruth, a licensed practical nurse, told a few of their neighbors that the family no longer could support Todd's skating. The friends offered to help. They held a clambake and raised some money. Others hosted parties at their homes, where videotapes of Todd's skating competitions were shown to entice pledges. They raised $10,000 the first year.

Todd Eldredge kept on skating.

Soon, Callaghan was off to take a job coaching at the prestigious Broadmoor Ice Arena in Colorado Springs, and Eldredge went along. Ruth Eldredge left her husband and other son behind in Cape Cod and moved to be with Todd, a high school sophomore rising quickly through the ranks in U.S. skating. They rented an apartment and sat there together to watch Brian Boitano win his Olympic gold medal in 1988.

But they soon were on the move again when Callaghan became director of skating for the San Diego Ice Arena. Ruth moved with them, and lived with Todd as he finished high school. By 1990, at eighteen, Todd had become the men's national champion. The townspeople of Chatham continued to raise money, a total that finally was estimated at $200,000 by the time Todd Eldredge began making a living in skating.

Eldredge won the national title again in 1991, and came in third at the world championships. The Albertville Olympics were a year away and Eldredge was a medal contender. Things were setting up perfectly for him.

But all his preparation for the Olympic year began causing troubles. His back hurt. Eldredge's right leg is about three-eighths of an inch shorter than his left. The discrepancy created rubbing in the joints between the vertebrae in his lower back. He had felt the pain before, in 1989, but had been able to rest and the problem went away. Coming into the 1992 Olympic trials, the pain had returned, more severe than ever. Eldredge withdrew from the trials, but was placed on the Olympic team by the U.S. Figure Skating Association's international committee because he was two-time national champion and a world medalist.

His back got better (he now wears a lift in his right shoe), and he competed in the 1992 Olympics. But he fell on a relatively simple jump—a double axel—in the short program and finished the competition in tenth place. Eldredge felt awful. He had bumped Mark Mitchell, the third-place finisher at the U.S. trials, from the Olympics. He began to doubt whether he should have been sent to the Games at all. His confidence waned.

By the 1993 nationals, Eldredge was still haunted by what had happened a year earlier. He looked like he was skating in slow motion. He finished sixth.

"People said, 'Oh, we shouldn't have sent him to the Olympics because of what ended up happening,'" Eldredge said. "I didn't qualify for it, and then was chosen over Mark. It was tough for me to deal with all that."

So Eldredge quit.

He was living in Detroit, the latest stop on the journey with Callaghan. He played golf all day. He made friends outside of the rink. When he wasn't playing golf, he was playing tennis. For three months, he did not skate.

Ruth, John, and Scott, Todd's brother, came to Detroit to visit. They weren't sure what Todd planned to do, although they were fairly certain it wouldn't take him back to the Cape.

Todd Eldredge got queasy on his father's boat.

"He likes his water frozen," his father said.

John didn't want his sons to follow in his footsteps anyway.

"I prayed they wouldn't. It's such a hard way of life."

Todd's family told him they would support whatever decision he made about skating.

"But we also let him know that he had much more to offer the sport," Ruth said.

One day, Eldredge wandered back into the Detroit Skating Club.

"Playing tennis was fun," he said, "but I had spent so many years of my life in this sport, it was kind of ridiculous that one bad year, or two bad years, were going to take it all away."

The Olympic schedule had been juggled to stagger the Winter and Summer Games, which meant another Winter Olympics was coming in February 1994. Eldredge threw himself into his training, with one very important difference. His attitude had changed. He realized there was life after a bad skating performance. If he missed something, he would get it into his next performance. He wouldn't be so hard on himself.

The Olympic trials were in Detroit. It was working out perfectly. His practices were superb. He was ready. He was going to make another Olympic team. He was sure of it.

He checked into the Westin Hotel in downtown Detroit, where all the skaters were housed. Two days before the short program, he woke up in the morning feeling awful and walked into the bathroom.

"I looked in the mirror, didn't look good, and passed out," he said.

Eldredge's head dropped into the sink. He immediately regained consciousness and called Callaghan, who found a doctor. Eldredge was diagnosed with the flu and a 104-degree fever.

Callaghan called Eldredge's condominium, where Todd's parents were staying.

"Todd has a hundred-and-four-degree fever, looked in the mirror, passed out, and hit his head," Callaghan said into the phone.

"You're kidding,' Ruth replied.

"No."

For two days, Eldredge ate nothing but soup and crackers. He showed up to skate, but had little energy and finished fourth. Two other men—Scott Davis and Brian Boitano—moved on to the Olympic Games in Norway.

Eldredge watched the Olympics on television, and was heartened by the strange things he saw. The big guns—Boitano, Viktor Petrenko, and Kurt Browning—fell. The younger skaters—Alexei Urmanov, Elvis Stojko, and Philippe Candeloro—swept the medals. His contemporaries ruled the Olympics.

"If I had been there," Eldredge said, "I more than likely would have been on the medal podium."

He told himself only one thing: "Now that you're over this flu, head into the next four years."

* * *

Eldredge won the national title in 1995. He was upset by Rudy Galindo in 1996, but came back to win the world championships two months later. In 1997, he again won the national title, his fourth over a remarkably long span of eight years. Over that same period of time, there had been seven different national women's champions.

"He's always been a fighter," said John Eldredge. "In the past, he's always been coming from behind, always fighting. He always does better when he's a little bit down."

By the mid-'90s, Eldredge had started to make a fabulous living in skating, well into the hundreds of thousands of dollars. After winning the 1996 world title, Eldredge stopped back in his hometown. He knew he had to return to Chatham.

He gathered some of the neighbors together, and presented them with a check for $10,000 to help young skaters growing up in the area. Eldredge told the townspeople he would have left skating in 1985 had it not been for them. Now, he wanted to make sure another child didn't leave skating too soon.

The people of Chatham assured him they would never let that happen. Never had, never would.

At the opening draw of the 1997 world championships in Lausanne, Eldredge pulled a bad number out of a hat. Three. There were thirty-one skaters in the men's short program. To have to go third was not good.

It's skating tradition that the nine judges, who are given the nearly impossible task of ranking skaters against those who are yet to perform, usually "leave room" with their marks for excellent programs later on in the competition. A performance that should earn 5.9, 5.9 will receive at best only 5.8, 5.8 if it comes early in the short program. It's not fair to the skaters who come at the beginning, but it's the way skating works, and everyone in the sport knows it and seems powerless to do anything about it.

At 1:35 P.M. on Wednesday, March 19, 1997, Eldredge skated a meticulous short program. His right ankle was 90 percent healthy, and he flew across the ice. His performance was, in the words of Brian Boitano, "the perfect short program." Callaghan said it was Eldredge's best ever technically.

But the problem for Eldredge was that it came three hours too early to put him into first place after one-third of the men's competition.

When the judges' scores were posted, there wasn't a 5.9 to be found, just 5.7s and 5.8s.

"The judges have to save their marks," Callaghan said. "There are a lot of great skaters coming up."

There was no doubt in Callaghan's mind that if Eldredge had skated the exact same performance at 4:35 P.M. that he skated at 1:35 P.M., he would have received bunches of 5.9s.

Elvis Stojko followed Eldredge seven skaters later. He executed his program to perfection, but was placed below Eldredge. Three judges gave him 5.6 for his presentation.

Michael Weiss, the young American, came right after Stojko. He skated to "The Quest of the Dream Warrior," an avant-garde program choreographed by Brian Wright. Weiss two-footed both landings of his triple axel–triple toe loop combination, and his scores reflected it; they dipped as low as 5.1 technically from a high of 5.6, and reached only as high as 5.5 and 5.6 artistically.

The men's short program was televised by ESPN2, with ABC's announcers. The Weiss team still was a mystery to them.

As Weiss finished his program, a camera was focused on Lisa Thornton, his jazz teacher, applauding by the boards near the ice.

"There's his fiancée and choreographer," commentator Terry Gannon told U.S. viewers on ESPN2.

He was half-right. She was his fiancée. Brian Wright was his choreographer, and he was watching on TV at his sister's home in Seattle, where he continued to fight AIDS. Wright was startled by the mistake. Thornton helped Weiss with some moves on the ice, but Wright was the one who created the programs. It was an indisputable fact: Wright was Weiss's choreographer.

In Seattle, some of Wright's friends watched the short program on television. After Weiss finished, they called Wright to tell him that because they heard on TV that he wasn't the choreographer, they didn't like the program.

They made Wright laugh, but inside, he was very sad. How could the TV people have forgotten him?

Audrey Weisiger, Weiss's coach, was pleased Michael had tried the tough jumps even if they had not been perfect. She waited for Weiss and sat with him in Kiss and Cry to watch his scores. On television, her name was mispronounced. It's "WHIZ-ager," but the announcers called her "WISE-ager." Then again, no one could quite figure out Ilia Kulik's name either. Was it "Koo-LEEK"? Or "KOO-lick"?

Either way, when Kulik skated from the seventeenth position in the draw, he was perfect, and edged close to Eldredge.

Although Kulik didn't do it, someone was bound to pass Eldredge. There were just too many good male skaters, and his performance had been sitting out there way too long, growing stale in the judges' minds.

Alexei Urmanov lucked into the delightful next-to-last spot in the skating order, and performed beautifully. When he hung on to a precarious landing of his triple axel–triple toe loop, he gave Eldredge the inevitable nudge to second place. Most of the judges had not given out their 5.9s, saving them for someone who skated cleanly near the end. So, with the short program all but over, they gave their top scores to Urmanov.

Urmanov leaped into first place, followed by Eldredge, Kulik, Stojko, and Alexei Yagudin, the other Russian. Because of the complicated skating scoring system, this meant Urmanov, Eldredge, and Kulik could win the world title simply by winning the long program the next night.

Stojko, however, was in trouble. His task was as difficult as Michelle Kwan's was in the women's competition. He needed help from a competitor. He had to win the long program, then hope that Urmanov came in third in the long program. If Urmanov wasn't two places behind Stojko in the long program, Stojko could not beat him overall for the gold medal.

With all the top skaters performing clean programs, Stojko was pushed to the back of the pack. It was not a good sign for him: All things being equal, the judges placed him fourth.

But if he was surprised, he certainly didn't show it. He reared back on his heels and fired away.

"I couldn't have done any better under the circumstances. I knew that after I skated clean and all the other guys skated clean, I knew I was going to be fourth. For some reason, I'm always put at the bottom of that group."

Weiss, with his nagging mistakes, fell to ninth place. But there was no disgrace in that. Men's skating was making great technical leaps. Eleven of the thirty-one competitors landed triple axel–triple toe loop combinations in the short program; only two men had accomplished the feat in the short program a year earlier.

One of those triple–triples, however, proved costly.

After landing slightly off-balance on his triple axel, Alexei Urmanov quickly jammed the toe of his left skate into the ice to launch himself into his triple toe loop. Because he was out of position on the finish of the first jump, it was an awkward move. Had it not been the world championships, Urmanov probably would have played it safe and tried a double toe loop. But he knew he needed a triple–triple to have any chance to win in Lausanne.

As he flew into the air on the rushed jump, Urmanov didn't feel pain, but something inside his left leg felt different.

"Something happened," Urmanov told himself.

Alexei Mishin, who coached Urmanov to the gold medal at the 1994 Olympics, always told his skaters, "Jump every jump like it's the last in your life."

Urmanov followed orders; whatever it was did not stop him in the short program. He completed all his jumps. As he finished and waited for his scores, he wasn't hurting. But he knew something had happened to the top of his left leg.

When he woke up on Thursday morning, the day of the men's long program, Urmanov felt stiffness and pain in his left groin. A Russian doctor told him there was nothing to worry about. But in practice, the groin felt worse. He tried to skate. He was in trouble. He received three painkilling injections, the last one twenty minutes before he had to come onto the ice.

He appeared in costume to join the other leaders for the six-minute final warm-up for the long program. In the practice, Urmanov landed one triple, then doubled a jump. With thirty seconds to go in the warm-up, he steadied himself against the boards beside the ice, put on his skate guards and trudged away.

A groin injury doesn't sound particularly threatening, but for a skater, it can be worse than a broken leg. Nearly everything a skater does on the ice tears at the groin muscle. There is no way to rest it. It's like a tennis player with a bad shoulder or elbow; it can bother them for months.

Ten minutes later, on the advice of a doctor, Alexei Urmanov withdrew from the competition, having to give up what would have been his best chance ever to win a world title.

"I am simply destroyed," he told ABC's Lesley Visser backstage.

After winning the Olympic gold medal in 1994, Urmanov had had nothing but bad luck. He failed to win a medal at the world championships in 1994, 1995, and 1996. He was the forgotten man. Who even remembered who won the gold medal in the '94 Games? Some Americans and Canadians considered his victory to be a fluke. Perhaps it would have been better if he had not won at all, if he had settled for the silver and bronze and disappeared back into the woodwork. Then few would have expected anything from him.

Coming into the Norway Olympics, Urmanov was known for two things: He was the man who came to competitions dressed as a Dutch Master, and he was the Russian skater who had landed a quad.

Then, at twenty, he won the gold over the likes of Boitano, Petrenko, and Browning. He was the darling of the European judging establishment. They plucked him from relative obscurity and made him their man.

"I didn't understand at all what the Olympic gold medal meant for me," Urmanov said. "I was just, 'Well, it happened. Okay.' All my friends say, 'You're the Olympic champion,' and I say, 'Oh, what of it?'

"I didn't understand. But pretty soon I realized I was the Olympic champion, and I was not allowed to fail. I was nervous for a few years. I realized I always had to skate well."

"He was sensitive after the Olympics," Mishin said. "He thought he was not able to do anything bad."

Urmanov did not receive a Western-style million-dollar Olympic payday, but his life did change. Before Norway, Urmanov sometimes took a taxi to practice in St. Petersburg. By 1996, he owned a Jeep Grand Cherokee. He made enough money that his mother, Galina, was able to retire from her job as a cook. He was building a three-bedroom home outside of town, but, for more than three years after his Olympic triumph, he lived in a two-room flat in a delapidated high-rise with his mother, and slept on a sofabed.

On the ice, the handsome Urmanov was a mystery. He performed so poorly at the 1995 world championships that he lost his regular spot on the prestigious Campbell's Soups skating tour. The tour paid him more than $100,000 for little more than three months of shows. But a fourth-place finish at the worlds was not good enough for Urmanov to keep his job in America.

It got worse in 1996, when he finished fifth in the world. That's not bad for a journeyman, but not good for the reigning Olympic champion.

But Mishin did not give up, and neither did Urmanov. He won the 1997 European championships, finished a credible third at the Champions Series final and came into the worlds on top of his game. He had literally taken the gloves off in Lausanne. He showed up for a fine qualifying round performance without his trademark apparel.

"It's just the costume," he said. "We're thinking that it's maybe a good idea to change the costume. We have to change something."

He was looking forward to the world championships. He wanted to win a big event again. He wanted to put himself at the front of the pack of great skaters heading into the 1998 Olympics.

"I feel better than last season," he said, "or the season before."

Mishin agreed. "He has accumulated in his skating everything a human being can collect in art and feeling and music and architecture."

And then Urmanov skated that magnificent short program, and felt "something happen" at the top of his left leg.

Urmanov's withdrawal gave Elvis Stojko the opening he desperately needed. Instead of being fourth and requiring help from others to win his third world championships in four years, he instantly moved up to third. Things were going Stojko's way.

Before Stojko skated, Kulik came onto the ice for his long program. He had moved into second place with Urmanov's withdrawal, with Eldredge in first.

All of a sudden, Kulik had only one person to beat to win the world championships, the one title everyone in his sport had been predicting for him since he captured the silver medal at the 1996 worlds.

But it was not to be. He had another long program meltdown, something that was becoming a regular occurrence for him. It was such a Russian thing to do: run out of gas and fall apart in the four-minute, thirty-second long program. Time and again, a chronic lack of training—sometimes exacerbated by a pack or two of Marlboros—doomed the Russians when it counted most. Kulik, not known as a smoker, but also not known as the hardest worker, turned his planned quadruple toe loop into a triple, then made three mistakes elsewhere in his program, and took himself completely out of contention for a medal of any color.

Stojko couldn't wait for his turn to skate. Nineteen days earlier, on another continent, Stojko had landed the first quad–triple in competitive skating. In Lausanne, he landed the first quad–triple in world championship history. The reaction was not nearly as demonstrative—it was Switzerland, not Canada—but the result was the same. His combination was big and overwhelming, as was the rest of the performance. Every judge gave him at least 5.9 for technical merit; the Italian judge could not restrain herself, and tossed out a 6.0.

But Elvis was jolted back to reality when the second marks, the artistic ones, appeared. Some dropped precipitously. Two judges gave him 5.6, including the suddenly subdued Italian. Only one of the nine judges handed out a 5.9. Everyone else went lower.

"From what I focus on, the marks mean nothing," Stojko said. "I will never, ever give the judges control over how I feel."

This was another textbook judging move to "leave room" for one other skater. In this case, it was Todd Eldredge. The very judges who "left room" for others to beat Eldredge in the short program now were returning the favor for Eldredge in the long program. Judges always hedged their bets, with good reason. Their marks were a ranking system, not a judgment of absolute value. If Eldredge skated fabulously, they didn't want to be stuck giving first place to Stojko.

The judges' scores for Stojko sent a message to Eldredge:

Skate cleanly, and we're giving you first place.

For three and a half minutes, that's just what Eldredge did. He was skating as he had in the long program in Canada. Eldredge was zipping along, flying toward a second consecutive world title, when he leaped into the air for his second triple axel—and popped it into an embarrassing, gaping single.

"What was that?" Eldredge said to himself.

He had one minute to go and one jump left. He had planned a triple toe loop. But because of his mistake, he told himself the triple toe was out. He would have to improvise. He needed the second triple axel to beat Stojko, he told himself as he skimmed across the ice. He would put it where the triple toe loop was planned, twenty-five seconds before the end of the program. That wasn't the ideal time to be putting in the difficult triple axel, at the end of a program when he was getting tired.

Eldredge considered his other options. There were no other options. He would have to risk it.

The same thing happened two years earlier, at the world championships in Birmingham, England. He threw in the triple axel and landed it, but still finished second to Stojko.

Inside the Malley Sport Centre, Eldredge calmly glided down the ice, turned to skate forward, and threw himself into the air. Immediately, he didn't feel right. He was not high enough. He completed only two and a half revolutions before his left foot came back to earth. Startled, unable to grip the ice with his blade, Eldredge slipped and fell. He scampered to his feet with ice still covering the seat of his pants.

He grimaced.

"Well, you're second," Eldredge told himself.

The battle with Stojko was over. He knew it. He had failed. On that missed jump, he had lost. He gamely spun to a bittersweet conclusion, crinkling his face, smiling bravely as he bowed. He had come so close, but it was not enough.

Eldredge calmly skated toward the door near the corner of the ice. As he approached it, he made a fist and angrily pounded the boards.

The final score was eight judges for Stojko, one for Eldredge (the U.S. judge, of course).

After Stojko and Eldredge came Yagudin, who only that week had turned seventeen. With everyone else falling by the wayside, the new Russian kid sneaked in for the bronze medal at his first world championships.

Without Urmanov, and with Kulik blowing up in the long program once again, the world championships might as well have been held in Michigan, or Ontario. Who needed the Europeans in men's figure skating in 1997? Just like the North American men who had come before—Scott Hamilton and Brian Orser in 1984, Brian Boitano and Orser in 1988—Stojko and Eldredge had turned their event into a Canada–U.S. border war.

Unless the Russian men could get their act together, it appeared on that March day in 1997 that Stojko and Eldredge were headed for one final confrontation in 1998, winner take all, in Nagano, Japan. Funny, wasn't it, that they would have to go half a world away to battle for backyard supremacy?

There was more irony in the competition in Lausanne. After the incessant talk about the quad, it turned out that all that mattered was one missing triple axel. Eldredge had been right all along. He did not need a quad.

The quad-letdown had begun even before the final group of skaters, when Michael Weiss didn't try his. He planned to do it, but didn't get the right takeoff and turned it into a triple instead. Weiss moved up two places to seventh overall with a solid performance that included a total of eight triples.

Once again when Weiss finished his program, ABC showed Lisa Thornton and identified her as Weiss's choreographer, failing to mention anyone else.

Sitting in front of the television in his sister's home in Seattle, Brian Wright couldn't believe they had forgotten him again.

* * *

The second- and seventh-place finishes for Eldredge and Weiss should have buoyed American hopes heading into the Olympic year. But something happened on the ice earlier in the week, in the men's qualifying, to dampen the spirits of the men's team.

The third U.S. man, Dan Hollander, skated miserably—he landed only one of eight planned triple jumps—and failed to make the cut into the main competition.

In previous years, this hardly would have been devastating news to anyone but Hollander. But the International Skating Union, the sport's worldwide governing body, devised a new system to determine the number of entries a country would have for the 1998 Olympics. Before 1997, if a nation had one skater who won a medal in the men's and women's competition—or placed in the top five of the pairs event—it could send three entries in that category to the Olympics (or world championships) the next year.

But, for Lausanne, the ISU came up with a complex point system designed to require all skaters from a certain country to perform well to earn the maximum three slots at the Olympics. In the case of the United States, or any nation with three skaters in an event in Lausanne, the sum of the placements of those skaters had to be twenty-one or less in order to send three skaters the next year.

If a skater failed to qualify for the main competition, he or she automatically was assigned sixteen points.

So, before the men's short program began, Hollander saddled the United States with sixteen points.

When Eldredge and Weiss came in with a total of nine more points, the ax fell on the third U.S. men's spot at the 1998 Olympic Games.

The Americans weren't the only ones sabotaged by the new rule. One of its provisions was that if a skater withdrew after the short program—for any reason—the skater's country would receive sixteen points. In one of the more ill-conceived moves in Olympic sports, the international federation weighed the situations of Hollander and Alexei Urmanov equally.

Perform horribly and miss the cut—that's sixteen points.

Withdraw due to an injury after leading the competition—that's sixteen points too.

As a result, Russia would not be allowed to send three male skaters to the 1998 Olympics. Russia! The greatest skating nation in history! Urmanov's sixteen points could not be offset by Yagudin's three and Kulik's disappointing five from a fifth-place finish.

While the Americans were smarting, their loss was minor compared to what the Russians—and the sport itself—were facing. The third U.S. man almost certainly would have little, if any, impact on the medals at the Nagano Olympics. But the three top Russians all have impeccable resumés, and each was considered a medal contender at the Olympics. Urmanov was the 1994 Olympic gold medalist. Kulik was the 1996 world silver medalist. And Yagudin had just become the 1997 world bronze medalist.

One of them was not going to qualify for the Olympic Games.

Unless, that is, the Russians could get that old Soviet camaraderie working for them again. Speculation mounted. Would a deal be made? Wouldn't it be only a matter of hours before Yagudin would miraculously gain citizenship in, say, Azerbaijan? That country had two men's spots in Nagano. Couldn't Mother Russia stash Yagudin there for the Olympic year?

But what the Russians would do with Yagudin, or Urmanov, or Kulik, was only part of the story of Lausanne.

What skating would do with Stojko was an equally intriguing question. He had won his third world title in four years, yet the judges were not entirely satisfied with him. It was the usual problem between them and Elvis: his artistry. If others made mistakes, he could win. But if Eldredge, Kulik, or Urmanov skated well, Stojko could be in trouble. The results of the short program proved that. Such uneasiness rarely accompanied a champion who was on such a roll.

"I'm not going to give in and I'm not going to go away," Stojko said. "I'm going to be in their face the whole time, whether they like it or not, because I'm part of this sport and I always will be part of this sport, and all the people who made a difference always had to go through that. And I want to make a difference. I don't want to just be another player and use it as a vehicle to make money and be famous and win a gold medal."

Stojko was riding the crest of an intriguing historical wave. He became the latest in an increasingly long line of Canadians to win the men's world title the year before the Olympic Games.

Not that this was particularly good news for him.

Since Scott Hamilton of the United States won the world title in 1983 and Olympic gold medal in 1984, the male world champions heading into the Olympic year all had been from Canada. Brian Orser was world champion in 1987 and Kurt Browning in 1991 and 1993.

Orser did not win the gold medal at the 1988 Olympics. And Browning did not win it in 1992 or 1994.

Stojko laughingly dismissed any historical connection between himself and his countrymen and said he wouldn't spend another moment thinking about it.

But there could be no denying he entered the Olympic year exactly as Orser and Browning had before him. Those world titles brought nothing but heartache to those two men the following winters at the Olympic Games.

Now came the next of their countrymen to try to do what no Canadian man ever had been able to do, win the Olympic gold medal in figure skating.

Perhaps Elvis Stojko would once again prove how different he was. Perhaps, with the mighty quad, he would do it. Perhaps he would escape the "Curse of the Canadians."

Then again, perhaps not.

Part III

*Spring–Summer
1997*

Preparation

THE CLASS OF '94

As spring arrived and the Olympic season officially began, every top skater's dream was to get to the Games and skate like Nancy Kerrigan or Oksana Baiul.

Kerrigan and Baiul staged a battle at the 1994 Olympic Games that defined the two essential aspects of skating. Kerrigan's magnificent athleticism was matched against Baiul's timeless artistry. The decision that gave Baiul the gold medal and Kerrigan the silver broke down along old East-West lines. But it was not political. It was a matter of taste. The five judges from the old Eastern bloc voted for the classical Baiul. The four Western judges went for the powerful Kerrigan.

Kerrigan skated better than she ever had at the most important time in her life, and Baiul, while she made mistakes, enchanted not only the judges, but a massive worldwide audience watching on television.

For Michelle Kwan and Tara Lipinski, for Todd Eldredge and Elvis Stojko, the dream was to go to Nagano and perform just as Kerrigan and Baiul had. To be as good as—or better—than they ever thought they could be.

The goal definitely was not to go to the Olympics and skate like Tonya Harding.

Harding got to Norway by threatening the U.S. Olympic Committee with a $25-million lawsuit. When she arrived, she realized she left her skate guards at home. The guards are the plastic runners that protect the skate blades, and they're rather essential. That wasn't the only problem she had with her equipment. Her skate lace broke during her long program. She cried and asked for a do-over. She got a second chance, finished eighth overall, had an asthma attack backstage, and ended the evening by throwing up into a trash can. Later, she was banned for life from the U.S. Figure Skating Association because of her admitted involvement in hindering the prosecution of those responsible for the clubbing of Kerrigan's knee.

The last time Oksana, Nancy, and Tonya were together was February 25, 1994, the night of the women's Olympic long program in Hamar, Norway. Tonya was sitting in Kiss and Cry looking at her scores as Oksana and Nancy were taking the ice for their warm-up.

But that wasn't the last time they were in the news.

In a span of less than two months, the following things happened:

On December 17, 1996, Nancy Kerrigan gave birth to a baby boy, Matthew Eric Solomon, whose father is Jerry Solomon, Kerrigan's agent/husband.

On January 12, 1997, Oksana Baiul got into her Mercedes after drinking "four or five" Long Island iced teas, skidded off the road at ninety-seven mph, and crashed into a cluster of trees.

On February 12, 1997, Tonya Harding was kidnapped.

This is how it happened, Harding told police. As she was walking to her pickup truck outside her home in Portland, Oregon, to get some cigarettes, a bushy-haired man abducted her and forced her to drive her truck to a rural area thirty minutes away. Harding slammed the truck into a tree and ran into the woods, where she hid behind a tree until the attacker ran past. She called a friend on her cellular phone and was rescued. The police confirmed that there were bumper marks on the tree, and said they were taking the matter seriously.

The kidnapping occurred early in the week of the U.S. nationals in Nashville.

Coincidental?

The USFSA thought not.

USFSA president Morry Stillwell was in the midst of a press conference on a variety of skating topics when someone asked if he had heard the news.

"Yes," he said. "*We* got kidnapped today."

He shook his head, later telling Filip Bondy of the *New York Daily News,* "It's a bunch of B.S."

Tonya Harding, the chain-smoking asthmatic who had more raw athletic talent than any other woman in the history of U.S. skating, was back where she wanted to be: dominating the news in figure skating once again.

Tonya just wouldn't go away. Although she had to perform 500 hours of community service in 1994 and 1995 as part of her felony plea bargain in the attack on Kerrigan, she still found time to skate once a week or so at her rink in the Clackamas Town Center shopping mall. People still came by to sip coffee and watch. She was a curiosity, and she liked it that way.

She got married again, this time to a machinist named Michael Smith. (Jeff Gillooly, the brains behind the knee-whacking, was her first husband.) The wedding was held on a yacht on a river, and tabloid TV cameras naturally were on the scene.

Three and a half months after the wedding, Harding filed for divorce from Smith.

Over Labor Day weekend, 1995, Harding launched a new career. She became a singer. She and her new group, the Golden Blades, performed at a riverfront concert in Portland. They sang three songs. Throughout the performance, spectators booed and threw soda bottles and cans.

By January 1996, at the age of twenty-five, Harding was understandably anxious to return to skating. No matter how bad she might have been, skating judges never booed or threw anything.

"If O.J. Simpson can make a comeback, why can't I?" she asked.

"O.J. Simpson has not made a comeback," a reporter replied.

"Well, everyone is making money in the sport but me."

"That's because you've been kicked out of the sport."

"But they're making money *because* of me."

Harding's skating career could not get a jump-start because almost everyone in the sport believed she was involved in the plot to club Kerrigan on the knee. No one in skating wanted to have anything to do with her. Some skaters had no-Tonya clauses in their contracts. If she showed up to skate at a pro event, they would go home.

"I didn't know, honest," Harding pleaded during that 1996 interview. "Jeff would always leave the house when he was planning the attack. Why doesn't anyone believe me?"

Harding was practicing her skating more often, even taking some lessons from Dody Teachman, the coach who guided her to the 1991 U.S. title and a silver medal at the 1991 world championships. Some of her triple jumps had returned.

She signed an agent, David Hans Schmidt of Phoenix, who was

desperate to get Harding back onto the ice in some kind of show or competition. It was time for her return, he said. He even gave it a name: "Tonya II, The Comeback."

Schmidt called the USFSA to tell them Tonya was coming back.

The USFSA had a message for him: No she isn't.

If Harding sought reinstatement, a USFSA spokeswoman told the Associated Press, "she'd probably get a letter back saying she's been banned for life."

Schmidt wasn't deterred. He specialized in this kind of client. He said he also did publicity for Gennifer Flowers, the woman who said she had an affair with Bill Clinton, and former Arizona Governor Evan Mecham, who was impeached.

Schmidt's motto was simple: "Celebrating a Decade of Aggressive Practice." Bad girls, bad boys: He'd take them all.

If the United States didn't want Tonya anymore, he would see if other countries would take her.

Norway popped into his mind. After all, she had such a great experience there in 1994.

"She already looks like your people," he said he would tell the Norwegians.

Bolivia also was on his shortlist.

"They don't have any skaters," he said. "It's one of our options."

After floating those ideas in the press and getting nowhere, Schmidt started to work on another "consequential project," as he called it. If Tonya couldn't skate in a legitimate event, or for another country, she would be the pregame entertainment at a minor league hockey game.

As she prepared for her return to the ice, Tonya Harding continued to smoke, stay out late, and visit her usual hangouts around Portland.

Good thing she did.

On one of those nights out, she saved an elderly woman's life.

Harding said God was behind her decision to stop at a suburban bar for a few minutes to play video poker. While Harding was in the bar, an eighty-one-year-old woman happened to collapse and stop breathing.

Harding called 911 on her cellular phone and then gave the woman mouth-to-mouth resuscitation.

A few months later came the kidnapping. Then, just ten days after she was abducted, Harding made her triumphant return to skating at the soldout Reno Convention Center in Nevada.

The event was quite a coup for Schmidt. It wasn't easy selling Tonya Harding in 1997. A survey of celebrity marketability placed her last out of eighty-five names, one spot below O.J. Simpson.

In the convention center, a banner greeted her: "Tonya Harding Go Home." Hoots and catcalls rained down from the crowd of 4,434 who came to watch the Reno Renegades play the Alaska Gold Kings. She wore a black, two-piece workout outfit. Her midriff was bare.

The crowd screamed and jeered so loudly, Harding could barely hear her music during the two-minute performance. She jumped twice. She landed a double axel and double salchow. (If she had done that kind of short program at the nationals, she probably would have received 3s and 4s from the judges.) She finished with a slide along the ice. Flower bouquets flew at her. So did two rubber police batons. There was a certain symbolism to the batons. A collapsible baton was the weapon used to hit Kerrigan on the knee.

"She didn't stumble," Bondy wrote in the *New York Daily News*. "She wasn't abducted. She was just booed."

Harding blew kisses to the crowd nonetheless.

"I felt great, my speed felt fine," Harding said. "I'm a grown-up woman. I skate for myself and the people."

She figured the crowd was "eighty percent positive, twenty percent negative."

Said Harding: "The twenty percent negative just wanted to watch the hockey game."

That was the last the skating world heard from Harding for many months.

Things were quiet on the Western front.

Too quiet.

There were not likely to be any more kidnappings—at least not while she was driving her truck. She reported the pickup stolen later in the spring.

One person familiar with the situation, though, said it was not stolen.

It was repossessed.

The silence was so deafening in Portland that a reporter made a call to Phoenix, to the office of agent David Hans Schmidt, to see what Harding might be cooking up in the future.

"I've got a deal we're working on," Schmidt said. "I've got to keep it confidential, but let me tell you, it's big."

However, Schmidt added, "if the deal doesn't go down, she'll do something. She might start a bonfire in Nagano. Something will happen. You can be sure of that."

Oksana Baiul won the world championships at fifteen.

She won the Olympic gold medal at sixteen.

She was washed up by seventeen.

No skater ever disappeared off the competitive sport's radar screen faster than the magical wisp from the Ukraine. Once revered as a skater for the ages, a magnificent prodigy who might win two—or even three—Olympic gold medals, Baiul instead was in danger of becoming the answer to a trivia question: Who won the Olympic gold medal in women's figure skating in 1994?

Beloved as the tiny orphan who captured the world's attention with her riveting—if flawed—skating at the Norway Olympics, Baiul turned into her sport's most poignant cautionary tale.

In the months following her triumph over Kerrigan by one-tenth of a point on one judge's scorecard, Baiul went on a joyride through life. She moved to America, got rich, bought a $450,000 house in Connecticut, dyed and cut her hair, bought new clothes, did photo shoots, changed her hair color again, left her coach, dumped her old friends, hung out with new friends—and occasionally practiced her skating. "I tried to talk to her, but it seemed like I was talking to a wall," said 1992 Olympic gold medalist Viktor Petrenko, who once was one of her dearest friends.

Other colleagues issued very rare—and very pointed—public criticism.

"It's a clear case of too much too young," commentator and 1984 Olympic silver medalist Rosalynn Sumners said on NBC Sports. "She's got people telling her what she wants to hear . . . her future's unclear . . . with all this heady stuff going on at a young age, the first thing to go is your fight and your desire to skate."

"If I got too out of hand at times, of course my family was the first one to knock me back down to earth and bring me back to reality," 1992 Olympic gold medalist Kristi Yamaguchi told NBC. "Unfortunately, Oksana doesn't have that source of family."

Baiul's mother, Marina, died of ovarian cancer when Oksana was thirteen. Her father, Sergei, divorced her mother when Oksana was two. She did not see him again until his mother's funeral.

Baiul admitted she was overwhelmed by her new life.

"It was so much," she said, "so much, way too much, having to deal with that."

As many rebellious teenagers have done before her, Baiul turned away from the adults in her life—and all but turned her back on the sport she loved.

She left the Olympic division and turned professional, signing a $1.5-million deal to skate in ten made-for-TV events in the year and a half after the 1994 Games.

In most sports, when an athlete turns professional, the competition becomes stiffer. But not in figure skating, and certainly not in the case of Baiul. She turned pro and kicked back. Some pros work very hard; people like Brian Boitano and Kristi Yamaguchi have distinguished themselves because of the way they've attacked their professional careers.

But even the best pros often do not fare well against Olympic division skaters, who are younger, with less wear and tear on their bodies. And there is a lack of intensity in the professional world because there is nothing that approaches the importance of the Olympic Games; the professionals already have had their Olympics, and will never find anything that demands as much from them in the professional ranks.

"Too Hot to Skate?"

"Battle of the Sexes?"

It's nonsense. Professionals in skating are adrift in a sea of silly events.

Boitano, who turned thirty-four in the autumn before the Nagano Games, could not go triple axel–for–triple axel anymore with Elvis Stojko. Stojko is nine years younger; his body has endured nine fewer years of jumping. And Boitano has reached the stage in his career where jumping is not quite as important to him as producing his own shows and pushing the envelope artistically.

Yamaguchi wouldn't want to go triple lutz–for–triple lutz with Michelle Kwan either. Artistically, the top pros usually can beat the Olympic skaters, but jump-for-jump, most would get eaten alive by the Olympic division skaters.

Among the pros, Yamaguchi was at the top end of the work-ethic scale, while Baiul was at the bottom. Within seven months of her Olympic triumph, Baiul dislocated her left kneecap and tore a piece of cartilage. She did this while curtsying at the end of a practice session in Sun Valley, Idaho. Instead of taking time off to heal, however, she went ahead and showed up to skate a full complement of made-for-TV events—and lost all but one of them.

In addition to moving to a new land and having all kinds of new demands on her time, Baiul was being betrayed by her body. It was changing rapidly: five-foot-two and 97 pounds at the Olympics, she was five-foot-four and 101 pounds by the end of 1994.

Never much of a jumper, Baiul lost her triples. And while she didn't have to jump at all to make an audience swoon, the rules of the professional events dictated skaters had to do the occasional triple jump.

But when Baiul tried to jump, she almost always crashed to the ice.

Within a year of her Olympic triumph in Norway, skaters and coaches wrote her off. As a competitor, they said, she was finished.

"She will never again be like we saw her at sixteen," said Viktor Petrenko. "She was nobody when Galina [Zmievskaia] took her. Galina built Oksana Galina's way. She built good programs, taught her how to jump, made it work for her, built her image. That was nice. Everybody loved it. She was a nice girl we all enjoyed to watch.

"But when she grew up, she decided to build her own image and she did it. The result last year was drunk driving. She has two sides to her personality. She still can cry and make everybody cry who looks at her. And then she turns around and she hates everyone and everybody."

By early 1997, Baiul was miserable.

"I had a nervous breakdown," she said. "I really didn't want to skate. I didn't want to do anything. I would just sit at home all by myself. My friends would talk to me and I would start crying. I was just a mess."

At nineteen Baiul had grown to five-foot-four-and-a-half, and weighed 120 pounds. She wasn't listening to Zmievskaia and she wasn't listening to Petrenko. She was very much on her own.

On the night of her car accident, Baiul went to an ice show in Hartford and then to a local bar, where she said she had "four or five" Long Island iced teas, a powerful drink that includes vodka, gin, rum, and tequila. At 2:30 A.M., she was driving her green Mercedes more than fifty mph over the forty-five-mph speed limit along a road in Bloomfield, Connecticut. When she crashed the car, her blood-alcohol level was .168 percent, well above the legal limit of .10. Baiul also was two years below the legal drinking age in Connecticut.

Baiul suffered a concussion and needed twelve stitches for a cut in her scalp. A passenger in the car, Ararat Zakarian, a thirty-year-old skater, suffered a broken finger.

When the case went to court, Baiul was ordered to do community service and was allowed to enter an alcohol education program. She wound up paying just a $90 speeding fine because her blood-alcohol test was given by the hospital where she was treated, not by the police.

Instead of losing her license, she went on *Oprah*.

"You were drunk," Oprah Winfrey said.

"Actually, no, I wasn't drunk," Baiul replied.

"Yes, you were drunk," Winfrey said. "You had to be drunk if you had four Long Island iced teas."

"I'm a Russian," Baiul replied.

"You're a Russian," Winfrey said with a bemused look on her face. "Okay. Okay. Forgive me. Okay."

That unrepentant exchange surprised Baiul's agents at the William Morris Agency. They tried to anticipate every question Baiul might face. They didn't expect her to be asked what she had been drinking. They never prepared her for that.

And, of course, she wasn't Russian. She was Ukrainian.

The *Oprah* appearance left a lingering question: Was Baiul taking the accident as seriously as she should have been? Or was she looking at it as just another of her numerous missteps, where she simply got up, dusted the ice off her clothes, and bowed to an adoring audience?

Zakarian, who was with Baiul in the car, certainly enjoyed *his* fame. A month after the accident, when he was introduced to a stranger, he shook hands and smiled broadly.

"I'm the passenger!" he said.

Baiul soon joined the fifty-nine-city Campbell's Soups tour. Although she still was one of the show's headliners, she could not live up to the billing. Her once-tiny body had grown thick; her face was full and rarely looked happy. Make-up could not cover patches of teenage acne. Her hair was cropped short and dyed very blonde.

She stumbled in the opening number when the tour kicked off with a show in Baltimore. Two months later, she slipped in Madison Square Garden trying to do footwork while twirling a long scarf, got up and looked around for a second, as if she was lost. The audience rustled uncomfortably.

"I'm falling all over the place," Baiul said.

But even with her mistakes, friends noticed a glimmer of hope.

"She's trying," Brian Boitano said. "This is the first time I've seen her try in a long time. She's actually practicing, trying new things, old things that are new things again."

In occasional press conferences at made-for-TV competitions, Baiul would laugh in short bursts and often look toward Nancy Kerrigan, or Kristi Yamaguchi, or someone, for approval or reassurance. She would lean on an elbow, or squirm in her chair, and pronounce herself "very" nervous. Once, she used seven "verys" in a row to describe how nervous she was.

When she finished an answer, she looked to one of the other women at the press table, often Kerrigan. And Kerrigan smiled and nodded her head, as if to tell Oksana her answer was alright.

Baiul said she got along fine with Kerrigan, and hated that outsiders thought she didn't.

"People said we used to fight a lot," Baiul said, "but I didn't speak English then so we couldn't fight."

"We get along," Kerrigan said. "People ask me if we're good friends. But I remind them that she's eight years younger than me. I have a husband and a child and a completely different life than she does."

By February 1998, a new women's Olympic champion would be crowned. Oksana Baiul no longer would be the reigning women's gold medalist. Her four-year run would be over.

"It will be tough for her to see how the new Olympic champion will be treated," Viktor Petrenko said.

Perhaps in anticipation of her new status in the sport, Baiul changed almost everything in her life prior to 1998. She found a new coach and a new choreographer. She sold her big house in Simsbury, Connecticut, and moved to the Boston area. She trained at a rink in Acton, Massachusetts, where a picture of Kerrigan greeted her every morning. It used to be Kerrigan's rink. There was a certain irony in that.

On the ice there, Baiul, who turned twenty in November 1997, dreamed of new things, and old.

"Maybe I will think about going back to being amateur again," she said. "I am not joking. If they would change the rules, I would. Figure skating is all about jumps right now, but for my heart, figure skating shouldn't be all about jumps. I have to have some dream, right?"

There were times Baiul thought about quitting her sport altogether, but even in her darkest hours, she never once wished she could undo what had been done. She never, ever thought that it might have been better not to win the Olympic gold medal, the prize that became more of a curse than a blessing the moment it was placed around her neck.

"Are you kidding me?" she said. "That's my life. I'm so happy with everything I've done. My mom used to tell me, 'Oksana, you can't write your life on paper. You have to fight all of your problems and find a way. You have to fight for everything. If you have a problem, you can't go away somewhere and say you really don't want to think about that problem.' That's what she used to tell me.

"So," Baiul concluded, "I am still on the ice because of my mother's words. And that is where I belong."

When Nancy Kerrigan returned to her hometown of Stoneham, Massachusetts, after the 1994 Olympic Games, she told her friends and her future husband that she was thinking of getting a job.

"I don't know what I'm going to do," she said. "I'm going to be home so often. Maybe I'll go to work."

"What can you do?" a friend asked.

"Well, I used to waitress."

The friend laughed.

When she told Jerry Solomon, he laughed too.

"Everybody was laughing at me," Kerrigan said.

Kerrigan, the millionaire skater whose name became a household word during the seven-week Tonya–Nancy ordeal, told them she was serious. She wanted to get a job. She wanted everything to return to normal.

After she graduated from high school in 1987, she took a year off before college and held down two jobs while skating. She waitressed at Friendly's and sold clothes at a discount store called Frugal Fannie's.

After the Olympics, she thought she'd do it again. She thought she would return to the way things used to be. She would return to her pre-Tonya life.

"It will be fun," Kerrigan told Solomon and her friends. "You can meet new people. I like to do that."

Everyone looked at her.

"Nancy!" they said. "You're famous now. You can't just go out and *waitress*."

Kerrigan shrugged.

"They all thought I was totally nuts."

Nancy Kerrigan's dreams never strayed far from home. With her fame and money, Kerrigan could have moved anywhere and had almost anything she wanted.

But she and Solomon and their young son live very close to where she was raised, just a ten-minute drive from her parents. They own one and a half acres in the Boston suburb of Lynnfield, where her fix-it man and part-time gardener also happens to be her father.

"Did you notice?" Dan Kerrigan asked his daughter as he dropped her off at home one day.

"Oh, the flowers? Dad, they're beautiful," she said.

If Nancy had her way, she and Solomon would live the life she did as a little girl growing up in Stoneham, where family vacations often were spent camping.

"It's so much fun," Kerrigan said. "You go by a lake and it can be very peaceful. But I'm not sure Jerry's really into camping. We haven't gone yet. We have a tent and a sleeping bag, so we're all ready. But Jerry probably won't go with me, so when Matthew gets a little bigger, he and I will go camping in the backyard in the tent."

What the media never understood about Nancy Kerrigan was how simple she really was, and is. She grew up in skating's old days, when a girl lived at home, trained in the area, went to school, and never figured on a career in the sport. She wanted to be a wife and a mother. As the sport changed and money rushed in, if she could keep a career going in professional skating for several years, she thought that would be fine too.

But her goal was the same: husband, kids, a house near Mom and Dad. She had started making money after winning the bronze medal at the 1992 Winter Olympics, and, even before the saga with Tonya, Solomon had engineered deals with Disney, Northwest Airlines, and Reebok, among others, that made Kerrigan a millionaire several times over.

Nancy Kerrigan refused to change. She stopped at her parents' home and read the paper to her mother, who is legally blind. She went to lunch with her girlfriends. She talked to her father or her brothers on the front lawn.

Her dad kept working his regular job as a welder; her parents stayed in the family home, where Nancy paid for a new, brighter kitchen so her mother was better able to get around.

"It was so dark," Kerrigan said, "she couldn't see, so as she was cleaning, she'd slap something off the table and send it crashing."

Everything revolved around the family. When Nancy signed up to do Elvis Stojko's tour of Canada in 1997, she immediately thought of her grandparents. They had just returned from a trip across Canada.

"It's so pretty, from everything they said," Kerrigan said. "I've only skated in Windsor, so I'm excited to see other parts of Canada. I especially can't wait to see Lake Louise."

People forget that they grew up together in skating, Tonya and Nancy, one on the West Coast, the other on the East. On international trips in the early 1990s, Kerrigan said she would ask Harding to join the group for dinner. Harding almost always declined. Tonya went her own way while Nancy joined the other skaters.

Kerrigan could never quite figure out Tonya Harding.

With Kristi Yamaguchi, Harding and Kerrigan formed one of the most formidable trios in U.S. skating history. They swept the medals at the 1991 world championships, the first time American women ever did that.

Yamaguchi won the Olympic gold medal in 1992, then turned pro. Harding and Kerrigan stayed in the Olympic side and planned to compete through the 1994 Games. Kerrigan won the national title in 1993, while Harding, who peaked in 1991, fell back into the pack.

The Kerrigan camp always enjoyed competing with Harding.

"I knew the first moment I saw Tonya at every nationals whether we had a chance or not," said Evy Scotvold, Kerrigan's coach. "I'd look at her butt and her legs and know immediately if we were going to win or if we were in trouble. If she was in shape, we were in trouble. Five to ten pounds could make Tonya the world's biggest jerk or the world's best skater."

Kerrigan wasn't a bad athlete herself. When she was on, she was practically unbeatable. Her jumps were technically superb. She gained fame by wearing Vera Wang dresses and being called the "Irish Katarina," but Kerrigan actually was a feisty tomboy disguised as a gorgeous figure skater.

After the Olympics, Kerrigan turned pro and had trouble motivating herself to compete in events that didn't matter. Her jumps suffered. She did not skate well. In 1996, during her pregnancy, Kerrigan gained twenty-three pounds, then underwent a rigorous training program to lose most of the weight by spring, in time for the 1997 skating tour.

She performed in twenty-five of the tour's fifty-nine cities. Her mother came along to help take care of Matthew on the road. Two of her triple jumps eventually returned, but she stumbled or put her hand down much more often than she liked.

"I'm close," she said. "I'm not there yet. But I'm close."

Kerrigan didn't like not landing her triple jumps, even as a twenty-eight-year-old mother. Some things were supposed to be certain in life. Her triple jumps were one of those things.

"You'll be doing triple toes when you're seventy," choreographer Mary Scotvold once told Kerrigan.

"I won't be on the ice then," Kerrigan replied.

"But if you are," Mary Scotvold said, "you'll be landing them."

Kerrigan rarely links herself with Tonya and Oksana anymore.

"We're so different," she said. "Everything's so different now."

Kerrigan doesn't like to discuss the attack on January 6, 1994, the day her sport was given over to the masses. But every now and then, if she must, she talks.

"People still remember. It's amazing to me. Children were very affected by what happened to me."

Dozens of children approach Kerrigan at skating events.

"Can I have your autograph?"

"Is your knee okay?"

Kerrigan looks at the children.

"Were you old enough to remember it?" she asks. "You're seven years old!"

"I remember. I cried."

"That's so sweet. I'm fine."

Kerrigan shrugs and takes a deep breath.

"That's so long ago to me, I don't even think of it. But these little kids, they remember. I guess people really do remember."

THE LONG, COOL SUMMER

9

If there was anything Carol Heiss Jenkins enjoyed more than coaching skating, it was predicting the outcome of skating events. Whether it was the Eastern Great Lakes regional competition or the Olympic Games, Heiss loved guessing what the judges would do well in advance of their decision. She was right much more often than she was wrong. As she stood at the end of the rink or sat in the stands in a beautiful mink coat with her golden hair pulled back, she could have passed for a woman born to luxury. But when she spoke—and Heiss was always talking with someone—she revealed herself as skating's most down-to-earth voice of reason. That voice, scratchy as sandpaper, came from Ozone Park, New York, where Heiss was the daughter of a baker, and even though she had traveled the world as one of the Olympic Games' grandest winter champions, she never let go of Queens. If Heiss hadn't become a skating coach, she could have been a bookie. And she would have been a good one.

Over the years, Heiss had become quite good with her predictions. Her grandest call came as she was commentating on television at the U.S. nationals in 1964. Watching an unknown fifteen-year-old skate for the first time as a senior lady, Heiss boldly predicted the teenager would win the 1968 Olympic gold medal. Calling Peggy Fleming's future was Heiss's grandest handicapping achievement.

Heading into the Lausanne world championships, Heiss bet her choreographer and sidekick at their rink in suburban Cleveland, Glyn Watts, that Tara Lipinski and Elvis Stojko would win. Standing in the airport in Geneva on her way home from the world championships, her eyes twinkled as she pumped her fist.

"We bet dinner and wine!" she said. "And I won!"

It wasn't that she was cheering for Tara and Elvis; she had her own skaters to worry about. It was just that Heiss loved being right.

She had had a gut feeling about the world championships; Kwan, of course, had been shaky, while Lipinski looked so certain. Tara was one of the very few skaters in the sport, male or female, who instilled confidence when they jumped, Heiss said. When Heiss watched some skaters take off, her heart leaped into her throat. But when she watched Lipinski launch herself into the air, Heiss knew from watching the takeoff that the landing would be fine.

Heiss loves trying to figure out figure skating. She enjoys the sport's politics and its many layers of intrigue. In football, a touchdown is six points. In baseball, if the ball leaves the park, it's a home run. But in skating, with the artistic marks and judges' opinions, who knows what might happen? You could talk for hours in the hotel lobby and still not figure out everything. Heiss loves skating for its quirkiness. She enjoys unraveling the mystery of why a judge ruined a skater's season with a low mark. She can't get enough of it. The best thing about skating is you could talk about it for hours, and still have more to discuss the next day. And Heiss loves to talk.

But Heiss also knows that for all its foibles, her sport almost always righted itself in an Olympic year. She loves to say that skating almost always picks the right person to win the Olympics. She, of course, had been one of those right people in 1960.

Time and again, she said, a skater for the ages beat someone who might even have been better that night to claim the most coveted title in the sport, that of Olympic gold medalist.

Look at history, Heiss said. The artist almost always triumphed over the jumper. The legend-in-the-making almost always won. John Curry beat Vladimir Kovalev. Katarina Witt beat both Rosalynn Sumners and Debi Thomas. Kristi Yamaguchi beat Midori Ito. Oksana Baiul beat Nancy Kerrigan. Alexei Urmanov beat Elvis Stojko.

In the end, in the long program, ties are broken by the second mark, the presentation mark. It's a significant distinction. The tie goes to the artist in skating. And most judging panels are dominated by European judges, who almost always will take an artist over a jumper.

Heiss knew that. And so, standing in the Geneva Airport, eleven months away from the Nagano Olympics, she matter-of-factly blurted out two names.

"Michelle Kwan and Alexei Urmanov," she said.

"They'll be the Olympic gold medalists. The judges will go with the artists. They always do. Kwan won't make a mistake in the short program again. She won't fall again.

"So it'll be Kwan and Urmanov."

In April, the world tour slowly began to grind to a start. It was time for skaters to do two things that created conflict in their lives: make money by touring outside of their rinks, and begin to work on their Olympic programs inside their rinks. Parents and skaters wanted the money; coaches tore their hair out waiting for the skaters to come back to work on their programs, knowing that no matter how much money they made in 1997, it wouldn't matter one bit if they finished fourth at the 1998 Olympic trials.

In the spring of 1997, Kwan and Urmanov were having troubles. Heiss knew that Urmanov had had to withdraw from the world championships with a groin injury, but she assumed—as many people did—that he would be fine in a month or so.

Kwan was another matter. Heiss had no idea that she sometimes was skating in pain.

Every now and then, Kwan complained that her left foot hurt when she took off for a jump. Her Riedell boots still were bothering her.

But skaters always had some ache or pain, so she kept on skating. She was on the three-month-long Campbell's Soups tour, which, while it was grueling, was not exactly heavy lifting. She performed an exhibition-style program with four triple jumps every night, which wasn't easy, but it certainly wasn't as difficult as competing.

Nonetheless, the word was out in skating that Kwan was having a very difficult time in the Riedells. It didn't take a genius to see that she had lost three consecutive competitions. Skating coaches and experts knew Kwan was too good to have such troubles.

Returning to their hotel in Lausanne after the banquet at the end of the world championships, Heiss chatted with Danny Kwan.

"Lose the boots," Heiss told him. "Whatever the money is, it's not as important as the gold medal."

"If you think so," Danny Kwan said, "they're gone."

Yet for several months, through many weeks of the tour, Michelle Kwan skated in the Riedells. There were two more seasons left on the contract Danny Kwan had negotiated with the company. But he said money wasn't the reason he stayed with Riedell. He was a fiercely loyal man, a man who remained true to his word. He had a contract, and he intended to fulfill it. What's more, Riedell officials were furiously trying to come up with a solution to Michelle's troubles. They offered a new pair of boots, they changed the mounting of the blades, they tried everything.

Meanwhile, Michelle Kwan skated on.

Urmanov returned to St. Petersburg, Russia, from Lausanne and took a month off to rest his injured groin muscle, which doctors discovered was partially torn. He came back to the ice in mid-April, and began jumping. His triple axel came back. Within three weeks, everything was fine. But one day at the end of May, he was practicing footwork on the ice and felt pain.

"Oh no!" he said.

Urmanov took off another month.

At the end of June, he joined some friends for a game of soccer. He stretched before he played. He thought his groin had healed, so he figured there was nothing wrong with a friendly game, nothing too intense.

"I felt it again."

By then, he had lost any chance to participate in the tour in the United States. He had been invited, and had been expected to join when he could, at the halfway point or whenever he could make it. But he never did. He would have made as much as $200,000 had he been on the entire tour.

In July and August, Urmanov joined his coach, Alexei Mishin, and the other skaters, including the third Alexei, the seventeen-year-old Yagudin, for a training camp in Spain. Urmanov did not jump, but he worked with Mishin and their choreographer to put in his new long program—a tango—for the Olympic year.

When they returned to Russia in September, Mishin was alarmed. Urmanov still could not do everything they wanted him to do on the ice. He still was in pain. So Urmanov went to Moscow and checked himself into a hospital for two weeks of physical therapy and medical treatment, including pain-killing injections.

By mid-September, Urmanov started getting worried. The hospital hadn't been able to help him get better. He had seen seven doctors by then: some in Spain, some in Moscow, some in St. Petersburg.

"So many doctors, so many different things," he said.

He could skate, and he could take off and land some of his triple jumps, but when he tried a triple axel, the difficult jump he absolutely had to have to compete in Nagano, he couldn't do it. Because it has an extra half rotation in the air, the triple axel requires a skater to pull his arms toward his body very tightly, cross his legs at his ankles in the air and hold the leg muscles very still and tight as he rotates. That was what got to Urmanov; he didn't have the strength in his upper left leg to hold his crossed legs together for the duration of the jump—no more than one second.

But Urmanov kept on trying. Throughout the summer, and into the early fall, he practiced. He did double jumps. He did his programs with everything but his triple axel and his triple lutz, which also hurt a bit.

He was puzzled.

"I am fine for the normal life," Urmanov said. "I can walk without pain, I can run without pain. I can do other things. But it's only when I practice on the ice."

When the injury happened in March, some Western coaches shook their heads and warned that a groin injury was just about the worst thing that could happen to a skater.

"A skater shreds the muscle every time he moves on the ice," said one coach.

As summer turned into fall and Urmanov still could not try all his jumps, he began to be haunted by one terrible thought: What if he didn't get healthy all autumn? What if this injury carried into winter, and the new year? What, then, would become of his chance to repeat as Olympic champion?

Michelle Kwan's troubles were not nearly as great as Urmanov's. She was skating every night. Nothing looked out of the ordinary. She stretched and ran backstage on tour, as always. She hung out with Elvis Stojko and Brian Boitano. Her mother, Estella, cheerfully accompanied her, as she almost always did on tour. While Michelle skated, Estella did more motherly things backstage, like the laundry.

In the spring and summer, even with her boot troubles, things seemed to be going Kwan's way. Two very significant developments occurred to help Carol Heiss have a chance to be at least half right on her Olympic predictions.

The first was personal: Kwan was loading up with two stunningly intricate and majestic programs for the Olympic year.

The second involved her sport's continuing tug-of-war between jumping and artistry. Figure skating judges and officials plunged into serious introspection in the summer of 1997. In international seminars planned long before Tara Lipinski's victory, the sport's leaders took a very hard look at artistry. They organized several "Second

Mark" seminars—named for the presentation mark judges give to skaters—in Europe and America. These Second Mark seminars were meant to remind judges that artistry mattered—and shouldn't be treated as jumping's stepchild.

Meanwhile, doubts about Tara Lipinski wafted over the sport. Skating could be awful in this way. It would anoint someone, then look back and try to figure out what it had just done. The U.S. Figure Skating Association did this too. It ran Tara up the flagpole as fast as possible. It was negotiating with Mike Burg to sign her to a multiyear deal to skate in future competitions whether she stayed on the Olympic side or turned pro. (The USFSA did the same for Kwan and Todd Eldredge, and signed all three to six-figure deals.)

Yet at a springtime seminar for skating parents, a question was asked.

"How can I get my daughter to be like Tara Lipinski?" a parent wondered.

"Are you sure you want your daughter to be like Tara Lipinski?" a USFSA official replied.

The official then listed the issues: moving around the country, not being in school, dealing with all the pressures of being on top, having to grow up on national television.

Lipinski read those nasty press clippings in Lausanne. She and her mother heard the gossip. They knew what some people were saying.

It bothered Tara.

"Yes, a lot," she told Jo-Ann Barnas of the *Detroit Free Press*. "I know that being on top there are people who don't like you. But I don't think I've done anything wrong. I could understand the criticism if I would have skated bad, but I skated the best I could and I won."

Tara tried not to pay attention to the criticism and did her best to enjoy the view from the top of her sport.

She appeared on *The Tonight Show with Jay Leno* in July. When she told him the family home was in Houston and she trained in Detroit, Leno exclaimed, "Quite a commute every day, I imagine."

Tara laughed.

She knew how to handle her national television appearances and interviews and all the other trappings of sudden fame. It was her sport that stumbled on, uncertain exactly what to make of her.

There were some elements of Tara's triumph that thrilled skating people.

"This is why our sport is better than it used to be," her coach,

Richard Callaghan, said. "Ten, fifteen, twenty years ago [an upset by Lipinski over Kwan] wouldn't have happened. We kind of knew who would win back then. It's nice not to know. It's why the sport is better than it used to be. It's got to be more interesting for everybody if they don't know what the hell is going to happen."

Pure, raw sports issues were one thing. But lifestyle issues were something else. Some of the sport's biggest names were concerned about the lives being led by America's teenage skating superstars.

"I don't like it that kids don't go to school," said Nancy Kerrigan. "I believe it's very important to meet different people, to see all different walks of life, because there's so much more in life than skating. You break your ankle and it could be over."

"You've got to have interaction with kids your own age who do something else besides skating," said Peggy Fleming, wondering about the trend toward tutoring the top stars.

Almost everyone wished the two American millionairesses had at least a locker and a homeroom.

Meanwhile, some agents were criticizing the sport's turn toward "gymnastics on ice."

"You take away our sex appeal, you've taken away much of our overall appeal for TV and shows," said Michael Rosenberg, who once was Dorothy Hamill's agent. "People want a beautiful ice queen, not short, gymnastic sixteen-year-olds."

Even older skaters were concerned.

"What's being rewarded now in skating is wall-to-wall jumps," said 1992 Olympic silver medalist Paul Wylie. "That rewards a certain type of performance, not necessarily the most entertaining performance."

It all was building in the summer of 1997. The pendulum was swinging back. Figure skating gave the appearance that it was massing for a very strong show of support for Michelle Kwan, the one young lady who embodied everything it wanted in a skater.

If she didn't fall again.

Between the world championships and the tour, Kwan went back to Lake Arrowhead to meet with a very familiar member of her team, choreographer Lori Nichol. They had become good friends by 1997, having worked together for five consecutive years, which was a lifetime in the volatile world of skating. The Kwans treated Nichol like a member of their family; two years earlier, when Nichol came to California to create "Salome" with Michelle, she brought her eight-month-old son, Austin. While Nichol and Kwan worked together on the ice, Estella Kwan had baby-sitting duty, which included driving Austin around the mountaintop retreat to get him to go to sleep, then sitting in the parking lot with the motor running so the baby would not wake up.

Working alongside coach Frank Carroll, Kwan and Nichol had a very important task to accomplish in two weeks in the early spring. It was time to create the long program that Kwan would skate at the Olympic Games.

For Nichol, working with Kwan on the ice in the spring of 1997 was the last stage of a fourteen-month process that had begun in her Mercedes, of all places. Nichol was listening to an FM station while driving to her rink near Toronto to give a lesson to one of her skating students in February 1996. As she was driving, she heard a piece of classical music and immediately thought of Kwan. This was a common reflex for a skating coach or choreographer. Audrey Weisiger, Michael Weiss's coach, always listened to tapes in her car while she drove, trying to find music for her skaters. Sometimes, Weisiger got so caught up in the music, she forgot she was driving. Seven times over fifteen years, while dreaming up programs for her skaters, Weisiger plowed into the car in front of her. No one ever was injured in her fender benders, but her insurance was canceled once for a few weeks.

Nichol didn't run into anyone when she heard *Lyra Angelica* on the radio, but what she did after hearing the music was a bit unusual. Nichol was the type of coach and choreographer who would show up for her teaching duties even if she had pneumonia. But once she listened to that music—"the most joyous piece of music I'd ever heard," she said—she decided she had to have the CD immediately. So she skipped the lesson and continued driving to downtown Toronto, to her favorite music store, where she found what she was looking for.

She played the music for Kwan at the Edmonton world championships.

Kwan didn't immediately fall in love with it.

Nichol gave her a tape of it anyway, and asked her to listen to it on the 1996 skating tour.

Months later, Kwan told Nichol and Carroll that she had changed her mind. She had grown to like the music very much. They all agreed it would be perfect for the Olympic year.

To build a skating program in her mind, Nichol always starts with the music. It dictates every path her skater takes. *Lyra Angelica* ("Angel's

Song"), a concerto for harp and string orchestra performed by the London Philharmonic, was light and flowing, ethereal rather than dramatic. It was just what Nichol wanted for Kwan after her previous two long programs, both mature, character-driven performances.

Nichol's goal was to create a program that had as its foundation one simple word:

Joy.

And as Nichol worked, she couldn't help but think of her favorite skater:

Janet Lynn.

Janet Lynn never won an Olympic gold medal or a world championships, but she is considered by many in skating to be the greatest skater who ever lived. She skated in the late 1960s and early 1970s, when compulsory school figures ruled the sport. Unfortunately, Lynn had a terrible time with school figures.

But when she took to the ice and skated her programs, there was no more beautiful performer, ever. She stood with a smile and listened to her music, letting the first note push her on her way. Nothing Janet Lynn did was rushed or forced. Even standing still, she was a delight.

"You just fell in love with her," Dick Button said. "Her eyes sparkled, she had that marvelous pixie haircut. She was a little angelic doll."

As a girl growing up in skating, Lori Nichol also fell in love with Janet Lynn. She was almost nine years old when Lynn won the Olympic bronze medal in 1972. At those Olympic Games in Sapporo, Japan, the last Games to be held in Japan until the 1998 Nagano Olympics, Lynn stumbled and fell on a sit spin—and smiled as she sat on the ice. Immediately, the Japanese people fell for the tiny American. Lynn began receiving thousands of fan letters a week from Japan.

Years later, as the mother of five boys in suburban Detroit, Janet Lynn Salomon occasionally looked out her living room window to see a Japanese camera crew coming up the front walk. She never knew how they found her. But they always did.

In 1976, thirteen-year-old Lori Nichol spent the summer training on Long Island, where she boarded with the family of a fellow skater. That skater's brother happened to be married to Janet Lynn.

During those long summer afternoons and evenings, as she hung around the home of the Salomon family, Lori Nichol found herself daydreaming. She would look at Janet Lynn's wedding picture in their house and imagine Janet skating to routines Nichol made up in her head.

"I was lying on the couch," Nichol said, "looking at Janet Lynn's wedding picture, remembering her beauty on the ice, and choreographing for her—to Barry Manilow music, of all things. I think the Salomons thought I was nuts."

When it came to Janet Lynn, skating people often went over the top. There was something about her that grabbed hold of little girls, coaches, whomever, and would not let go.

Nichol couldn't shake thoughts of Janet Lynn from her head four years after the 1972 Olympics.

And it was the same for the others in 1997. At the pro-am event in Japan in January, where Kwan won as Pocahontas, Yuka Sato skated to Debussy's "Prelude to 'The Afternoon of a Faun.'" As Sato's music came over the loud speaker in the arena in Tokyo and she began to skate, a curious thing happened in the stands, where a few skaters, coaches, and officials gathered to watch practice.

They began talking about someone without mentioning her name.

"I don't know if anyone else can skate to this," someone said.

"Yeah, it's really hers."

"But if anyone can, Yuka can pull it off."

Frank Carroll was nearby.

"We considered having Michelle skate to this, but decided no one else could do it."

"Prelude to 'The Afternoon of a Faun'" was Janet Lynn's signature piece, music she skated to for exhibitions in the 1970s.

Twenty-five years later and half a world away from the United States, the skating community heard the music and immediately thought of Janet Lynn. A forty-three-year-old homemaker living in the suburbs of Detroit still held that kind of magical grip on her sport.

At Lake Arrowhead in the early spring of 1997, Nichol was trying to tell Michelle Kwan about Janet Lynn, to explain how, when Lynn skated, you saw her soul, and you saw the joy she felt for skating. Kwan had never met Janet Lynn and had seen only a few minutes of her skating on a highlight tape. But Nichol wasn't trying to re-create Janet Lynn in her skater. These were two different girls. Kwan was more exotic, more complex, and more inquisitive than the spiritual, naive Lynn. Nichol simply wanted Kwan to express her love for skating the way Lynn had years earlier. It was a lofty mission.

But Nichol had a few things working in her favor. Kwan had come to skating as a child because she loved the feeling of flying on the ice. "Think of yourself as a bird flying through space," Nichol said.

Nichol also stressed that one word: joy.

Nichol and Frank Carroll hoped that a program that exhibited the simple joy Kwan felt while skating would help her forget the difficult months of February and March 1997 and carry her through the nerve-racking year of the Olympic Games. If things got too intense, she could seek refuge on the ice, of all places. Her long program would be her ultimate escape.

"There is such phenomenal pressure at the Olympic Games that I thought the music would be comforting," Nichol said.

And so the program developed. For the opening position, Nichol decided there would be no opening position. In her years with "Salome," then "Taj Mahal," Kwan had played a strong, female role. There was no role for the Olympic year; Nichol wanted simplicity. So Kwan began the program by simply standing still. Nichol wanted her to hear the music, come to life, and begin skating. Not coincidentally, that's the way Lynn started some of her programs.

"I wanted to take the message of hope that Janet showed twenty-five years ago and give it to a skater today," Nichol said.

Nichol was doing everything she had dreamed of while lying on the Salomons' couch two decades earlier—minus the Barry Manilow music.

Nichol, Carroll, and Kwan certainly were marching to the beat of a very different drummer in their sport in 1997. They eschewed the trend toward using movie soundtracks, something their chief rival, Tara Lipinski, chose again for the 1997–98 season in both her short and long programs. They didn't go for the familiar, like Gershwin's *Rhapsody in Blue,* which Ilia Kulik was using.

While much of the rest of the U.S. skating world was revving up for the upcoming Michelle–Tara Olympic year rivalry, Nichol and Carroll were paying absolutely no attention. They went their own way, and proudly so, planning and plotting and loading up to try to create something masterful for Kwan. That included using music that had never been used before, as far as they knew.

"I think it's good to challenge yourself all the time," Frank Carroll said approvingly.

Conventional wisdom in skating says that it's easier to skate to movie music than to classical music. It's easier to find movie soundtracks. They're usually sitting at the front of a music store. The classical music is in the back, or in the basement.

Although some movie soundtracks can be quite complex and might involve classical music, they also give a choreographer and skater a picture of how to interpret the music. Classical music that never has been used for a movie is more challenging because there is no mental picture for the skater and choreographer.

"Movie music fits the chase scene or the battlefield scene," said U.S. skating judge Joe Inman, a musician and piano teacher. "It's much harder to skate to really hard, classical music because there's so much to it, there's just so much there."

Beautiful music always will be the backdrop of the sport, its drumbeat, its lifeline.

To get her attention at home, Peggy Fleming's husband still sometimes hums her music from the 1968 Olympic Games, Tchaikovsky's Symphony no. 6, *Pathétique*.

When Audrey Weisiger and Michael Weiss chose Beethoven as the theme for Weiss's 1997–98 long program, they immediately ruled out the *Moonlight* Sonata as a possible selection. Ekaterina Gordeeva and the late Sergei Grinkov won the gold medal skating to that at the 1994 Olympics.

"I'm not going to compete with that," Weisiger said.

All musical memories were not quite as enchanting. When some skating people hear the music from *Jurassic Park,* they squirm. It's not the dinosaurs. It's the fact that Tonya Harding skated to the soundtrack during her infamous romp through the 1994 Olympic Games.

Nichol sometimes uses movie soundtracks with other skaters for whom she choreographs, but for Kwan, movie music just wasn't right. Nichol and Carroll both believed Kwan was so exceptional as a skater and an artist that she had to be pushed. Heading into the Olympics, they felt they really had developed a rapport, the three of them, over their five seasons together. They didn't want to sound crazy, or arrogant, but they most definitely were looking far beyond an Olympic gold medal in 1998. They all wanted the gold medal for Michelle Kwan, that was for sure. Neither Carroll nor Nichol ever had worked with a skater who had won the Olympic gold medal. The gold medal meant a lot to them.

But they wanted even more. They wanted Michelle Kwan to create a lasting image for their sport, to skate a performance—two performances actually, once they figured out what the short program would be—that would be remembered for the ages.

"I'd like the sport of skating to have these performances," Nichol said. "I'd like to give them to skating. I'd like Michelle, when she's sixty years old, to watch the tape and still remember how her heart felt, how much she loved skating, how much joy she felt as she skated the long program. Even if she doesn't win the Olympic gold medal, I'd like her to look back decades from now and go, 'Wow, was that me?' "

Because they felt they were doing something very special, the Kwan gang shrouded the long program in secrecy through the summer and early autumn of 1997, until its unveiling at Skate America in Detroit in late October.

This was serious business. When Nichol was asked by reporters what her plan was for Kwan's Olympic season, she playfully declined comment. When she played the music for a friend in Canada, the woman cried. But that woman wouldn't tell what it was either.

No one was talking. It was a state secret. Or, at least, a skate secret.

Nichol had her reasons. Sometimes choreographers and coaches kept their musical choices to themselves, especially heading into a big year. No one wanted a competitor to get any ideas from them. And no one wanted to show up at the party wearing the same dress. It happened in Calgary in 1988, when both Katarina Witt and Debi Thomas came as Carmen.

With a Michelle–Tara rivalry brewing, and media interest certain to reach a fever pitch, Nichol and Frank Carroll decided to keep the long program under wraps and allow it to have a glorious debut—or so they hoped—at Skate America.

It wasn't only the Kwan camp that was interested in Janet Lynn. Not long after the world figure skating championships, two skaters met for the first time at the Detroit Skating Club. One was a forty-something suburban housewife in stretch pants trying to stay in shape.

The other was Tara Lipinski.

A woman who works at the club thought the two should meet, so she escorted Lipinski from one rink to another, where they found the middle-aged woman. No one thought it strange that the new world champion would trudge off to find the virtually unknown homemaker. Most places, you'd figure it would be the other way around. But at the Detroit Skating Club, they understood.

They knew that Tara Lipinski went to Janet Lynn, not the other way around.

The two spoke for only a few moments. Lynn congratulated Lipinski on her world title, something Lynn never earned. Lipinski said it was a pleasure to meet Lynn. They went their separate ways.

Before the meeting, Lipinski fired some questions at her choreographer, Sandra Bezic.

"Who's Janet Lynn? Why do I keep hearing this name? She didn't win the Olympics or a world championships. Why does everyone talk about her?"

Bezic smiled and suggested Lipinski watch some old skating videos.

"That joy that Janet had for skating, with such freedom and honesty, has really been my goal with Tara," Bezic said.

Unlike the Kwan camp, however, they did not particularly push the envelope musically with Lipinski heading into the 1997–98 season. Bezic tried, but had no success. When Lipinski visited her home in Toronto in the spring, Bezic played dozens of classical pieces for Tara for short program music in the Olympic year.

Lipinski turned down every one.

"Tara's eyes didn't light up," Bezic said. "We went everywhere, every movie score, every classical piece."

As they kept searching for the music for the short program, Bezic and Lipinski had more success with the long program, which they went ahead and choreographed first. It was another movie soundtrack, *The Rainbow,* about a girl growing up and coming of age, combined with another piece of music by composer Lee Holdridge. "At a big competition, when you're skating great, it's going to feel wonderful," Lipinski said. They had had great success with movie soundtracks the year before, Tara's championship year. There was no reason to back away from them then.

Bezic had no trouble with having Tara skate to a movie about a young girl. Bezic rather liked the idea of allowing Tara to be what she was on the ice. It would have looked ridiculous for her to try to portray an older character, or an exotic role. Unlike Kwan, she could not begin to look the part.

"I'm not trying to fool people into thinking she is older," Bezic said. "She lives the life of a fifteen-year-old, maybe younger. She lives the life of a skater. She loves it. I don't want to get in the way of that face. When you see that joy, you can't knock it."

Bezic had not been the one in the Lipinski camp to suggest putting Tara's hair up into a bun, for instance.

"That's not me," she said. "I'd be quite happy to see a ponytail bopping around. Kristi [Yamaguchi] won with a ponytail."

Richard Callaghan said it was his idea.

Bezic, known most of all for helping Brian Boitano win the 1988 Olympic gold medal and Yamaguchi win in 1992, did not work with many Olympic division skaters. She created Tara's programs, and Lu Chen's.

Bezic's biggest assignment every year was directing and coproducing "Stars on Ice," the touring show starring Scott Hamilton and Kristi Yamaguchi, among others. She also worked for NBC Sports and the Canadian Broadcasting Corporation as a skating commentator.

The Lipinskis got in touch with Bezic through a business associate of agent Mike Burg's, and she agreed to take on Tara in 1996. It was quite a coup for Tara to have Bezic. They worked together for a couple of weeks in the spring and summer of 1996, and again in 1997. Bezic offered to help later in the year, saying she would gladly "drop everything" to work with Lipinski if she needed her.

But the task of reworking the programs in late summer and autumn—something Lori Nichol did in person with Michelle Kwan—would fall to another choreographer, ice dancer Susie Wynne.

And when Wynne got busy with television work herself in November, as the Lipinskis knew she would, Tara would rely on her ballet teacher or Richard Callaghan—or would be on her own.

Nichol and Bezic both were having trouble finding short program music for their respective skaters for the Olympic year.

After turning the house upside down and playing practically every classical piece of music she owned with no success, Bezic wasn't certain what she would do for Tara's short program. One day, Mike Burg gave Tara the new soundtrack from *Anastasia,* an animated movie to be released late in the autumn. She loved the lyrics and the music and immediately thought she could skate to it.

"And I supported that," Bezic said. "The most important thing for any competitor is to be completely honest, to be who they are and not try and be what anyone else thinks they should be."

Before they made the final decision, however, Tara wanted to see the movie. So, in the summer, Burg arranged for a private screening in a small theater at the Fox executive offices in Hollywood for Tara, her mother, himself, and one of Tara's dogs, who sat on Tara's lap throughout the screening. The movie was not yet completed; some of what they saw on the screen was nothing more than drawings.

Tara was sold. And so was Bezic.

"We had to go that way," Bezic said. "There was simply no choice."

Burg helped them get Fox's permission to use the music without the vocals, the soundtrack was cut and edited, and Tara had a short program.

But Team Tara was taking a big gamble tying into an animated children's movie for her short program, especially after picking a childhood theme for the long program as well. After all the talk of Lipinski's age at the 1997 world championships, they were playing right into the critics' hands.

As the summer wore on, Nichol, Carroll, and Kwan had not settled on Kwan's short program music. They were considering some Spanish music that Kwan liked, but Nichol and Carroll had problems with it. So they kept searching.

Nichol also choreographed for Michelle's older sister Karen, who was still skating while going to Boston University. Nichol decided on piano music by twentieth-century composer Sergei Rachmaninoff for Karen's long program and, as she edited it, there was a section of the music, less than a minute in length, that she liked but couldn't use. Nichol kept it in the back of her mind for Michelle. But she still thought of the Rachmaninoff music as Karen's, not Michelle's.

One day on the phone, Nichol asked Carroll to try to pick up a copy of that particular Rachmaninoff CD at a music store in Palm Springs so he could hear the music.

"There was one lousy Rachmaninoff CD there," he said. "I turned it over and there were none of the pieces I wanted."

He was about to put the CD back when he noticed the price: $4.95. He bought it.

Carroll walked to his Jeep Grand Cherokee and tossed the CD on the passenger seat. It was July in the California desert. The temperature was over 100 degrees. "That CD sat on the seat and was just baking in the sun," Carroll said.

As he drove back "up the hill" to Lake Arrowhead, Carroll popped in the CD just to assure himself that there was nothing on it that he and Nichol could use for Karen Kwan. After listening to well over an hour of music, Carroll suddenly heard something that had him turning off the road and stopping his car.

"Oh my God," he said. "This is fabulous."

When he got to his home in Lake Arrowhead, he called Nichol in Canada.

"This is it!" he told her. "I've found something perfect for Michelle."

But the dramatic music was too short for the two-minute forty-second short program. They'd have to find something to go with it.

After spending a few days in "panic mode," Nichol woke up in the middle of the night. She had figured it out. For Michelle's short program, they would use the music Carroll found, plus the unused music from Karen's long program—as long as that was alright with Karen.

Karen Kwan agreed, and Nichol and her music consultant, Lenore Kay, edited the two pieces—seventy seconds of Karen's extra music first, followed by ninety seconds of what Carroll had found—and gave Michelle a tape.

Kwan listened.

"It's good," she said hesitantly.

She was still hoping for something else.

Nichol felt the Rachmaninoff piano music was worth fighting for, so she faxed Michelle a four-page letter, listing fifteen reasons why Rachmaninoff was perfect for her. Nichol's main points were that the Rachmaninoff music was "phenomenal," and that it worked better with the way she was envisioning the placement and flow of the eight elements of the short program.

Kwan read the fax, listened to the music again, and called Nichol to tell her she agreed.

Rachmaninoff it was.

Nichol flew to California for two weeks in July and August to work with Michelle to create her short program. The second time Kwan ran through the program, it was flawless.

Nichol was thrilled.

"I love that it actually was part of Karen's music," Nichol said. "I love that each sister is stepping onto the ice carrying a piece of the other sister with them."

The troubles of the two choreographers had been the same; the results could not have been more different. Nichol ended up with Rachmaninoff for her seventeen-year-old; Bezic with *Anastasia* for her fifteen-year-old.

Bezic tried to get Tara to skate to classical music, or anything that wasn't an animated soundtrack. She really tried. But Bezic had been with Tara and the Lipinskis for just two years—actually, just a couple of weeks each year—and while her rapport with Tara was excellent, ultimately, Tara would call the shots. "We had little history together," Bezic said. "Had she gone along with my idea [for classical music], it would have been a blind leap of faith, and that's a lot to ask of anyone."

Nichol, on the other hand, had built up five years of trust with the Kwans and Carroll. She already had challenged Kwan with "Salome" and "Taj Mahal." She had a track record of grand success with her skater.

When that fax came through, Michelle Kwan knew Nichol was serious. And she also knew that when Nichol and Carroll were that certain about something, she probably should go along.

Tara Lipinski did not raise the bar musically for the 1998 Olympic season, but she was trying new things technically and artistically. In the rink in Detroit, she went back to what she loved most—jumping. Richard Callaghan worked on her double axel, trying to teach her to leap into it rather than spin off that precarious edge. They began practicing two new triple-jump combinations: triple lutz–triple loop and triple toe loop–half loop–triple salchow. They thought they would raise the stakes athletically to a point where no one, not even Michelle Kwan, could touch them.

But they also knew that triple jumps alone would win them nothing in 1998. Tara needed to become more artistic. And Callaghan hoped that would happen by osmosis on the tour. Tara spoke of trying to mimic Oksana Baiul's eyes and ice dancer Maia Usova's hands. Usova, the 1994 Olympic silver medalist, was especially helpful to Tara on tour. When Tara skated her number, Usova came out from backstage and stood in the corner of the dark arena to watch.

"I felt," Tara said, "like I was skating for her."

The one American woman who could have taken the Olympic gold medal away from Kwan and Lipinski was in no position to do so throughout the summer. Nicole Bobek ran into the boards on the skating tour on July 4 and injured her ankle.

The injury was the second most momentous event involving Bobek on the 1997 tour. Bobek and ice dancer Oksana Grishuk—who changed her name to Pasha to avoid being confused with Oksana Baiul—had a confrontation over a man Bobek was seeing. Grishuk said that during their argument, Bobek slapped her. Bobek said she didn't.

For Grishuk, it wasn't the first boyfriend-related incident with another skater on tour. In 1992, she had a widely reported affair with rival ice dancer Alexander Zhulin, who was married to Usova, his dance partner.

Usova got her revenge during the tour when she walked into Spago, the famous Hollywood restaurant, spotted Grishuk sipping a margarita at the bar, walked up behind her, grabbed her by the hair, and smashed her head into the counter.

Bobek avoided any bar scenes with Grishuk and began preparing to skate in a memorial tribute to Carlo Fassi in August. She performed two numbers, although she could not jump well. Nonetheless, she still looked great. If only she could get herself in shape for the coming year, anything seemed possible.

But something else momentous—and potentially career-threatening—happened to Bobek in August 1997.

She turned twenty.

Leaving the teenage ranks was not a good thing for a skater, even one with as much natural talent as Bobek.

On the tour, someone mentioned to Evy Scotvold, Nancy Kerrigan's coach who taught Bobek for a month, that Bobek would be the highest-paid woman in the history of her sport if she won the Olympic gold medal.

Scotvold didn't disagree, but he issued an ominous reply: "Too late."

He explained: "For years, she didn't put in the work. It's too late for her to do it now. Not at twenty."

It was like trying to withdraw money from a bank without making deposits for years. Bobek, who was going to stay in Lake Arrowhead and work with Christa Fassi, Carlo's widow, would have to perform a miracle to win an Olympic medal in Japan.

The top three men in figure skating also were juggling tour life while creating new programs for the Olympic year. Elvis Stojko, Todd Eldredge, and Ilia Kulik trained just hundreds of miles apart: Stojko near Toronto, Eldredge near Detroit, and Kulik near Boston.

As he began to put together his short program, the rebellious Stojko received help from an unusual source: a skating judge.

Canadian judge Sally Rehorick, who was living in Japan for two years teaching English, sent Stojko a tape of traditional Japanese Taiko drumming. Stojko, who had been toying with a rock-and-roll piece, listened to the tape and immediately decided that the unusual music, with its tremendous speed and offbeats, was perfect for him.

"I thought Elvis would be interested in this," Rehorick told reporters in Canada. "But I kept it to myself and didn't say anything to any of the judges I know [in Japan] because, frankly, I thought one of the Japanese skaters might [steal] the idea. Until Takeshi Honda [Japan's top male skater] had chosen his music, I didn't say anything."

What a change this was for Stojko. The year before, he was criticized for standing still on the ice.

The drum music ensured that Elvis would be moving in 1998.

While Stojko went down a new road for the Olympic Games, Todd Eldredge took the same old path. After buying thousands of dollars worth of CDs, Eldredge decided to keep his old short program, "Walk on the Wild Side," and to reprise one of his favorite long programs, "Gettysburg."

Going through CDs one day, he popped in his 1994–95 long program, a selection of music from the *Gettysburg* soundtrack. The music meant a lot to him. "It was the start of my new career, my second career," he said. "It was the program I used to get back on the scene again."

After missing the Olympic team in 1994, he used the soundtrack the following year, and with it, finished second to Stojko at the 1995 world championships.

Eldredge decided to use different cuts from the soundtrack for the Olympic year, but the theme would remain the same. For the frantic 1997–98 season, he, like Kwan, would find comfort in reassuring music in the long program.

Then there was Ilia Kulik. Everything he was working on in the summer of 1997 was grand. It was big and it was bold. He was going to overwhelm his competitors with his massive jumps and his swinging arms and his brilliant artistry at the Olympic Games. Or he was going to go down in a blaze of glory.

It was always one or the other with Kulik.

"For me, it's more interesting when I'm doing something between the jumps," he said. "This is figure skating. It's not jumping. It's not just going into the jump and out of the jump and waiting for the next jump. I want to show the program. I want to show the step sequences. I want to do this. That's what figure skating is."

At the 1997 world championships, Kulik certainly looked like he might become the odd man out with only two Olympic slots available for Russian men. But as Urmanov's injury did not heal, things began looking better for Kulik. That's what Kulik was thinking in August, as he arrived at practice after sleeping in late in his adopted home of Marlboro, Massachusetts, a place where a beautiful ice rink sat empty, waiting for him.

Twenty minutes after Kulik set foot on the ice, he put on his music, Jean-Michel Jarre's "Revolutions," and began practicing sections of his short program.

A silent alert must have gone through the huge, four-rink facility, because, at that moment, three ponytailed girls came in to watch, followed moments later by four more. The girls leaned forward, elbows on knees, watching Kulik's every move.

He was dressed in a black, long-sleeve T-shirt, gray sweat pants, black leggings pulled down low over his black skates, and black gloves with the fingertips cut out. His hair was flying. His cheeks were flaring.

The girls were mesmerized.

It was Ilia Day at the rink.

Unlike most American skaters who allow their music to play from start to finish, when Kulik didn't like something he had done on the ice, he flew to the tape machine and snapped off the music. He was sharing the ice with two Ukrainian ice dancers. On occasion, they skated over and stopped Kulik's music. He returned the favor and stopped theirs as they were skating. The ex-Soviets were demons with tape machines.

Start, stop. Start, stop. No wonder they ran out of steam when they competed; they weren't used to skating a program without stopping.

After an hour of alternatingly skating and racing to the tape machine, Kulik gathered his things and left the ice.

The girls scattered to other rinks.

Ilia Day was over.

Kulik practiced without his coach, Tatiana Tarasova, who was in New York City picking up his costumes. He was going to wear something light and flowing for the short program, and a very strange selection for the long program, which was skated to Gershwin's *Rhapsody in Blue*.

Tarasova had chosen a yellow-and-black vinyl shirt, something akin to an animal print. She thought it looked like clothing people wore in Gershwin's time in America.

Within a few months, critics would have a few other thoughts about what it looked like.

Three days later, Kulik was on crutches. As he was going up for a triple lutz in practice, his right toe pick got stuck in the ice. The blade from his left skate sliced through the top of his right skate all the way to his big toe. The blade reached the bone and lacerated a ligament.

At first, Kulik didn't realize he was injured. He continued skating for a few minutes until he spotted a little hole in his boot. Moments later, blood was spurting from the hole. Other skaters called 911 and he went to the hospital, where a pin was put in his toe, the ligament was stitched together, and his foot was put in a cast.

He was off the ice for less than a month.

"It's no problem," he said.

Stojko. Eldredge. Kulik. They, along with Alexei Yagudin, were the brightest lights in men's skating in the summer of 1997.

But they weren't the only ones getting ready for the Olympics.

Even before the Lausanne world championships, Audrey Weisiger called Brian Wright in Seattle to ask him to choreograph for Michael Weiss in the Olympic year. Wright wasn't sure what to say. He wasn't sure if he would be dead or alive by February 1998. He had good days when he felt surprisingly strong; he had awful days when he could barely remember his name and couldn't get out of bed.

Lesions on his brain, caused by AIDS, affected his memory. On his rare out-of-town trips to work with skaters, he often misread his ticket and went to the airport on the wrong day. He did that four times prior to one trip, and it cost him nearly $300 in cab fares. Wright actually laughed at himself; going back and forth to the airport four days in a row was quite funny, he thought.

But what wasn't so funny was the fact that he asked his sister to stash sixty sleeping pills in a safe place in case he ever needed them. "It takes ten to kill you," he said. "If I ask her for them, I'll want her to give them to me."

On the phone with Weisiger, Wright sounded uncertain, which surprised her.

"I'm asking for you emotionally, if not physically," Weisiger said.

"I don't know."

Weisiger wasn't going to let Wright wallow in sadness.

"Listen," she said, "why do you keep running toward the darkness? Why don't you run toward the light, as long as you can see it? I know you are dying of AIDS and I know this is difficult for you but I need you. I need you as a choreographer. Mike needs you. Now make up your mind."

"Okay," Wright said. "You're right. I'll do it."

Wright flew to Washington in late April to help Weisiger create the short program, then moved onto the ice and worked with Weiss to help him learn it. Weeks earlier, Weiss heard another skater's music playing at Fairfax Ice Arena and liked it. It was Spanish. He wanted something like that for his short program.

Weisiger went through the figure skating CD-listening ritual and came up with new-style flamenco music by guitarist Jesse Cook. But the music didn't have enough variety to it.

"It needs some spice," Weisiger said.

"It needs a big finish," said Weiss, who heard a rough cut of the music.

Weisiger knew just who to call on to add the spice and big finish. One day, she took Wright to a Falls Church, Virginia, recording studio. There, the two of them joined fellow skating coach Linda Reynolds and Stuart Ridgway, the studio president and an accomplished musician, to create their own version of Weiss's short program. They added various sounds and instruments to the music: tambourine, shaker, cymbal, and even rhythmic clapping.

The clapping was important; it lasted the final minute of his performance, and was designed to energize the program.

"Are we clapping too loud?" Weisiger asked Ridgway when she, Reynolds, and Wright emerged from the soundproof studio.

"I think it's okay," Ridgway said. "I'm thinking of that crowd in the arena in Philadelphia next January."

The arena in Philadelphia was the CoreStates Center, site of the 1998 U.S. nationals and the Olympic trials, where Weiss would try to win one of two men's spots for the 1998 Olympic Games.

"Yeah, it might sound great," Weisiger said with a chuckle. "Do you think people really will begin to join in and clap?"

"Oh yeah," Ridgway said.

"Stuart," Weisiger said with a chuckle, "maybe you can go to Philly and lead the rhythmic applause."

He shooed them back into the booth to clap some more.

Weiss's long program demanded no rhythmic applause. He was skating to Beethoven.

Weisiger piled dozens of Beethoven CDs into Weiss's arms after practice one day.

She gave him more several days later.

Lisa Thornton, then Weiss's fiancée, looked at Weisiger and laughed.

"No more CDs, okay?"

Weiss also rented the movie *Immortal Beloved*, the story of Beethoven's life. He watched it at least five times by the end of the summer, and he and Thornton sketched out the idea for his costume based on what they saw on the videotape. Weiss even read a couple of books on Beethoven. He couldn't believe how quickly he had plunged into Beethoven's life, but he had to, because he was quite serious about this.

"I don't want to be stereotyped as the guy who skates in a tie-dye shirt to Santana," Weiss said. "I don't want to be the same type of person every year."

Originally, Weisiger planned to have Christopher Dean, the 1984 Olympic ice dancing gold medalist with Jayne Torvill, choreograph the long program for Michael. She decided to not have Brian Wright do the long program because she wanted Michael to go in a completely different direction for that season. But Weiss told Weisiger he wanted to create his own program, and Weisiger went along.

So Weisiger, Thornton, and Weiss joined forces to choreograph the long program.

They picked the *Egmont* Overture and the piano sonata no. 8, *Pathétique,* as the music. And once again, Weisiger wasn't satisfied with the way the music sounded.

But this wasn't Jesse Cook.

This was Beethoven.

Weisiger didn't care. She decided to hire three respected musicians, playing the cello, piano, and clarinet, to improve on Beethoven.

"This," she said, "was risky."

As Ridgway conducted in his studio with a pencil, Beethoven's piano sonata became a cello, piano, and clarinet trio. Weisiger thought Weiss needed stronger music to skate to, and also wanted a richer sound resonating in the arenas where he would perform.

She would do anything for her skater, even if it meant fiddling with Beethoven.

Music was one element of Weiss's life as a skater.

Jumping was another.

"He coulda done five!"

Nick Perna, one of the coaches at the Fairfax Ice Arena, couldn't believe his eyes. Michael Weiss had just gone up for a quadruple lutz, a four-revolution jump never landed before in competition. He had gotten so high off the ice, there was room, Perna thought, for another revolution.

On a ninety-degree early July afternoon in Fairfax, Virginia, two stars of U.S. figure skating—one current, the other for the future—took turns practicing historic jumps on opposite ends of the rink. Weiss landed quadruple lutzes on one end of the ice—holding on to shaky two-footed landings that wouldn't count in competition—as a tiny eleven-year-old named Elizabeth Kwon landed triple axels on the other end while wrapped in a jumping harness being held like a fishing pole by Perna.

It was 2:45 P.M. Freestyle skating was in session. Ten skaters, including Weiss and Kwon, covered the ice, taking turns when their music came on to practice the long and short programs they would use in the 1997–98 competitive season. Only one of them—Weiss—had a shot at the 1998 Olympic Games. But that didn't matter at Fairfax. Weiss waited his turn as half a dozen other skaters played their music before his came on.

Weiss had a task to work on while he waited. He had a secret weapon for the coming Olympic season. He had come close to landing the quadruple toe loop at the 1997 nationals. Now, he and Weisiger planned to up the ante for the coming year's nationals and Olympics. He wouldn't try the quad toe loop. He would do the quad lutz.

"Without it, he won't be on the medal stand at the Olympics," Weisiger said. "There are too many great skaters who have been around longer than he has. If he makes it to Nagano and he's fourth or tenth, what's the difference? He wants to be in the top three, and to do that, he's got to do something really big to break through."

The lutz was the second hardest jump in the sport, after the axel. To try four revolutions of that jump was excruciatingly hard. The lutz was so difficult because skaters had to pick in to launch themselves with the right foot while holding onto the outside edge on their left skate, then immediately throw themselves into the air spinning to their left. The body had to go one way, then another, in a split second. Only someone with the technique and upper body strength of Michael Weiss would dare try a quad lutz.

"A lot of things could rock his world, but his triple lutz will always stay," Brian Wright said of Weiss.

So, why not a quad?

As Weiss navigated through skating traffic to pound out his landings, the little Kwon girl, nicknamed Lisa, landed two impeccable triple axels and two-footed two more in fifteen minutes of practice in the harness.

Lisa Kwon was about to enter the sixth grade in the Washington suburb of McLean, Virginia. In April, she won the national intermediate championships, a big step in a little skater's career.

She immediately moved up to the novice level, from where she would try to make nationals in 1998. After one year in novice, her father said, she would advance to juniors. Then, at the junior level in 1999, she would unveil the triple axel, John Kwon said.

He wasn't the first parent to entertain such a dream, even if it was extremely unrealistic.

Wright, Weiss's choreographer, had flown in for the week to work with Weiss and some of the up-and-coming Fairfax skaters.

He was watching the triple axels out of the corner of his eye.

"Chick spins fast," he proclaimed with a laugh. Slyly, he added, "Did we mention she's Asian?"

Of the previous nine women's world champions, six were Asian, or of Asian descent: Midori Ito, Kristi Yamaguchi (twice), Yuka Sato, Lu Chen, and Michelle Kwan.

Why do some Asian women become such great skaters?

"It's our drive and it's our bodies," said Weisiger, who is of Chinese descent. "You get the right personality, the family pushing its kids to succeed. You get the right body type. Asians genetically don't have breasts, and we're small-boned."

Lisa Kwon was born in the United States. Her parents came from Seoul, South Korea, in 1978 "for the better life," said John Kwon, who runs a contracting business.

Lisa was born in 1986 and began taking skating lessons at age three from Debbie Prachar, one of Weisiger's and Perna's colleagues at Fairfax Ice Arena.

"Lisa," Brian Wright called to her later on, taking her tiny hand in his gloved hand and gliding out onto the ice with her. "Let's work on your arm movement."

With that, Wright placed his arm in the air, extending his fingers, striking a pose. He then suggested she raise her arm, encouraging her to do just as he had done.

On her first try, Lisa Kwon mimicked him exactly.

The handful of coaches at the Fairfax Ice Arena were exchanging students with a delightful vengeance in the hour-long afternoon session. Weisiger was keeping her eye on Weiss, but working with two other skaters, girls whom she had coached for years, but girls who will never make it to nationals, or make her famous. She didn't care;

Weisiger, like Frank Carroll, and many other coaches around the country, found joy in taking skaters with limited talent to heights they never would have reached on their own. Sometimes these coaches had more fun with these skaters than with their stars. A gem like a Michelle Kwan—or perhaps a Lisa Kwon—came along rarely. The kids who rejoiced at a third-place finish in the South Atlantic regionals and a chance to compete at the Eastern sectionals were the norm on ice surfaces like Fairfax.

Figure skating was unusual in this way: Top coaches coached the best in the world, and also coached the no-names. It would be as if a football legend like Don Shula had coached both the Miami Dolphins and Pop Warner youth leagues. It never happened in football, but it happened all the time in skating.

The skaters without the big names made only one concession to the emerging greatness of Michael Weiss in the summer practice session. After he stayed out of their path, giving way when necessary as they performed their programs, they completely cleared the ice for him when his long program began playing over the loudspeaker at the rink.

As the others hung on the boards to watch, Weiss began ticking off his triple jumps, two-footed his quad, and went through a summer version of the long program that would need to be perfect by the autumn. As he neared the finish, he stopped skating and looked down at his skate lace.

"Did you break it, Tonya?" Prachar asked with a grin.

"Yeah," Weiss said.

As another coach stopped the tape player, Weiss tied the lace together, the music came back on, and he picked up where he had left off, finishing with a flourish.

It was just this kind of attitude that made Weiss one of the hottest properties on the skating landscape in the summer of 1997. Agents were swarming around him. There was just one problem, however: Weiss already had an agent, Nancy Kerrigan's husband, Jerry Solomon.

They had been together for several years, Weiss and Solomon, and the relationship had been good for the young skater, who made some money as a tag-along on Kerrigan's shows.

But after Weiss nearly landed the quadruple toe loop in Nashville, the relationship soured. Weiss expected Solomon to be able to promote him as the "Man with the Quad." Yet Weiss made nothing off the jump, except for loads of good publicity. This wasn't unusual for a male skater; endorsements usually went to the female stars of skating, not the men. Still, Weiss wanted more from Solomon.

"Jerry did a lot for me when I was first coming up," Weiss said, "but he wasn't really prepared for the quad to happen, not being at the national championships, not having a plan if it did happen."

Of course, officially, it didn't happen.

"The quad was a great effort and Michael is a really good kid," Solomon said, "but those two things don't make a whole lot of impact."

In June, Weiss and his father told Solomon that they thought it was better if they went their separate ways and did not renew their contract.

For months, Weiss did not sign with anyone else.

But his phone rang constantly. Agents knew about Weiss's potential. They had a pretty good idea that Weiss, even if he was the understudy to Todd Eldredge in 1998, would be the future American male star of his sport leading up to the 2002 Olympic Games in Salt Lake City.

Agents were everywhere in figure skating. You could tell a lot about skaters and their families by the agent they selected.

Michelle Kwan had Shep Goldberg, whose firm was called Proper Marketing Associates.

Tara Lipinski was with Mike Burg, whose company was named Edge Marketing and Management.

Proper. Edge.

Kwan. Lipinski.

While Goldberg kept a very low profile, Burg took the skating agent business to places it had never been before.

"I just saw a three-month-old I'm thinking of representing," he said with a laugh.

Sometimes agents worked for people they didn't even represent. Michael Rosenberg was performing just such a duty for Russian coach Tamara Moskvina's new pair, Elena Berezhnaia and Anton Sikharulidze.

Moskvina asked Rosenberg to put the pair on Elvis Stojko's tour across Canada in September. Rosenberg was the tour's producer and promoter. The money was low by tour standards, but terrific by Russian terms: $20,000 for the pair for nearly two weeks of work.

Moskvina, who also served as the pair's agent, didn't care what they earned.

"I would have paid Michael to have them on the tour," she said. "They got important experience. I wanted them to have a chance to skate on tour."

Moskvina also snagged another opportunity for the pair. They played the skating roles of Ekaterina Gordeeva and Sergei Grinkov in a CBS made-for-TV movie based on Gordeeva's best-selling book.

It wasn't the movie that Moskvina envisioned for them, the story of Berezhnaia's comeback from her head injury. That might happen someday, depending on their results in Nagano.

But at least it was a start.

As the skating tour wound down, Michelle Kwan took off her Riedell boots, put on a pair of SP-Teris, and went onto the ice for practice one day.

That was how she changed back to her old boots.

When the tour moved west, Danny Kwan took those boots to his local shoemaker in San Bernardino, California. For three dollars, he had a few changes made, and his daughter was set.

With two years still left on the contract, the Riedell boots were history. Michelle Kwan was back in the boots in which she won the world championships.

"It's not Riedell's fault," Danny Kwan said. "I loved the endorsement, I loved the company. It's not their fault. It's my fault."

He told Riedell he was breaking the contract, and encouraged the company to discontinue its advertising featuring Michelle. But throughout the late summer and autumn, the ads kept running.

When Michelle returned home from the tour in July 1997, she began to feel a nagging pain in the second toe of her left foot. She had felt it off and on through the year, but this was worse. She gritted her teeth and made it through her triple toe loop and triple salchow—jumps that put particular pressure on that toe—but something wasn't right.

In August, Danny Kwan took his daughter to a doctor in Los Angeles, where she underwent x-rays and magnetic resonance imaging (MRI).

As the Kwans joined him in his office, the doctor pointed to something on the MRI.

There was a stress fracture on the second toe of Michelle's left foot, near the spot where the toe connected to the foot.

Danny Kwan's heart skipped a beat.

"A stress fracture?" he asked.

"With six months to go until the Olympics?"

"But it's good news," the doctor told Michelle Kwan and her father. "That fracture happened a year ago. It's already ninety percent healed."

Danny Kwan felt terrible. He didn't know if the Riedell boots had contributed to the injury. He didn't know if the stress fracture had occurred over many years of jumping. He didn't know what caused the injury.

But he knew this: As she entered the Olympic season, his daughter was injured. She had been injured for a full year. It turned out that she had been hurt at the Nashville nationals, at the Champions Series final, at the worlds in Switzerland.

And yet she had kept on skating because she hardly ever complained.

When Danny and Michelle Kwan returned to Lake Arrowhead, Danny Kwan decided not to tell Frank Carroll about what they had learned from the doctor.

"I didn't know," Carroll said later. "Not in August. They told me in October."

"I asked myself, 'Why bother telling Frank?'" Danny Kwan said. "She had had pain, and she had skated. She was ninety percent healed. I thought it was a tissue problem, not a bone problem. That was the mistake I made."

Carroll was not at all pleased when Danny Kwan finally told him about the injury, but for Michelle Kwan, the decision to stay on the ice seemed right. She had skated with the injury for a year, and the doctor said it was nearly healed.

The Olympic year was coming. That was no time to be off the ice.

So Michelle Kwan kept on skating.

10

THE LAST HURRAH

By his tenth fall Scott Davis had had enough. Ten times he went up for his triple axel in the chilly ice rink as a mid-August morning heated up outside in Simsbury, Connecticut, and ten times he crashed to the ice.

The tenth time he stayed down.

Scott Davis never got mad, which is something that had bothered some of his friends and colleagues over the years. "You've gotta get angry," Scott Hamilton used to tell him. "You've gotta get mad."

"That's just not me," Davis shrugged.

As he lay on the ice, Davis *almost* got mad. Almost. After a few seconds, he pulled himself up to a kneeling position, then grudgingly stood up and dusted the ice off his pants.

He ran his fingers through his hair. Galina Zmievskaia, his coach, was standing on the other side of the ice in her Asics sneakers. She pointed to her head and screamed to him in staccato English.

"Scott! Head! Think!"

Davis threw his hands down as he glided around the spot where he had just fallen. Without a triple axel, he was dead in the Olympic season. Dead. He almost certainly needed to land three—one in the short program, two in the long—at the 1998 nationals to have a chance to be one of the two U.S. men to go to the Nagano Olympics.

Five months from the nationals, he couldn't land one.

Viktor Petrenko, the 1992 Olympic gold medalist who trains in Connecticut with Davis, wheeled toward Davis, bent over, and glared at the ice. He was looking for clues at the scene of the crime. He studied the marks Davis's skate blades left on the ice, to see if he could notice what Davis was doing wrong on his takeoff.

"It looks really good," Petrenko shrugged. "Why didn't you land it?"

"I have no idea," Davis said.

Petrenko scratched his head and glided away.

He wasn't the first person to scratch his head when he thought of Scott Davis.

A week later, as Tonia Kwiatkowski took the ice in Lakewood, Ohio, to run through her short and long programs for the Olympic season, one of her skating students brushed alongside of her.

"I did all my doubles in my program!" sixteen-year-old Kelda Vopnford told Kwiatkowski.

"Great!" Kwiatkowski said. "Sorry I didn't get to you today, but I promise I'll get to you tomorrow."

"No problem," Vopnford said.

Kwiatkowski and Vopnford and four other skaters warmed up on the rink before Kwiatkowski glided to the tape player and popped in her music for her Olympic season long program, selections from a new Broadway musical, *The Hunchback of Notre Dame*. It was a different kind of music for Kwiatkowski. At twenty-six, she was making some changes, retooling her classical image and going to more contemporary music for the last of her eleven senior national championships. She went through at least one hundred CDs before her agent, Lee Marshall, who produces Broadway shows, suggested the musical. But on the CD there was singing—and there's no singing allowed in Olympic division skating music. So a technician stripped the vocals off the music, and Kwiatkowski had her long program.

Kwiatkowski went to center ice and waited for the music to begin. Carol Heiss Jenkins, her coach since she was eight, was in Europe at a competition with another skater. Kwiatkowski was on her own, just her and the kids. That was fine with her. After undergoing surgery in the spring to remove a cyst the size of an egg from her right ankle, she was taking it slow in the summertime.

"I'm just doing doubles," she shouted. "No triples yet."

The five other skaters stopped as Kwiatkowski began, but within seconds, four of them left the boards and trickled back onto the ice to practice, careful to avoid Kwiatkowski's path.

But one last girl in a black skating dress refused to move. She stood and watched the whole time.

Kelda Vopnford, one of ten students Kwiatkowski coached when she wasn't practicing, knew what it was like to have someone watching you as you churned through a program alone on the ice. She felt more certain when her coach stood by and paid attention. She liked having Kwiatkowski stand watch over her practice sessions.

Vopnford also knew how important every run-through was to Kwiatkowski as the days ticked away to the nationals in January in Philadelphia.

That August day in the suburbs outside of Cleveland, Vopnford simply took four minutes out of her practice time and returned the favor.

Washed up. Left for dead. Written off. Forgotten.

Scott Davis and Tonia Kwiatkowski were all of the above.

It was awful getting old in skating. It was terrible knowing you could not win on your own anymore, that someone would have to make a mistake for you to have a chance at the Olympics. An advancing age in figure skating—Kwiatkowski turned twenty-seven the week the 1998 Games began, Davis turned twenty-six two weeks earlier—was worse than a bad costume. It was worse than falling on the combination jump. It was worse than having your skate lace break.

"It's frustrating," Kwiatkowski said. "They don't stop talking about how old you are. They say, 'You're even older now.' I say, 'Oh my God, stop it.' I'm not that old and I don't feel old so no one's going to tell me I'm old."

Yet the voices still sang out:

Tonia, you're old. Scott, you too, although some of your competitors are still your age, and confidence probably is your biggest problem.

"I know," Davis said. "One slight mistake and you're third. Two and you're tenth. It's the last hurrah for me. I want to go out feeling good about my skating, showing people I'm a good skater, that I deserve to be out there, on top of the sport."

Hanging on for one last try at the Olympics made them feel like outsiders. They were different. Disposable. Even unnecessary. They were not old for life, but they were old for skating. Kwiatkowski looked ahead of her and saw a fifteen-year-old (Tara Lipinski) and a seventeen-year-old (Michelle Kwan). Davis had twenty-one-year-old Michael Weiss blocking his view of the medal stand, although four-time national champion Todd Eldredge was half a year older than Davis.

But, for Davis and Kwiatkowski, this was a no-brainer. One year to the Olympics? Of course you went for it.

In 1997, both had missed the world championship team. Neither skated on the tour, costing them earnings of over $100,000, money that they both had earned the year before. Both had time on their hands, plenty of time to get their short and long programs finished early. The good thing about having nothing to do was that by August, when their competitors were scrambling to get their music selected and costumes made and choreography finished, they knew their routines inside and out. The bad thing was that it meant, for whatever reason, the tour did not want them.

For Kwiatkowski and Carol Heiss, the conversation was inevitable. They dreaded the moment, yet knew they had to have the little chat. Who wanted to discuss being washed up? Who wanted to talk about quitting? Who wanted to look into the eyes of the person they had been working with every day for nearly two decades and say it was time to give up?

Kwiatkowski had had a rough nationals in 1997, finishing sixth, her worst performance at the U.S. championships in seven years. She went to her first nationals as a junior skater in the winter of 1986, when Tara Lipinski was three and a half years old. Her first senior nationals was 1988. Brian Boitano and Debi Thomas won the men's and women's titles at that event. That's how long Kwiatkowski had been hanging around.

She began skating at the age of five, in 1976. Kwan, Lipinski, and even Nicole Bobek weren't born yet.

It was a long time. In some ways, too long.

"You might want to think about going pro," Heiss told Kwiatkowski at dinner after the 1997 nationals. "You know Tara and Michelle are going to make the Olympic team. There's just no doubt about it. But you never know what Bobek's going to do, and there's Angela Nikodinov and there's Sydne Vogel and there's . . ."

Kwiatkowski interrupted her coach.

"Look, I know that. But I don't want to look back when I'm forty and say, 'You know, I wonder what would have happened if I had trained another seven or eight months. Could I have made the team?' I don't want to be sitting there watching nationals in my living room, looking and saying, 'You know, if I would have skated a decent program, I could have made the Olympics.' I just don't want to do it. I don't want to look back and wonder if I should have done this or I should have done that. It's only another eight months or so. I'm staying in, Carol."

For Davis, there wasn't going to be a conversation. There was a simple reason for this. He and Zmievskaia didn't speak the same language.

But Davis, the two-time U.S. champion whose career was in a two-and-a-half-year free fall, had had enough conversations for the both of them. Scott Davis talking to Scott Davis.

He had begun calling himself "Mr. Fourth Place." He hadn't won an event since the 1994 nationals. Self-doubt had become his constant companion.

"You hear those little voices in your head saying, 'Can I do this?' Instead of saying, 'I can do it, let's be confident, let's show 'em.' It's the best when you're younger and you don't know any better and you're just skating."

But Davis wasn't young anymore. By the 1998 nationals, which were the Olympic trials, the voices in his head were screaming.

"My last shot, my last year," Davis said. "I really want to go back to the Olympics. Last time, I got distracted with the outcome rather than the performance. This time, I know what I want. I've always really admired people who are consistent, like Todd and Tara and Michelle. They pretty much go out there and do it every single time. I really want to do that my last year. I want to go out there and do two clean programs. I've never done that. I've never, ever done a clean long program in competition. Never. Just realizing that pushes me every day."

Tonia Kwiatkowski was a mom-and-pop operation in a world increasingly dominated by big chain stores. At Winterhurst Ice Rink in Lakewood, Ohio, she shared the ice with then-singles skater Jenni Meno and ice dancer Elizabeth Punsalan. All three of them were still around in 1997, trying for the 1998 Games. Nationally, she grew up in skating with Nancy Kerrigan, Kristi Yamaguchi, Tonya Harding, and compulsory school figures. At the 1987 national championships in Tacoma, Washington, they all were bunched near the top of the junior ladies results. A skater named Jeri Campbell won, followed by Yamaguchi, Kwiatkowski, and Kerrigan, second through fourth. Meno, who later became a wonderful pairs skater, was eighth.

Yamaguchi, Kwiatkowski, and Kerrigan all did poorly in the school figures, then bounced back with good short and long programs. In the long, Yamaguchi was first, Kerrigan was second, and Kwiatkowski was third. It was clear back then that when the sport jettisoned school figures, those teenagers were going to explode onto the scene.

"I was part of a different era in skating," Kwiatkowski said. "And I think I've done well with the transition. By the time they got rid of figures, my figures were starting to get good. 'Don't do this to me!' I said. Of course, my figures get good and then . . . oh well, I liked the free skating better anyway. But every now and then, I wonder what would have happened if I had been part of this era. When I was fifteen and went to nationals, I had all my triples. I had a triple lutz then . . . and I was a junior.

"If the rules then were like they are now, I would have moved up quicker, but I don't know if that would have been good. I don't know if I would have been able to do college if that had happened. So, it's just the luck of being born when you're born."

And she could take her time in the sport because her body cooperated.

"It changed very slowly. It gave me enough of a chance to kind of regroup, get my feet back underneath me, and then it would change a little more. Some girls got curves and if the hips started to go, they were dead. Dead. There's just no way to turn in the air then. But for me, it was gradual."

She actually weighed less in 1997 (just 103 pounds) than she did as a teenager. Kwiatkowski and Michelle Kwan, both five-foot-two, were almost exactly the same size.

In the early 1990s, Kwiatkowski's peers came and went. Yamaguchi is exactly five months younger than Kwiatkowski, yet she got her Olympic gold medal and got out of the so-called amateur world six years before Kwiatkowski planned to leave, in 1998. Six years is a long time. Why did Kwiatkowski stay?

Because it fit in with her life. She was able to go to college, graduating in 1994 with degrees in communications and psychology from Baldwin-Wallace in the nearby Cleveland suburb of Berea. She lived in the dorms and had just a fifteen-minute drive to the rink. As a college student, she loved to escape to the ice and train.

"I didn't mind coming into the rink two to three hours every day," Kwiatkowski said. "There was no reason to stop skating."

Even when Tonia was in high school, the Kwiatkowskis stressed to their only child that she would have a normal life. Back then, all the top girl skaters stayed in school. There was no money to be made in the sport. Plus, until they graduated from high school, they were "buried," to use Kwiatkowski's word, by compulsory school figures.

Kwiatkowski actually survived life without a skating tour and televised shows and million-dollar deals. She had to settle for the

National Honor Society. And Friday night hockey games with her friends. And living in the same home in which she was raised, with both parents.

Her parents are decidedly middle-class. Phil Kwiatkowski works for a heavy equipment company, sometimes driving a tractor-trailer to construction sites, other times going to auctions to examine machinery the company might buy. He worked hundreds of hours of overtime to pay for his daughter's skating. When Tonia began earning money in the sport, she returned the favor with typically utilitarian gifts: a new garage door and a new front door.

Corinne Kwiatkowski accompanied her daughter as she rose through the ranks in skating. She wanted just two things from skating: for Tonia to get one trip to nationals and for both of them to skate on the rink at Rockefeller Center.

"We did it all in the same year," her mother said.

The 1986 nationals, where Tonia finished fifth in juniors, were on Long Island. They stayed in New York a few days after the competition, and Tonia, Corinne, Jenni Meno, and Carol Heiss all went one day to Rockefeller Center, paid to get in, and skated with the general public. None of the people around them realized an Olympic gold medalist (Heiss) was among them, although Kwiatkowski put on an impressive jumping display when she found the room to maneuver.

Experiences such as that shaped Kwaitkowski's career. When she qualified for her first world championship team in 1993, then failed to make the cut into the regular competition in Prague, she was devastated. However, instead of heading home, she and her mother toured the city. By the end of the week, there wasn't a cathedral or museum they hadn't visited.

For Tonia Kwiatkowski, skating was just another experience, not her sole existence. Unlike some of her young competitors in 1997–98, she didn't reconstruct her life for the sport. She never stopped going to school, although she did have a tutor for three years in middle school for two periods each day for spelling and reading. She went to school for five periods, then skated. She received a gym credit for the skating.

"It's a different sport now," she said. "I can't imagine what it's like for Michelle and Tara."

There was no doubt in the minds of Phil and Corinne Kwiatkowski that this was the right way for their daughter to grow up.

"People really don't care what happens in the rink when you walk out the door into society, into life," her mother told her.

* * *

The last competition Tonia Kwiatkowski won prior to the 1997 autumn season was the 1995 World University Games. The only other big competition Kwiatkowski ever won was the 1991 World University Games. She never had won a national title, although she finished second behind Michelle Kwan in 1996, then went to the world championships and finished eighth, a few places lower than many believed she deserved because she skated very well, without a fall.

"I couldn't have done any more at those worlds," Kwiatkowski said. "It made me feel good about myself. People thought Carol and I were nuts, skipping out of the place like we just won."

During Olympic years, things didn't go so well for her. She missed the 1994 U.S. Olympic team by four spots; the 1992 team by two places; the 1988 team by eight.

She was a journeywoman, praised for her persistence and criticized for what some saw as her predictable choreography, outfits, and jumping style. Judges and other critics suggested to Heiss heading into the 1998 Olympic year that it was time for Kwiatkowski to soften her hairstyle, which had been a tight bun for a few years. The complaint was it was an older look, and Kwiatkowski didn't need anything else to remind people of her age.

Kwiatkowski told Heiss she wasn't going to listen to the critics. She was staying the way she was.

The costumes for 1998 changed slightly, becoming more glamorous and shorter. Her short program, "Madame Butterfly," inspired by thoughts of the Japanese Olympics, was designed to be slower, to help her settle down. Both Heiss and Kwiatkowski knew Kwiatkowski's last, best chance to make an Olympic team hinged on skating a clean short program at the nationals. If she fell in the short program, the judges would put all the teenagers and younger skaters ahead of her. But if she landed the jumps, she would have to be in the mix.

Anything, then, might happen in the long program.

But Kwiatkowski knew it was a long shot. She knew Kwan, Lipinski, and Bobek were the favorites for the three spots. She knew the judges didn't really want her on the Olympic team. She wasn't as dynamic as the other three, all of whom had won a medal at a world championships in the past three years. Kwiatkowski, medal-less, was steady and sure. Steady and sure didn't get very far in skating in the 1990s.

Kwiatkowski was given this message in numerous ways. In the

summer, when international assignments were handed out for the Champions Series events, Kwiatkowski got dealt out. She didn't get any of the six. She was assigned to lesser events, international competitions in Vienna, Austria, and Hamar, Norway. And she was told by the USFSA that she would have the honor of qualifying for the 1998 national championships in the Midwestern sectional competition. While Kwan and Lipinski competed in Skate America on national TV, a month later, it would be Tonia and the twelve-year-olds in a rink in Dallas.

Even when things supposedly were going well, she got no respect. In 1996–97, she qualified for the Champions Series final in Canada, but, hampered by the cyst on her ankle, finished last. Fox televised the event and showed three Russian women skate every last second of their long programs, even though none of them finished better than third behind Lipinski and Kwan. But when Kwiatkowski skated, Fox went with a Kwan feature that obliterated all but the final fifty-three seconds of Kwiatkowski's four-minute program.

Kwiatkowski got over it. She got over everything.

What taught her how to cope?

Skating.

"Life doesn't go as planned, ever," she said. "No one is going to hand you everything. There are times you may do a great job and still not get something. Skating teaches you all that. It teaches you a lot."

It was hard to figure out exactly what Scott Davis had learned from skating. His career was very different from Kwiatkowski's. There had been more pure talent, more international success, more acclaim, more puzzlement. He was a two-time national champion, a 1994 Olympian. The man who defeated Brian Boitano at the 1994 nationals. The best spinner in the world.

And then it all went up in smoke—and he found himself in exactly the same place Kwiatkowski did coming into 1998. On the outside, looking in.

"When I won my national titles, I didn't know any better. Then you win and you realize what you did and you ask yourself, 'Can I do it again?' You get distracted with things you have no control over—judges, money, medals—instead of focusing on what you can control—me, my confidence level, my skating."

Davis cringed when he heard the news that because of Dan Hollander's horrid qualifying round performance, the United States would be able to send only two men to the 1998 Olympic Games. That third spot, conventional wisdom said, was Davis's spot to fight for. If Todd Eldredge and Michael Weiss skated cleanly in Philadelphia, based on the results of the 1997 nationals and worlds, the first two spots were theirs.

Davis had an agent, International Management Group, and he knew if he didn't make the Olympic team, IMG would find him work on one of its tours. He had a high school diploma and a couple of years of college. He had a life. "Skating is a small part of the whole picture," he said. "When I'm eighty, I will look back on my life and skating will be a part of it, but there will be so much more."

Yet skating defined Davis. And in recent years, bad skating defined him. There were two moments in particular that signaled Davis's collapse. The first came at the Norway Olympics, when he was in fourth place after a slight mistake on his combination jump in the short program.

Two days separated the short program from the long. Davis spent a good portion of those two days thinking about what it would be like to win a medal, rather than thinking of skating cleanly.

"I can win a medal, I can do this, I can do that," he told himself.

Half a minute into his four-minute, thirty-second long program, he crashed on his first jump, a triple axel. He felt like someone punched him in the stomach. He finished eighth.

The second disaster came in 1995, after Davis qualified for the world championships in Birmingham, England.

He again got himself into position to win a medal in the short program, then made three mistakes in the long program and dropped to seventh.

Within the following year, Davis would suffer from vertigo, fail to qualify for the 1996 worlds, and leave his coach of nine years, Kathy Casey.

Casey and Davis were from the same hometown, Great Falls, Montana. Scott left home when he was fifteen to take lessons from Casey, who was working in Tacoma, Washington, then in Colorado Springs. Scott always was quite shy, and never said much. As Casey watched him self-destruct time and again, she wondered aloud what more she could do to help him.

It was perplexing. Here was the son of a high school assistant football coach who admitted he simply was not very competitive. When he got into position to win a medal at the worlds or Olympics, instead of moving in for the kill, his mind wandered and he fell apart. His career suffered from vertigo too; the higher he went, the worse he did and the faster he fell.

Finally, in the winter of 1996, after a fourth-place finish at nationals, Casey and Davis talked about their careers together.

"Do you want a change?" Casey asked him.

"Well, maybe," Davis said.

Davis and Casey were finished.

Davis was a glorious spinner in the days he won the 1993 and 1994 national titles, forcing Todd Eldredge to spend extra time on his spins to try to keep up. As a boy, Davis used to push himself to see how fast he could go, and he and the other skaters in the rink had a strange contest. Because of the centrifugal force created by spinning, small blood vessels often pop in a skater's arms. Davis used to love to see how many tiny vessels would pop on his arms, creating dots on the surface of his skin like chicken pox. He and the other skaters would compare dots; Davis sometimes had twenty or thirty on his arms.

As Davis prepared for the 1996 nationals, he began having problems with his spins. He grew disoriented out of a spin and took ten seconds to figure out where he was. He was in a restaurant with his choreographer of seven years, Brian Wright, who also was Michael Weiss's choreographer, when he shook his head and told Wright, "I see lots of you."

During one choreography session with Wright, he slipped going into a triple jump and landed on his back and head on the ice.

Doctors said it could be that all the spinning and jumping Davis had done in his career had caused the vertigo.

Davis's spins had not been the same since the vertigo, even though he said the condition never flared up again. He and Zmievskaia chose not to accentuate his spins in the program they built for 1996–97, and they avoided big spins again for the 1997–98 season. (They also avoided the dancing in front of the judges for 1998.) Few could figure it out. If it wasn't the vertigo, what was it?

Questions surrounded Davis as he headed into the Olympic season. Unlike Kwiatkowski, he was assigned two major international events: Skate America and NHK Trophy in Japan. Unlike Kwiatkowski, he wouldn't have to wait until the 1998 nationals to work on an Olympic berth. If he did well in the autumn events, he could put some pressure on Eldredge and Weiss. He could get the judges talking.

But never before had Davis been able to apply any pressure to anyone—except himself. He had never done a clean long program in competition. It was stunning. Never. He had never put it together when he had to for four and a half minutes.

But Davis still thought he could. After waiting through two decades of skating, why not?

"The perfect program still is out there," he said. "It's still attainable for me. To have the people on their feet, to skate that well. It's out there for me. Somewhere."

The Olympic Games were out there, somewhere, for Kwiatkowski too.

"You work your whole life to do something and you want to get it," Tonia said. "At least I'm giving it my best shot. If I don't make it, it's not the end of the world."

Her mother and Heiss, the women closest to Kwiatkowski, were not quite as matter-of-fact.

"I'd be so sad for her if she doesn't make it," Corinne Kwiatkowski said, her voice trailing off.

"I'd like her to have that experience," Heiss said. "I guess I'm not too old to dream."

Kwiatkowski thought of the Olympics, smiled, and shrugged.

"It would be a great way to end my career, but if it doesn't happen, I'll be fine. It's not like I don't have anything else to do."

PART IV

Fall 1997

THE OLYMPIC SEASON BEGINS

11

THE PENDULUM
SWINGS BACK

The lights were up in Detroit's Joe Louis Arena; the girls were warming up for the short program at Skate America. It was opening night of the Michelle and Tara show. Wearing their new dresses, arriving for the warm-up as if it were the first day of school, Kwan and Lipinski were about to unveil their new programs. The Olympic season was beginning right then and there, on that six-minute warm-up.

Tara Lipinski looked as steady as ever. Summertime had been kind to her. She had grown just an inch or so, and gained six pounds. The weight was well distributed; she was showing no signs of developing anywhere. With the Olympic Games less than four months away, Lipinski still was blessed with the perfect little jumping body. Mother Nature obviously was cooperating fully.

Michelle Kwan, on the other hand, was looking positively Nashville-esque.

Midway through the warm-up, she lifted off the ice for a triple lutz—and had to spin around to hold onto a precariously poor landing. She tried another lutz in the same corner of the rink. Her hand reached for the ice to prevent a fall. A few moments later, she stumbled over her feet. Finally, attempting a double axel in the middle of the ice, she slipped and fell.

Kwan stopped at center ice, hands on hips, and stared into space. What was going on? Could it possibly be happening again? Quickly, she shook her head. No! This was only the warm-up, she told herself.

It was no problem. That's what Frank Carroll would tell her if she glided over to see him by the boards. Don't worry. You're only warming up the jumps for the short program.

"You're thinking too much," Michelle Kwan told Michelle Kwan. "Just let your body do it."

Kwan had quite a few conversations with herself. And with Carroll. Some were very public: The two of them engaged in entertaining introspection in front of the media at a press conference two days earlier. They analyzed everything: the falling in Nashville, the stumble in Lausanne, the weather in Detroit.

"After last year, I asked myself, 'Why am I here if I don't love it? Why am I torturing myself?'" Kwan said. "As I go to sleep, I'm thinking, 'What's going to happen in four months? Am I going to be Olympic champion? . . . What happens if I trip on a spin? Oh my God, that could cost me the Olympic gold.'

"Then I say, 'Forget it, Michelle, how many times do you trip on a spin?'"

Carroll said he was trying to think of ways to become a better coach for Kwan, to try to help her become more positive and happy on the ice.

"What did you come up with?" a reporter asked.

"A lobotomy," Carroll chuckled.

"For her or you?"

"Both of us," he said. "We're going in for a group rate."

One reporter suggested afterward that they be given their own sitcom. Kwan and Carroll put on quite a show; and the fact that it all was so brazenly honest further endeared the two of them to reporters.

But those same journalists wondered: How could anyone who had so many thoughts bouncing around in her brain possibly shut them all out and skate perfectly on the ice? How could this inquisitive seventeen-year-old close out the world in the most important year of her life? Or was it conceivable that all the talking and thinking was good, that Kwan found her question-and-answer sessions to be helpful, even cathartic?

The answers would come where they always did. On the ice.

Two nights later, back in Joe Louis Arena for the short program, Kwan knew it was alright to make mistakes in the warm-up, but in twenty minutes she would skate for real, and she would have to clean up all those errors. In twenty minutes she would have to be perfect. If she wasn't, the horrors of competitions past would come back to haunt her. Each had a name: Nashville, Hamilton, Lausanne . . . and Detroit? Might the list grow and grow?

Kwan had been pointing toward this moment for months. She joked that she had been "hidden in a closet for a while," which meant that she had been working in seclusion in Lake Arrowhead, California, waiting to debut her new programs. She had RSVP'd for Skate America the moment the U.S. Figure Skating Association invited her in the summer. She couldn't wait for the season to begin.

"It's time to skate well," Kwan said, "and I know I will, because I feel really good."

After all those press conference doubts and concerns, Kwan simply uttered that sentence and smiled.

But while she entered the season with the highest hopes, she still was bothered by the stress fracture in the second toe of her left foot. It was on the mend, but still causing troubles. Kwan usually skated three forty-five-minute sessions a day at Lake Arrowhead. Prior to Skate America, she could handle only two.

Yet no one outside the Kwan camp knew this. Even Frank Carroll found out only a few weeks earlier. The injury was a secret.

"Why make excuses?" Danny Kwan asked.

Tara Lipinski was gunning for Skate America too, even if her camp had been far less anxious to come than Kwan's. There was an unwritten rule in skating that top competitors didn't meet until the end of the season, at the nationals or Champions Series final. But this was the dawning of the 1998 Olympic season, and it was unprecedented to find two national and world champions from the same country returning to skate against each other. The USFSA knew it had something special going on in 1997–98; it wanted the two Olympic gold-medal favorites on the same ice at the same time at its big autumn event.

For both skaters, there was a risk in showing up. As long as the two did not meet, each skater—and each of their agents—could claim the title of gold medal favorite. But by meeting early in the year, one would emerge as the leader in the race for the Olympic gold medal, and the other would fall a step or two behind.

Lipinski's camp felt this pressure most of all, and took its time to decide if it wanted to travel thirty minutes down I-75 from the Detroit Skating Club to Joe Louis Arena to meet Kwan.

But Tara came, and, at 9:35 P.M. on Friday, October 24, 1997, the Olympic season officially began for Michelle Kwan and Tara Lipinski. That's when they stepped onto the ice at Joe Louis to begin their warm-up. Kwan would be the third skater of the group, Lipinski the fourth. There were eleven women in the field—from Russia, Japan, France, and elsewhere—but there were only two who really mattered: Michelle and Tara.

Lipinski popped out from backstage in a new dress made of frilly light-yellow lace with a blue dirndl-style vest. She was skating to the soundtrack from the children's animated movie *Anastasia*.

More than two hundred media credentials were requested for the competition, and one of them was hanging around the neck of Jere Longman of the *New York Times*. He took one look at Lipinski's outfit and blurted out, "Tara's saying, 'I'm going to my first communion and I intend to yodel.' "

He wrote those words in the *Times*. Philip Hersh printed the comment in the *Chicago Tribune,* and later described the costume as "something the youngest Von Trapp child might wear in *The Sound of Music.*" Never had a skater's costume been critiqued so severely so quickly.

When he saw the articles, Mike Burg, Lipinski's agent, pointedly suggested that the journalists see the movie before they picked on Lipinski.

"Do you think the Hungarian or Ukrainian judge at the Olympics is going to see the movie?" the reporters replied.

The controversy over the dress showed that everything the two teenagers did would be scrutinized in the Olympic year. Everything. Seasoned journalists who were required to analyze the behavior of millionaire athletes in other big-time sports were not going to spare a teenager from this criticism. The high school–aged girls had come into the public eye because they or their parents wanted to be there. It was their choice to compete in the most popular Olympic sport of all. Once Tara Lipinski and Michelle Kwan and all the other skaters stepped off the sidewalk and joined the parade, they were fair game for reporters.

There also was a valid reason for the journalists to bring up Tara's outfit. After all the criticism of Tara's little-girl image at the world championships in March, she was dressed, interestingly enough, as a little girl.

As the warm-up ended and the skaters left the ice, Kwan calmly looked into Frank Carroll's eyes. While she put on her skate guards and climbed off the ice, they spoke briefly about the troubles she had had on each jump.

"It's the warm-up," Carroll said. "It's no big deal. You're supposed to warm up, and you just did."

In no time at all, Kwan was back on the ice for real. Dressed in a sleeveless red-and-cream dress, she took a deep breath and waited for her music, those two dramatic pieces of piano music by Rachmaninoff, to begin.

Skaters always feel pressure in the short program because of the deductions that must be taken if mistakes are made. But for Kwan, the pressure was worse. She absolutely had to perform well to reassert herself as the favorite, and to remind herself of just how good she could be when she didn't fall or stumble out of triple jumps. If she made a mistake in that short program, the next would be that much more difficult. And so on. And so on.

"Just let go," Carroll told her by the boards as she went off to skate. He looked calm, but his stomach was churning. He always got tense when Kwan skated. And he felt especially nervous as Kwan glided into the most important element of the short program: the triple lutz combination jump.

Carroll steadied himself with technical thoughts.

"Is she standing up straight?"

"Is she leaning or going up crooked?"

But technique only went so far. He also said a little prayer.

"It's in your hands, God."

Praying, in the end, was all a coach could do as his skater sped into the corner for the triple lutz.

Twenty-seven seconds into her short program in Detroit, Kwan glided into that triple lutz, using the old, familiar, long-line approach on her trusty SP-Teri skates. She flew through the air without hesitation. She landed solidly, straight up and tall, then picked into the ice with her left foot for a smooth double toe loop. The landings on the two jumps were as precise as they had been in 1996, her world championship year. She had what she wanted: a clean combination.

Kwan effortlessly flew through the rest of the two-minute, forty-second program. A satisfied smile—not a wide grin, but an assured smile—appeared as she landed her other jumps, the double axel and the triple toe loop, with ease. She soared into a long, lingering spiral that glided on one edge of her blade, then another, before she finished.

"Exquisite," Dick Button gushed into the ABC microphone. "Gentle, light . . . effortless."

"Inspired skating," added Peggy Fleming.

Delighted, Kwan raised her arms as the sparse crowd stood and cheered. She was back. It was that simple. One clean short program in a pressure-packed situation was the antidote to Kwan's "coma," as she laughingly called it, of the previous February and March.

She joined Carroll in Kiss and Cry to see her marks as Lipinski shot onto the ice to get ready for her turn in the short program. The first set of scores, the technical marks, were all 5.7s and 5.8s. Good. Solid. Just what she and Carroll expected.

Then came the marks for presentation:

"5.9, 5.9, 5.9, 5.9, 5.9, 5.9. 5.9, 5.9, 5.9."

It was as if the judges hung a banner from the rafters of the arena: "Welcome back, Michelle!"

The scores were stunning, almost surreal. With the reigning world champion biding her time on the ice, yet to skate at the opening event of the Olympic season, the judges had gone wild over someone else.

Although Lipinski told herself to ignore the scores as they were read over the public-address system, the judges already had put Kwan back on top of their sport. Tara had never received such high scores internationally. There was no way she was going to beat those marks. For all intents and purposes, the short program was over before Lipinski skated.

That's how nine international judges welcomed Lipinski back from her summer vacation: They held a Michelle Kwan lovefest.

In the corner of the stands, sitting by herself near an entrance way, was Kwan's choreographer, Lori Nichol. Nichol, who had driven in from Toronto for the weekend, sat strategically near an entrance so she could get up and walk around the concourse without bothering anyone if her nerves got to her as Kwan skated.

Nichol never left her seat.

From the moment Kwan took the ice in the warm-up to the split second she finished the short program, Nichol concentrated on nothing but her skater. She wasn't particularly worried about the stumbles in the warm-up. But the short program was something else. That was a big deal for Nichol. After keeping both the short and long programs under wraps for months, her work was out in the open for the entire world to see.

When Kwan finished the short program, Nichol smiled and nodded her head.

"She's baaaack," Nichol said to herself with a laugh.

Nichol had felt great about the short program from that second time Kwan ran through it in the summer. Her instincts had been confirmed.

And when the scores came up, and that row of 5.9s flashed from the scoreboard, Nichol nodded once again.

The judges got it, she said to herself.

They understood the program—and they really liked it, Nichol thought.

She had one other thought.

"It would have been great to see a 6.0."

Don't get greedy, Nichol told herself. Be patient. Kwan was only going to perform the program better and better throughout the season.

Next, Tara Lipinski moved into position. There was nothing more frightening for a skater than standing alone on the ice, waiting for the crowd to quiet, waiting for the music to begin, waiting to start skating. With those 5.9s echoing in her ears, Tara had to go out and begin *her* season. The wait was only a few seconds, but it was excruciating. She wanted to plow right into her program; she wanted to show that she, too, was ready for the Olympic year. Standing on the ice, as the selections from *Anastasia* rang through the arena, Lipinski pushed every thought out of her mind, every doubt, every worry, and began to skate.

She was her bubbly self, and, as usual, performed more difficult jumps than Kwan or anyone else. She wobbled slightly on her combination spin near the end, but otherwise she was solid. It was a delightful start.

What happened next, however, was quite ominous for the diminutive world champion.

Even though Lipinski had the tougher jumps, her marks for the required elements were below Kwan's on six of the judges' scorecards. She received a 5.5 from the German judge, and four 5.6s. The bobble on the spin had been noticed, but, even so, those were remarkably low marks for the returning world champion. Especially for a girl known as a technical marvel.

She must have made another mistake, journalists said to themselves. But what was it?

No one could figure it out.

The artistic marks appeared, and they plunged in comparison to Kwan's:

"5.7, 5.8, 5.7, 5.8, 5.7, 5.8, 5.7, 5.7, 5.8."

One judge, the Japanese judge, judge No. 4, gave first place to Tara. The other eight went for Michelle.

How overwhelming was Kwan's victory? The seventh judge, from Russia, gave Kwan 5.8, 5.9. She gave Lipinski 5.6, 5.7. The gap between the two was so wide mathematically that the judge could have placed more than a dozen skaters between them.

Dick Button wasn't judging, but his television analysis was just as devastating for Lipinski:

"Tara just does not quite have the fulfillment, the maturity, the charm and the joy that Michelle has."

Tara Lipinski didn't understand the scores. What were they doing to her, the reigning world champion? She wanted to go into the press conference after the short program at Skate America and sit beside Michelle Kwan and say she was confused, and throw the issue right back at the judges. She and her parents and Mike Burg talked about it before she went into the press conference, but they decided against it. Tara instead calmly sat beside Michelle and said all the right things.

An example: "I see the first competition as a big hill. I just want to get over it and it starts the season for me."

And: "I've been working so hard and I was really happy with tonight."

There was no reason to get mad at the judges two minutes and forty seconds into the season.

Nonetheless, Lipinski was perplexed. Somewhere between those serendipitous days of March in Switzerland and the cool days of October in Detroit, she began to believe she was the best skater in the world.

Burg had sent out a press packet that read: "Tara Lipinski is America's premier skating star . . . national champion, world champion, Olympic hopeful . . . and getting better every day."

Lipinski had let her true feelings slip at a press conference the day before the short program, when she said that having a competitor (Kwan) "right under you always pushes you."

She truly believed Kwan was beneath her. But Lipinski was mistaken; Kwan never had been underneath her. She always had been in control. That was the lesson of Nashville, of Hamilton, of Lausanne. If Kwan skated flawlessly, she should win every time, because she was the skating package the judges—and the sport—wanted most of all. She could jump, and she had become elegant on the ice. Kwan nearly won the world championships despite a key mistake in the short program. Kwan won the long program at worlds despite doubling one of her last triple jumps.

Had the Lipinski gang forgotten this?

The sad fact for Lipinski was that she would win only when Kwan let her win.

Just as Carol Heiss had predicted seven months earlier in the Geneva Airport, the pendulum was swinging back. Kwan made it easy for the judges, because she skated exquisitely. But the judges also were beginning to scrutinize Tara more critically. In February and March 1997 she shot like a rocket to the top of her sport and gave the judges very little time to look at her jumps, to really analyze her. At Skate America, the judges had the time to watch her closely. The Skate America judges were an entirely different group of judges from the ones at nationals or worlds. Nonetheless, they started to look for Tara Lipinski's faults.

Figure skating, Frank Carroll said after the competition, was more than a jumping contest.

"Michelle's footwork in the short program and her spiral sequence in the short program are equally as difficult as the triple lutz–triple toe loop," he said. "There are more things besides triple-jumping that are difficult in skating. We seem to be sidetracked and thinking only jumping is difficult. I don't think there's a girl in the world who could do that spiral sequence except Michelle."

Obviously, the judges agreed.

It was just the first night of a long season, but already the pressure was getting to the people closest to the two American girls. When Kwan skated, Shep Goldberg, her agent, paced in one concourse entrance to the stands, while Mike Burg paced in his entrance on the other side of the arena when Lipinski skated. Neither man could sit down. And it was only October.

After the event, in the dimly lighted bowels of the arena, Jack and Pat Lipinski were having an intense chat with Richard Callaghan by the loading dock. The conversation went on for dozens of minutes, long after all the spectators had gone home. The Lipinskis were concerned about the judges' marks for their daughter, and they also were not pleased that Callaghan had arrived three minutes late to Tara's afternoon practice session that day. The reason Callaghan was running late also was a problem for them; he had been with Todd Eldredge attending a series of media interviews arranged for reporters through Eldredge's agent. "I got stuck behind a garbage truck," Callaghan said. "I plead guilty to being three minutes late."

This was just another reminder to the Lipinskis that their coach—the man they selected on their nationwide search after the well-known breakup with their former coach—was responsible for another skater as well as Tara, a skater whom he had coached for sixteen years at that point. Callaghan would try hard to please the Lipinskis, and would go out of his way to make sure he was giving Tara equal time in practice, but he could not devote all his time to one skater. And everyone who knew Callaghan knew his devotion to Todd Eldredge was unshakable.

The Lipinskis understood, but they weren't entirely happy with the situation. Whenever they looked at the kind, protective, fatherly way Frank Carroll took care of Michelle Kwan, they saw something their daughter did not have. Although Carroll coached other skaters back at Lake Arrowhead, Kwan was his one and only Olympic medal prospect. The devotion and affection the two had for one another was obvious to everyone—including Tara's parents. It also was a fact that Kwan and Carroll had been together for nearly six years, which covered most of Kwan's competitive career.

The Lipinskis longed for Carroll-esque loyalty from Callaghan, but they could not get it. They had been with Callaghan not even two years at that point, and they had a history of not staying anywhere very long, having already moved from Houston to Delaware to Detroit in four years. Loyalty in figure skating had to be earned over years, not months.

But even in paradise, there was grumbling. As Danny Kwan pushed open an arena door to head back to the Westin Hotel after his daughter's magnificent short program, he shook his head.

"She's too nervous. She's too nervous," he said as he slipped outside into the chilly night air.

Ever so slowly, the Michelle–Tara battle was driving the parents a little bit crazy.

The next evening, Saturday night, was the long program. Kwan once again skated before Lipinski, this time with one skater between them.

Three days earlier, Kwan revealed to reporters at her press conference that her long program was skated to *Lyra Angelica,* composer William Alwyn's concerto for harp and string orchestra.

"What was that again?" one sports writer asked.

Carroll and Kwan took out a piece of paper and spelled the name for the journalists.

"It represents freedom and a lightness on the ice," Kwan explained. "I hope everyone will see the joy I have in skating."

As Kwan skated onto the ice for the long program and simply stood still, with her arms by her side, Lori Nichol thought her heart would jump out of her chest.

She was sitting twenty rows up from the judges, trying to look at the program the way they would see it at ice level. She was not on the aisle, but one seat in. A friend of hers was in the aisle seat. If she had to get up to pace or walk around, Nichol knew she could leap over her friend and escape without causing a scene. There must have been a shrink sitting at a booth in the concourse somewhere, just waiting for all the agents and parents and choreographers to come by.

But, once again, she was able to sit still.

"Listen to the music," Frank Carroll told Kwan on the ice. "Just let yourself go. Have fun."

His advice was similar to the words Janet Lynn's coach, Slavka Kohout, told her in the 1960s and 1970s before she skated: "Go out and tell a story."

Kwan drew spontaneous applause at least five times for intricate footwork, difficult spins, or an elegant spiral. Who knew that American crowds even recognized spins and footwork anymore, what with all the jumping going on?

Two and a half minutes into the program, Kwan spun in one direction, then another, then back again the other way, something no one else in the world tried. It was like trying to write with the wrong hand. She bobbled slightly, but it was a bold attempt, and certainly worthy of the recognition a triple jump received.

Of course, Kwan did plenty of those too. She landed seven triples, including two difficult triple lutzes.

The scores from the judges were consistent: all 5.8s for technical merit and all 5.9s for presentation. It had become her mathematical mantra: "5.9, 5.9, 5.9 . . ."

The grand debut of the program that Nichol, Carroll, and Kwan created for the 1998 Olympics went off without a hitch.

But Kwan's long program was not beloved by everyone. "It didn't have quite the impact that the short program did," Button said on ABC.

Other critics were so used to seeing Kwan play a dramatic role that they didn't know what to think when she just *skated*.

But Kwan knew exactly what to make of it.

"When I'm eighty years old and I'm looking back [at the Olympic year], I don't want to see Salome or any character, I want to see me."

Carroll stood in the dark hallway under the stands and exclaimed that he was "absolutely delighted both programs got standing ovations.

"That's a real tricky thing at the beginning of the year," he said. "When you work on them, it doesn't mean that they're going to go over. They can bomb. You can pick the wrong music or people won't react the way you want them to. I'm just delighted that they seemed to go over so well."

But Nichol wasn't entirely satisfied. It was her job to critique her own work from her seat twenty rows up from the judges. And there were things she saw in the program that she did not like. The minute-long slow section in the middle of the program, which featured footwork and intricate hand and arm movements, particularly bothered her.

"It's not grabbing me by the throat and pulling me in," she said to herself.

It wasn't Kwan's fault.

If fingers had to be pointed, Nichol said, blame the choreographer.

"My work was not up to the standards I had set for myself," she said. "She's better than the vehicle I provided her. When I work, I call it the 'gasp' factor. I didn't feel that the program made you gasp."

Nichol wasn't certain what to do, so she and Carroll talked about it after the performance. They knew that Michelle already had performed the program hundreds of times in practice over the previous six months. Changing things less than four months from the Olympics was risky. They discussed Kwan's comfort level, her muscle memory.

Why not leave it as is?

On the other hand, they knew it could be better.

Didn't they want to give Kwan the best possible program for the Olympic Games?

Carroll and Nichol decided that weekend that they would not make a hard-and-fast decision. They absolutely wanted to make the changes, but they wouldn't force the issue. Michelle had enough to worry about with her injured toe and the building pressures of the Olympic year. If a chance to work on the long program presented itself, they would take it. If not, they would live with the program as it was.

But within weeks, Nichol realized she couldn't do that. Even though these were subtle things—little nuances that a casual observer might not even notice—they bothered Nichol.

The slow part had to be changed, she told herself.

How she would present it to Michelle, and when she would do it, she had no idea.

Back on the ice, Kwan was finished, and Tara Lipinski, the toughest competitor in the sport, was in trouble even before she skated. How could she beat Kwan with those scores?

She tried. She definitely tried.

Did she try too hard?

Eighty seconds into her program, she drew back her right leg, slammed her toe pick into the ice, and muscled into her triple lutz. Coming down, she crashed to the ice. Tara hadn't fallen in almost a year. It was a shock to see her on the ice.

Then, near the end of her program, she got tangled up in a sequence of triple jumps with a hop between them and ended her program three seconds too late. When her music, the soundtrack from the movie *The Rainbow,* stopped, she was still spinning. She hit her ending pose and threw her left arm into the air in deafening silence.

Peggy Fleming suppressed a nervous laugh on air as Dick Button rushed to explain the problem. It was an embarrassing moment. Rarely was a top skater so far off her music.

The fall on the triple lutz undoubtedly slowed her down, but, by late October, Lipinski was a confused little skater. Sandra Bezic gave her the programs, Susie Wynne helped Tara interpret them, ballet teacher Marina Sheffer added her artistic advice, and coach Richard Callaghan offered his thoughts.

There were all kinds of voices filling Tara Lipinski's head.

Lipinski's scores for her long program were 5.6s, 5.7s, and 5.8s. She lost all nine judges to Kwan. There was no need to question the marks. They were exactly what they should have been. Second place was where she belonged.

Lipinski shrugged and took her defeat quite well.

"I just made one mistake," she said. "I was glad I came back strong afterward. This gives me something to work for. It's a good spot for me."

Kwan and Carroll, on the other hand, were thrilled.

"Wow!" Kwan said. "Yes! I did it! Every time I landed a jump solidly, I looked forward to the next. By the time I knew it, I was at the end.

"I feel different this year. I have more to skate for, I have so much more love for the sport. Last year, I didn't love it as much. Now, it's back again. I love it more than I ever did."

Immediately, there were signs of distress in the Lipinski camp. Tara canceled a planned appearance at the U.S. Olympic Committee's media day in Salt Lake City, which was to be the day after Skate America ended. Kwan and Carroll went and were the hit of the event. Kwan appeared on the front page of the local paper. And Carroll, ecstatic over the triumphant return of his skater, mused about the changes in Kwan from one year to the next.

"She now has a woman's body, and a beautiful one," he said. "It was a kid's body, flat everywhere. Now, it isn't flat. Michelle felt uncomfortable jumping and didn't know why. The whole balance changed. She wasn't at ease. Every time she put it on the line and went out to compete, there was fear involved."

Nichol drove home, quite pleased overall with what she had witnessed—except for that bothersome minute in the long program.

"This is just confirmation of what I knew in August," she said. "That Michelle felt good, and if Michelle feels good, there's nothing she can't do."

In raw sports terminology, it was a blowout. Michelle Kwan had demolished Tara Lipinski.

Said one member of the chagrined Lipinski camp, "We probably shouldn't have faced Michelle this early."

In the men's competition, Todd Eldredge was expected to win easily.

He did win.

But it was an adventure.

His right shoulder popped out of its socket when he tripped over an ice chip during the warm-up for the long program, but he popped it right back in as he lay on the ice and came back to compete ten minutes later. He skated gingerly but still landed five triples and won easily, receiving a 6.0 for courage—if not artistry—from the Canadian judge, his first ever in a real competition.

For Eldredge, who writhed in pain on the ice for four minutes as he was being helped by Richard Callaghan and medical personnel, the freak injury brought back horrible memories of Olympic years past.

"Lying there for a while, I was thinking about a lot of things," he said.

In 1992, a back injury forced him to miss the nationals (Olympic trials) and gave him such trouble that he finished tenth at the Olympic Games. In 1994, he passed out two days before the short program at nationals due to the flu, and failed to qualify for the U.S. team.

"I'm sure [he thought it was happening again]," said Callaghan, who walked onto the ice to assist Eldredge. "He didn't say it, but I'm sure."

Doctors told Eldredge he had a severely sprained shoulder and would have to miss several days of training, at the very least.

His mind wandered: "How bad is it? Will it affect the rest of the season?"

One question he did not ask was "Why me?" the famous words Nancy Kerrigan cried out after being hit on the knee in Detroit at the 1994 nationals.

"We're in the wrong building for that," Eldredge said with a smile.

He fell in Joe Louis. Kerrigan had been practicing next door at Cobo Arena when she was attacked.

One of the many people to praise Eldredge was Alexei Mishin, the Russian mastermind who was in Detroit not with the ailing Alexei Urmanov, but with one of his bright young stars, fourteen-year-old Evgeni Plushenko.

Mishin nodded toward Callaghan and said, "His skater was the hero today."

But Mishin also knew that he had witnessed quite a debut for Plushenko, his "very skinny chicken." Plushenko finished a surprising second, defeating Scott Davis, who dropped to fourth after making mistakes on all three of his triple axels in the short and long programs.

On the first triple axel he attempted in his new long program, Davis popped it into a single in midair, at which time a woman in the audience screamed—for no apparent reason. It was believed to be the first single axel–scream combination in the history of the sport.

"She must have thought I did something good," Davis said. "But that really wasn't good."

He was not at all pleased with his fourth-place showing, including being beaten by a kid born in November 1982.

"In previous competitions, I'd be sad," said Mr. Fourth Place. "This time, I was angry. I wanted to show everybody I was still alive. I don't know if I accomplished that or not."

As for Mishin, he showed that, as a coach, he was very much alive—and that he was the master of turning out skaters who could step in for other skaters and not miss a beat. If Urmanov couldn't perform because of his injured groin muscle, Mishin brought someone else to Detroit from the rink in St. Petersburg—and took home second place with him.

Plushenko was so green, even Mishin wasn't certain how high he could soar. Too young to shave, Plushenko was the only male skater flexible enough to be able to pull off the difficult "Biellmann Spin," in which a skater holds one foot above his or her head while spinning.

"His mother pulled him and pulled him and one day, he did the Biellmann Spin," Mishin said playfully.

Mishin also cautioned reporters not to count out Plushenko for the second spot on the Russian Olympic team, after his very own Alexei Yagudin, of course—or Urmanov, if he ever got healthy. Mishin loved touting his young, unknown skaters from the rink far away; he loved toying with Western journalists.

And, most of all, he loved being right.

Prior to Skate America, one silly yet prophetic battle took place in an unusual ice skating venue: Daytona Beach, Florida.

It was a U.S. Figure Skating Association pro-am, the men against the women, held in early October, the first time most of the skaters had seen one another since the tour ended in July.

During a practice session, as Tara Lipinski and Richard Callaghan talked beside the boards, Michelle Kwan flew into the air and landed a triple loop–triple loop combination several feet away.

"That's *my* combination," a stunned Lipinski told Callaghan.

Callaghan smiled. Later, he told Jo-Ann Barnas of the *Detroit Free Press* how he explained to his young skater that "there's no patent on jumps."

Kwan was trying the triple loop–triple loop because the loop was a jump that did not hurt her injured left toe. The more common and easier triple combination—the triple toe loop–triple toe loop—bothered her too much to try.

Ironically, because she was injured, Kwan actually was practicing more difficult jumps.

In the meaningless competition, something else surprised Lipinski and Callaghan. Kwan received all 6.0s but one for her short and show programs. But Lipinski's scores were not as strong, dipping as low as 5.7s and 5.8s for presentation.

And this was the kind of competition where forty-one-year-old Dorothy Hamill would receive all 6.0s for simply stepping onto the ice.

Something strange was going on, Callaghan said.

"It bothered me. I didn't think it was accurate. I disagreed, but it's not the first time I've disagreed. I felt Tara skated great and as world champion, I would have liked to have seen some higher marks. I felt Tara was undermarked."

Kwan and Lipinski were dueling on many fronts in the autumn of 1997.

A press release came from the office of Shep Goldberg on September 29:

"The first marks of the season are in and with scores ranging from 3.5 to 4.0 you would think Michelle Kwan would be unhappy. On the contrary. The seventeen-year-old skating champion is thrilled because the marks refer not to her skating prowess but to her high school grades."

The release announced Kwan's grade point average (GPA) for the eleventh grade as 3.8, with her cumulative high school GPA at 3.53.

It went on to say Kwan's classes for her senior year were English, French, U.S. government, economics, and computer science. She planned to graduate on time in June 1998 and was expressing interest in attending Harvard.

"So will Kwan bring her books and schoolwork to the '98 Winter Olympics?" the release concluded.

" 'Absolutely,' she says. 'Conjugating French verbs will help me relax.' "

Responded *Los Angeles Times* sports columnist Randy Harvey: "It certainly hasn't helped Surya Bonaly."

Bonaly, the veteran French skater, continued to have problems throughout the autumn and was fighting to make the French Olympic team for a third consecutive time.

Asked if he was going to respond with his own press release on his tenth grader's grade point average, Mike Burg laughed and said no.

But he did not miss a beat the previous month when, after a media day at the Detroit Skating Club, reporters piled into their rental cars and drove to the Lipinskis' home to witness a momentous event: Tara being tutored.

There was also the battle of the bookshelves. Both teenagers already had written their memoirs. The children's books looked alike, with similar crowd-pleasing titles: Kwan's *Heart of a Champion*, and Lipinski's *Triumph on Ice*.

Kwan's book was more thoughtful and introspective; Lipinski's, lighter and childlike.

Skate America was the first event in the six-competition Champions Series, which served as a traveling, worldwide, pre-Olympic warm-up. The circuit moved to Germany the next week for the event called Nations Cup.

There, Elvis Stojko unveiled his new programs and won over the hearts of the judges for the first time in months, easily winning the men's event. He landed the year's first quadruple toe loop and seven triples overall.

Michael Weiss and Audrey Weisiger were there too. It had been an eventful autumn already for Weiss; on September 28, he and Lisa Thornton were married in the Virgin Islands. There were some people in skating who, when they gossiped, happened to wonder why the twenty-one-year-old Weiss was getting married so close to the Olympic Games.

Weisiger, who had as much riding on Weiss's devotion to skating as anyone, reminded her sport's busybodies that Weiss had the right to do whatever he wanted with his life.

"He's happy," she said. "If he's happy, I'm happy."

Weiss perplexed skating's gossips. He was so different from the stereotypically single-minded athlete, it scared them. They couldn't control him. It drove them crazy.

Weiss laughed when he thought about the gossip he was generating. And he also knew if he landed his quadruple lutz, all the doubters would think the marriage was the greatest idea ever.

Weisiger sat at the bar in her hotel in Gelsenkirchen, Germany, on Thursday night, October 30, and ordered herself a glass of champagne. Surrounded by Germans, she felt a little self-conscious celebrating alone.

That afternoon in practice, Weiss landed a quad lutz, the most difficult jump in figure skating history. It was just a practice session, not a competition, but Weisiger saw it. What's more, Lisa captured it on her video camera in the stands.

Clean. Not two-footed. Perfect.

Weisiger was not celebrating the quad lutz by itself, however. She smiled to herself. She had been coaching Weiss for thirteen years, the entire time he had been skating. With the four-revolution jump, she had taught one skater—Weiss—a single, a double, a triple, and a quadruple of the same jump. How many coaches could say that?

During the competition, however, Weiss made mistakes. He was fourth in the short program because he backed off his triple axel–triple toe loop combination and did only a double toe loop. He tried the quad lutz in the long program, skated to Beethoven, but stumbled badly and put both hands to the ice. He made a few other mistakes and actually dropped a place to fifth.

It made sense in a way: Beethoven's Fifth.

There was one reporter at the event for the Associated Press who said Weiss tried a triple lutz and fell. Not a quadruple. A triple.

USA Today took the wire service's report and printed it.

A triple lutz.

So did other publications. That was embarrassing to Weiss. He landed triple lutzes in his sleep.

But this wasn't just a tiny error to be ignored and forgotten. It could have become a big problem for Weiss. Word-of-mouth meant everything in a sport where events were televised weeks later on tape delay. Lisa Thornton Weiss was so concerned that judges might get confused and think Weiss was slipping that she called the U.S. Figure Skating Association to make sure the word was out that it was a quad he tried, not a triple.

The Weisses had had experience with these kinds of mistakes. A few years earlier at the nationals, one judge mistook his attempt at a quadruple toe loop for a triple. Falling on a quad was a badge of honor in skating; falling on a triple was an invitation to disaster.

There were two grand plans working for Weiss at the same time in the autumn of 1997.

The first was Weisiger's four-year plan for his skating success. Weiss didn't just happen into Beethoven for the Olympic year. Back in 1995, Weisiger plotted a specific course for Weiss. She had him skate to Mozart in 1995, followed by two years of Carlos Santana. It was important to her, as it was to Frank Carroll and Lori Nichol, to try something new every year to broaden her skater's artistic reach. Weisiger and Weiss ran the gamut from 1995 to 1998, but ended smartly and safely with the bold, classical composer for the Olympics. Santana was fine for 1997. But not 1998.

There was a plan off the ice for Weiss as well. After splitting with agent Jerry Solomon in June, he signed with Advantage International, a major sports marketing and management firm near Tyson's Corner, Virginia, just five miles from Weiss's rink. Advantage represented Olympians, including Bonnie Blair and Matt Biondi, but it never had worked with a figure skater.

After signing him in October, Advantage kicked off its representation of Weiss in its fourteenth-floor boardroom overlooking the Virginia urban sprawl on a cold and damp day in mid-November. Sixteen people were seated at the boardroom table. Six were from Advantage. Five came from Team Weiss: Audrey Weisiger, Michael, Lisa, and Michael's parents, Greg and Margie Weiss. And five were reporters.

They had the media outnumbered.

Advantage was as perplexed as Weiss about the mixup on the quad lutz in newspapers around the world.

"We thought we were going to have to get our message out to the sports community," Advantage's Tom George said of trying to sell a figure skater. "We didn't realize we had to inform the skating community first."

By trying the quad lutz, Weisiger and Weiss were going against all conventional skating wisdom. This didn't bother them. In fact, it was their specific goal.

Weiss was landing only one out of ten a day in practice, two-footing or falling out of the other nine. A 10 percent success ratio is awful on a jump. There wasn't a coach in the country who would put a jump into a program with that kind of percentage; 75 to 80 percent is more like it.

Except Weisiger.

"I don't want him to just hit a home run," she said. "I want him to knock the cover off the ball."

Weiss said he didn't care. He trusted Weisiger. He loved the thrill of trying something new. She sent him out at the world junior championships in 1994 and told him to do a triple axel combination when he never had landed one in competition in his life. And he did it. So why not try a quad lutz for 1998?

Weiss's success rate even went up to two out of three, or two out of four, in practice sessions at competitions.

"The thing I've always relied on is adrenaline," he said.

The bottom line was: They knew he wouldn't have a chance to

reach the medal podium in Nagano without it. He needed the jump "as something to separate myself from the other guys doing quads," Weiss said. "I can't just go twelve rounds with the champion. I have to knock out the champion."

While Stojko triumphed and Weiss bombed in Germany, a once familiar face reemerged as a major player in the women's competition heading into the Olympics.

Another Tanja.

For eighteen months, Tanja Szewczenko of Germany slept sixteen hours a day, her face gray and swollen. She had to stay indoors during the day because the sun hurt her eyes. When she tried to read a book, she would forget what she had read the minute she turned the page. She cried when she watched the 1997 world figure skating championships on television. After winning the 1994 world bronze medal, she thought she probably would never skate again.

She couldn't walk up a flight of stairs without having to rest. She once told her mother she thought she would die.

For months, doctors were puzzled, unable to help, until an immunologist figured out what was wrong. She was suffering from Epstein-Barr and Coxsackie B, two life-threatening viral infections that had spread to her heart.

Szewczenko's treatment was extreme. Each Friday, she flew from her home in Dortmund, Germany, to Munich. One week, doctors would remove some of her blood and treat it. The next week, the blood would be put back into her body. Medical bills neared $100,000. Her family almost lost its home.

Skating people had been wondering what happened to the beautiful young German skater. She had had a foot injury, but that was all anyone knew. The woman best known for colliding with Oksana Baiul during practice before the women's long program at the Norway Olympic Games had simply disappeared.

Then, she won Nations Cup—and the $30,000 first-place prize money—with a stirring and nearly flawless performance. Overnight, she was reborn. This was the European woman for whom international skating judges had been waiting: twenty years old, gorgeous, and still able to land a triple lutz.

Fox television analyst and ex-skater Christopher Bowman said it best: It looked like Szewczenko had "jumped out of the pages of Cosmo, not off of a hospital bed."

* * *

The next week, Michelle Kwan went to Skate Canada in Halifax, Nova Scotia, where she won the short program with seven 5.9s and took the long and the overall title with three more 5.9s.

The fact that she received any 5.9s in the long program was stunning, because she did not skate well. She doubled two triple jumps and fell on her final move, a flying butterfly spin.

"A dead butterfly," she called it.

She still won and collected the $30,000 first-place money—to go along with the $30,000 she earned at Skate America—because almost everyone else fell too. In all, there were sixteen falls among the dozen women in the four-minute long program. The only competitor who didn't fall was Surya Bonaly, who finished third.

"There haven't been this many unfortunate collisions with ice since the Titanic lost an edge," wrote Canadian sports journalist Steve Milton.

"There's something wrong with this picture," Canadian figure skating association chief David Dore told the Toronto Globe & Mail. "Do we really want to come and watch all that falling? I defy anyone to sit there and enjoy it."

Frank Carroll thought there was something wrong with this picture too. By the midpoint of the season, Carroll and Danny Kwan were having a disagreement over Michelle's schedule, especially because she still was dealing with her injured toe, which remained a private matter.

Kwan wasn't originally slated to go to Skate Canada. Her two Champions Series events were Skate America and NHK Trophy on the Olympic ice in Nagano. But top skaters were allowed to enter a third event not for series points, but for experience and prize money. That's what Danny Kwan decided to do—enter Michelle in Skate Canada.

Kwan also received an appearance fee reported to be as high as $100,000 to go to the event and bolster a weak field for television ratings on Fox.

"Fox requested that Michelle do it," Danny Kwan said. "They wanted the top American to go there."

Carroll said he didn't know about the money and, furthermore, he didn't care about the money. He didn't want Michelle to go to Skate Canada, and when Danny and Michelle both insisted upon it, Carroll refused to go with her. While his Olympic gold medal favorite was in Canada, Carroll spent the week at the USFSA's Southwest Pacific regional competition in Anaheim, California, with fourteen unheralded skaters he also coached.

"She was not slated to do it and she didn't have to do it and she had an injury to her foot," Carroll said. "I chose to go with the students I coach who were at the biggest competition of their year. I didn't want to go see Michelle skate a competition she didn't have to go to and I didn't want her to go to."

So Danny Kwan accompanied his daughter to Skate Canada as her "coach," and whenever they were asked, they said Carroll simply had a conflict and had to be with his young skaters in California.

Another American woman showed up in Canada—sort of. Nicole Bobek made her Champions Series debut there, and fell on her triple lutz in the short program to wipe out any chance for a top finish. She ended up fifth. Later, she would go to Cup of Russia, fall on the easy triple toe loop, and finish sixth.

"I'd rather get the bad stuff out of the way now and save the good things for nationals and the Olympics," she said.

There was no reason for Bobek to worry. So what if she wasn't in shape, she was falling all the time, and she appeared totally incapable of running through her program without getting winded? It was only November. There were many weeks to go until January.

Bobek hardly ever was ready for anything until after the first of the year.

She had plenty of time.

The weekend of Skate Canada, ABC Sports finally televised the Michelle–Tara competition from Skate America. On the broadcast, Peggy Fleming analyzed a replay of Tara Lipinski's triple lutz in the short program, the program where she received the lower-than-expected technical marks.

To try to explain the bad scores, Fleming described how Tara rocked from the correct outside edge of her blade to the inside edge a split second before taking off on the jump. That change of edge turned the jump from a lutz to a flip, an easier jump. The flawed jump had a name in figure skating slang: It was called a "flutz."

For several years, Lipinski had been known to commit the technical flaw; it was the reason her mother and former coach argued at the world junior championships in Australia. She wasn't the only skater who did a "flutz"; many women who don't have the strength to muscle into the jump off the harder outside edge end up rocking over to the easier inside edge before taking off.

But those other women and girls weren't the reigning world champion. Lipinski was. She might have "flutzed" a year earlier and gotten away with it, but she was being held to a much higher standard in 1997. The judges were watching her closely. And they were finding things to pick apart.

The next week, Tara Lipinski and Todd Eldredge traveled to Paris for the fourth event of the Champions Series, Trophy Lalique.

Philip Hersh of the *Chicago Tribune* went too. He had watched the ABC telecast and heard the talk about the "flutz." After Lipinski received some extremely low technical marks—two 5.4s and one 5.5 out of seven judges' marks—for what appeared to be a very good short program in Paris, Hersh asked Lipinski if she thought the judges were penalizing her for doing a "flutz."

"A lot of girls are [doing a 'flutz']," she told him. "I'm doing it and I'm trying to fix it. I think it's a lot better than last year."

Tara Lipinski made figure skating history that night. She became the first skater ever to be asked if she turned her lutz into a "flutz."

And the first to say, honestly and refreshingly, that indeed she did.

It wasn't the smartest move a skater ever made.

Because the judges sit so far away from the corner where the lutz usually is attempted, some have trouble telling exactly what edge the jump takes off on. If a judge isn't certain, he or she gives the skater the benefit of the doubt. But when Lipinski admitted it, she tipped off the judges to a possible deduction of one-tenth to three-tenths of a point from her score for required elements.

The next day, Richard Callaghan fired back in Tara's defense.

"If a world champion comes out and skates a short program like that, you don't give her 5.4," he said.

That day, Saturday, November 15, 1997, turned out to be quite a day in the lives of America's three top skaters.

Rattled by the "flutz" controversy, Tara Lipinski lost in Paris to a woman affectionately known as "The Human Zamboni."

Todd Eldredge fell apart on that same ice, finished fourth, and spent two hours sitting by himself around midnight under a pedestrian bridge in a cold Paris rainstorm.

And Michelle Kwan had her left foot put in a cast back home in California.

Tara Lipinski had a cold that day in Paris, and felt rather lethargic. Still, there wasn't a person among the 8,000 gathered at Palais Omnisports de Bercy who thought she would lose at Trophy Lalique.

Who could beat her?

Lu Chen, who had secured an Olympic berth at a qualifying event in Vienna a month earlier, had come to the event. But Chen looked too much like the Lu Chen of Lausanne, not the Lu Chen of Birmingham or Edmonton, the world championships where she finished first and second.

Laetitia Hubert was there, but she was not the kind of skater who figured to beat the reigning world champion. Hubert was a twenty-three-year-old journeywoman best known for having one of the worst long programs in Olympic history.

At the 1992 Olympics in her native France, she skated last, after eventual gold medalist Kristi Yamaguchi, and fell at least five times, "or maybe it was six or seven," she said cheerfully. And it was just a four-minute performance.

Hubert finished eleventh of eleven skaters at Nations Cup just two weeks before Paris, and admitted she had a terrible fear of failure. She also had been one of the outspoken critics of the rise of young skaters like Tara Lipinski, whom she called "baby gymnasts" after her sixth-place finish at the Lausanne world championships.

Admittedly discouraged by her low marks the night before, Lipinski skated her long program right before Hubert. She was slow and uncharacteristically distracted. Although she did not fall, she turned her triple lutz into a double, and later made a big mistake on her trademark triple loop–triple loop combination, doing just a triple–single.

When she reached the slow part two minutes into her long program, a moment that was designed to generate at least polite applause, the arena was silent. Only one pair of hands applauded. They belonged to Mike Burg, her agent.

Her scores were quite low; the Hungarian judge gave her 5.3, 5.5. Most of the scores hovered around 5.6.

Lipinski was in trouble.

Hubert landed the same number of triples as Lipinski—five—but was much more energetic, even if her skating was sloppier. But she was skating at home, literally. She trained in that very rink. And, when her marks appeared, she defeated Lipinski, five judges to two.

Lipinski put on a brave face and handled herself beautifully in front of the French media, saying she was perplexed by the marks, and perhaps a bit unfocused because of them. But she found solace in the fact that she had been third in Paris the year before, and was second in 1997.

"I'm moving up," she said strongly. She had no tears. She even smiled. Losing to "The Human Zamboni" did not seem to rattle her.

Hubert, on the other hand, was ecstatic. While she said she liked Lipinski and her skating, she felt vindicated by the results.

"TV wants a new star to attract audiences and they could do it with the idea of the youngest," she said. "Tara is impressive but she is incapable of expressing herself the way an older woman can."

Soon, everyone in the sport was talking about Tara. The judges who gave her the world title in March suddenly were finding all kinds of flaws in her skating in November. (The judges weren't the same people, but they were from some of the same countries.) Tara snuck up on them in the spring. By late autumn, they were getting to know her. They were watching her more carefully. And she was making mistakes, something she had not done in her run to the world championships.

There was the fall at Skate America, then the problems in Paris. When she made errors, she did not have a strong artistic mark to fall back on as Michelle Kwan did, for instance. Kwan filled the ice; Lipinski did not. She was getting better, but she was not the artist Kwan was. So if she made mistakes, she was in trouble.

"I knew there was always going to be doubt," Lipinski said. "Once you are the world champion, you do have a little more pressure to stay on top."

"We knew that a lot of people were upset that she won. We knew that," Callaghan said of Tara's victory at the world championships. "But it's not her fault. She showed up and trained and it happened to go that way. Now, I don't think they're being fair with her."

Todd Eldredge won the short program at Lalique also, and came into the long program ahead of Russia's Alexei Yagudin, France's Philippe Candeloro, and others. But he still was in pain from his fall at Skate America three weeks earlier, and had been able to practice seriously for just four days before going to Paris. His shoulder was getting better, but in his fall, he apparently strained muscles in his rib cage, and those muscles caused stabs of knifing pain when he tried his triple axel.

Nonetheless, he landed the triple axel in the short program, and figured he would be fine in the long program as well.

But he wasn't. Eldredge front-loaded his program to be able to get all the hard things out of the way in case his stamina was not yet back to where it needed to be. He leaped forward for a triple axel, and popped it into a gaping single. He came around the ice again. Another triple axel. Another single. There were three minutes to go, but Eldredge was done. He managed just four triples and disgustedly ran his hands through his hair as he awaited his scores.

When he saw them—nothing higher than 5.7—he stormed out of Kiss and Cry, took off his skates in the locker room, and dashed out of the arena.

Wanting to be alone, Eldredge walked through a chilly autumn rain into a park, squeezed past a wire construction barricade, climbed over construction debris, and sat under a pedestrian overpass.

He thought about many things. He told himself he probably shouldn't have gone to the competition. But he never gave up; he was known as a skater who always competed.

Eldredge also was embarrassed, even though he knew he could readily attribute his troubles to the injury. He couldn't remember the last time he skated so poorly. That wasn't like him, popping two triple axels and dropping out of the top three.

And most troublesome of all, the Olympic Games, the Games he had been awaiting for nearly four years, were just three months away.

The news wasn't announced until the next week, Tuesday, November 18, in a one-page press release that did not include a statement from Michelle Kwan.

Kwan's foot was in a cast.

The release said she suffered a stress fracture in the second toe of her left foot in August 1997, and reinjured it during the week of Skate Canada. It was revealed later that that was the reason she slipped and fell on the butterfly spin at the end of the long program. Kwan would be out for ten days to two weeks, according to the announcement.

The release made news around the world. But it wasn't news at all. The injury that Danny and Michelle Kwan had thought would go away, did not go away. And the release did not mention that the injury actually occurred in August 1996, not 1997.

Kwan's cast went on November 15 and came off November 26, the day before Thanksgiving. In an unusual move, the name of the doctor, or where he worked, was not released.

"He doesn't want to be known," Frank Carroll said of the doctor. "He doesn't want to be bothered about this, or to have the nurses bothered."

A strange aura of secrecy surrounded the news about the toe. Publicly, Kwan didn't talk about it until December, more than a month after the initial announcement.

"At first, in August, I felt I could deal with the pain," she said. "But it got worse and worse at Skate Canada. I said, 'Okay, something is wrong.' When I fell on the butterfly, it hurt, but I didn't want to say it was a stress fracture . . . I didn't want to announce my foot hurt. It could have been a muscle spasm. I didn't want to go, 'Hey, I have muscle spasms.' "

"This is just taking precautions to get the situation permanently fixed because we are concerned about the nationals and the Olympics," Carroll said. "It hasn't been anything that serious and we don't anticipate anything serious or any complications. She had this condition at Skate America and skated beautifully."

Because of the injury, Kwan missed NHK Trophy, and the Champions Series final in Munich.

That was fine with Carroll.

"I don't give a damn about the Champions Series final," Carroll said. "I care about nationals and the Olympics."

Three days after Michelle Kwan's cast came off, Lori Nichol flew to California. Frank Carroll was going to be away at the Pacific Coast sectional competition, and they decided someone should be with Kwan as she slowly returned to the ice, just forty-five minutes a day, with no jumping allowed.

Nichol went to the Kwans' home near the rink.

"Would you like to watch your Skate America performance?" Nichol asked Kwan.

Michelle said she would.

They went into the TV room, popped in the tape of the long program, and watched in silence.

When it finished, Kwan looked at Nichol.

"There's something missing," she said to her choreographer.

Nichol couldn't have heard more delightful words.

They began talking about the minute-long slow part of the long program, the section that troubled Nichol at Skate America. Kwan, like Nichol, thought it needed to change. The music was intimate and very personal, but they agreed Michelle needed to reach out to the audience more, to better translate her feelings about the music for those who would be watching.

Nichol then put another videotape into the VCR. She had brought a short tape, just six or seven minutes long, of two of Janet Lynn's performances.

It was the first time Kwan watched Janet Lynn skate an entire program.

She was riveted.

When the tape wound its way to the end, Kwan again was the first to talk.

She was most impressed by the way Janet Lynn focused on the ice without making it look like she was concentrating.

Nichol was thrilled. Michelle had picked out the one thing watching Janet Lynn that Nichol hoped she would. Michelle had cracked the case; she had figured out an important facet of the mystique of Janet Lynn.

If Michelle could take that feeling to the ice, it would be breathtaking, Nichol thought.

And there was no reason to think she couldn't do that.

"Once Michelle sees what she needs to do," Nichol said, "she always takes care of it."

The tapes over, the talking done, it was time for Kwan and Nichol to put their thoughts into action.

All alone in the TV room, the skater and the choreographer got up from the couch and joyfully danced around the room like a couple of school girls.

While Kwan was away, Mike Burg decided it was time to elicit sympathy for Tara Lipinski and what the judges were doing to her by holding a telephone conference call with sportswriters from around the country.

Tara was on the December 10 call, as were Richard Callaghan and choreographer Sandra Bezic.

It didn't go as Burg planned.

Following a couple of questions about the little-girl music for Tara's short and long programs, Bezic strongly defended her choices, saying jovially that Tara "leads the process, she is extremely opinionated and extremely headstrong."

Bezic said the programs were "true and honest."

But, by December, she had not seen Tara for four months, had not seen any of her competitions on television, and, while she said she offered to work with Tara prior to the nationals, the Lipinskis never took her up on it. Bezic was completely out of the loop.

"If Tara had called, I would have dropped everything," Bezic said later. "If she had called and asked me, 'What do you think?' I'd have made sure I got the videotape of her performance and responded. That's the kind of relationship I had with Brian Boitano in 1988 and Kristi Yamaguchi in 1992."

On the conference call, sympathetic questions about judging quickly turned into microscopic queries about Tara's triple lutz. Lipinski honestly admitted to everyone on the call that she did in fact "flutz."

Callaghan followed up by saying most of the top women "flutz," even Michelle Kwan.

Frank Carroll received a few phone calls that day from reporters wanting a comment on Callaghan's comment.

Michelle, Carroll said, does not "flutz." And he invited Callaghan to, one, come out and see for himself or, two, mind his own business.

For one day, figure skating was embroiled in "Flutz Wars."

Yes, she does.

No, she doesn't.

Much more significantly, a conference call designed to portray Tara in a favorable light ended up creating a damaging headline in the next day's *New York Times:* "Mechanical Flaw May Hurt Lipinski's Chances for a Medal in Nagano."

Every judge in America—and perhaps the world—was alerted to look for the error.

Heading into the Champions Series final in Munich less than a week before Christmas, Tara was in trouble.

And then she won.

Kwan did not show up, and did not watch on television. She was busy rehabilitating her foot, skating gingerly, staying in shape off the ice, and resting.

But the next five best women in the world came, and put on quite a show.

No one fell in the long program. There were twenty minutes of skating and no falls. In women's skating in the late 1990s, that was a rarity.

Tanja Szewczenko, the hometown favorite who also won NHK Trophy in Kwan's absence, nearly leaped through the ceiling at Olympiahalle. She landed seven triple jumps and finished with her face buried in her hands.

As the arena erupted, Tara Lipinski took the ice. It seemed she always had to skate after someone else's terrific performance.

"Pretend we're back at C rink and it's just you and me working," Richard Callaghan yelled over the crowd.

Lipinski laughed.

C rink at the Detroit Skating Club? With the crowd going crazy in the arena where Olga Korbut won her gold medals at the 1972 Olympics?

Yeah, right.

But when her music came on and the crowd quieted, Lipinski skated delightfully, better than she had all season. She put together her first clean short and long programs of the year. She landed seven triple jumps, the same as Szewczenko.

But Szewczenko was a grown woman. Lipinski still looked like a little girl.

What would the judges do?

They gave Lipinski marks of 5.7, 5.8, and 5.9—eight 5.9s out of a possible fourteen—and she edged Szewczenko, five judges to two.

"To be second in both events before, and to get first place back, was great," Lipinski said, a wide smile crossing her face. "I'm just so happy. This is going to be the best Christmas."

Tara Lipinski was back. The judges were on her side again. The Champions Series final was the first title she ever had to defend in her skating career. And she did it successfully. She was convinced that her worst days were over, that the tough scrutiny of autumn was giving way to a glorious winter of triumph. She had another title to defend in three weeks, the U.S. national championships. She felt great about that. Things were going her way.

Tanja Szewczenko was just as pleased to be second.

She had been asked a question that startled her two days earlier.

"Do you think you can beat Kwan and Lipinski at the Olympics?"

She looked around for a moment.

"Me?" Szewczenko asked.

She laughed at the thought.

"To skate my best, that is for me a victory."

On Saturday, December 20, Tanja Szewczenko did skate her best, and came quite close to defeating the world champion.

But on Monday, December 22, she had to go back to the hospital.

It wasn't serious.

She just needed to have her tonsils and breathing passages examined.

* * *

Back in Lake Arrowhead, Michelle Kwan was worried.

"My foot's not doing too well," she said on a conference call with reporters three days before Christmas.

But she also said she felt less pain in her toe than she did at Skate America, when she turned in the finest performances in the world all season.

She sounded confused. She said she had had tears in her eyes when she was told back in November she would have to wear a cast. She never had taken off more than two days from skating; to be off the ice for nearly three weeks was awful.

While the injury gave her enough time to make all the subtle changes she and Lori Nichol wanted to make in her long program, it also affected her jumps.

"I'm at seventy percent accuracy," she said. "My confidence level is in the middle. I'm trying to get it motivated to move up."

Someone mentioned she had been on top of the world at Skate America.

Did she feel like she still was there?

"It's really hard to say," Kwan answered meekly.

And she was leaving for nationals in thirteen days.

12

"I Can't Do
My Lovely Job"

The black Jeep Grand Cherokee pulled up beside the tiny Russian
Ladas in front of the nine-story concrete block apartment building,
kicking up some stones and dust as it came to a stop. It was 3:15 in
the afternoon on a clear, crisp, mid-November day at the intersection
of Solidarity and Bolshevik streets on the outskirts of St. Petersburg,
Russia. The wide streets were lined with apartment buildings, each
one as drab as the next. Two miles away, drug dealers had taken over
a desolate farmers' market. In that neighborhood, heroin turned a
bigger profit than potatoes.

In less than two hours, by 5 P.M., the sun would go down on those
apartment buildings, and the miseries of the landscape would disappear into the darkness for another night.

Alexei Urmanov stepped out of his Jeep, slammed the door, and
pushed the remote control lock. The lights on the Jeep flashed once.
Urmanov walked toward the decrepit building, pushed open a green
wooden door, and walked into a concrete stairwell. The lights were
out in the stairwell; the air had a sickeningly pungent odor. It was the
smell of urine. Urmanov turned toward a tiny elevator and waited for
it to return to the ground floor to get him. When he got in, he nearly
filled the elevator, and he is a slight man, of average height, five-foot-
ten. There was graffiti on the walls, mostly in Russian, some in English. The smell was even worse in the elevator, although Urmanov was
so used to it, he did not notice.

Urmanov felt the elevator slowly lurch upward. He got off on the next-to-last floor, the eighth. Three empty vodka bottles sat on the landing above his floor. One fluorescent light brightened the entry way for the four doors. Urmanov reached for the door on his left, put his key in the lock, and turned the knob.

The 1994 Olympic gold medalist was home.

"It's unbelievable that we love this country, because this country is terrible," Urmanov said. "It's a crazy country. But we love this country because we were born here. And if I move to the United States, I never will be American. I am still Russian. My mother is here, my friends are here, everything is here. If you go to America, what do you do there? Just practice."

To the average Russian, Urmanov is indescribably rich. He lives with his mother, Galina, in their tidy, two-room apartment, where there is no rent to be paid. (The government has taken care of that simply because he is a Russian citizen, not an athlete.) Prior to his Olympic triumph, Urmanov and his mother had no choice but to live there; she had lost her factory job and was working as a cook. She couldn't pay her son's skating expenses. That was not a problem when the Soviet Union was thriving and subsidizing its athletes, but when the country fell apart, Urmanov's coach, Alexei Mishin, picked up the costs.

After the 1994 Olympic Games, Urmanov no longer had to rely on Mishin's financial kindness. He made more than $100,000 per year on the American skating tour in 1994 and 1996. It was a fabulous sum for a Russian (factory workers make less than $100 a month), but there could have been so much more. He was dumped from the tour in 1995 after a bad performance at the world championships, and he missed out on about $200,000 in 1997 because of his groin injury.

Still, a few hundred thousand dollars goes a very long way at the corner of Solidarity and Bolshevik streets. Urmanov bought the Jeep from his old girlfriend, Olympic pairs gold medalist Natalia Mishkutenok. He bought another city apartment for $30,000 and was building a $70,000, three-bedroom house in the country. An only child, Urmanov told his mother to quit her job, and she did. He bought a Panasonic television and a fax machine. A shiny breakfront and wall unit came from Scandinavia. "It's not real wood, though," Urmanov admitted.

Yet, with all his money, the twenty-four-year-old Urmanov insisted on staying with his mother in their tiny, eighth-floor apartment, where he had lived every day of his life.

Urmanov slammed the apartment door behind him, shutting out the stench of urine and the sight of graffiti in the glow of fluorescent light. He walked into an apartment that was warm and inviting, and humming with activity. His forty-nine-year-old mother was busy preparing for guests. She moved the round table in the corner of the living room a few feet into the center of the ten-by-twenty-foot room. Two visitors sat at the table on a brown Naugahyde sofa, which, at night, became the Olympic gold medalist's bed. Also in the apartment was a small bedroom, where Galina slept, a tiny kitchen, and a closet-sized bathroom.

"Where's your gold medal?" someone asked Urmanov.

"I don't know," he said.

He set out to find it.

He crouched low, opened a cabinet in the living room wall unit, and began searching through a Reebok shoe box.

No luck.

He shrugged.

"I need time to find it because I don't know where it is."

Urmanov moved to another cabinet above a closet in the hallway. He rustled through some plastic bags.

"Here it is," he said, dangling a beautiful gold and granite medal on a thick blue and purple ribbon.

He nonchalantly handed it to his guests and left the room.

Later, one of the visitors pointed toward one of a dozen framed pictures sitting on a table. It was from the 1994 Winter Olympics. Urmanov was in costume, on the medal stand, smiling at the photographer, with his gold medal hanging proudly from his neck.

"Great picture," the guest told Urmanov.

Urmanov nodded his head and said nothing, immediately reaching for another picture.

"This is nice too," he said.

He was holding a photograph of himself and his mother, arm-in-arm.

Urmanov cared so much about his mother's feelings that he found himself lying to her in the autumn of 1997.

"I usually try to say to her, 'Yeah, it's better,'" Urmanov said sadly, brushing his dark bangs out of his eyes.

The fact was that his injured groin muscle was not getting better. Every day he came home from practice, his mother would be there waiting for him, wondering how his left leg was doing.

"Don't worry," Urmanov said to his mother. "Everything is going to be fine. It's better."

"You know how much I love you," Galina replied. "I am sure that my love will help."

"Of course, everything will be fine," Alexei said. "Don't worry about it."

But everything was not fine. Urmanov still couldn't land a triple axel, nor a triple lutz. He withdrew from his two Champions Series events, including Skate America. He watched from afar as the other skaters went on with the autumn schedule without him. This was to have been his year. He might have won the world championships in Lausanne had he not injured himself doing his triple–triple combination jump. He could have been in position to become the first man since Dick Button in 1948 and 1952 to win two Olympic gold medals. He realized he was barely known outside skating; winning the gold medal in 1998 would have changed everything for him.

But what was he to do when he could not jump?

"If I am coming to the practice and if I practice real nice, I love myself," he said. "If the practice is not so good, I hate myself. This period is terrible for me. I can't skate and I can't jump. For half a year, I hate myself.

"It takes so long a time and I can't do my lovely job, my figure skating, the most clever thing for me. It's very difficult to be without your job."

Still, every day, Urmanov drove eight miles from his apartment to the center of town. His journey took him from "Leningrad" to "St. Petersburg." That's the way the citizens of St. Petersburg talk about the city of four million people. The ragged outskirts with their cell block buildings are derisively called "Leningrad"; the beautiful center city, built in the image of Paris by Peter the Great, is "St. Peterburg." Urmanov lives in the depressed world that Lenin, Stalin, and Brezhnev left behind. But he works near the cradle of Russian culture.

Yubileiny Palace is a ten-minute drive from the Hermitage, one of the world's grand museums, and it's no more than a fifteen-minute drive to the Mariinsky Theater, home of the Kirov Ballet. They form a triangle, those three buildings, a triangle of artistic excellence unparalleled throughout the world. Without the other two points of the triangle, Yubileiny—and the St. Petersburg school of figure skating that is housed there—would be vastly different, and might not exist at all.

But even with all of the built-in cultural advantages, the figure skaters have not had an easy life since the Soviet Union disbanded in 1991 and the government all but abandoned its athletes.

The long hallway inside Yubileiny Palace is cold and desolate. Eight fluorescent lights hang from the ceiling; an eerie yellow glow comes from the only one that is working. The smell of perspiration lingers in the hallway, while farther down the corridor, the strong odor of urine rushes from the grimy locker rooms.

At the far end of this hallway, there is a door. It's made of heavy metal, and with a good shove it swings open, revealing an old, rutted ice rink.

When Alexei Urmanov pushes on the door, he enters the center of the figure skating universe.

Every day, a procession of skaters with the world's most remarkable resumés comes down that hallway, opens that door, and steps onto that ice. Artur Dmitriev, the 1992 Olympic pairs gold medalist and 1994 silver medalist, trains there with partner Oksana Kazakova. Elena Berezhnaia and Anton Sikharulidze are there too. They train at Yubileiny because it's the base of operations for their coach, Tamara Moskvina. When 1984 Olympic gold medalists Elena Valova and Oleg Vassiliev prepare for a professional competition in the United States, they work there with Moskvina too. Even rival pairs skate beside Moskvina's skaters: Marina Eltsova and Andrei Bushkov, the 1996 world champions, also work on that ice.

When the pairs aren't there, Alexei Mishin's male skaters come in to practice. Urmanov is one of them, even though he was injured and had been taking it easy since March. So is Alexei Yagudin, seventeen, the 1997 world bronze medalist, and Evgeni Plushenko, the 1997 world junior champion.

Of the eight Olympic figure skating gold medals won during the first two Games of the 1990s, two have gone to Yubileiny skaters (Dmitriev and Mishkutenok, and Urmanov). Only one gold medal has been won by an American: Kristi Yamaguchi in 1992.

In Olympic competition in 1992 and 1994, one miserable rink in Russia outproduced the entire United States of America.

Yet Mishin and Moskvina were not entirely satisfied. They were not stopping. They were not leaving for America, at least not yet.

They wanted more. The two of them—former pairs partners and dear friends—loved nothing more than driving the rest of the skating world absolutely crazy.

"We knew that with our heads and our hearts, we could make something from nothing," Moskvina said. "We knew we could make an achievement that America, a very wealthy country, would be surprised about."

Surprise might be too mild a word. Russian skating, with all its troubles, was thriving. There may have been few new children coming up, but the ones already in the pipeline were going to make it. In addition to his biggest names, Mishin had two other international-level male skaters, as well as a few young kids on the rise. When they all were on the ice, Mishin beamed. Unlike many coaches, he didn't wear skates when he taught. He walked among his skaters in high-top Fila boots, leaving footprints wherever he traveled on the frosty ice.

"My main weapon is out," Mishin said, referring to Urmanov, "so I have to attack with my garbage and my refuse."

Yagudin was Mishin's "garbage," Plushenko, his "refuse." Most places, they would be national wonders. At Yubileiny, they received second and third billing to Urmanov, even with his bad groin.

"The coach against the country," Mishin boasted. "With these skaters, I could compete against a select team of Canada or the U.S., and I could win."

Mishin pointed toward a blond, blue-eyed boy, a thirteen-year-old named Andrei Griazev.

"Even with this little piece of shit."

Little Andrei Griazev smiled. (He doesn't understand English.)

"Go out and do a double axel without arms," Mishin shouted in Russian, ordering Griazev not to use his arms to help throw himself into the air on the two-and-a-half revolution jump.

The boy succeeded.

"Next year," Mishin said, smiling mischievously, "we will demonstrate a double axel without legs."

If only it were so easy. If only one could do a jump without legs. As Mishin's other skaters danced and jumped in the ballet room before heading to the ice, Urmanov tied an elastic strap around the end of a radiator, then put it around his left ankle, and began his stretching exercises. His routine was shockingly rudimentary, like something out of the nineteenth century.

When a doctor who has worked with U.S. Olympians heard of Urmanov's training methods, he shuddered.

"The Russian way, unfortunately, is to grin and bear it," said the U.S. doctor, who requested anonymity. "Rehabilitation in the United States is four or five steps ahead of what Alexei Urmanov is getting in Russia. What a shame this is for him. It's a very delicate muscle, but he should have been able to come back within a few months of the injury, at the very latest."

What was going on in that ballet room around Urmanov was nearly as eye-opening—for all the right reasons. The boys were completing three-revolution jumps from a standing position on the floor. Mishin and his choreographer, Evgeni Serejnikov, who once worked with the Kirov, walked up to the skaters and tapped them under their chins.

"Up, up, up," Mishin said.

Posture meant everything to the Russians.

Chin up.

Shoulders back.

Arms out.

In four years, or eight, Mishin figured, Olympic judges would look at these kids and be in ecstasy.

That's how Urmanov won the 1994 Olympic gold medal. He began working with a choreographer three times a week at the age of seven. Most American boys would be dragged kicking and screaming into ballet or choreography classes.

And if American boys weren't doing the kicking and screaming, it's likely their fathers would be.

But in Russia, it was different. Ballet was something to be revered. St. Petersburg was home to the first school of Russian dance in 1738. It was the cradle of ballet. For years, Moskvina brought ballet tickets to practice, gave them to her skaters, and strongly suggested they go to that evening's performance of the Kirov.

"Some people took the tickets and stayed home, but I went," said Artur Dmitriev.

"It was not only the ballet, but the museums, fashion shows, drama and the theater," said Elena Valova, Moskvina's professional pairs skater. "We were doing all this as teenagers."

They are serious about their art in St. Petersburg. At the Hermitage, the grand Winter Palace of the czars beside the beautiful Neva River, there is an abundance of riches. The museum doesn't have just a few

Rembrandts; it has rooms full of Rembrandts. One of them, the masterpiece *Danaë,* was attacked in 1985 by a man who threw sulfuric acid on the canvas and slashed the painting with a knife.

Recently restored, it hangs on a wall in a place of honor in the Hermitage.

It is guarded by a man with a machine gun.

Yubileiny (Jubilee) Palace, built to commemorate the fiftieth anniversary of the Russian Revolution in 1967, has something in common with the Hermitage. Inside both are great treasures. But because times are so hard in Russia, the structures themselves suffer.

At the Hermitage, hundreds of oil paintings of military leaders from the War of 1812 can barely be seen—because the room in which they are hanging is pitch black. Electricity bills are hard to pay, so money can be saved when the lights are off. Many other paintings are hung by windows, where direct sunlight bakes them by day.

At Yubileiny, which is part of a sports complex visible from some windows of the Hermitage, the zamboni sometimes fails to sufficiently smooth the ice—and other times does not work at all. Skaters tell stories of having to buy gasoline to get the machine back up and running. Sometimes, they can't even *find* the zamboni driver because he's out back in the parking lot, washing cars for the very significant sum of $5 apiece.

Back inside, the air around the rink is so cold, skaters can get sick. And the ice never is perfect, like it is at a top U.S. rink. The skaters know there will always be something wrong.

"That's our secret," said Valova, the 1984 Olympic gold medalist in pairs. "When we skate on other ice, it's like heaven for us. On this ice, we have to push two times harder, so every time we go to a skating competition, we can fly on the ice."

That explains part of the Russian phenomenon, the fact that no one but a Russian pair has won the Olympic gold medal since 1964, or that skaters from the former Soviet Union won every Olympic gold medal in the 1992 and 1994 Games but Yamaguchi's.

The rest of the Russian success story is embodied in the extraordinary lives and antics of the sport's two great masterminds, Tamara Moskvina and Alexei Mishin.

Tamara Moskvina, the giant of her sport, is four-foot-ten. She is the oldest of three girls in her family, and by far the shortest. Her two sisters each are a good six inches taller than she is.

"There's a reason," Moskvina said. "They were not born in the war. I was."

Tamara Bratus was born June 26, 1941, in Leningrad (now St. Petersburg). On September 29, 1941, Adolf Hitler issued a directive. It was short and to the point. The city of Leningrad, he said, should "be wiped off the face of the earth."

The siege of Leningrad began when Tamara was three months old.

German forces surrounded the city and cut it off from the Soviet Union and the rest of the world. For 900 days, until January 27, 1944, the four million residents of St. Petersburg were linked to the outside world only by air drops and one road, "The Road of Life," a path that was laid across the frozen waters of Lake Ladoga during the long, harsh winters.

At one point during the siege, only half a slice of bread was allocated to each resident per day. In the winter, there was no heat or electricity.

Nearly one million people—one out of every four—starved to death.

Tamara Bratus survived.

She was one of the lucky ones. She and her mother were evacuated to the Ural Mountains in Siberia when the siege began, and stayed there until it ended. Their life was extremely difficult, but still far better than what they would have faced at home. Each person received the same half a slice of bread a day, Moskvina said, but she often revieved extra from family members because she was a child. Even so, they ended up eating tree roots.

By the age of ten, she was skating on a river across the street from the boardinghouse in which she grew up. Her family—all five of them—lived in one room and shared a bathroom at the end of the hallway with seventeen other families.

For the next ten years, Tamara received free group skating lessons and got to be quite good, becoming the first Russian woman ever to land a double lutz, and the first person in the world to perform the "Biellmann Spin." The move is named for 1981 world champion Denise Biellmann of Switzerland, who was believed to be the first skater to try it.

But Moskvina actually accomplished the feat in 1957, five years before Biellmann was born, and she has the pictures to prove it.

Should it be called the "Bratus Spin"? Or the "Tamara Spin"?

"No," Moskvina said with a wave of her hand. "Forget it."

In 1961, Tamara's father, an air force engineer, died. She applied for and received a scholarship that amounted to 120 rubles a month. Tamara, her mother, and her two sisters lived on the stipend, which, at the time, provided a respectable living in the Soviet Union.

Tamara represented the Soviet Union internationally as a singles skater in the early 1960s, where she met a British skater named Sally Stapleford. Tamara's English was quite poor, so Stapleford gave her some books she had brought with her to a competition. They were Agatha Christie mysteries. At every competition, Stapleford—now the International Skating Union's figure skating technical committee chair, and the referee of the men's competition at the 1994 Olympics—brought more Agatha Christie novels for Tamara, and Moskvina read them all.

"I liked the psychology more than the mystery," she said.

Tamara Bratus's coach at the time was Igor Moskvin, the coach of the legendary Protopopovs, the 1964 and 1968 Olympic pairs gold medalists from the Soviet Union.

In 1962, Tamara and Igor began dating. In 1964, they were married. Tamara became a pairs skater that year. After her first partner retired, Moskvin suggested a strong male singles skater he coached: Alexei Mishin.

Moskvina and Mishin, who is three and a half months older than Moskvina, were together for four years, from 1965 to 1969. They were sturdy and fast skaters who performed lifts and double jumps, but none of the throws that are common in present-day pairs skating.

Moskvina said Mishin never dropped her, although one time in practice, on a twist, she fell out of his arms and into his knee, leaving a tooth mark. The accident happened in a church.

"In those years," Moskvina said, "because it was the Soviet Union, we didn't use the churches, so instead of using that church for storage, they made it into an ice rink."

In 1969, Moskvina and Mishin won the Soviet national title in a grand upset. On grit and guile, the two skaters-who-would-be-coaches defeated two of their sport's great legends: the Protopopovs and Irina Rodnina and Alexei Ulanov. The Protopopovs had won the two previous Olympic gold medals, and Rodnina and Ulanov would win the next, in 1972. (Rodnina also won the 1976 and 1980 Olympic gold medals with another partner.) In 1969, at the world championships in Colorado Springs, Rodnina and Ulanov won the gold, but Moskvina and Mishin captured the silver.

They soon retired. They weren't going to have a better year than that.

Unlike most Russian pairs of the day, Moskvina and Mishin were not romantically involved.

"People still think and suspect," Moskvina said with a twinkle in her eye. "But I know. I was married then. I would never do that."

Moskvina and Mishin are great friends, however. They often travel together to or from competitions on the one flight coming or going from St. Petersburg that day.

When Moskvina naps at an airport gate before boarding an international flight, Mishin warns others not to "wake up my partner."

When there is waking up to do, Mishin takes on the duty himself. He gently rubs Moskvina's ear lobe until she opens her eyes. He even takes her hand to help her down a step, even though they both are happily married—to someone else.

Several years ago, Mishin broached the subject of the romantic relationship they never had.

"You never gave me any sign," he said.

"You never gave *me* any sign," she replied.

"Let's start now," he said.

She laughed.

He laughed.

They didn't start anything.

Moskvina and Mishin both began their coaching careers soon after they quit skating together in 1969. After finishing second at the world championships, Moskvina received a new apartment from the Soviet government which she had to pay rent on, and was given the right to buy a car without having to wait in line.

The Soviet government paid her the equivalent of $13 a month to coach.

When she and her skaters began taking trips to competitions in the United States and other Western nations, they received a per diem of much more: $25 a day. That money became too precious to use for food. They brought sandwiches from Russia for their meals, and used the per diem to buy clothes and other necessities for their families and friends back home in the Soviet Union.

"We might have been hungry, but we were very happy," Moskvina said. "We came home from competitions slim. It was the special nutrition system for Russians."

Even in the privacy of their hotel rooms, Moskvina and her skaters were wary of talking about their purchases. Concerned that "U.S. spies" had bugged their rooms, they never uttered the words "shopping mall," Moskvina said.

They always substituted the word "museum."

"We said we were going to the 'museum,' " she said. "Woolworth's was our favorite 'museum.' "

Moskvina began having great success coaching pairs; winning the 1981 world title with one pair before Valova and Vassiliev won three world titles and the 1984 Olympic gold medal in Sarajevo.

That same year, a tall sixteen-year-old boy from a nickel- and diamond-mining town near the Arctic Circle came to St. Petersburg to train with Moskvina. The Soviet skating federation thought all tall boys should skate pairs.

This boy liked everything in skating except pairs.

No matter.

The Soviet skating federation had spoken.

Artur Dmitriev became a pairs skater.

He already was six feet tall and weighed 170 pounds. Within a couple of years, Moskvina brought two women skaters to him. One was Elena Bechke, who had skated pairs before and already had her own style. The other was Natalia Mishkutenok, who had been a pairs skater for just one month.

Dmitriev picked Mishkutenok. "I prefer to make a different style," Dmitriev said. "For me, it was easy to make from zero."

Moskvina always had one or two other pairs in the rink at the same time as Mishkutenok and Dmitriev, including Bechke and her eventual partner, Denis Petrov. (They won the 1992 Olympic silver medal behind Dmitriev and Mishkutenok.) But there was something about the way Moskvina and Dmitriev clicked that told her that of all her skaters, he would be with her for a long, long time.

They both had vivid imaginations. Moskvina taught Mishkutenok and Dmitriev a unique, upside down spin in which Dmitriev stood upright and Mishkutenok held onto his ankle spinning upside down.

"I stole it from a Canadian couple," Moskvina confessed. It soon was called the "Natalia Spin."

Dmitriev came up with a spin in which the woman remained flat as a board, looking like she was being whipped around as he held her vertically in the air.

"We try a lot of things and maybe put in half of them," he said. "Usually the ideas are my inspiration. It's just in my head. When I copy something, it looks like a copy. So we do a lot of elements no one has ever done before."

When Moskvina gave her skaters tickets to the Kirov, Dmitriev was one of the ones who went. He wanted to learn about the ballet. He even watched a videotape of the great male stars of Russian ballet. With his thick, tangled, dark hair, Dmitriev himself looked like a creation of the Kirov when he leaped off the ice and flew through the air.

Moskvina loved what she was creating in Dmitriev. He was the perfect male pairs skater: big, handsome, athletic, and always a gentleman on the ice. Moskvina made sure of that. She demanded triple jumps, and she demanded manners.

"Don't forget the women in the stands," Moskvina told all her male skaters. "Skate with a passion that women in the audience will be satisfied with."

Mishkutenok and Dmitriev dramatically captured the Olympic gold medal in 1992, but soon were having trouble. Dmitriev developed back problems from all the lifts and throws, and picked up a pack-a-day smoking habit while touring in the United States, away from his wife and young son. His weight ballooned to 196 pounds.

Mishkutenok also gained weight, Moskvina said.

"She is a cloud," Moskvina told reporters, explaining Mishkutenok's role in a new skating program.

"A heavy cloud."

Moskvina spared no one with her comments. When Dmitriev had trouble landing his triple jumps throughout 1996 and 1997, Moskvina blasted him too.

"He is a thunderstorm."

Mishkutenok and Dmitriev split several months after winning the Olympic silver medal at the Norway Games. It would have been the logical time for Dmitriev, who would turn thirty right before the Nagano Games, to quit or turn professional. But that was the furthest thing from Dmitriev's mind.

"It's much more interesting to skate amateur than professional," he said. "I'm lazy a little, and to keep my training at a high level, I need to skate amateur."

Dmitriev and Moskvina searched for a new partner for him, settling on Oksana Kazakova, a skater in their rink who turned twenty the year they came together, 1995. Dmitriev and Moskvina became her sponsors, each paying half of Kazakova's expenses.

Dmitriev could afford Kazakova because of the six-figure income he made on the U.S. tour; Moskvina could afford her because, years earlier, she had cleverly made herself the agent for all her pairs. When they toured in the United States, she made a significant percentage, and while she said she wasn't earning $100,000 a year, she certainly was making a very nice living.

"I prepare them all those years," she said, "why then would I give up the money? Why do you need a middleman? I learned what I needed to know. I knew the price for Russian skaters was low. I asked and I learned."

Both Dmitriev and Moskvina live the good life in St. Petersburg. Unlike Urmanov, they have big apartments in nice buildings; Dmitriev's has two floors and three bedrooms, while Moskvina's has exquisite high ceilings.

"I am used to the modest life, not the wealthy life," Moskvina said. "I could buy a Rolex, but why do I need a Rolex? I already have a watch, and it works."

Unlike Mishkutenok, Kazakova already had been a pairs skater, so Dmitriev had some work to do.

"She had a style already," Dmitriev said, "and I was asked to correct this style. My skating depended on what she did and how we put this together."

Their timing was off on almost everything when they began, but they quickly grew together on the ice, and won the prestigious European championships in 1996. After winning the bronze medal at the 1997 world championships, they won Skate Canada in November 1997, but Kazakova fell and hurt her lower back when she slid into the boards during practice at NHK Trophy in Japan, forcing them to withdraw.

Mostly, though, it was his mistakes that cost them higher placements.

"He teaches her and forgets about himself," Moskvina said.

They came back to finish third in the 1997 Russian nationals and third in the Champions Series final in Munich, awaiting the dawning of 1998 and Dmitriev's third Olympic Games. He knew that he could become the first man in history to win Olympic gold medals with two different pairs partners, but he said he did not particularly care about that achievement.

"I don't think about my first Olympics, second Olympics, third Olympics," he said. "Now I must do something for Oksana."

Moskvina had taught him well. He was thinking only of his partner.

Dmitriev also was not entirely pleased that the Olympic year was moving along so quickly, that within three months of a cold, gray day in November in St. Petersburg, it would all be over. He loved his work. He did not want it to end. He enjoyed the process more than the result.

"To win a medal for me is a very bad feeling," he said in halting English, "because it means I am done with this program. It means I am finished. To do something better is the best feeling. It's more important to me to create a new program than to finish first or second or third at the Olympics."

Back at Yubileiny, Moskvina had to perform a balancing act in the year leading up to the Nagano Olympics. She had another pairs team there, Elena Berezhnaia and Anton Sikharulidze, and they quickly caught and surpassed Dmitriev and Kazakova in international rankings.

This pleased Dmitriev in a strange sort of way, because he looked at Sikharulidze as his protégé. Kazakova, however, had trouble with the competition. Teamed with Dmitriev, she expected to be the one moving toward the Olympic gold medal. But, by the autumn, she and Dmitriev were only the second-best pair Moskvina was coaching. Berezhnaia and Sikharulidze were soaring; they finished second to 1997 world champions Mandy Woetzel and Ingo Steuer at Nations Cup in Germany, then upset the Germans at Trophy Lalique in Paris.

Before her young pairs skaters performed in Paris, Moskvina looked into their eyes to gauge their nerves, gave them a final word of encouragement, and sent them onto the ice. Then she left the boards, ran to a set of stairs, waved her credential at a security guard, and dashed into the stands.

This was highly unusual behavior for a coach, running away from the ice as her skaters glided to their opening position.

Moskvina quickly found an empty seat in the third row in the Paris arena, where she sat on the edge of her chair to watch their long program. She wanted to see how the program played to the judges and the spectators. Moskvina left nothing to chance.

Moskvina had seen a marked improvement in Berezhnaia—"Skate in the Head" to those cynical journalists—and Sikharulidze in the time they had been together. They were put together late for a Russian pair, which is why she pushed agent Michael Rosenberg to take them for Elvis Stojko's tour. They needed the seasoning.

"I want them known now," she said. "I want them on top now. But it's hard. Even the pie needs time to be cooked. But you can put it in the microwave."

By the time of the Nagano Games, they would not have been skating together for even two years.

When Sikharulidze brought Berezhnaia to St. Petersburg after her ex-partner's skate hit her in the head in January 1996, Moskvina became both coach and sponsor to the new pair. It was worth the risk. She loved the challenge of creating something from nothing.

"This is my hobby," Moskvina said. "I was a mediocre skater. These skaters are nobodies, and I put them together, teach them, and that makes people enjoy. It makes people happy. I didn't think I'd ever be a great skating coach. I just work, work, work and then it happens."

As Berezhnaia slowly recovered from her head injuries in 1996, Moskvina realized Sikharulidze, who is half Georgian, had quite a temper. A partner with a temper was one thing the fragile "Skate in the Head" did not need. Her previous partner, the one who accidentally kicked her in the head, had a short fuse too, and sometimes hit Berezhnaia, Moskvina said.

Moskvina knew this relationship wouldn't work unless Sikharulidze calmed down.

She decided to seek help from her most trusted pupil, Artur Dmitriev. Both Moskvina and Dmitriev talked to Sikharulidze, who is eight and a half years younger than Dmitriev. They suggested he watch the way Dmitriev kissed Kazakova's hand each time they finished a program, the way he gently helped her off the ice.

Within weeks, Sikharulidze was offering to carry Berezhnaia's bag at the rink.

Moskvina nodded her approval.

"If she falls, he helps her up," Moskvina said. "The audience will see this and say, 'Oh, what a man.' The majority of a skating audience is women, of course."

In their first year together, Berezhnaia and Sikharulidze began dating, but were no longer seeing each other by the autumn of 1997, Moskvina said.

"It's my very, very good friend," Sikharulidze said of Berezhnaia.

Berezhnaia, standing near her partner, smiled softly and said that she lived by herself in an apartment in St. Petersburg.

"Ah-ha!" Sikharulidze exclaimed, as if he had just learned a secret about her social life.

Their friendship was so strong that when Berezhnaia said she didn't want to show reporters the scar on her head from the skating accident, Sikharulidze took over for her and obliged.

He drew an imaginary square in the air over her tiny head, symbolizing the drastic surgery she had that opened up her skull to remove bone fragments.

Berezhnaia's ex-partner's skate left a one-and-a-half-inch scar above her left ear, but the operation required an incision all the way around her skull.

Reporters raised their eyes in shock. Few had realized the extent of the surgery.

Berezhnaia smiled politely, and said nothing.

Sikharulidze nodded, put his arm gently around his skating partner, and escorted her from the room.

After finishing behind 1996 world champions Marina Eltsova and Andrei Bushkov at the Russian nationals, "Skate in the Head" and her partner won the 1997 Champions Series final, defeating Woetzel and Steuer in Munich. (Eltsova and Bushkov missed the event when Bushkov injured a groin muscle.)

Distraught, Steuer buried his face in his hands. They had had to water down their program because of an injury. After having both his knees operated on in the off-season, he was the victim of a bizarre hit-and-run car accident in early December in which the arm that he used to lift Woetzel was hit by the mirror of a passing car.

First, "Skate in the Head."

Then, "Car in the Arm."

What was next, Dr. Seuss skating to "Cat in the Hat"?

Berezhnaia and Sikharulidze skated perfectly to the same long program they performed the year before—the Hollywood Bowl Symphony Orchestra's "Dark Eyes."

Asked why she hadn't changed the program, Moskvina replied: "Do you change your husband every year? If he's good, you keep him."

When the Germans and Kazakova and Dmitriev made their mistakes—Dmitriev once again stumbled on a triple toe loop—Moskvina's youngsters won easily.

"Now comes the most difficult part," Moskvina told Sikharulidze, "the burden of being the best."

She was thinking on her feet even as she stood on her tip-toes. Moskvina could barely see over the boards in Munich's Olympiahalle to watch her two pairs come in first and third. Only her head was visible over the barrier, but she saw enough to know that two Olympic medals were possible for her pairs—and that Kazakova and Dmitriev still had a chance at the gold if the big guy didn't stumble out of another triple toe loop.

In many ways, Moskvina was just like Dmitriev. He already was feeling the sadness of a season winding toward its inevitable conclusion. And she, too, already was searching for a new challenge with her younger pair, thinking beyond 1998 even before the new year dawned.

"Last season, I wanted them to just stick together," she said in her deep, playful voice. "This year, I added more elements. Next year, I will invent something special for them."

Alexei Mishin's mind also was hard at work. He was a graduate of "The University of Life," he said, and, by 1997, he clearly was working on an advanced degree. His top skater, Alexei Urmanov, was injured and missing all his fall events, yet Mishin had come up with two other skaters who he thought could more than fill the void.

This was Mishin's crowning achievement: skaters as interchangeable parts.

He had come a long way since the days in the 1970s when he was banned from traveling for three years by Soviet officials because he was intelligent and spoke English and just might take off and never return. Or the days when 50,000 copies of his book, *Figure Skating for Everyone,* were ripped up and destroyed by the government. Or the times that Soviet television was forbidden to show him at a competition.

Mishin had become the toast of Russian men's skating.

He was having one long, last laugh.

"Now, nearly all coaches leave Russia—but me," he said.

While he labeled Urmanov's groin injury a "tragidity" (the Russian-English version of "tragedy"), he pressed on with his teenagers, his "garbage and refuse," and he showed the world that he was a mighty force, a masterful coach, a superb judge of talent.

Alexei Yagudin, the seventeen-year-old who once was believed to be the odd man out of the two-man Russian Olympic team, had matured almost overnight into a serious gold medal contender.

After upsetting Todd Eldredge in Paris, he flew home and competed the next week in Cup of Russia in St. Petersburg. He didn't come home in the best of shape. In surprisingly strong English—Mishin was preparing him in all ways for a future life of skating abroad—Yagudin said he was tired. He explained he was competing for the second time in a week. This kind of wall-to-wall scheduling was new in skating; in years past, skaters might have competed two times in the entire autumn, not twice within the same week.

But in the short program, skating before his family and friends in the cavernous SKK Arena, Yagudin uncorked what might have been the highest triple axel ever landed.

Tired? Burned out?

The kid was only seventeen.

Mishin said that never in the history of his sport had there been a triple axel with more air underneath it, although he certainly had not seen every one ever performed.

Even the Americans were in shock.

"That kid could beat Elvis Stojko," said U.S. Figure Skating Association President Morry Stillwell, staring from the stands in disbelief.

"Mishin said we will start to try a quadruple axel in the spring," Yagudin said, smiling broadly.

Most likely it was hyperbole, but Yagudin was on a rampage through his sport. Looking much more mature than he had in Lausanne, Yagudin stormed to a huge victory with a magnificent long program that included eight triple jumps and a clean quadruple toe loop. When he finished and the 8,500 spectators rose to their feet to salute him, he put his hands to his face and shook with joy.

"For me, that was fantastic skating, the best performance of my life," he said.

Evgeni Plushenko, his training partner, finished second for the second time in a Champions Series event. As Mishin joined the two at a press conference, he was ebullient.

"Nobody has skated as well this year as these two skaters did," Mishin said.

Mishin knew why they were so good. It was because they were hungry. It was because they had nothing.

Yagudin was so embarrassed by his living conditions that he refused to speak about them when Russian reporters were within earshot. He, his mother, and his grandmother lived in two rooms of an apartment that they shared with another family. They had their own living room and bedroom, as did the other family. The two families shared the kitchen and bathroom.

Asked if he knew and liked the other family, Yagudin said softly, "We don't speak with them."

Plushenko was so poor that Mishin paid the $60-per-month rent on a room he and his mother shared in a St. Petersburg boardinghouse—until Plushenko's success at Skate America in Detroit. When he finished second to Eldredge, he won $18,000.

"Now he can pay the rent," Mishin said.

"This is an unbelievable situation for Americans to comprehend," he added. "Never a coach pay for a skater. A skater usually pay for a coach."

Left in the wake of the two Russian teenagers was Michael Weiss, the twenty-one-year-old American who all of a sudden was feeling quite old. Weiss had been given two faraway Champions Series events—Nations Cup in Germany, and Cup of Russia. He had not been particularly happy with the assignments, but the USFSA had its reasons for sending him far from home. Looking at the field in those two events, the USFSA figured Weiss could finish second or third in both events and qualify for the Champions Series final in Munich. The U.S. association had high hopes for Weiss. Jerry Lace, the organization's executive director, said the USFSA was working on a lucrative, six-figure deal to keep Weiss skating in Olympic division events another four years, heading to the Salt Lake City Olympics in 2002. Looking at a dearth of strong, star-quality male skaters, the USFSA needed Weiss more than he needed it.

"We should pick our Olympic team right now," Lace said with a smile before the competition began in Russia. "If it's not Eldredge and Weiss, we should shoot the international committee [the USFSA group that had the final say about the Olympic team]."

After the competition in St. Petersburg, the USFSA might have had second thoughts. Following a disappointing fifth-place finish in Germany, Weiss wobbled to a miserable fourth-place showing in Russia. He ended the season mired in eleventh place in the Champions Series rankings and failed to qualify for the six-man Champions Series final. Even Scott Davis, who finished a dismal fourth at Skate America but a strong second in Japan, outranked Weiss by the end of the autumn. Davis was eighth overall, the same place Weiss finished the previous season.

While Davis was on the rise, Weiss was dropping.

In the short program in Russia, Weiss took the easy way out with a triple axel–double toe loop, which guaranteed he could not pass the two Russians, who easily performed triple–triples. (Weiss had done the same thing in Germany: a triple axel–double toe loop. That might earn him second place at the U.S. nationals in January, but it would get him nowhere internationally.)

But as Weiss, dressed in basic black, performed his flamenco-style short program in front of several thousand stern Russian fans, something interesting happened. In the final minute, the music erupted with the sound of rhythmic clapping. It was the section of Weiss's music that coach Audrey Weisiger, choreographer Brian Wright, and fellow coach Linda Reynolds created in Stuart Ridgway's recording studio in Virginia in the spring.

As their clapping filled the arena on tape while Weiss skated, the Russian audience took the hint and joined in.

Back in April, Ridgway had assured Weisiger that the crowd at the 1998 nationals in Philadelphia would pick up on the clapping. He didn't know at the time that Weiss was going to Russia first.

Eight time zones away from that studio in Falls Church, Virginia, Ridgway had been proven right.

In Weiss's long program, there was little room for applause of any kind. He suffered a shocking meltdown. He didn't attempt his quadruple lutz; he did a smooth triple lutz instead. But then he doubled or singled four planned triples, and fell on another.

"I had no attack at all," Weiss said calmly afterward. "I don't remember doing that many singles in my life."

He smiled and shrugged. That was as angry as Weiss ever got.

"As they say, 'In order to enjoy it when you skate well, you've got to skate badly.' And I skated badly. The Russians came out and flat out kicked everybody's butt here. Sometimes you've got to admit to that. I just got my butt kicked here.

"But this kind of stuff motivates you to go home and work harder and make sure that this doesn't happen again."

The USFSA was getting antsy. With Scott Davis's track record of disaster in big events, it was banking on Weiss to be its up-and-coming superstar. Weiss had a "watch-me" presence on the ice. He was cocky, young, and extremely masculine. What more could anyone want?

"We'll let Audrey and Michael take care of it," USFSA president Morry Stillwell said in Russia. "We'll let them figure it out and work it all out."

But Weisiger knew the phone calls would start coming, from USFSA officials and judges and coaches and friends, all offering suggestions on how to snap Weiss from his autumn slump. Weisiger wasn't looking forward to the advice, but she admitted she might listen because she was puzzled. She knew Weiss performed best when he was cornered, when he had no choice but to fight. In that sense, losing wasn't always the worst thing to happen to him. But this was ridiculous. He was too good to perform so badly. This was the Olympic year. What in the world was he waiting for?

"Mike almost needs to be desperate before he skates well,"

Weisiger said. "The Russian kids clearly are desperate. I just hope Mike is disgusted enough now."

Weisiger left Russia bothered by nagging questions about her skater, while Mishin figured he was providing his sport with all kinds of glorious answers.

He was certain that two skaters no longer were factors in his life: Todd Eldredge and Ilia Kulik.

And he had theories about both of them.

Eldredge was history. Mishin was sure about this. Other Russian coaches—not Mishin—had come up with an elaborate conspiracy theory that linked Eldredge's Skate America shoulder injury to his fear of Evgeni Plushenko, Mishin's "very skinny chicken."

This was the theory: Eldredge began his Olympic season using the previous year's short program and a long program that was similar to the one he used in 1994–95. In other words, he had developed nothing new for the most important year of his career.

He also came into the year without a quad, even though he was practicing it. He didn't try one in competition all autumn. This put him well behind the curve; every other top men's Olympic medal hope had one.

The Russians said that when Plushenko landed a quad–triple combination in practice at Skate America (a practice in which Eldredge skated poorly) and another quad in the warm-up for the long program in Detroit, Eldredge was spooked.

Then, the theory went, he took a dive so he wouldn't have to skate and lose to Plushenko, which would have been very embarrassing. Eldredge had a wide open path to victory in Skate America; no Michael Weiss, no Elvis Stojko, no Ilia Kulik. To lose to a then-fourteen-year-old would have been devastating to his Olympic medal hopes.

The Russian theory continued: After Plushenko skated his long program and made some mistakes, Eldredge decided to skate anyway, with the shoulder injury, and won the competition.

It was a mouthful, that story. And as they told it, the Russians actually thought it to be true.

Eldredge heard about the story in Paris, and laughed it off.

It definitely was not true, he said.

"It's kind of like they're searching for the single-bullet theory," he said, playfully mixing his conspiracy theories. "If they had strong enough stomachs to watch the tape on ABC, they would have seen my shoulder pop out."

That was one problem with the Russian theory. Eldredge's shoulder did in fact pop out when he took his "dive."

"I guess I find it a little shocking that something like that would get out there," Eldredge added. "It's such an important year, people are trying to play different games. Maybe it is to put doubts in the minds of the judges about how I feel about my skating and how I fit into the picture, if I do at all."

Eldredge, always a good sport, found the theory rather amusing.

"[Taking a fall] isn't something I would do to help my career out," he said.

Nonetheless, Mishin thought his two teenagers had Eldredge beat.

"Eldredge is not a problem," Mishin said dismissively after Yagudin and Plushenko went 1–2 at Cup of Russia. "Stojko? He's more of a problem."

Having dispensed with Eldredge, Mishin moved on to Kulik, a countryman and a rival, coming from Moscow, not St. Petersburg.

Mishin's task to dismiss Kulik was a little more difficult because there was nothing old or tired or stale about the twenty-year-old blond Russian rocket.

But Mishin figured Kulik had grown soft training by himself at the beautiful, four-rink facility in Marlboro, Massachusetts, and the season's performances didn't disprove this theory. Kulik finished second to Elvis Stojko in Canada and won NHK Trophy in Japan, but both times he made mistakes on an important axel jump—the double axel in Canada, the triple in Japan—in the short program, popping it into a single each time. Kulik was up to his same old maddening tricks; nearly perfect, except for one devastating mistake.

Skating to Gershwin's *Rhapsody in Blue,* for the long program, he held audiences spellbound until he made some other silly mistake.

He also was annoying everyone—spectators, journalists, other skaters, and judges—by wearing perhaps the most distracting outfit ever worn by a skater of his magnitude. Although the music was *Rhapsody in Blue,* Kulik wore nothing blue. His outfit was a black and yellow spotted vinyl shirt with a white vinyl vest and black pants.

A reporter cornered him on the subject of his shirt.

"Is it supposed to be a cow print, or are you dressed more like a giraffe?"

Kulik: "It's not a cow or a giraffe. It's something from the time of Gershwin, the United States of the '40s and '50s. I think it looks good. Don't you like it?"

Reporter: "No."

Kulik: "Why not?"

Reporter: "It's distracting."

Kulik: "Well, my coach spent a long time picking it out. Talk to my coach about that. I'm tired of answering this question."

Perhaps he and coach Tatiana Tarasova, the ice dancing specialist, became confused. Did they mistake *Rhapsody in Blue* for *Rhapsody in Moo?*

For the short program, Kulik wore flowing wings. It was very Russian, designed to accentuate his graceful moves. His short program, like the long, was marvelous. But both costumes were so distracting it was hard to notice how marvelous the programs were.

Mishin had no quarrel with the costumes—who was he to talk about men's skating outfits?—but he assumed Kulik was too Americanized to do much damage anymore.

"If you are in the motherland, you have roots," he said. "If you leave, you don't have roots. If you lose your roots, you don't have the source of your power."

Mishin also said that Kulik's camp had made a strong effort to convince Alexei Yagudin to move to Massachusetts to train with Kulik, who made his move in 1996.

"To be alone as a competitor is the beginning of the death," Mishin said. "They tried to steal athletes from me, to give him someone to train with. They tried to steal Yagudin to make a sparring partner for him, to make Kulik's life more relaxed. He would become a shadow of Kulik. Now, though, he's a competitor of Kulik."

Kulik said he never wanted Yagudin to come and train with him.

"I have no idea what he's talking about," Kulik said of Mishin.

Yagudin, a strong-willed, talkative young man, said he was going nowhere.

"I love Russia," Yagudin said, "and I will never leave, not like Kulik."

As his skaters entered the Russian nationals, followed a week later by the Champions Series final in Munich, Mishin thought the hard life was the right life for his boys. He brought his two teenagers to the nationals to beat Kulik, then to Munich to beat him again.

But Mishin miscalculated. In his zeal to create two top Olympic medal contenders, he burned out both boys. They lost to Kulik at the nationals, then lost to him again at the Champions Series final.

Yagudin ran out of gas in his long program at the Russian nationals in Moscow, but hung on for second place behind Kulik, whose only mistake was putting his hand to the ice on a triple axel.

In Munich, Yagudin made two mistakes in his short program, and finished last among the six contenders. He slid out of the landing of his huge triple axel, then nearly fell on his triple lutz. The kid was exhausted, having competed in six different events in the autumn, including four major competitions—Trophy Lalique, Cup of Russia, the Russian nationals, and Champions Series final—in five weeks.

It was one thing to overcome fatigue in his hometown, as he did at Cup of Russia. It was quite another to be physically drained and trying to beat the world's best skaters.

With all that skating, Yagudin, one reporter said, had become "Ya-bad-in."

Even though he was the only competitor to cleanly land a quad in the long program, Yagudin moved up only to fourth place, while Plushenko finished fifth. Mishin's skaters were not on the podium.

It was a time of confusion in Mishin's camp. Wire reports said Alexei Urmanov had been eliminated from possible selection to the Russian Olympic team, but both he and Mishin said that wasn't true, that there still was a chance if his groin muscle miraculously healed by January.

But who would the Russians bump from their two-man Olympic team in that case? Yagudin had won two Champions Series events. Kulik was the gold medal favorite coming out of Munich. And Plushenko, the third-ranked Russian male skater who was gunning more for 2002 than 1998, also had had a terrific season.

If only the Russians had that third men's spot back, they all thought.

If only the International Skating Union had thought through its new points system, and made some dispensation for a skater who was injured after leading the short program.

If only Russian doctors could have treated Urmanov better.

If only . . .

"Who knows?" Urmanov said. "Maybe tomorrow I will feel fine."

Little was going right for the men from St. Petersburg as 1998 neared. Yubileiny Palace was going to be closing for a year and a half to be refurbished to host the world hockey championships in 2000. It was thought the rink would reopen better than ever, but who would be left to skate there? Mishin was talking with officials at a rink in Phoenix, Arizona. Moskvina was considering her options in the United States as well. Everyone might scatter.

"In one and a half years, everything will be destroyed," Mishin said. "If our skating school is closed, this generation will be the last. After the Olympics, everyone will forget us immediately, the next day."

In eight weeks exactly, the men's Olympic gold medalist would be crowned in Nagano. The Champions Series final was a sneak preview of the Olympic Games; the event gave a wide-open jumpfest some semblance of order.

Three men sat at a table in the interview room after the competition in Munich, each having learned something very valuable from the Champions Series final.

Ilia Kulik realized, finally, that if he skated cleanly, he could be the judges' favorite. He had never been as close to perfection as he was over those two days in Germany. He finally skated a clean short program, and he was nearly flawless in the long program; putting his hands to the ice to brace himself on his quad toe loop was his only error.

He was second after the short program, but won the long program, and finished first overall.

Kulik rarely let down his guard with strangers, but he admitted in Munich that his problems over much of 1996 and 1997 were caused by a lack of confidence with the four-minute, thirty-second long program. After finishing second in the world in 1996, he had assumed that things might come easily for him. He had assumed wrong.

"I didn't have enough experience," he said. "Now, I have a base. Even if I miss something [a jump], I still have a base. Last year, I wasn't so confident in my free skating. That always was a big problem for me."

Elvis Stojko was second. He fell on his quad toe loop two minutes into his long program; that was his only mistake over two days.

Stojko was heartened by a short program victory that indicated international judges liked him much more in 1997–98 than they did the previous year. Nine months after finishing fourth among equals in the short program at the 1997 worlds, Stojko was first.

"Five of us skated clean, with triple–triples," he said. "And I came out on top, all firsts."

The judges were coming around, believing he was true to his music and himself, even if they still didn't entirely love the performances.

"They say, 'Oh, we see what he's doing now,' " Stojko said.

During his long program, Stojko said he never quite felt "over" his feet, but he wasn't worried about it.

"Better it happens here than at the Olympics," he said with a confident smile.

He vowed to go home and work on the little things that would put him back on top of his sport. He was not concerned about Kulik; that was not his way, to worry about others.

"I'm just getting prepared and getting in the miles and the run-throughs," he said.

He even found some strange satisfaction in coming in second. It would calm down Canada. By the end of 1997, the nation was obsessed with its men's Olympic hockey team, and with Elvis. If one or both didn't win the gold medal, the country might take months to recover.

"It really shows it's not going to be that easy," Stojko said. "Instead of winning everything, now I know what it really takes. When I fell in Edmonton [at the 1996 worlds], people realized, 'This is difficult. He is human.' It's not like it just happens."

Overall, Stojko was pleased as he left Munich. He was second to a man who rarely was able to put together two grand performances in a row. Odds were Kulik would make a mistake the next time he skated in a big event. And that next big event was the Olympic Games.

Finishing second to Kulik was not a bad spot to be in, Stojko told himself. Not bad at all.

Todd Eldredge was third. And he was in trouble.

He skated beautifully, the best he had since the previous year's Champions Series final. As usual, he did not attempt a quad, but he made no mistakes on his seven triple jumps. His shoulder was fine. So were his ribs. Although he was having trouble with his skate blades, his spins were wonderful, his footwork was superb, and his overall skating was crisp and clean.

And he was third.

Two judges—the Russian and the Canadian—placed Eldredge fourth in the short program, below Evgeni Plushenko. Overall, he came in third in the short, and third in the long program.

In the long program, one judge—Joan Gruber from the United States—placed Eldredge first. Two judges put him second. Two more placed him third. And two more had him fourth, behind Alexei Yagudin.

When it came to Todd Eldredge, the judges were all over the map.

"I think it's good," Eldredge said jauntily. "It keeps the competition between the three of us really close. It keeps you in suspense for Japan."

But what if Yagudin had skated cleanly in the short program, then landed his quad in the long program?

Might not Eldredge have been bumped to fourth place?

It became clear in Munich that Eldredge was not the international skating community's top choice for the Olympic gold medal. Without a quad, with old programs, with the same reliable Eldredge look, he no longer was the judges' favorite skater.

In March, in Lausanne, he could have won without the quad.

In December, in Munich, he could not.

The Olympic gold medal still was out there to be won, but Eldredge would need some help to do it.

Eldredge knew when he left Munich that he would be in for the fight of his career to try to win a medal of any color in Nagano.

Right before Christmas, Alexei Urmanov met with Alexei Mishin at Yubileiny Palace.

"You're still not able to skate the normal way," Mishin said, staring into the sad gray eyes of his Olympic gold medalist.

"I know," Urmanov said.

"The Olympics are less than two months away," Mishin said.

"Yes, I know," Urmanov said. 'It's just not possible. I can't go."

Mishin nodded his head.

He stared at his skater. This was unbelievable, Mishin thought. Urmanov jabbed the toe of his left skate into the ice to launch a triple toe loop in March, and it ruined him for a year.

What was it that Mishin always told his skaters?

"Jump every jump like it's the last in your life."

Mishin tenderly patted Urmanov on the shoulder.

There was nothing more to say.

Urmanov's mother was waiting for him in the apartment when he walked in the door.

"The Olympics, . . ." he said, shaking his head, "the Olympics just are not possible."

She wrapped her arms around her son.

"Everything will be fine," she said.

"I'll keep skating," he said. "I'll come back."

He looked around the room. He saw all the items the 1994 Olympic gold medal had provided for them: the furniture, the fax machine, the television.

Urmanov smiled at his mother.

"It's going to be okay," he said. "We'll watch the Olympics right here, together."

PART V

January 1998

THE
NATIONAL
CHAMPION-
SHIPS

13

"6.0, 6.0, 6.0, 6.0, 6.0, 5.9, 6.0, 6.0, 6.0"

At 8:45 A.M. on Tuesday, January 6, 1998, the telephone rang in Room 1768 of the downtown Philadelphia Marriott.

Audrey Weisiger was trying to sleep in.

She reached for the phone.

"Hello?"

"Is this the most important day of your entire career?" a friend asked.

Weisiger was startled by the wake-up question.

"Well, that's a little better than the question Debbie Prachar asked me the other day," Weisiger said of one of her coaching colleagues. "She said, 'Don't you feel like you're going to throw up all the time?' "

It was the day of the men's short program at the 1998 U.S. national figure skating championships, where the two men who would represent the United States at the Olympic Games would be selected over two days of competition.

Michael Weiss, Weisiger's skater, was expected to be one of those chosen, but it was no guarantee. Nothing was guaranteed in the short program. It was two minutes and forty seconds of skating agony. One fall and you're out. Or, at the very least, one fall and you're in big trouble.

Weiss had become a poster boy for U.S. short program troubles as a senior-level competitor at nationals:

In 1994, he put a hand down to the ice on a jump.

In 1995, he fell.

In 1996, he stepped out of a landing.

In 1997, he put both hands down on a jump.

His track record was dismal: four short programs, none clean.

His fifth short program as a senior-level skater would be that night.

Weisiger and Weiss had spent thirteen years together as coach and skater. Very few coaches could say they took a skater from his first steps on the ice to the Olympic Games. Weisiger had been at Fairfax Ice Arena the day eight-year-old Michael showed up to join his older sister, who was coached by Weisiger.

And she was with him in Philadelphia the day a twenty-one-year-old skater's career would be made—or broken.

Years from then, when they looked back on it, Weisiger and Weiss would be able to point to the short program at the 1998 nationals as the competition that launched him on his way to the Olympics, or sent him spiraling into a non-Olympic skating netherworld, a sports purgatory located closer to hell than to heaven. A mistake that night could become the defining moment of his life. How many cocktail parties would he have to endure over the course of his life where people would find out he had been a skater, then ask the obvious question: "Did you go to the Olympics?"

And he would have to answer, "Well, no, I didn't," and think back to that night in Philly in the winter of '98.

It could be a debilitating thought: thirteen years of skating wrapped up in two minutes and forty seconds. And, more specifically, thirteen years all tied up in the dreaded triple axel–triple toe loop combination, which came fifty seconds into his program. If he landed it, and didn't bomb the rest of the way, he would be in great shape for Nagano.

If he fell, he might be headed for fifty years of nagging cocktail party questions.

The last practice session for the men was in the empty CoreStates Center, Tuesday at 5 P.M., two hours before the spectators streamed in and more than three hours before Weiss skated the short program.

"This is it," Weiss told his wife, Lisa, as they left the hotel and went to the warm-up. "The chance for the Olympics is what everybody asks you about when you're younger. It gets closer and closer and all of a sudden, it's right on you, and here it is."

After Weiss warmed up for just fifteen minutes, he grabbed his skate guards and his water bottle and left Weisiger sitting in the first row of seats in a corner of the arena. Weiss went back to the hotel. Weisiger stayed in that first row of seats and chatted with a friend.

Weisiger was calm. That surprised her. She normally was anxious watching Michael skate at big events. She sobbed uncontrollably in Nashville when he finished second. Most of her friends expected her to be a wreck with an Olympic berth on the line.

"It's really not the nerve-racking moment people think it is," she said as the next group of skaters came onto the ice, and Scott Davis caught her eye and said hello as he sped by.

"In terms of what I've done for his career, my work is basically finished. He's ready. I think he will skate clean tonight. And even if he doesn't, it's all been a success. It's been a really long, rewarding journey."

She felt a strange sense of satisfaction overtake her, the way students who have studied hard for a test feel as they walk into the classroom knowing they can study no more, that they're as ready as they'll ever be.

After coming home from Russia in late November, she watched Weiss instantly buckle down in practice to skate cleanly day after day. Perhaps that awful performance in St. Petersburg had "disgusted" him just enough. One day in December, Weisiger handed Weiss a tape of *Chariots of Fire* and suggested he watch it. She was hoping it would fire him up.

Weiss shrugged when he brought it back to her.

"It was alright," he said.

He didn't need to get psyched up by a movie, it turned out.

"He was almost scaring me because he was so on," Weisiger said.

As he prepared for the Olympic trials, Weiss still had to negotiate traffic and thread the needle during crowded practices at Fairfax.

One day, Weisiger politely shouted to all the kids working on their double toe loops to move toward the boards so Weiss could run through his programs without running into them.

"Hey, everybody, Mike's trying to make the Olympic team," she shouted.

Frank Carroll and Richard Callaghan never had to make that kind of announcement at their rinks. But Fairfax Ice Arena was where Weisiger and Weiss belonged, the way Linda Leaver and Brian Boitano belonged in various unassuming rinks around San Francisco more than a decade earlier.

The legacy of loyalty that Leaver and Boitano left to the sport—the housewife/coach training the talented boy skater from childhood to the Olympic Games—was proudly being carried on by Weisiger and Weiss. They formed the same tandem: the wife/mother/coach and the promising young skater. They had not reached the level of success that Leaver and Boitano achieved, and they never might. But together they certainly planned to try.

It wasn't always easy. In the spring of 1995, looking for advice on how to help Weiss improve, Weisiger met with Leaver when she came to Washington with Boitano for the Campbell's Soups skating tour. Weisiger rarely sought out anyone for advice; Leaver was one of the few people she trusted and respected enough to ask. They sat in the lobby of the Four Seasons Hotel in Georgetown, sipped coffee, and talked about bringing up a talented young man in their sport.

"How do I get him to deal with the pressure and deliver consistent competition performances?" Weisiger asked.

"If he's having trouble with the triple axel, if you're having trouble with his consistency on that jump, water down the program so he skates a clean program every time," Leaver told Weisiger. "You want him to gain consistency and confidence."

Weisiger listened.

"But you're doing fine," Leaver said. "You're doing a great job."

In December 1997, hoping to energize the national prospects of their two top skaters, Weisiger and fellow coaches Nick Perna and Debbie Prachar invented a contest between Weiss and eleven-year-old Elizabeth (Lisa) Kwon, who was competing in the novice ladies event at nationals.

"Every day," they said to the two skaters, "we'll see who does the cleanest programs."

All of a sudden, Weiss was competing against an eleven-year-old girl. The coaches figured out a way to equalize the two: His quad lutz equaled her triple loop; his triple axel equaled her triple toe loop.

They weren't certain Weiss would find this interesting.

But the first day, Weiss showed up at the rink after Kwon's afternoon session.

"How'd Lisa do?" he asked one of the coaches.

"She was clean."

"Hmmm."

The next day, she asked how *he* did.

"Mike did a clean short," Perna told her.

"Hmmm."

One day, the two went to Washington's new MCI Center to get the feeling of skating in a big arena. This was especially important for Kwon, who never had skated in a place so big.

When Kwon returned to Fairfax, she proudly proclaimed, "I beat him. I had to, otherwise he'd be two days ahead of me."

They arrived in Philadelphia tied in their little competition, but Kwon swiftly moved ahead by winning the national novice ladies title on Monday, the day before the men's short program. Skating with speed and determination, she made no mistakes in either her short or long program, in which she landed four triple jumps.

The novice ladies competition was held across the parking lot from the CoreStates Center at the Spectrum, where the 1968 nationals had been held. There, Peggy Fleming won her fifth national title and went on to win the Olympic gold medal, while, in the novice ladies event, a skater named Audrey King from Washington, D.C., finished third.

"That's really special to me," Audrey Weisiger said, "that baby Kwon won where I started at nationals thirty years ago."

Fairfax's Lisa Kwon had become America's next hot little girl skater.

The pressure was on Weiss to answer her.

At 8:30 P.M., Weisiger was standing by the boards, as she always did, when Weiss took the ice for his flamenco-style short program, the music she and Brian Wright and the others had created in April.

Wright was not there; he was in Los Angeles choreographing for a professional skater. That day, he had trouble standing on the ice. He had cramps in his abdomen. He didn't feel good. But he certainly planned to watch Weiss perform the program he created for him later that night on television.

Back in Philadelphia, Lisa Thornton Weiss stood by the boards with Weisiger. It was a new season, but ABC Sports' announcers, working on ESPN2, once again mispronounced Weisiger's name. And, once again, they identified Lisa as Weiss's choreographer, which, for the short program, was wrong.

"It got to the point where I didn't even pay attention anymore," Wright said when he heard the broadcast.

One ABC staffer said she was frustrated that the network could not get the information right; that Wright was the choreographer for the short program (and the choreographer for the short and long in 1996–97) and that Weisiger, Lisa, and Michael combined on the long program. She said the mistake kept being made because Lisa was officially listed as one of Weiss's choreographers and needed to be identified in some way when shown on the air.

Weiss began by taking his opening position while standing on the huge U.S. flag that was painted on the blue ice of the CoreStates Center.

In twenty seconds, he landed his triple lutz, as smooth as ever, a warm-up jump for him.

Thirty seconds later, he sped across the center of the ice and, turning forward, kicked his right leg into the air.

This was his triple axel. This was the combination.

His takeoff was not perfect. He flew into the air not perpendicular to the ice, but slightly askew. Weiss rotated three and a half times and slammed down on the blade of his right skate. Ice sprayed as he dug in to hold onto the landing. It was jarring, but he had done it. A triple axel.

Immediately, Weiss's left leg reached back and he launched himself into the air again. This was the combination jump that had injured Alexei Urmanov so severely that he still could not compete. Weiss rotated: one-two-three. It was a triple toe loop, not the double he settled for in Germany and Russia.

But because he had been off balance taking off on the triple toe loop, he came down out of position. He landed on his right foot—his left foot never touched the ice—but he swung around in a full circle to hold onto the landing.

"Good save!" Wright screamed into the TV set in Los Angeles.

Weisiger watched stoically. Like Frank Carroll, she never betrayed her emotions until her skater was done. Then, unlike Frank Carroll, she sometimes did.

The triple–triple was what she was waiting to see. For her, it was a sign. Weiss's triple axel was worse than the one he landed in Germany, but he still tacked a triple toe loop on the end of it. This was a signal that Weiss finally was ready to compete.

Weiss still had a double axel to do, and spins and footwork, but the tough stuff was over. He was flying.

Another fifty seconds went by before his music changed and the rhythmic applause began. The crowd was not great in the arena that night, just 5,425, but the people joined in.

"They're clapping," Weisiger thought to herself, smiling. "The fans are clapping."

*   *   *

Weiss finished his program by sliding on one knee. He pumped his fist. He had not made a mistake. It was his first clean short program ever at the senior level. It had been dicey on the triple toe loop landing, but it was clean.

As Weiss waved from center ice, Weisiger opened her purse and pulled out a familiar visitor to national competition. The pony. The plastic pony had made the journey from Fairfax once again. She reared back and fired, sending the little toy flying across the ice. It picked up speed until it lodged in the bottom of the boards surrounding the ice.

Weiss joined Weisiger in Kiss and Cry, where a backdrop of blue sky and mountains had been erected to make it look pretty for the TV cameras.

"I really pulled that one out," Weiss said to her, referring to the combination.

"Yeah," Weisiger said, "good work. You prepared. You were ready. This is what happens when you prepare."

As they awaited his marks, the flower girls and boys brought the loot that had been tossed onto the ice.

Weisiger searched through it.

No pony.

"Mike, they didn't get the pony."

"Where is it?" he asked.

"It's still on the ice."

Weiss's eyes grew wide.

The next skater was already circling around, waiting to skate.

It was Todd Eldredge.

Weisiger glared at a flower girl.

"There's a toy pony out there, sticking out from the boards," she said. "Go get it!"

The last thing they needed was for Eldredge to trip over the pony—thrown by the coach of his greatest rival—and fall. They didn't want any repeats of Eldredge's Skate America crash.

"Please," Weisiger told the girl, "get that pony!"

The flower girl arrived with the pony as Weiss's marks arrived on the scoreboard. There were a majority of 5.6s, 5.7s, and 5.8s. Weiss was in fine shape.

Most importantly, he had survived the short program.

Todd Eldredge, Mr. Reliable, was skating his old short program, "Walk on the Wild Side," for the last time, he said. He was planning to jettison it for the Olympics, but kept it for nationals because he had no time to make the change in the fall, what with his injury and all his travels.

The deliberate Eldredge skated better than Weiss, with a more controlled triple–triple combination, and was placed above Weiss by all nine of the judges.

Weiss and Eldredge had drawn the fourth and fifth skating positions out of eighteen competitors. Normally, those positions would be a bit of a problem, because judges have to leave room for skaters who come later. But, because of their impeccable resumés, Weiss and Eldredge received fine scores, leaving just the slightest opening for two other men who were yet to come, Dan Hollander and Scott Davis.

Hollander, the ninth skater, had a difficult task. As the man who lost the United States its third spot at the Olympic Games by missing the cut at the Lausanne world championships, Hollander would have had to hang from the rafters to earn a trip to Nagano. Instead, he performed the sports equivalent of hanging himself when he stepped out of his triple axel–double loop combination, then performed an airy single axel where his double had to be.

If he wasn't history prior to the event, he was finished after skating for less than three minutes. He was seventh by the end of the evening.

The fourteenth skater was Scott Davis, the last man who had a chance to pass Weiss—and even Eldredge, perhaps, if he skated well. Performing to blues guitar music, Davis set out quickly and effortlessly, progressing toward his triple axel–triple toe loop. The axel was his nemesis all summer and all fall; a chance for a trip to Nagano was riding on it.

He went up—and landed cleanly. But he chickened out—as Weiss had in Europe—and went only for the double toe loop on the end of it.

Already, he was behind Weiss.

Moments later, disaster struck when Davis picked into the ice with his right toe for his triple lutz, caught the tracing of another skater's triple lutz, and didn't get the lift he needed, popping the jump into a single.

When he finished, Davis shook his head in disbelief.

"Can I go out and do it again?" he asked.

Another year, another disaster.

But the judges gave him a going-away present—assuming he wasn't going to Nagano after the long program—by placing him third, ahead of journeyman Shepherd Clark, who did not make a mistake, but happened to skate first. The judges gave Clark low scores, and when Davis did not skate perfectly, five of them still put a stumbling Davis ahead of Clark.

"I'm lucky to be third," Davis said.

Davis said his problem was that he was thinking too much before he skated.

He shrugged.

Mr. Fourth Place was third.

"I'm kind of kicking myself right now," he said softly. "It's like a wake-up call, I guess."

Whatever it was that plagued Davis in 1996 and 1997 most definitely was back in 1998.

Davis was not alone in his agony. The men's short program had been extremely messy.

"I saw some wonderful things and some positions that were not worthy of novice or junior or skating pond competitions," ABC's Dick Button told reporters afterward.

Ironically enough, though, if Weiss made a few big mistakes in Thursday's long program, Davis could be in the running for the second berth on the Olympic team. For that matter, Eldredge still was in a precarious spot, although no one thought he could be denied an Olympic slot.

To compare skating scoring to football, Eldredge and Weiss should have held a 50–0 halftime lead over Davis.

But in skating, all the judges' scores were turned into ordinals, which then were turned into factored placements. And because anyone in the top three after the short program could win the overall competition by winning the long program, that meant the real score between the three men, in football terms, was 0–0.

Skaters like Eldredge and Weiss could lead by a mile, but there was no way for the skating scoring system to show it.

This didn't matter to Weiss. He skated so well that he thought he would soar on Thursday night. After the short program, he talked with reporters at the front of the interview room; he also talked with reporters at the back of the interview room. He was accessible and agreeable. He was new and different. He was broad-shouldered and handsome. He was a story. A good story.

"I just got this big smile on my face today," he said, "because I realized, when I was eight, when I first started skating, the question was, 'Do you want to go to the Olympics someday?' This is what everybody asks you about your entire life. And here you are, it's right before you."

As Weiss spoke, Weisiger stood outside a blue curtain separating the interview room from the hallway. She could hear her skater, but couldn't see him. She was alone, simply staring into the curtain.

Someone motioned her to come in.

"No thanks," she said, staying in the hallway, "I've already seen everything that I needed to see today."

The women didn't compete until Thursday afternoon. That gave them hours of practice time in front of big crowds at the various rinks being used in Philadelphia.

Spectators saw jumps and spins and beautiful practice outfits.

But when they walked away and went back to the hotel lobby, they remembered one thing: Michelle Kwan crashing to the ice.

Kwan changed her short program back at Lake Arrowhead, replacing her triple toe loop with the more difficult triple flip. The switch occurred because of the stress fracture on her left foot, where her second toe met her foot. The toe loop required her to pick into the ice with her left foot. On the flip, she picked with her right. Kwan and Frank Carroll changed the triple jump in her short program to avoid the stabbing pain she sometimes felt when she picked in with her bad toe.

"I put that toe in there and it's just like, 'Wow! Ouch!'" Kwan said.

But the only problem with their strategy was that when Kwan ran through her short program in practice, she often fell on the triple flip.

The toe was all the rage in Philly. It was the No. 1 topic of conversation.

"Michelle, how's the toe?"

"Did it hurt today?"

"Are you thinking of withdrawing?"

She was taking Advil for the pain, nothing more, and trying just one triple toe loop and one triple salchow in practice each day. Doctor's orders: just one a day.

Ironically, the injury forced her to scrap an easier jump and put a harder one in for the short program. Tara Lipinski did the triple flip as her second, by-itself triple jump in the short.

Kwan matched her. She was doing one too.

At least she was trying to do one.

"I tell her, 'Remember what your book is called, *Heart of a Champion,*'" Danny Kwan said. "'You have to have what your book said.'"

When her music came on in the big arena at a Tuesday afternoon practice, and she pretended she was skating for real, she tore down the ice for the triple flip—and fell.

When she went to the Pennsylvania Convention Center and practiced on makeshift ice there Wednesday afternoon, she fell on the triple flip once again.

"The triple flip?" Frank Carroll said cynically that day on the eve of the short program.

"Fabulous! She never misses it."

He laughed.

"She's not one hundred percent yet. She's doing her best to stay tough. I'm not aiming at perfect here. I'm aiming for her to do a really good job."

Carroll always took a philosophical view of a skater's falls.

"If you're not falling, you're not improving," he said. "When your falling days are over, your skating days are over."

Carroll also knew that Kwan usually turned practice trouble into perfect programs. That was her track record. She was a gamer. She did it in the short program at Skate America and she did it many times in 1996 prior to Nashville. Carroll believed Kwan focused better and got sharper as the week wore on at every competition; he was banking on that again in Philadelphia.

Kwan and Carroll did their usual press conference before the event, and put on their usual show. They didn't seem to be alarmed, even though Kwan hadn't been able to do clean run-throughs in her minimal practice time back at home, either.

They were upbeat. They were chatty. The psychologist's couch was open for business.

They knew that Kwan didn't need to be in Philadelphia, that she would have been given a free pass to the Olympics by the U.S. Figure Skating Association if she wanted one. That was her right as the 1996 world champion and top women's skater in the world in the autumn of 1997. This wasn't cheating; it was the smart thing to do. The United States sent athletes to the Olympics in all kinds of ways: Gymnastics did a little picking and choosing to go along with its trials; track and field went strictly with trials results; NBA players were picked in meetings. The United States absolutely wanted to send Kwan, if she was healthy, to the 1998 Olympic Games.

Kwan also knew there was a risk competing at the nationals. What if she fell and lost to Tara Lipinski? What would that do to her confidence? What would international judges think coming into the Olympics? She could have taken a nice, long, easy approach to her training and simply showed up ready to go, albeit a bit rusty, on February 18 in Nagano.

But Kwan decided that option was not for her.

"I thought, 'No, I don't want to do that. I want to earn this spot to the Olympics,' " Kwan said. "This is the moment. This is the year that everything will happen. And there's no guarantee that I'll be perfect at the Olympics. This is kind of like a test.

"If I can't make it through this, how am I going to make it through the Olympics?"

Kwan threw that question into the air without hesitation. She was unique in that way, challenging herself in the public eye. Reporters often wondered if her comments were a sign of weakness, but Kwan later said they in fact were an indication of her strength. Talking it out with the press made her feel good.

Reporters who had covered the sport for the past four or five years also realized something else about Kwan; she had grown up in front of their eyes. On the ice, this was obvious. In 1995, she was the awkward junior skater. A year later, she was Salome, and on her way.

Off the ice, a plain little Chinese girl had become exotic and beautiful. When Kwan popped up on Jay Leno, all made up for television, she looked as if she should stay right where she was, on a Hollywood set, and never leave.

Tara Lipinski and Michelle Kwan were in different practice groups at nationals, and Lipinski looked invincible on the ice. So much so that when her music came on, reporters knew if they had to turn away and interview someone, they would miss nothing.

She never fell.

Coaches watching the two skaters thought they saw a pattern: a shaken, injured, unreliable Kwan, and a tough-as-nails Lipinski. Tara would win the national title, some of them said privately. She was on a roll after Munich. They were sure of it.

But within the Lipinski camp, there were the usual signs of tension.

Agent Mike Burg canceled a press conference that had been tentatively scheduled for early in the week. Tara, he said, was "hurt" by media attacks, including the old costume controversy and the newer "flutz" controversy.

But her mother said a few weeks earlier that Tara didn't read the papers.

"I keep it all away from her, but I read it and then I guess she can't understand why I look sad sometimes," Pat Lipinski said. "But she always says, 'Mom, I know you read something. Will you just forget it and get on with it?' She's good like that. I just respect her so much because she's everything that I could probably never be."

Tara's inner circle also took a significant hit from Philip Hersh in the *Chicago Tribune* in a lengthy piece on Sunday, January 4:

Hersh wrote about the family's "defensiveness," saying it turned into "sideswipes at Kwan.

"They cannot understand how Kwan at fifteen could have earned universal praise along with her world title," Hersh wrote, even though there was the considerable questioning Frank Carroll and Danny Kwan received over Kwan's portrayal of Salome at that young age.

The article continued:

" 'Tara is fifteen now, and when Michelle won at fifteen, the whole world stood still,' Pat Lipinski said . . .

" 'I know Tara's competitor,' Pat Lipinski would say a few minutes later, when the subject of financing a skating career came up. 'Sixteen years old, and her mom and dad don't work. Who is paying those bills?' "

Shep Goldberg, Kwan's agent, was angry about those comments, but decided not to show the article to the Kwans or say a word about it in public.

The Lipinskis were preoccupied with the Kwans. One member of Team Tara waited no more than a half hour after Lipinski's triumph at the Champions Series final in Munich before asking, "What's Michelle going to think when she hears about this?"

Kwan later said she fell asleep back home in Lake Arrowhead and didn't watch the competition.

By the morning of the women's short program, Brian Boitano, working the men's event for ABC Sports, was a little concerned about Michelle Kwan.

He called her at home in December to see how she and her toe were doing, then didn't see Kwan all week at nationals. By Thursday morning, having been told how her practices were going, Boitano decided to call her room at the Marriott to give her a pep talk. He never got an answer.

Kwan was gone from the room by the time Boitano called, but she had slept late that morning—missing her final practice session—after having trouble sleeping all night. She tossed and turned and kept wondering, "How am I going to do? What's going to happen?"

She was scheduled to skate at 2:17 P.M., and she arrived an hour or so beforehand to stretch and warm up. She was dragging her portable suitcase when she spotted Boitano, who went backstage specifically to find her.

"Think," he said. "Just think."

He gave her a hug and off she went.

Kwan was in the building, and so was Lori Nichol, her choreographer. Nichol had flown in to Philadelphia just that morning, but it took her no time at all to get into the spirit of the competition.

"I'm not going to be able to sit down," she said with a smile as she stood in the bright arena concourse. "I might go and stand outside. I don't know."

She was talking with a friend, Jonathan Geen, and watching the skaters on a TV monitor in the wall beside a concession stand. She could hear the music wafting through one of the portals as one skater after another went through her short program.

Kwan was the fifteenth of eighteen skaters; Nichol still had an hour to wait.

The first skater in the competition had been Tonia Kwiatkowski.

After she and the three other skaters in her group warmed up just after noon, the others left the ice and trudged backstage.

Kwiatkowski stayed and waited for her turn to skate.

The public-address announcer had not yet called her name. But there she stood, a skater waiting for her last short program at her thirteenth national championships.

The applause began in the sections close to where she was standing. It caught on spontaneously and traveled like wildfire until it encircled the ice. The 6,100 spectators were clapping for the woman in white in front of them.

A college graduate was trying to compete in the land of the teenyboppers. A loyal soldier was giving it one last go. Someone who actually was old enough to watch Dorothy Hamill win the 1976 Olympic gold medal on television was still alive and kicking.

News flash: There actually was one adult lady left in ladies figure skating!

And there she was, all alone, on the ice.

Tears welled in Phil Kwiatkowski's eyes the day before the short program. "This is the last one, so it feels a little different. You just really hope it works out for her. She's worked so hard. You'd just like to see it happen for her."

His wife, Corinne, took one look at him and began crying too.

Kwiatkowski was not the type of man anyone would expect to see crying at a figure skating practice. Big and friendly, he works with heavy machinery for a living.

But he also knew that his daughter was a survivor. He and his wife watched Tonia grow up in a sport that was changing rapidly around her. They knew she wasn't the favorite to win an Olympic spot; all things being equal, the three-member U.S. team would be Kwan, Lipinski, and Nicole Bobek, the three previous national champions.

But they also knew their daughter had paid her dues, and where they were from, paying your dues meant something.

"My kid always accepts what's given to her," Corinne Kwiatkowski said. "Carol [Heiss, her coach] says she's too nice, but we raised her that way. If she's your friend, she's your friend."

"She represents the Winterhurst Figure Skating Club in Lakewood, Ohio," the announcer's voice boomed. "Tonia Kwiatkowski!"

In 1995, at the nationals, Tonia Kwiatkowski unluckily drew the first skating position in the short program, skated perfectly, and won that portion of the event.

In 1998, with all the weight of the world on her shoulders, she skated flawlessly once again. Kwiatkowski was known as a strong tactician who usually nailed the short program, and, in her last nationals, she did it again.

The judges gave her strong scores—5.5s, 5.6s, and 5.7s—and kept her in the mix for an Olympic berth. Because she skated cleanly, she would be a factor Saturday night in the long program.

Seven skaters later, Nicole Bobek came along. November was long gone; it was a new year, and Bobek was ready. Reggie Jackson became baseball's Mr. October in the 1970s; Nicole Bobek was skating's Ms. January of the 1990s.

She skated cleanly too. She leaped over Kwiatkowski and remained very much in the running for the Olympics. Bobek hadn't shot herself in the foot, at least not yet. This created a happy air of anticipation in the arena; with Bobek, anything was possible.

But there was some confusion over her program.

It involved the kind of triple jump she was attempting on her combination. She called it a triple lutz, the jump all the top women try. But it looked distinctly like a triple flip, coming off the easier inside edge.

No, Bobek said, it was a lutz.

A compromise was reached:

Reporters called it a triple Bobek.

The first skater in Group No. 3, the tenth skater overall, was Tara Lipinski.

By not speaking to reporters all week, she kept herself focused on the one thing that she already concentrated on best: skating. If Kwan was a bit of a mystery psychologically, always questioning herself, Lipinski was an open book. She was a fierce competitor, a strong type-A personality, a girl on a mission. Although jumping was her passion, she spent hours in front of the mirror at home, working on her presentation. She would do anything for success in skating.

The familiar strains of *Anastasia* came over the public-address system. Dressed in her controversial "yodeling" costume, which she steadfastly refused to change, Lipinski tore into her program. She landed her triple lutz–double loop combination one minute and five seconds in, then came around the ice to prepare for her triple flip.

But something happened. She rushed the jump. She hurried to pick into the ice. Her right toe didn't get a strong foothold in the ice and she flew into the air off-balance. She was doomed. Tara Lipinski, the kid who never missed, was about to do just that.

She thudded to the ice, sat there for a split second, then got up.

The audience was in shock.

A fall in the short program is figure skating death.

"It's drastic," Richard Callaghan said later.

Tara was in shock too. She cried later, her face looking like Michelle Kwan's in Nashville by the time she met the press. For a while, Tara sat slumped on the floor backstage, surrounded by her mother and father and agent, sobbing.

Lipinski couldn't believe it. Of all things, she fell on a triple jump. A triple jump! Her jumps were her life. She practiced them dozens of times a day. They had driven her into "frenzies" in Delaware. They meant everything to her.

Who could believe this sentence: Tara Lipinski fell on a triple jump in the short program?

How could a triple jump betray her?

After four more skaters and one last warm-up, Michelle Kwan took the ice.

Lori Nichol couldn't watch.

She didn't have to watch.

She knew exactly what Michelle Kwan was doing on the ice, seventeen rows below the portal between sections 119 and 120, which was where Nichol was standing. Because she didn't want Kwan to look up and possibly see her, and because she was nervous and wasn't sure if she wanted to watch or not, Nichol stood behind Jonathan Geen's back and poked her head out on occasion to take a peek.

Kwan skated to the center of the ice. As Rachmaninoff—the music that led Nichol to fax Michelle—filled the arena, she began her program.

Kwan's hands appeared to be cupping an imaginary ball as she brought them up toward her head.

Nichol knew that move.

As they worked near midnight on a Friday night the previous July, just the two of them in the rink at Lake Arrowhead, Nichol skated over to the tape player to rewind the music so they could hear it again. As she did, she turned her head to keep an eye on Michelle, who was moving around on the ice, trying to come up with something to begin the program.

"What was that?" Nichol said.

"What?" Kwan said.

"What you just did, that cool thing you just did?"

To Nichol, it looked like Kwan was cradling a crystal ball in her hands, looking into it, then turning it.

Kwan did it again.

"Yes! That's it."

"This?"

Kwan did it again.

"Yes," Nichol said. "Start like that, okay? Do that!"

*   *   *

Kwan did that, then kept going. In other short programs in other years, Kwan performed a spiral at the beginning of her program, then looped around and glided into the difficult triple lutz. But not this time. Nichol and Frank Carroll were concerned that one of Kwan's troubles with the lutz the year before may have been that she stretched her muscles for too long while performing the spiral and didn't have sufficient time to recover before going into the triple lutz, where quickness was critical.

So Nichol rearranged things. The spiral would come later. The lutz would come . . .

Now.

On the ice, Kwan was building to the big jump.

"There is such a joy to her skating," Dick Button said into his ABC microphone. "She seems to embrace us with it. And I hope she embraces this triple lutz combination."

Kwan glided in on the outside edge of her left skate blade, picked into the ice with her right toe, and flew into the air. A moment later, she landed self-assuredly, as though she somehow had seen the tape of the performance already, and knew it was going to turn out just fine. She lingered for the slightest of moments, as if to take it all in, then picked in for a double toe loop.

A perfect combination.

"Exquisitely done," Button said in the booth. "Just fine."

"I was holding my breath," sidekick Peggy Fleming added.

"We all were," Button replied.

On the ice, Kwan was talking to herself.

"One step at a time," she said as she moved from element to element. "One step at a time."

"Breathe, baby, breathe," Nichol said in the tunnel between sections 119 and 120.

Kwan flew into the air again and delicately landed the double axel less than a minute into her program.

"I believe that this short program will be remembered as a signature piece for Michelle," Fleming said into her microphone. "It's absolutely extraordinary."

The music changed. It grew dramatic. It sounded as if something important was going to happen. Nichol knew the music's every beat, for she had put it together the previous summer. The music dictated Kwan's every move, her every gesture.

In this case, the music was building to the triple flip, the jump Tara fell on, and the jump Michelle kept falling on in practice all week. As Kwan moved down the ice, the music signaled one of two things: impending doom or total ecstasy.

Michelle, take your pick.

Dick Button was shouting into his microphone.

"And it's a higher difficulty than what most of the . . ."

Kwan picked into the ice with her right foot.

". . . skaters are doing!"

Kwan was flying through the air.

In a split second, she landed.

"Oh! Wonderful!" Button said, exhaling.

Nichol exhaled too. The jumps were finished.

Kwan soared effortlessly across the ice. Her blades were barely leaving a tracing of where they had just been.

Nichol knew what was coming next. She had Kwan build to it, as if to say, "Here it is, here it is."

It was the spiral, where Kwan lifts her left leg to the heavens and glides majestically on the inside edge of her right blade, then makes the difficult and swift transition to the blade's outside edge as she continues to glide along.

"And look at this inside edge," Button gushed.

"Oh!" Fleming replied reverently. "I just forget that we're watching a short program when I see her do this. She just blends all these elements so beautifully."

Soon, Kwan spun to a finish, and one of the most appreciative standing ovations a figure skater ever received overtook the arena.

"Spectacular!" Fleming said on the ABC broadcast.

"Have you ever seen it rain teddy bears?" Button asked.

"Who said anything about an injury?" colleague Terry Gannon wanted to know.

Nichol couldn't take her eyes off Kwan. She stood and applauded with Geen and a few other friends, including Don Laws, her coach from her skating days, and waited for the scores.

It took a few minutes. Finally, the marks for required elements popped up: all 5.9s except for one 5.8.

Laws turned toward Nichol in the few seconds before the presentation marks, the ones choreographers take extremely seriously, appeared on the scoreboard.

"Let's see what they do," Laws said. He was smiling. "Let's see what they do."

Nichol grabbed the hand of the man who once coached her and

squeezed it hard. The judges' marks popped onto the scoreboard hanging over the center of the ice.

"5.9, 6.0, 6.0, 6.0, 6.0, 6.0, 5.9, 6.0, 6.0."

The scores hit Nichol like a thunderbolt. Laws hugged her. Geen hugged her. People she didn't even know hugged her.

"I told you!" Laws said, pointing at Nichol. "I told you!"

Tears welled in Nichol's eyes. She kept looking at the scoreboard.

At Skate America, Nichol hoped for 6.0s. Little more than two months later, there they were, seven of them, staring her in the face.

The scores wrote skating history. Never before had a woman received even one 6.0 in the short program at the U.S. national championships.

Kwan had just skated the most well-received short program by a woman in U.S. figure skating history.

And Nichol had been the one to give it to her.

She had hoped the short program would become one for the ages, that when Kwan skated it at the Olympics, it would be revered as one of the great performances of all time.

Nichol had been right about everything, except for the part about the Olympics.

Little did she realize that even before Kwan reached Nagano, the program and its skater already would be legendary.

Sitting beside the ice as Kwan skated was Judge No. 2, Joe Inman. Inman, who began judging in 1972 and worked his first nationals in 1986, knew months earlier that he was going to judge the nationals. When he found out, he asked the chief referee of the event to not put him on the men's event. He had his reasons.

Inman, who lives in Alexandria, Virginia, had been a U.S. Figure Skating Association monitor of Michael Weiss for many years, often suggesting changes or additions to his programs. He also was a good friend of Audrey Weisiger's. They went to dinner together on occasion, and talked often on the phone. Inman wanted to avoid any appearance of conflict of interest, and asked, if possible, to judge the women in Philadelphia.

In his twenty-six years as a skating judge, Inman never had given out a 6.0. He thought he never would. A musician, he was a stickler for artistic perfection on the ice. His standards were so high that he believed there might never be a skater who could impress him enough to punch the "6" on the keypad in front of him.

"It's a moment in time," he said. "It would have to be a moment nobody could touch."

Throughout the fall on television, Inman watched Michelle Kwan and Tara Lipinski progress. Inman had been quite complimentary of Lipinski at the Lausanne world championships, believing her to be a breath of fresh air for the sport. But by the autumn, Inman noticed some changes.

"The skating had a different sense to me this year," he said of Lipinski. "She was the reigning champion. She had other baggage to carry. Last year, she had a freedom to her skating, she had nothing to lose. This year, this girl was carrying a lot of new pressure on her shoulders."

Inman was thrilled, however, to see how Kwan was skating. He loved her musical selections; the harder the music, the better Inman thought it was, provided the skater could pull it off.

When he watched her skate to *Lyra Angelica* for her long program on television, Inman shook his head in admiration.

"This piece of music requires a terribly sophisticated skater," he said.

But he also knew that watching on television was very different from judging a performance at ice level, where everything was right there in front of him and larger than life.

Before Kwan skated, Inman sat on the edge of his seat as Lipinski came onto the ice. He already had given Kwiatkowski 5.6, 5.7, and Bobek 5.5 and 5.8. That meant he had Kwiatkowski ahead of Bobek, because he tied them both at 11.3, but ties in the short program were broken by the first mark, and Kwiatkowski's was higher than Bobek's on Inman's scorecard. Inman gave the nod to Kwiatkowski because her second triple jump was a flip, while Bobek's was the easiest triple, the toe loop.

Certainly, he had left plenty of room above them for Lipinski and Kwan, the two world champions.

When Lipinski fell, Inman had to take the required deduction of .4 off her first mark, the technical one. In his mind, he gave her a base mark, a starting point, of 5.8. He took off the .4 to reach 5.4, then took off another .1 for her change of edge on her triple lutz—that "flutz."

So Inman punched 5.3 into the keypad, followed by 5.7 for presentation.

Kwan came onto the ice thirty-five minutes after Lipinski, and Inman, pencil in hand, watched intently. He had been at the practice sessions; he had seen Kwan miss all those triple flips. But Inman went to practices not to prejudge the competition, but to look at the quality of the entire group of skaters to get an idea of who was doing what.

He also went to hear the music. He tried to shut his eyes as a skater's music came on and picture what he should be seeing. Then, the second time the skater's music was played in the next practice session, he would watch to see if what the skater was doing made sense to him, Joe Inman, the music man.

Nonetheless, Inman said, a skater had to skate. Inman was a tough judge, and a dedicated one. Although he and his fellow judges were paid an honorarium of $500 for the week, he lost money every week he volunteered for the USFSA.

Yet he kept on doing it, year after year.

Halfway through Kwan's program, as she moved elegantly from element to element, Inman felt a chill travel up his spine. Very few things surprised Joe Inman, but that did.

When she finished, tears welled in Inman's eyes. This, too, surprised him. He certainly didn't expect to have an emotional reaction as he sat along judges' row at nationals.

Through his tears, Inman punched in his scores, then looked to his right, to the judge sitting beside him, Steve Winkler.

Winkler had tears in his eyes too.

"Wow!" Inman said to Winkler.

The marks popped onto the scoreboard, the marks Lori Nichol had watched from the portal.

Judge No. 2 gave Kwan 5.9 for required elements.

And, for presentation: 6.0.

For Inman, Kwan's performance was especially meaningful. Within a four-month period in 1997, Inman's mother and his best friend died. It had been a terrible time for him. For those very few minutes that Kwan was on the ice, he found something to take his mind off his sadness.

"How wonderful," he said, "to have something in my life to lift me out of my doldrums."

There was one very sad little girl and three very happy older girls backstage after the short program.

Lipinski was fourth but in absolutely no danger of missing the three-woman Olympic team. She and Kwan were world champions in 1997 and 1996. There was an unwritten rule in figure skating: If you have world champions, send them to the Olympics. Everyone knew it, and there was no arguing about it. Tara and Michelle were going to the Olympics if they both finished out of the medals. It was a done deal. Bobek, who finished second to Kwan in the short, and Kwiatkowski, who was third, were fighting it out for the third spot.

Lipinski called her fall a "fluke," then walked out of the press conference and buried her face in her mother's shoulder. Many older and richer athletes wouldn't have had the guts or the class to show up and talk to reporters at such a devastating moment. Tiger Woods blew past reporters after a bad first round at the 1997 U.S. Open, an annual event that, while laden with tradition, did not hold the career-breaking significance to a golfer that the quadrennial Olympic trials held for a skater.

But Lipinski didn't do what Woods did. She showed up, looked into the eyes of reporters, and talked.

ABC Sports did a number on Lipinski when the event was shown on television that night before the men's long program. The network showed her fall on the triple flip, but first showed two replays of her triple lutz, with Button and Fleming pointing out that Lipinski once again rocked over and did a "flutz."

At Skate America, that was a pertinent issue.

But not at nationals.

Showing the triple lutz when the story was Tara's fall on the triple flip was like focusing on the problems in the boiler room of the *Titanic* rather than on the iceberg.

When ABC Sports asked to interview Tara the day after the short program, Mike Burg said a swift no.

Carol Heiss Jenkins met Tonia Kwiatkowski with a shudder of laughter in Kiss and Cry, and they smiled for two consecutive hours, the two of them.

"I heard it," Kwiatkowski said of the spontaneous applause that engulfed her as she stood on the ice before she skated. "It's kind of nice to have the crowd behind you before you even do anything."

"How wonderful!" Heiss said. "Oh, how wonderful that was for her!"

But for all their joy, Heiss and Kwiatkowski were concerned that, all things being equal, Kwiatkowski wasn't going to make the

Olympic team. Bobek, Lipinski, and Kwan were the three previous national champions, and they were appearing together in a Campbell's Soups commercial that was airing that week.

It was as if the Olympic team had already been selected.

"Hopefully," Kwiatkowski said, "I'll skate really well and they'll have to change [the soup cans]."

But the talk of the short program was not the second- or third-place skater, but the one who was first.

"Michelle!" said competitor Brittney McConn. "Wow! Wow! Wow!"

"I thought it was one of her best moments," Frank Carroll said. "I thought it was great. It was not so much what she did as it was the way she did it. There was a wonderful look of ease on her face and of confidence and there was a performing aura about it rather than just a technical aura."

Carroll didn't say it, but Kwan had mastered the essence of skating like Janet Lynn. That was what Lori Nichol and Kwan talked about as they watched that tape after Thanksgiving: making it look so effortless when of course it was not.

"When you're under a lot of pressure and stress to do these very difficult things," Carroll said, "to make it come off with great ease and like you're just having a wonderful time is difficult to do and I think that's what Michelle did today."

Perhaps that stress fracture was a blessing in disguise.

If Kwan hadn't been injured, Nichol might not have gone to California to spend time with her.

If Kwan hadn't been off the ice, she might never have watched the videotape of Skate America, or Janet Lynn.

That night, the men skated their long programs. And while the intrigue centered on who would make the two-man U.S. Olympic team, there were rumblings backstage that Todd Eldredge, the most conservative guy around, might be doing something quite extraordinary.

He might try a quad.

Of the Big—and Only—Three in the event, Eldredge was the first to skate, followed by Scott Davis and Michael Weiss.

Stung by repeated criticism that he was not daring enough to give the big jump a try, Todd Eldredge opened his "Gettysburg" long program with a big surprise. After crash-landing a quad in the warm-up session, he decided he would, for the first time in his career, try a quadruple toe loop for real.

He came down the ice forty seconds into his program, picked in with his right toe, spun four times, and landed. But the moment he came back to the ice, his left leg collapsed underneath him and he slid off the edge of his skate, thudding hard to the ice.

Eldredge picked himself up and carried on.

The fall shocked no one. The attempt was the thing.

The audience cheered appreciatively.

But the quad took its toll. It sucked the life out of the rest of his program. He appeared to be going through the motions, as if he were practicing, or as if his old, familiar music had lulled him into feeling like he was in a peaceful, private skating lesson.

The quad could have that kind of overwhelming effect on the other elements of a program. In Munich a few weeks earlier, Eldredge constantly practiced the quad, and found it to have a chilling effect on his practice success with his tried-and-true triples. The jump is demanding. It requires a skater to hit a tiny sweet spot on the ice. Elvis Stojko, the master of the quad, said that the "balance point" for a quad is the size of a dime. But the balance point for a double jump, he said, is as big as a basketball. Quads, he often said, don't just happen. They can take years of effort. And the twenty-six-year-old Eldredge, the king of the balanced program, didn't have years to devote to that one jump.

He did land six triple jumps, including an eleventh-hour triple axel, which served as an exclamation point on an otherwise extremely dull sentence.

The judges, clearly thrilled to see Eldredge try to keep up with the other top male skaters around the world, gave him a collective pat on the back with scores of mostly 5.8, with six 5.9s for artistry. *Sports Illustrated* later would call the judges the "Todd Squad."

Eldredge was the four-time national champion going for his fifth title, and this was the Olympic year. Send-offs always were cheerier at the nationals before the Games.

Scott Davis came next.

Harboring his own sincere hopes to make the Olympic team, Davis imploded on his first jump.

He fell on the triple axel, the jump he kept falling on in his summertime session in Connecticut, the jump that always caused him problems.

He later went up for another one and turned it into a single.

The perfect long program had eluded him again. The judges sent him away with 5.5s, 5.6s, and 5.7s.

Davis looked at his scores and shook his head.

A quizzical look crossed his face.

"I should be having fun and skating with a lot of heart. And it didn't happen."

For the second year in a row, the last skater in the men's event at the nationals was Michael Weiss.

And, for the second year in a row, he came out gunning for a quad.

As Beethoven's *Egmont* Overture built, Weiss sped over the flag on the ice and glided tantalizingly on the edge of his left skate, waiting, waiting.

When it was time, his right toe jack-hammered into the ice.

One-two-three-four revolutions.

He didn't fall.

Ice sprayed under his feet. Both feet touched down. It was obvious. But Michael Weiss was still standing.

No one on earth had come closer to landing the most difficult jump ever attempted in figure skating.

ABC's Dick Button liked the effort: "It looked awfully, awfully good."

His sidekick Brian Boitano noticed the flaw immediately: "It was definitely two-footed."

Audrey Weisiger leaped, put her hands to her face, and disappeared from view by the boards. She didn't fall. She simply began crying, and decided to tuck herself behind the Kiss and Cry curtain so Weiss wouldn't see her and get distracted when he came by.

"Come and watch," Lisa Weiss said to her.

Weisiger stayed back.

"I didn't see much of the rest of the performance," she said. "I was crying too hard."

After the quad, Weiss still had four minutes left to skate.

"I've never felt anything like the adrenaline I felt from that crowd," he said.

Energized by an audience that knew it had seen something quite incredible, Weiss tore into his triple axel–triple toe loop without a care.

It was flawless.

He had skated little more than a minute, and he looked like the new national champion.

But there were three and a half minutes to go.

As quickly as he sent himself soaring, Weiss came tumbling back to earth. He bobbled a planned triple flip–triple toe loop, turning the whole combination into one ugly double flip.

He had had trouble with the combination all autumn. For the third time in as many competitions, he failed to land the jumps.

There was more trouble. Weiss held onto shaky landings on another triple axel and a triple loop before easing into two more triples at the end.

He wobbled in the middle, but was exquisite at the start and finish.

Weiss pumped his fist. The crowd roared louder than it had all evening.

"This crowd believes that we have a new U.S. champion," Terry Gannon proclaimed on ABC.

But the judges didn't believe that.

By a seven to two count, they stuck with Eldredge, giving him that fifth U.S. title.

They had some very valid reasons.

With his mid-program slips, Weiss did not deliver a knockout punch to the champ.

And, what kind of message would it have sent the Olympic judges if Eldredge had been defeated in his own country? What would that have done to his medal chances in Nagano? He, after all, was the country's top men's hope; Weiss was an up-and-comer who was unlikely to end up on the medal stand. This was figure skating, where resumés still meant something.

Then there was Eldredge's psyche after the strangest of seasons.

"The judges really wanted Todd to be confident going into the Olympics," Weiss said on a local television show back home in Washington.

Weiss could be a happy No. 2.

Eldredge could not.

Eldredge was not entirely pleased with himself that night, and he was not at all pleased when he watched the videotape of his long program when he got home to Detroit.

He tore the program apart piece by piece, revamping various sections.

"I didn't like a lot of things," he said.

He was not certain about the fate of the quad in that program, but he had a pretty good idea what he was going to do with it.

After one try, he was leaning toward going back to what he did best—skate a complete program and leave the quad to all the other guys.

Scott Davis was a disheartened No. 3.

He shrugged and raised his eyebrows and said he would go home and think about his future. Most likely, he would turn professional and move on.

"I think people will remember me as a two-time national champion, as a good presence on the ice with a lot of fans out there, and someone who was fun to watch."

He shrugged.

Scott Davis left what most likely were his last nationals with one last shrug.

The next evening, Friday, January 9, was to have been the showdown between the top two pairs teams in the land: 1997 national champions Kyoko Ina and Jason Dungjen and Jenni Meno and Todd Sand, the champions of the previous three seasons.

But, after staying at home and training much of the autumn, Meno and Sand suffered another in a year-long series of infuriating injuries, and Ina and Dungjen easily earned their second consecutive title.

Meno jammed her right ankle in a landing in practice the day of the long program and was diagnosed with a bruised bone and a strained ligament in her foot. She and Sand were forced to withdraw from the competition, but were placed on the Olympic team after receiving clearance from a U.S. Figure Skating Association monitoring team.

In their absence, Ina and Dungjen skated as fluidly as they ever have, and rode into the Olympic Games with a huge blast of confidence.

"On any given night, anybody in the top six [pairs in the world] can medal," Dungjen said enthusiastically.

The odds were that the two U.S. pairs would not be able to defeat the Russians and the Germans, but, that night, Dungjen thought anything was possible.

"It's who can hold it together at the Olympics."

*   *   *

The lobby of the Philadelphia Marriott was still at 8:45 P.M., Saturday, January 10. Six miles away, 19,000 people were sitting in the stands of the CoreStates Center, already listening to beautiful music and watching young ladies skate.

Standing together in the lobby, waiting, were Frank Carroll and Shep Goldberg.

Mike Burg talked on a house phone fifty feet away.

Other than one lonely clerk at the registration desk, they were the only people in the spacious room.

Within minutes, Michelle Kwan and her parents swooped into the lobby from the elevators. Michelle, wearing a warm-up suit, with her hair already up and her make-up on, held her mother's hand. As they passed, Carroll and Goldberg fell in line, and they all charged past Burg and disappeared through the revolving door.

They climbed into their rented Buick, with Michelle in the front and Goldberg at the wheel, and pulled away.

The small blue sedan moved carefully down I-95. Within minutes, out Michelle's window, the arena came into view. It was bathed in white light, with spotlights crossing above it in the night sky. It couldn't have looked more inviting.

It just sat there, waiting for her.

There were six skaters in the last group on the last night of the national championships. Nicole Bobek drew the first spot in the skating order, followed by Tara Lipinski. Amber Corwin and Angela Nikodinov, two fine young skaters with promising futures, came next, allowing the fans to take a deep breath before the final act: Michelle Kwan and Tonia Kwiatkowski.

Kwiatkowski's draw was awful in one way, terrific in another. After warming up for six minutes, she would have to take off her skates backstage and wait more than forty minutes before her turn. She would run and stretch and stay by herself—and, perhaps worst of all, she would think.

On the other hand, if she were going to make the Olympic team, she would have to skate the long program without a mistake. If she performed flawlessly at the end of the evening, the audience that so warmly received her in the short program might force the judges to place her in the top three.

But for her to get that spot, she needed Bobek to make a mistake. She needed her to run out of gas, as she usually did. Kwiatkowski was too fair a player to say or even think that, but it's exactly what she needed.

If Bobek skated cleanly, she almost certainly was going to Nagano.

Ms. January charged into her four-minute long program with abandon, and within a minute, was heading into the triple Bobek, the lutz-flip-whatever. She landed the jump, but failed to tack on a double toe loop. It was a cautious move, and a smart one. There was no reason for Bobek to take any chances that night.

She landed two more triples before doubling a planned triple loop, a jump that ruined her chances for the world title in 1995 at the same juncture of her program.

"Keep your focus," Bobek told herself. "It's okay."

"She looks like a very serious Nicole out here this evening," Peggy Fleming said on the air.

In other competitions in other years, Bobek fell apart in the final minutes.

Not this time. Although she slowed down, she completed two more triples and her second double axel, then smiled the entire length of a finishing spin.

She put her hands together and prayed, thinking only of Carlo Fassi, her late coach. She glided off the ice and into the arms of Christa Fassi, who did exactly what her husband asked her to do on his death bed: please stay with Nicole.

What Bobek lacked in jumping firepower—no triple combination, no triple loop—she more than made up for in a commanding artistic presence. Joe Inman gave her 5.6, 5.8; others went as high as 5.7, 5.9.

All the rest were yet to come, but it was almost certainly a done deal: With that program, and those scores, Bobek was going to the Olympic Games, and Tonia Kwiatkowski was going to be shut out. Even if Kwiatkowski performed perfectly, it was extremely unlikely she would pass Bobek.

Backstage, Frank Carroll and Michelle Kwan found their hiding place, their "cubbyhole," to spend their half-hour wait together. They hunkered down behind blue curtains in the skaters' stretching area. It was not soundproof; they could hear the scores, just as they did in Edmonton at the 1996 world championships.

But they weren't paying attention to the scores.

"Frank, how would we ever describe to anybody what it feels like to have to sit and wait for this?" Michelle asked.

They talked about the excruciating ritual of watching the minutes tick by, of timing when the stretching should begin, the running, the retying of the skates.

"But you know something?" Kwan said. "I like it."

Tara Lipinski was up next on the ice. For this fifteen-year-old girl, the following four minutes would be war. Tara against the ice; Tara against her triple jumps.

And Tara knew who was going to win those battles.

Peggy Fleming knew too.

She warned the other skaters ahead of Tara to beware; having Tara coming from behind, Fleming said on ABC, was like having "a fighter jet on your tail."

Tara still thought she could recapture the national title. If she won the long program and Kwan had trouble, it was possible. She had to think that way. It always was possible to win.

Her former coach, Jeff DiGregorio, said it best: "For her, coming in second would be a loss."

But winning wasn't Lipinski's only thought. She also wanted to stay on her feet. She was under extreme pressure to not fall again, and to make the Olympic team in her own right, without being voted onto it by the USFSA's international committee. She did not want to be a charity case.

Possessed by these thoughts, Lipinski flew onto the ice. Her first jumps were shaky: a tiny double axel, a crooked—but successful—triple flip.

By the time she reached the slow part of her program, nearly two minutes into her performance, the audience offered her little more than polite applause. Just as in France in November, the spectators were waiting for something more.

Lipinski, however, was so concerned with her triple jumps that she all but ignored the "in-betweens," skating slang for everything else but the jumps. Going into four of her seven triples, she did nothing but prepare for the jump. No footwork, no connecting elements, no nothing.

Lipinski was connecting the dots.

She sped into the tough triple loop–triple loop combination, her signature move. She landed the first jump cleanly, but had trouble with the second landing. She came out of the jump too soon and sneaked the final half revolution on her skate, on the ice. The judges noticed; they couldn't miss it. It happened in front of them.

Soon, Tara entered her final, difficult maneuver, a triple toe loop–half loop–triple salchow. She did it all, but she took too much time setting up each element.

When her music ended, she still was in the midst of a camel spin.

She ended three seconds later, just as she did at Skate America.

It was a sloppy finish for a skater of her caliber.

But Lipinski was thrilled about the jumps. She raised her hands to an appreciative crowd, and gulped in their applause. The attention made it all worthwhile.

She had landed all the triples, a whopping seven of them.

Tara had won the battles.

"I know I can do anything now," she said.

When she watched Tara's performance on television from her home in Toronto, choreographer Sandra Bezic wished she had had the opportunity to follow through with Tara prior to nationals. The programs were good, among the best in the world, but they could have been better.

"Some of the moves are not moves I would have done," she said. "The subtleties had been lost from the programs."

Richard Callaghan said that after Bezic created the programs and Susie Wynne helped in the early autumn, "no one" had been working with Tara choreographically in the two months leading up to the nationals. Callaghan also said Bezic "volunteered" to work with Tara, but the Lipinskis never called.

So Tara worked on the ice with her ballet teacher, and Callaghan.

"Tara had to take time to really learn the programs," Callaghan said. "There was so much correct emphasis placed on her presentation that I think she goes out [onto the ice] with a heavy thought in her head, trying to show people she has developed what they didn't think she could do."

The working situation was not what Bezic was used to.

She always had a "very close" working relationship with the coaches of the skaters for whom she choreographs. But she said she and Callaghan had spoken on the phone only once in two years.

"The biggest issue is the follow-through," Bezic said. "The coach must be the leader, I respect that. But I think we've all been compartmentalized instead of working as a unit."

Lipinski's scores were strong, better than Bobek's. She moved ahead of Bobek on the strength of her technical merit marks. Joe Inman gave Tara 5.8, 5.7, becoming one of five judges to drop Tara's presentation mark below the technical mark. That was an accurate evaluation of her performance, but not a good sign for Lipinski.

The lesson of the judges' marks was clear to both Bobek and Lipinski. If Bobek could master a triple jump combination, she had a chance to be a factor at the Olympics.

And Lipinski had to do more than just travel from jump to jump.

But, all things being equal, the judges did not want to drop the reigning world champion below the reigning free spirit. It was smart for the United States to send Lipinski to the Olympics ahead of Bobek.

The next seventeen minutes were an intermission of sorts as Corwin and Nikodinov skated and received their marks.

While Danny Kwan walked around the concourse and Mike Burg raced downstairs to find Lipinski, Don Laws, Lori Nichol's former coach, stood near the portal for sections 119 and 120, waiting for her. "Just in case she comes by."

Nichol, however, was seated in a box in section 123, high above the corner near Kiss and Cry. She vowed to stay in her seat and watch every moment of Kwan's performance. She was encouraged by Kwan's warm-up, which had been flawless. She noticed a serenity in Kwan's presence on the ice.

A serene skater made for a slightly less stressed choreographer.

Nichol felt good about what was going to happen as her skater took the ice.

Still, this was figure skating.

Nichol's heart immediately leapt into action.

Three other important people were watching Kwan as she glided into her opening position—the non-pose pose in which she simply stood still and waited as Janet Lynn used to do—near the far corner of the rink.

"No way am I giving another 6.0," Joe Inman told friends before the women's long program. "Nothing's going to give me these emotions again."

Judge No. 2 held onto his pencil, put his notepad in front of him, and put his eyes on Kwan.

Brian Boitano warned everyone to stay away from him.

He told everyone not to talk to him.

He stared at Kwan from the ABC booth. When Kwan skated, Boitano felt as if he were skating too.

Lori Nichol looked down from her seat at Boitano, a friend for whom she had choreographed a program that season. She knew Boitano was staring at Kwan, so she stared at Boitano staring at Kwan. Their laser-like gazes would have formed a triangle in the arena, except that one point of the triangle was missing: Kwan wasn't looking at either of them.

In the suburbs north of Detroit, a middle-aged housewife sat at home in front of her TV screen. Her twin sons, away at college, both called that day to remind her the skating was on that night.

Janet Lynn Salomon watched Kwan move into position and wait for her music to bring her to life.

It was a nice beginning, Janet Lynn said to herself.

Other than that, she didn't give it a second thought.

Before 19,000 people in the CoreStates Center and the rest of the country on television, Michelle Kwan stood on the ice and smiled.

When her music came on, she kept smiling.

No one ever smiled like that to begin the most pressure-packed four minutes of their year to date.

Actually, one person used to, but she was long gone and had to resort to watching skating on television.

When her boys called to remind her.

Kwan had been skating for little more than a minute when Dick Button said it.

She landed her triple flip, the third flawless triple jump of her program.

"Perfect landing position, straight up and down," Button said on ABC's live, prime-time telecast, "reminiscent of Janet Lynn."

Janet Lynn heard Dick Button mention her name. She and Button were friends; he had been her agent, and he had married her coach, Slavka Kohout.

It was very nice of Button to say that, Lynn thought.

"Here I am, hiding in my house for fourteen years, raising children."

Imagining angels and clouds, Kwan glided along.

"You can see the peace in her face," Fleming said softly.

Originally, Kwan didn't love the music, *Lyra Angelica,* when she heard it nearly two years earlier. But Nichol gave her a tape, figuring—and hoping—it would grow on her.

It did.

As they edited more than two dozen versions of Kwan's long program, Nichol, Carroll, and music consultant Lenore Kay inserted Erik Satie's *Gymnopédie No. 3* for the slow part, which was filling the arena at that moment, note by delicious note, light as air.

As Kwan glided effortlessly through the section of the program she and Nichol had reworked barely one month earlier, everything she did was accentuated by the startlingly simple dress she wore. It was ice-blue velvet, and it was the plainest dress in the competition.

Kwan wore a different dress in the autumn, busy and bluer, that looked as if it were made by Speedo.

"I wasn't very thrilled about my costume," Kwan said after watching a tape of Skate America. "It didn't look right on me. It was too distracting. People would be looking at my costume instead of my skating."

There was no danger of that in Philadelphia.

Two and a half minutes into the program, Kwan spun counterclockwise, her usual way, on a layback spin, switched to a clockwise camel spin, then rotated back the other way into a sit spin. It was perfect.

Nichol smiled up in section 123.

She had encouraged Kwan to try the spins in different directions when they put the program together in April. Nichol knew Kwan could do what no one else in the world was doing; she just needed a little nudge.

Leaving the spins behind, Kwan skated backwards and moved her arms in time to her graceful music, as if she were plucking a harp.

Back to the jumps.

Kwan reeled off a triple salchow, one of the jumps that forced her to push off on her injured toe.

She glided into her second triple lutz, and landed magnificently.

"Oh," Button said into the ABC microphone. "Wonderful! Wonderful! What a joy!"

Kwan fired out of the triple lutz and breezed down the ice. Across the middle of the ice she went, launching into her lingering spiral.

"She is just breathtaking to watch!" Fleming said in the ABC booth in awe.

With just fifteen seconds left, Kwan had one jump remaining.

The triple toe loop.

The one that required her to launch herself off her bad toe.

She didn't need to do it.

She did it.

She landed and turned her palms up to the crowd, with her head held high.

Nichol noticed.

It was a spur-of-the-moment, all-Kwan move.

Nichol had never seen her do that before.

But she loved that she did it.

Kwan flew into a death drop, swirled into a sit spin, and stood up, in the middle of the ice, by the stripes on the big U.S. flag.

Her music had only a few notes left.

First, Kwan did something Nichol suggested during her visit after Thanksgiving. Kwan delightedly brought her hands to the sides of her neck, creating a dramatic, endearing moment.

Then, for her final move, Nichol had given Kwan a piece of advice: Wing it.

"It's your Olympic moment," Nichol said. "You do whatever."

It was lunchtime on an early December day in California. They both were hungry. They left the rink.

When Kwan came to that moment on the ice in Philadelphia, Nichol had no idea what she would do.

Kwan simply threw her head back and tossed her arms rapturously into the air.

The audience already was standing. The noise was deafening.

She was finished.

"She is absolutely brilliant!" Fleming said breathlessly.

A *Sports Illustrated* photographer captured Kwan's ending pose from above.

It filled a full page in the magazine's next issue.

ABC Sports had to pick one shot with which to go off the air fifteen minutes later.

It picked the "wing it" shot.

Kwan felt a tear come to her eye as she bowed in the middle of the rink and spotted her sister, Karen, who had driven in from Boston to surprise her.

Boitano wiped a tear from his eye.

Nichol wiped a tear from her eye.

Joe Inman wiped a tear from his eye.

Inman couldn't believe the thoughts that once again forced their way into his mind.

"Everything was just floating out there."

When Kwan stopped, Inman reached for the keypad.

He pushed 5, then 9.

And enter.

He pushed again:

A 6, followed by 0.

"I was mesmerized," he said later. "Every move of the hand, every turn of the head, everything was done for a reason, everything made sense with the music. It's got to take somebody very special to skate like that."

Kwan sat in Kiss and Cry with her eyes on the scoreboard.

"And now her marks for presentation: 6.0, 6.0, 6.0, 6.0, 6.0, 5.9, 6.0, 6.0, 6.0."

All but one.

No long program ever had received as many 6.0s at the U.S. figure skating championships, which began in 1914.

And Tonia Kwiatkowski had to follow that.

The flowers were cleared from the ice; the crowd settled down.

Kwiatkowski didn't know exactly how Bobek had skated; she, like most skaters, didn't watch the people who came before her.

She didn't know the Olympic team was almost out of reach before she skated.

She didn't want to know.

After landing her triple lutz combination, she pulled back on her triple flip, and doubled it. That wasn't good, but this was worse: She fell on a triple salchow less than a minute later.

She fell later when she tried the triple flip again, and finished the evening fighting back tears.

Carol Heiss patted her hand as she came off the ice. With ABC in a commercial, they had several minutes to kill. Kwiatkowski alternated between smiling and crying.

The audience, Kwiatkowski's audience, filled the void as best as it could.

"We love you, Tonia," one section yelled.

"We do too," another chanted.

"So do we," responded another.

Minutes later, Kwiatkowski, who finished fourth, met with reporters for the last time in her career at the nationals.

"I gave it my all, I worked hard all year, I didn't give up out there and I'm really proud of myself for that."

As a tear tumbled out of her eye and fell onto her leg, she excused herself and walked away.

The winners' press conference featured Kwan, Lipinski, and Bobek, who finished in that order, and their delighted coaches.

"Tonight's performance proved we can be one-two-three at the Olympics," said Christa Fassi. "I think we have the dream team for these Olympics."

A team of strong individuals, others said.

"It's not like we're in a bobsled where we're all pushing and in the same sled," Frank Carroll said. "If they fall on their butts, they do it alone."

Kwan was asked about her performance, which, combined with her short program, gave her the finest overall effort in the history of the U.S. nationals.

"I was thinking of angels and clouds and the feeling of flying," she said. "Nothing can stop me. At the end, it's like, 'I'm free. I'm gone. Cloud 9, here I come.' "

Bobek, sitting near Kwan at the table on the dais, rolled her eyes.

Fassi elbowed Bobek in the ribs.

Even if Bobek thought it ridiculous, Kwan had taken her sport to a very new and different place.

For three days, at least, journalists weren't counting triple jumps. (For the record, Kwan did seven.) Instead, reporters were writing about a "falling leaf" (a small jump hidden in Kwan's long program), about lingering spirals, about spinning in two directions.

Sports Illustrated's E. M. Swift said that Kwan "left the impression of a girl skating in a secret garden." The sports magazine, which featured a muddy Green Bay Packer on its cover, also wrote that Kwan's long program "was filled with so many subtle treasures that it will be revisited on tape for years to come."

That night, many skating people found themselves transported in time as they watched Kwan.

"I flipped back to Janet Lynn in that yellow dress in 1973," said former skating referee Gary Clark. "This is the next great female performance since then."

It dawned on Joe Inman after he left his seat in the row of judges.

"It is nice we have somebody on the horizon with the whole sensibility of skating," he said, referring to Kwan. "I thought of Janet Lynn. This is the first person since her who has that. I wish Janet Lynn had been here to see it."

Kwan, Inman said, impressed him most by skating from "the skate up." Oksana Baiul, for instance, skated at the 1994 Games "from the waist up."

Janet Lynn always skated from the skate up.

Unlike Tara Lipinski, who had that brief meeting with Lynn after the world championships, Kwan had never met her. But she and Lynn had become pen pals of sorts.

"We've written many times back and forth," Kwan said. "When she writes, it's her talking to me."

Lynn even sent Kwan inspirational books.

Kwan said Lynn played a "big role" in her skating sensation of "flying and angels and stuff."

"She had that spark in her eyes," Kwan said. "It's just the freedom of it all."

Before the Nashville nationals, Kwan told the *New York Times* that she wanted to be a legend, "like Dorothy Hamill and Peggy Fleming."

That was the quote that got picked up and reprinted around the country.

But there was more to it.

"Janet Lynn didn't win an Olympic title," Kwan continued in the quote, "but in every skater's mind, she's a legend. I want to leave a little mark: 'Michelle Kwan was a great skater, artistically and technically. She had the whole package.' I want people to remember me after one thousand years when skating is weird and people are doing quintuple jumps."

Janet Lynn Salomon was thrilled by what she watched on TV from Philadelphia.

"At this point in time, it was the most inspiring night of skating I've ever watched," she said.

She meant all three of the top skaters, but, in particular, Kwan.

"I felt the joy in her skating," Janet Lynn said. "Even when she was waiting to go on, the joy was evident."

Joy.

There was that word again, the one word that Lori Nichol used as a foundation for Kwan's long program.

A deeply religious person, Janet Lynn Salomon went upstairs in her home to read her devotional book, which included passages from the Bible's Letter of Jude.

A quote jumped off the page: "Faultless . . . with exceeding joy."

"That's it," she said. "Those are exactly the words I'd use to describe what I just saw."

Back in the arena, not everyone was overcome with joy. Jack and Pat Lipinski leaned against a cinderblock wall near the press conference area and glumly watched the proceedings.

Sitting at the table in front of dozens of reporters, Tara was excited: "I trusted myself under pressure, and I did it!"

Her parents, however, looked like they were attending a funeral.

"Will someone tell them their fifteen-year-old daughter just made the Olympic team?" a reporter whispered.

The next day, during the meaningless exhibition, Tara tried her triple flip and stumbled out of the landing.

When she finished, she skated to the boards, grabbed her skate guards and stomped off.

The Lipinskis were finding out, as the Kwans had the year before, that the pressures of defending a national title were tremendous. They would need to find a way to cope, or the sport might devour them.

There were fears it was already happening. The *New York Times* reported two weeks later that "many in the skating community are concerned that by publicly showing their disappointment, her parents and publicists are placing unnecessary pressure" on Tara.

After midnight at the Marriott, Michelle Kwan stopped by the traditional competitors' party, but didn't stay long. She wanted to spend time with her sister.

As Michelle and Karen stayed up late talking in Michelle's room, Nicole Bobek breezed through the lobby bar with two men in tow. One was her boyfriend, the other a friend of theirs.

But they had other titles.

"They're my make-up men," she said. "And my bodyguards."
Make-up men who doubled as bodyguards.
Only Bobek.

Frank Carroll came back to the hotel, took an elevator up to his nine-teenth-floor room—and stayed there. He was exhausted. The last thing he wanted was to wade into the masses in the hotel bar and have everyone tell him how wonderful he was.

"I don't need world recognition for what just occurred," he said. "I know what happened."

A few friends stopped in, including Lori Nichol. Carroll eventually shooed everyone out of the room, and did the one thing he absolutely had to do in the early morning hours of January 11.

As the U.S. skating community celebrated the most warmly received long program in its eighty-four-year history, Frank Carroll opened his suitcase and packed.

Back in the lobby at 2 A.M., Brian Boitano took Nichol by the arm and whisked her away.

He had someone for her to meet.

"Oh my gosh," Nichol said, her face brightening.

Standing by a pillar near the registration desk, waiting with Boitano's coach Linda Leaver, was Slavka Kohout, the woman who coached Janet Lynn.

"I'm so honored to meet you," Nichol said.

"I've admired your work," Kohout said to Nichol, "especially tonight. That was wonderful."

Nichol told Kohout the story about her teenage days spent day-dreaming of choreographing for Janet Lynn.

"To Barry Manilow, if you can believe it!" Nichol said, laughing.

Kohout chuckled.

Boitano and Leaver smiled, but they didn't say a word.

They couldn't take their eyes off Nichol and Kohout, whom Janet Lynn Salomon calls "the person who taught me everything I knew."

Nichol and Kohout talked for only a few more moments.

"I'm getting old," Kohout said in the lobby. "My choreography is not so good anymore."

"With what you've created," Nichol replied, smiling reassuringly, "you can never grow old."

*   *   *

They soon went their separate ways.

On the night that Michelle Kwan stood on the ice and smiled like Janet Lynn, it was only fitting that Lori Nichol would meet Slavka Kohout.

Everything had come full circle.

PART VI

February 1998

THE
OLYMPIC
GAMES

14

RUSSIAN ROULETTE

The phone rang at the worst time in Artur Dmitriev's two-floor apartment in St. Petersburg, Russia, on Thursday morning, February 5, 1998. Dmitriev was packing and about to leave for the airport to go to the Winter Olympics. On the other end of the phone was a reporter in Nagano, Japan, asking for a few minutes of his time.

The journalist, Jere Longman of the *New York Times,* wanted to know about Dmitriev's preparation for his third, and presumably last, Olympic Games.

"Tamara Moskvina says you are living like a monk," Longman said into the phone in the press center at White Ring arena, the figure skating venue in Nagano.

"What's a monk?" Dmitriev asked.

"Well," Longman said, searching for words, "a priest."

"Prison?"

"No, uh, Tamara says you cut out smoking and drinking to get ready for the Olympics?"

"Oh, okay," Dmitriev replied. "Yes, for me, it's important to concentrate on skating. I'm thirty years old now. For me, it's very important to do this for my family."

An hour later, Dmitriev carried his bags into the tiny international airport on the outskirts of St. Petersburg for his 11 A.M. flight to Moscow. He was traveling with Moskvina, his coach since he was sixteen, and the three other pairs skaters from Yubileiny Palace: Oksana Kazakova, Elena Berezhnaia, and Anton Sikharulidze.

They were beginning their twenty-one-and-a-half-hour journey eastward, across Siberia, to the Olympic Games.

Moskvina's version of their itinerary was unique: "One-hour flight to Moscow; sit in the bar for five hours in Moscow; drink good cognac; ten-and-a-half-hour flight to Tokyo, in coach; five-hour bus ride to Nagano."

By the time Moskvina and her two pairs arrived in Nagano, tired and bedraggled, it was Friday evening. In little more than forty-eight hours, they would have to be ready to perform their short programs on the milk-white ice of White Ring, the big silver spaceship sitting on the outskirts of town. They were cutting it awfully close, giving themselves just two days of practice six time zones away before the most important competition of their careers. But while other skaters arrived a week in advance of their competition, Moskvina wasn't worried. She tossed a hand in the air. Coming in so late was nothing, she said. Two days of advance work in Nagano was plenty.

"If you're in New York in a nice Sheraton, shopping, watching Broadway shows, and eating in nice restaurants, you're not so concentrated on what you have to do. But here, after two days, you'll be climbing the walls. That's why we came in late. It's plenty of time for my skaters to get ready."

The Olympic Games meant everything to Moskvina and her pairs. To win there would be to catapult themselves into a world of their wildest dreams, a place where U.S. dollars flowed freely, where the U.S. skating tour beckoned, where doors opened wide to the poor skaters from Russia. Dmitriev already had tasted that life, and found it both intoxicating and infuriating. He loved the money, the cars, and the big apartment, complete with sauna, that it afforded him in St. Petersburg. But being away from his wife and young son, Artur Jr., was hard on him. He had become so nervous he began his pack-a-day smoking habit. He knew skating overseas was what he had to do to earn a very good living, but he didn't have to like it. If only he could keep creating programs for himself and Kazakova in St. Petersburg, without having to partake of the spoils of victory in the West. That would have made him extremely happy. He was unusual in this way, a man who loved his work, not necessarily its deserved rewards.

Dmitriev came to the Olympics with mixed feelings. If he and Kazakova upset Berezhnaia and Sikharulidze, their high-flying rivals, for the gold medal, he would make history. He would become the first man ever in the Olympics to win gold medals with two different pairs partners. In 1992, he won the gold with Natalia Mishkutenok. In

1994, they won the silver medal behind Ekaterina Gordeeva and the late Sergei Grinkov.

Back at the Games again, this time with Kazakova, his partner of three years, he wanted to win not for himself, but for her. He came to complete his work, the process he loved so much: creating something new, "from zero," he often said in English, and seeing it through to the end. Kazakova had been rough around the edges when he picked her as his new partner; she had grown into a worthy colleague by the Olympics. Dmitriev took great pride in that.

But he knew when they were finished, when their long program came to a close, whatever the result, his work would be over, and he would not be pleased. He hated endings, even happy ones.

Berezhnaia and Sikharulidze arrived at the Games with the grandest expectations. They were kids who had nothing. They had made little money. They had tiny apartments. They weren't even certain what success really means in their sport. They had won the prestigious European championships in January, and had become, at twenty and twenty-one, the Olympic gold medal favorites. They tried not to listen to the hype surrounding their chances. Skating people said their names and smiled. Who didn't love their skating: so smooth, so effortless, so youthful and fresh? And who didn't love her story, coming back from that awful head injury in 1996?

Moskvina didn't want them to listen. She knew they thought too much at the 1997 world championships, and plummeted from third to ninth in one horrendous four-minute, thirty-second stretch. She thought they might be ready to win in Nagano, but she wasn't sure. She knew Dmitriev could win with his new partner because he had won before; as for the others, she just didn't know.

Moskvina had to pull off quite a balancing act getting her two pairs ready for the Olympics. In the last few months leading to Nagano, she put her pairs on different practice sessions in St. Petersburg.

"I didn't want the competition to take place before the Olympics," she said.

The men were fine with the rivalry. Dmitriev and Sikharulidze were friends. They roomed together on the road; in the Olympic Village, they shared Suite 1001 in Building D-1 with Ilia Kulik, who joked that he arrived in Japan early to claim the biggest room. Dmitriev and Sikharulidze were far enough apart in age never to feel like fierce rivals; Dmitriev saw to that, making sure he went out of his way to help Moskvina make her young pair better.

But Kazakova and Berezhnaia couldn't help but compete. Kazakova was jealous of Berezhnaia's stunning success. And Berezhnaia was also preoccupied with some of the things Kazakova and Dmitriev were doing on the ice.

This was only natural, Dmitriev said.

"Girls is girls."

The short program took place in White Ring starting at 8 P.M. Sunday, February 8, the day after the Opening Ceremonies. One and a half hours into the three-hour-long event came the twelfth pair in the random draw, Oksana Kazakova and Artur Dmitriev.

Skating to the music from *2001,* Richard Strauss's *Also sprach Zarathustra,* dressed in black (him) and white (her), sporting nearly identical hairstyles, the two skaters tore down the ice, preparing for their side-by-side triple toe loops. The triple toe loop was Dmitriev's nemesis; the element doomed the pair time and again, including at the 1997 world championships.

The previous season, the husky Dmitriev looked like a DC-10 trying to become airborne as he moved into the triple jump. He was overweight, he was drinking, he was smoking, and he was about to turn thirty. It was a deadly combination for a skater.

Moskvina was getting antsy.

"Listen," she told him in the summer of 1997, "the Olympics are close."

"I know, I know," Dmitriev said. "Don't worry."

In the four months leading to the Olympics, he stopped drinking. He lost nine pounds. He didn't stop smoking; he couldn't do that. But he got himself into the best shape he could. "It was an exam for me: can I do this again?"

Twenty-two seconds into the short program, Dmitriev picked into the ice with his left toe pick and hurled himself into the air for the triple toe loop. This was the element he had to land. This was the reason he lost the weight. But Dmitriev wasn't thinking about that. He was thinking about nothing. "Nothing but the jump," he said.

Kazakova picked into the ice too, by her partner's side. They spun three times in unison. They landed softly, their left legs kicking out simultaneously behind them. Dmitriev was not sprawled on the ice. He was not reaching out to steady himself with his hand. He had landed perfectly, upright and tall. The triple jump had come off without a hitch.

Her head barely visible above the boards, Moskvina watched without changing expression at the other end of the rink. But in her heart, she knew this was good.

The two skaters moved through their other elements with ease until they came to the death spiral, the move that Jenni Meno and Todd Sand had fallen on at the 1997 U.S. nationals. This maneuver required Kazakova to lay out over the ice, hold Dmitriev's hand, and spin around him on the outside edge of her right skate blade. But Kazakova did not know how to do the move, and when Moskvina tried to teach her the previous year, she told her coach she would learn it by herself.

As the weeks went by, Moskvina saw Kazakova was having trouble with the maneuver. She called her 1984 Olympic champions, Elena Valova and Oleg Vassiliev, and asked them to nonchalantly ask Kazakova about the death spiral the next time they came by the rink, to see if they might help her.

No luck. Kazakova was stubborn. Finally, Moskvina gave up.

"Okay, you don't want to do it, you eat your dirt yourself," Moskvina said to herself.

With twenty seconds left in the program, Dmitriev put out his hand and Kazakova tried to bend over to do the outside edge death spiral. But she could not do it. She looked like someone with a bad back trying to figure out a way to lie down. She was crooked, and she never bent over far enough to allow her skate to reach the proper position. It was ugly and amateurish, an awkward move in an otherwise stellar program.

"It was not a death spiral," Moskvina said later. "This is my coaching failure."

That night, back in the village, Kazakova finally asked Moskvina to teach her how to do it right.

There were some strange things going on with Kazakova. She skated with a picture of her husband propped on the boards.

"He hypnotizes her through the picture," Moskvina said laughing.

"Hypnotizes?"

"Mesmerizes," Moskvina replied. "Whatever."

When her pair finished, Moskvina didn't immediately join them in Kiss and Cry. She needed to be in two places at once. The next warm-up was beginning, which included Berezhnaia and Sikharulidze. Moskvina quickly whispered some words of advice to them, then dashed around one end of the ice in her high heels to meet Kazakova and Dmitriev in Kiss and Cry. After seeing their fine scores—mostly 5.7s and 5.8s—she ran back to "Skate in the Head" and her partner.

She pulled Sikharulidze aside.

"Are you okay?" she asked, still catching her breath.

"Yes," he answered.

During their short program minutes later, he crashed to the ice on his triple toe loop. It was "a real banger," said U.S. pairs coach John Nicks.

"Sometimes," Moskvina said, assessing her short conversation with Sikharulidze, "people lie."

Sikharulidze was one big bundle of nerves heading into the competition. "He saw Olympic gold too early," Moskvina said. When Sikharulidze scrambled to his feet, he stumbled again slightly, forcing Berezhnaia to wait for him to catch up. But their short program, skated to *Swan Lake,* was otherwise perfect, and with their impeccable resumé over the previous few months, the gods of figure skating smiled upon them.

Although the U.S. pair of Kyoko Ina and Jason Dungjen did not fall, seven of the nine judges placed the Russians ahead of the Americans. The order in the short program went: 1. Team Moskvina (Kazakova and Dmitriev); 2. Germans Mandy Woetzel and Ingo Steuer; 3. Team Moskvina (Berezhnaia and Sikharulidze); and 4. Ina and Dungjen. Anyone in the top three could win the gold medal by winning the long program. And the judges definitely wanted Berezhnaia and Sikharulidze in the running for the Olympic title.

The Americans did not rant and rave. They were not angry about finishing behind the Russians because they knew that jumps were not always as important as spectators in the United States thought they were. There are eight required elements in the short program, and the third-place Russians were better than the Americans on six of those eight. The deduction for a fall is .3 of a point on the 6.0 scale; the deduction for mistakes on lifts and spins also can be that much. Berezhnaia and Sikharulidze received no score higher than a 5.6 on the first mark (reflecting the deduction), and overcame the U.S. pair with much higher scores on the presentation mark.

The other Americans, Jenni Meno and Todd Sand, made one mistake in the short program (he put his hand down on his triple toe loop) and were mired in sixth place. The three-time U.S. national champions, bothered by injuries for much of the past two seasons, made numerous mistakes in the long program and dropped to eighth.

There was a day between the short and long programs, and Tamara Moskvina used the time to make herself completely available to every reporter in the universe. She didn't wait for reporters to come to her; she went to them.

"We will have coffee in the press room," she said.

Most coaches didn't know where the press room was. Moskvina, however, had been there so often, she had a table with her name on it.

Reporters pressed her on her personal feelings about the pairs. Did she want Dmitriev to win his second gold medal? Or the fragile Berezhnaia to win her first?

"If you have a fourteen-year-old daughter and a two-year-old daughter, do you have a better feeling about one?" she replied. "I don't have a heart. I only have a brain. My heart is at home."

The day of the long program, Moskvina stayed busy. Sikharulidze needed her; he was a mess. He forgot his credential to get into practice, and finally got inside White Ring after twenty minutes of negotiations with rink officials that were won, of course, by Moskvina.

She tried her best to calm him down. He was too nervous. Berezhnaia was serene; it was clear she was becoming the rock of the pair. That day, Moskvina gave her only one piece of advice: "Remember when you were in the hospital? Compared to that, this is nothing."

She gave equal time to her other pair. She told Dmitriev not to get too anxious and get going too quickly early in the long program, and she told Kazakova to forget that she was at the Olympics.

"Close your eyes," Moskvina said to her. "Forget about the judges and the people. You're on our ice rink in St. Petersburg. There are the dirty walls. My husband is beside me. It's a dark atmosphere. Picture that."

The top four pairs skated near 11 P.M. Tuesday at White Ring. Woetzel and Steuer—whose arm and shoulder, injured in the bizarre December car accident, could tell changes in the weather—took themselves out of gold medal contention with a stumble and two shaky landings.

Berezhnaia and Sikharulidze skated next. Sikharulidze wore a maroon jacket with tails. "He's either going to park my car or be the best man in someone's wedding," Jere Longman said.

By the end of the evening, reporters generally agreed he was dressed more like a carriage driver in Central Park. How, they wondered, could he skate in tails?

He and Berezhnaia gripped each other's hands and glided onto the ice to begin their program. The triple toe loops went fine. But thirty-five seconds in, she got around only two and a half times on a triple twist, and came back to the ice facing the wrong direction. She clicked her skates as she landed a triple loop halfway through the program, but they looked to be cruising along quite well until the final six seconds of their program. Coming down out of a star lift, Berezhnaia landed strangely and caved into Sikharulidze, with both of them toppling to the ice in a heap.

As they finished, Berezhnaia looked at him with wide, bright eyes and buried her head in his arms. They couldn't believe it.

"It's new finish pose," Sikharulidze said in his halting English. "If you don't like it, we will change it."

He was laughing about it later, but Moskvina was steamed. She stood with her hands on her hips by the boards on the other side of the ice, glaring past the heads of the nine judges. It was a ridiculous mistake that might have cost them the gold medal.

Their marks were predictably strong, including four 5.9s, and they moved ahead of the Germans. When Ina and Dungjen made a slight mistake (he put his hand down on his triple toe loop), they were out of the running.

Moskvina went backstage to find the evening's final pair, her pair, Kazakova and Dmitriev.

She didn't tell them their training partners had fallen.

"Skate beautifully," Moskvina said. "Nobody has skated beautifully yet."

That was all Dmitriev had to hear. He relied totally on Moskvina. She had told him just enough.

Onto the ice they went. Artur was wearing black and yellow, matching Oksana, with a sash that looked like he was playing flag football. They had front-loaded the program to get the tough things out of the way early; they were finished jumping before they hit the halfway point.

During one of those jumps, their second side-by-side double axels, Dmitriev managed to hide Kazakova's only mistake—her singling of the jump—from the judges. He was so big, he blocked their view as he leaped in front of them.

They made no other errors. They finished with the remarkable "Natalia Spin" (named for Mishkutenok) in which Kazakova is upside down, hanging onto his leg, with her right leg in the air.

Exhausted, Dmitriev leaned his head on Kazakova's shoulder. He gave every last ounce of energy to the four-and-a-half-minute program. The big guy was done. Kissing Kazakova's hand, one, two, three times, he knew he had won.

As they glided to Kiss and Cry, Moskvina, wearing a black suit, made the long walk around the boards by herself to meet them.

She knew too.

As they had so many times before, Dmitriev sat beside Moskvina, grabbed her hand, and watched a row of skating scores pop onto the television screen in front of them. They won eight of the nine judges (the Germans won the German judge). Dmitriev leaned over and gave Moskvina a long, lingering kiss on the cheek.

Dmitriev made history: the first man to win gold medals with two different pairs partners at the Olympic Games. While he won the gold, his younger rivals took the silver (Sikharulidze said he was "happy there was no more skating here"), and the Germans won the bronze.

Moskvina was accumulating quite a cache of medals. Since 1984, her pairs had won three gold medals and four silvers; that's seven of the fifteen Olympic medals available the previous fourteen years.

She refused to say she felt sad for Berezhnaia, who came close to making a miraculous journey from a hospital bed to the Olympic gold medal in two years.

"I think she must be happy. She's like a hero," Sikharulidze said.

Dmitriev was melancholy. He didn't smile much. He knew it was over. That long process that he loved so much ended the moment he won. What a strange thought that was: his moment of triumph, over-shadowed by his own feelings of wanting his skating to go on forever.

"It's a little sad," he said. "It's over. The movie's over. It's sad for this reason: Amateur sportsman finished great time."

He said he didn't even think about himself. "I am happy for Oksana first. It was difficult but also interesting. I also am very happy for Tamara, much more than myself."

As he finished his third Olympics, he thought about what might be next. Would he be back for another?

"Maybe if the Olympic Games are next year," he said. "Four more years? We'll see."

He was asked again four days later. He was much more definitive.

"I am already thinking about new programs, new steps, new work," he said. "The 2002 Olympics? Why not?"

Elvis Stojko came to the Olympic Games with the hopes and dreams of most of Canada riding on his shoulders. Elvis and the NHL hockey team. Somebody had to do something for Canada in the two sports Canadians cared so much about: men's hockey and figure skating.

Stojko was in the same position as Brian Orser and Kurt Browning before him; he came into the Games as the reigning world champion. Orser and Browning both lost; the "Curse of the Canadians" began. No Canadian man had ever won the gold.

Stojko was going to give it a try.

"See those circles," he said to his coach, Doug Leigh, gesturing to the Olympic rings as he walked into White Ring for the first time.

"That's what I'm here for. I've prepared all my life for those circles."

But Stojko came to Nagano harboring a big secret. He was injured. He pulled his right groin muscle at the Canadian national championships in January, but told no one outside his inner circle. Much like Michelle Kwan, he would keep the injury quiet for as long as possible. He didn't want any excuses. And skaters also knew that they never wanted to tip off the judges—Elvis's good friends—to a potential problem.

By the evening of the Opening Ceremonies, Stojko also was sick. He'd caught the flu, which brought headaches and a fever. Within two days, he was taking fluids intravenously. Again, he told no one outside his camp. If anyone could get through it, Stojko could. He would do anything to perform well at the Olympics.

Russia's Alexei Yagudin, coach Alexei Mishin's only skater at the Games, also caught the flu, and ended up with a 102-degree fever. This was all Mishin needed. He had thought Yagudin could be the Russian to beat at the Olympics. Ilia Kulik, the Massachusetts Russian formerly from Moscow, skipped the European championships with a pinched nerve in his back, and Yagudin won with a quadruple and seven triples. (Kulik and Yagudin earned the two Russian Olympic slots.) But the flu threatened to ruin everything.

Michael Weiss, the second-ranked American who wasn't considered a medal favorite, also was injured. He fell on a triple axel the day before he left the Washington area and bruised his hip. He had to curtail his practices at the Games, but he also kept the injury a secret. He didn't want any excuses either.

Kulik was not entirely healthy, but compared to his rivals, he was doing quite well. He felt pain shoot through his lower back only occasionally; he considered himself ready. He said so, nodding his head quietly. There was no reason to doubt him. He won the Champions Series final in Munich; he was the Olympic gold medal favorite. But the last man to win the Olympic gold medal in his first Games was Dick Button in 1948. Kulik's goal would be no small task.

His coach, Tatiana Tarasova, was hoping for a unique double at the Games. She coached Pasha Grishuk and Evgeni Platov, the ice dancing favorites, as well as Kulik. They lived near each other in Marlboro, Massachusetts; Tarasova was coach, den mother, and cook. She even washed Kulik's clothes.

When asked about the prospects of winning both the dance and the men's, Tarasova grinned proudly.

"I dream about singles [the men]," she said.

Todd Eldredge, the five-time U.S. champion, was neither sick nor injured. He had worked very hard in the month prior to the Games, creating a new, peppier short program to *Les Misérables* and revamping his "Gettysburg" long program. He and Richard Callaghan danced around the quad issue, but there was no chance after the nationals that he was trying that again. "It's not a priority," Eldredge said. He thought his artistry was good enough to pull out a medal, and perhaps win the whole thing. He knew the artist—the spinner, the skater with the deep edges and nice line—was most welcome every four years at the Olympics. That was his forte. If the other men went for the quad, and failed, there was a chance for Todd Eldredge.

Lightning and thunder crashed overhead the day of the men's short program, Thursday, February 12. By luck of the draw, the competition was top-heavy. Twenty-nine men were in the event. Weiss picked fifth, followed by Kulik in sixth, Philippe Candeloro seventh, Japanese sensation Takeshi Honda eighth, Yagudin tenth, and Eldredge eleventh.

There were six men in the second warm-up, covering Kulik through Eldredge. Five were well-known. Then there was Yourii Litvinov of Kazakstan, skating ninth. He didn't even have a triple axel.

"Oh my God," Litvinov said. "How did I get in that group?"

Of the big guns, the only one left for later was Elvis Stojko, who sat in twenty-second.

"There is no gradual buildup," said Audrey Weisiger, Weiss's coach. "The judges have to be ready to give the marks right off the bat."

But Weiss knew he would not get particularly high marks. His draw was not good. A perfect program would receive just 5.6s or 5.7s in position No. 5. He and Weisiger knew it, and were prepared for it.

Because of his bruised hip, Weiss also had had some bad practice sessions. That made things even worse for him. If the judges had seen him doing great things, it might have helped his marks.

Weiss's father told him before he came to Nagano that, notwithstanding the draw, he had the perfect situation at the Games. "Your first Olympics always is the easiest to medal in," Greg Weiss, the 1964 Olympic gymnast, told Michael. "The pressure is not on you. It's on the other guys."

Weiss took the advice seriously. He was thrilled to be competing in Japan, just as his father had in 1964 when the Summer Games were in Tokyo. Michael even warmed up for the short program in his father's 1964 USA sweater.

Weiss skated at 7:30 P.M. His whole family had flown in from Washington, as had Weisiger's husband and daughter and Nick Perna, one of the coaches at the Fairfax Ice Arena.

"For thirteen years, this whole group has been waiting for this moment," Weisiger said. "I told them Mike skated early, so they better not arrive late and miss it."

They witnessed a good fifty seconds of solid skating before disaster struck.

After landing the best triple lutz in the Games, Weiss charged toward the middle of the ice for his combination, the triple axel–triple toe loop. He leaped into the air awkwardly, as if he were backing into the jump. He came down on his hands and knees. He had fallen on the combination. Any chance at a medal was gone.

His scores dipped into the 4s for required elements, but rebounded as high as 5.6 for presentation. Weiss ended up in eleventh place.

CBS tape-delayed the men's short program, as it did all the skating, and showed it hours later in Seattle. Brian Wright had been in the hospital after returning from a choreographic assignment in Los Angeles during the time of the U.S. nationals. Fighting AIDS, he was bleeding internally and doctors couldn't figure out how to stop it.

After more than a week, Wright's condition was brought under control, and he went home to his sister's, where he was heavily medicated. He watched on television that night as Michael skated the short program he created for him.

"It was really cool," Wright said. "I love sitting at home rooting on the Olympics from an armchair perspective, as a total spectator. But then I thought about my involvement, and that kind of caught me off guard."

Unlike other skating broadcasters, CBS did not forget him. On the contrary. The network ran a feature on him.

As he watched Weiss skate, Wright listened to the crowd in Japan pick up the rhythmic applause in the final minute of the short program the way it had in Russia in November and in Philadelphia in January.

"What a crack-up that is," Wright said to himself. "All these skaters have these great musicians and we're these three schlocks clapping our hands in a studio booth."

The murderer's row of skaters came after Weiss. Kulik, dressed ridiculously as a gypsy moth with flesh-colored webbing, skated cautiously and was clean. "It was nothing special," he said. Yagudin was flawless. So was Eldredge, who had had a bad warm-up and relied on a psychological pep talk from Callaghan to go out and skate his new short program without a mistake.

And, finally, there was Stojko.

He looked pale, but when he was asked if he was sick, he said only that his throat was dry. The truth was he had nearly passed out three days earlier because of the flu, and just that day in his practice he had re-injured his groin muscle.

But nothing would stop Stojko. He had put it all into Elvis-style perspective two months earlier.

"I've prepared the best way I can prepare. And I'm just going to go out there and do my job and enjoy it. And if I deserve to win, I will. And if I don't, that's the way it goes. And I accept that. But if I do what I was supposed to do and plan to do, then I've won, regardless if I win a medal, because you just don't have that control."

He was reminded of that after he skated flawlessly and saw his scores. The Canadian judge who had suggested the music for his program gave him a 6.0 for presentation, but six judges dished out 5.7s. Stojko laughed when he saw them.

He had come off the ice pumping his fist. Doug Leigh had been ebullient. But when they saw the marks, they grew grim. Stojko could manage just second place behind Kulik and ahead of Eldredge. At the Champions Series final, he had been a unanimous first-place choice. The same program two months later was a solid second. He was sick, he was injured, and he was dropping in the standings.

But he still was one of three men who were in it, all of whom trained within 800 miles of each other in North America. They traveled half a world away to battle for the heart and soul of men's figure skating. Kulik, the artist and jumper with such promise; Stojko, the old warrior, fighting his own battles with the sport; and Eldredge, who was just happy to be in the mix.

A fourth man in the equation was Yagudin, who had been hammered by the judges and put in fourth place for what might have been the best short program of all. Mishin couldn't believe how things were falling apart around him; he now saw that the sport was telling his seventeen-year-old to wait for 2002, and it gnawed at him. Russian judges and officials at the Olympics were pushing Kulik; Yagudin, who had given the performance of the year in St. Petersburg in November, had become the odd man out. This was particularly sad because Yagudin most of all could have used the fame and fortune of an Olympic medal. With some money, he could have moved his family from that apartment they shared with another family. Mishin shrugged. It was the nature of his sport. First Urmanov and that eleven-month-old groin injury, now Yagudin with the flu. It was Russian roulette, skating-style. The St. Petersburg men were on the outside at the Olympics, looking in.

Kulik, however, knew if he skated cleanly, he would win. The Champions Series final taught him that. He was the chosen one. But he drew the first skating position in the last group, so he would have to perform flawlessly, or his scores might not hold up.

Eldredge drew second, followed by Yagudin, Candeloro, and finally Stojko. It was a good draw for Stojko. As for Eldredge, who knew what he would do? He looked like the judges' compromise candidate if Kulik and Stojko both faltered, but he also had had a very strange season. He couldn't help but think of his long struggle for a medal, from 1992 through 1994 to 1998.

"Before I came, I was thinking about what it would be like to be on the podium. I do think it would be a great ending, like John Elway, like Dan Jansen, like Paul Wylie. To end that way would be fantastic."

Candeloro, however, was worried for him.

"I have seen Todd under big pressure," he said. "He can miss the program. He's very strong, but when you play with the Olympic title, it's not something small."

As a prelude to the final act, Michael Weiss emerged once more as Beethoven. After falling on his attempt at the quad lutz, he skated beautifully. He first landed his triple axel–triple toe loop, and then, for the first time all season, his triple flip–triple toe loop. None of the top skaters had managed two triple–triples by the end of the evening. Only Weiss. He landed seven triples in all, and leaped to seventh place. He and Weisiger wondered where he might have been had he not fallen in the short program.

As he sat in Kiss and Cry with Weisiger and his wife Lisa, Weiss strangely took a bite out of a grapefruit. It was not a random act of citrus-tasting. Weiss had mentioned to Advantage International, his agents, that he loved grapefruits and oranges; his agents thought they might be able to make some money off of his affection for citrus, and suggested it might be wise to show the Vitamin C people how much he loved the stuff on national television.

Advantage was working hard for Weiss in other ways. He shot a McDonald's commercial in Nagano (saying how much he liked Japanese food, as he held some French fries) for an estimated $7,000 and he appeared in a print ad for AT&T that earned about $20,000.

The idea was to sell Weiss as America's hope for the 2002 Games as Eldredge likely moved into the professional ranks.

The more people who were exposed to Ilia Kulik's long program outfit, the more thoughts there were on exactly what it was.

"A giraffe getting hit by a school bus," said one reporter.

"A bumblebee," someone else said.

"A bumblebee getting hit by a school bus," was another idea.

Tatiana Tarasova was the one who picked the yellow-and-black animal print shirt for Kulik. It represented freedom, she said.

"It's yellow, the color of the sun. It's a young man walking in New York in 1935 or 1937, and the sun hits him. Why not the yellow color?"

Why not?

The flight of the bumblebee was superb. "Rhapsody in Moo" was terrific. Whatever Kulik looked like, when he landed his quad toe loop twenty seconds into the program, it didn't matter. He was rolling. The great boy skater had turned into a man. There were no more Kulik meltdowns. At twenty, he was on top of his game.

Within a minute and a half, his cheeks were flaring. He was shrugging to the music another thirty seconds later. His hair was flying. After a quad and eight triples, he was finished. His scores closed the competition before it began. All 5.8s and 5.9s, except for one 5.7, out of eighteen scores. It was difficult to imagine anyone beating that.

Kulik went to the locker room and got on his cellular phone. He called his parents and his girlfriend in Russia. He talked to keep his mind off what was happening on the ice. He didn't want to know. He was too nervous to watch.

Eldredge came after Kulik. If the gold medal was gone, the silver still was available.

But Eldredge turned his first triple–triple into a triple–double. And then his second triple–triple into another triple–double. He couldn't afford to do that in the Olympics. The field was too strong.

At the four-minute mark, he popped his second triple axel into one of those Lalique-like singles, and the crowd inside White Ring groaned. This was skating by procrastination. He kept putting the tough stuff off, and he had just thirty seconds left.

At 4:16 of the program, Eldredge went up for a last-gasp triple axel. His left leg caved in as it grabbed for the ice. He went sprawling on the multicolored Nagano flower at center ice.

Eldredge assumed he was out of the medals—until Yagudin skated and did even worse.

Eldredge was ahead of him.

Unless Candeloro pulled out another performance as he did to win the bronze medal in 1994, Eldredge would be assured of his long-awaited Olympic medal.

Candeloro did it again. The swashbuckling D'Artagnan of *The Three Musketeers* not only outperformed Eldredge, he outjumped him. Candeloro, who was about to turn twenty-six and had fought an ankle injury for the past year, landed two triple axels. He swept ahead of Eldredge.

The only man remaining with a chance to win a medal, perhaps the gold, was Stojko. He looked uncomfortable as he took the ice; no one yet knew about his groin injury or his illness. But when he failed to attempt a quad—his jump—it was clear something was wrong. He skated tentatively and fought for each of his eight triple jump landings. The moment he finished, he grimaced in pain and reached for his right leg. His marks were not good enough to touch Kulik's; they didn't even reach Candeloro's long program scores. Stojko fell to third in the long program, and second overall.

It was another silver medal for Canada.

Stojko was in such pain that he left the arena without talking to the media and went to the Olympic Village to receive treatment.

Doug Leigh had his fourth Olympic silver medalist: Brian Orser (1984 and 1988) and Stojko (1994 and 1998).

"People will start calling me Hi-Ho-Silver," Leigh shrugged.

Stojko spoke two days later, and mentioned something about the 2002 Olympics. Perhaps he would try again in four years.

"I used to go to sleep at night thinking of myself at the top of the Olympic podium after a great performance," he said. "I thought about it last night: Why didn't it happen? I believe in it so much, but it's because I believe in it that I was able to get through this."

After Kulik and Stojko came Candeloro, Eldredge, and Yagudin. Those were the final standings.

Todd Eldredge was randomly chosen for drug testing as the three medalists—including Stojko hobbling in sneakers—were honored on the ice.

"Maybe I wanted it too badly," Eldredge said.

Something was wrong with this picture. Candeloro, a comical showman known for taking off his shirt during exhibition numbers and making teenaged girls squeal in delight, had two Olympic bronze medals.

Todd Eldredge, the five-time U.S. champion and 1996 world champion known for his impeccable work ethic, his solid jumps, and his superb spins and footwork, had none.

"The medal was something I wanted," Eldredge said. "But everybody doesn't get what they want."

Alexei Urmanov watched the men's event on Eurosport in his apartment in St. Petersburg. He saw the entire short program, and the whole long program, sitting with his mother on their pull-out couch.

"You can compete with those guys," Galina told him.

Urmanov grew sad watching. "Everyone was nervous, I think. Kulik was quite good. He was lucky that he was first in the last group. I think Todd was nervous after Kulik's marks. But the short program was good."

Urmanov did not know what happened to Stojko. Two days later, he found out it was a groin injury.

"Oh," he said, "that's not good."

Urmanov had only recently returned from the United States, where he saw a doctor about his groin. While he was training there, he cut his knee as he slid on the ice during a finishing move. That took him off the ice again.

Urmanov was getting restless. It had been eleven months since he hurt himself in Lausanne. His groin still was not better. Surgery was being discussed. So, too, was his retirement.

"I want to compete for the gold every time I skate, not just compete," he said. "I think this problem isn't over for me. If it doesn't get better, I think I will be finished competing. If at the start of next season it still hurts, I will stop competing. This is too hard for me."

15

THE SILVER LINING

The cameras and reporters were poised for Michelle Kwan's first Olympic practice just before noon on Tuesday, February 10. CBS Sports was televising it live back to the United States; it was primetime back home, and big news. Dressed in black, Kwan was on the ice; *Lyra Angelica* was playing over the big loudspeakers in the massive, barn-shaped practice arena beside White Ring.

The practice itself was not expected to be much. Kwan was tired and jet-lagged. She had been in Nagano for only ten hours after her overnight journey the day before from Los Angeles, which included an eleven-hour flight and a five-hour van trip from Tokyo's Narita Airport up to the Japanese Alps and Nagano.

Kwan began with her triple lutz, as she always did, and she fell. The fifty journalists standing beside the boards made a note of it: The Olympic gold medal favorite fell on her first official jump at the Games.

But she kept on skating. One triple jump turned into another. She landed everything else in her long program, the other six triples, and her double axel. She refused to stop. She looked calm, happy, even carefree. If she was feeling pressure, she didn't show it. Frank Carroll had told her that if she could get through the long program on the first day, running full out, she could get through it anytime.

No other skater had come in and attempted a complete runthrough of their long program the day after arriving in Japan. No one but Kwan.

"That's the Olympic gold medal!" several reporters exclaimed after she finished. The fall was incidental. The stamina and discipline were what caught their eyes.

Carol Heiss Jenkins, the 1960 Olympic gold medalist who was coaching a South African skater at the Games, was watching.

"It's important that everybody realizes the significance of that," she said. "She showed everyone from Day One she's here to win."

Heiss, the one who predicted Kwan would win the gold medal eleven months earlier at the Geneva Airport, was so impressed, she said it again.

"I want to welcome her into the Olympic gold medal family," Heiss said.

Kwan came to the Games a bit late, after the Opening Ceremonies. Because her competition came near the end of the Olympics, she stayed at home to receive treatment on her injured toe, and to keep everything as normal as possible as long as possible. She was sad she missed the ceremonies, but there were larger issues at stake for her. With her picture on the cover of some major national magazines, with all expectations on her after her superb Philadelphia performances, Kwan had to win. She knew it, and relished it. She said she liked the pressure. She needed that gold medal to solidify her place as the next great American ice legend.

When she and her parents and agent arrived in Japan, they checked into the Holiday Inn Express in the center of Nagano, a twenty-minute drive from White Ring. Kwan was not going to be staying in the Olympic Village; she was one of only two of the nearly 200 U.S. athletes who did not (Nicole Bobek was the other). Michelle wanted to treat the Games as if they were just another competition; her routine was to hole up with her parents in a hotel at Skate America or the U.S. nationals or the worlds. They didn't plan to change for the Olympics. They took some heat in the press for it, but it made sense to them. Many top athletes don't live in the village in the Summer Olympics; it's all a matter of the preferred routine for high-profile athletes at the most important event of their careers.

That didn't mean, however, that Kwan wasn't caught up in the Games the moment she arrived.

"Seeing the Olympic rings," she said, "I really want to cry."

At Lake Arrowhead, before she left, she had been skating "scary great," Frank Carroll said. "So sharp, fabulous, just fabulous.

"I'm nervous as hell," Carroll said. "I want this for Michelle."

He also wanted it for him. Most mornings when he woke up, his stomach began churning before he brushed his teeth. It had been eighteen years since Linda Fratianne controversially lost the Olympic gold medal. Eighteen years was a long time to wait for what might be his last, best chance at coaching an Olympic gold medalist.

Tara Lipinski, Kwan, and Bobek all were scheduled to practice together at the Games, but the other two were not at White Ring to see Kwan that day. Bobek still was in California, and Lipinski had been at the Olympics so long, she already had come and gone.

Lipinski arrived at the Games well before the Olympic flame did, and in many ways, she shined as brightly.

She was practicing with more life than she had shown at the nationals, or anytime throughout the autumn except for the Champions Series final in Munich. "She's barely clearing the boards, yet she took over the building," said Sandra Bezic, Lipinski choreographer-turned–Canadian TV commentator, who watched Tara skate for the first time since August from a television booth. She would do no work with Tara at the Games; she saw her only to say hello and give her a hug.

"It's a little frustrating for me," Bezic said. "Whoever she talks to, I haven't been able to talk to. There's the Susie Wynne layer, there's the ballet teacher layer, there's the Richard layer."

Richard Callaghan, known for wanting to be in complete control of the lives of his skaters, was the man in charge of Lipinski. Bezic understood that, but she was used to communicating with the coaches of the skaters she worked with, and that wasn't happening with Tara.

Before the ladies event began, Bezic was sitting in the press room at the skating venue and looked up to see Callaghan walking toward her.

"Hi, how are you?" Bezic said cheerfully.

"Good, how are you?" Callaghan replied.

"Good luck," she said.

"Thank you," Callaghan said.

As Tara's coach passed Tara's choreographer, he never broke stride.

But Lipinski's Olympic existence wasn't entirely consumed by skating. During the first week, she giggled with 516-pound sumo wrestler Akebono, had eighteen alterations made on her official but too-big U.S. Olympic clothing, lived in the athletes' village, marched in the Opening Ceremonies, worked on needlepoint in the athletes' sewing room, lingered in the village cafeteria, and barely ever saw her mother or her agent.

After the nationals, Mike Burg and the Lipinskis—mother, father, and daughter—talked on the phone. Burg noticed how glum Jack and Pat had looked when their daughter finished second in Philadelphia; Mom and Dad hated second place as much as Tara. But something had to change, Burg said. They had to let Tara be Tara. They were smothering the little kid. They all had to have more fun.

So it was agreed; Tara needed to be set free. But this would not be easy for the Lipinskis. After having their meeting, Team Tara went right back to their old ways and put Tara under wraps again. They kept her out of sight for the rest of January, allowing CBS just one interview. Burg told CBS officials that if he didn't like how it turned out, he might not allow Tara to talk to the network during the Games.

The arsonist was setting another fire.

When the CBS piece came out syrupy sweet, the firefighter unleashed Tara.

By staying in the Village and rooming with other U.S. figure skaters, Tara barely saw her mother and Burg, who had rooms at the Matsuchiro Royal Hotel. Pat Lipinski came to practice and waited backstage so she could talk to her daughter for ten minutes a day. Then Tara dashed back to the Olympic Village to have more fun, and her mother returned to her hotel. Tara had never spent so much time away from her mother.

Because Olympic security was extremely tight, even during practices, Burg also couldn't be near Tara. During practice sessions, he had to stand outside the arena near a snowdrift, or wait in the CBS compound of trucks and makeshift offices.

He didn't have a credential until the second week of the Games, when he mysteriously showed up wearing a pass that made him a chaperone of the French delegation. When someone mistakenly said Burg had a Russian credential, he winked and corrected them: "I'm French!"

But even that credential didn't get him into the practice rink. He and others, including Danny Kwan and some of the other skaters' parents, found one window outside the practice arena where they could see two-thirds of the ice. "The Peephole Gang" gathered there in the cold and took turns peeking in.

Being left alone by the adults in her life was the best thing to happen to Tara Lipinski. At the nationals, she was shut off from reporters and was a bundle of nerves by the time she took the ice for the short program, in which she fell.

But at the Olympics, Tara made herself available after nearly every practice. At the Games, the rules are that reporters must gather backstage in a place called the "mixed zone," where a waist-high fence separates them from the athletes as they walk by. Often, journalists have to shout to athletes or coaches to ask them to come over and talk.

Day after day, Tara gladly showed up without ever being beckoned. She gave daily reports of what she had been doing in the village. One day, she happily accepted a reporter's cellular phone to talk to another reporter who couldn't be at the skating venue at that moment.

"Are you where Picabo Street just won?" Tara asked excitedly into the phone.

She was loving the Games so much, she lamented how quickly they were passing. "Every day that goes by," she said, "it's almost over."

After more than a week of this, reporters had seen enough. These were the same journalists who had been critical of Tara's unusual upbringing and little-girl outfits, of her nomadic childhood and her two–time zone family life.

But they couldn't help themselves.

Even before the women's competition began, they awarded Tara Lipinski the gold medal.

For the mixed zone.

Things weren't quite so cheerful for Pat Lipinski, who was alone for much of the Games until Jack showed up in the second week. She told complete strangers that she didn't think her daughter was going to win the gold medal.

"Michelle's going to win," she said one day. "Michelle's going to win."

Pat Lipinski always was measuring her daughter against Kwan. And she thought the judges never would allow Tara, who was two years younger and less artistically advanced, to beat her.

But, true to form, Tara had a far different take on things at the Games.

"I really like being the underdog," she said at a press conference two weeks before the women's long program. "It gives me a lot more things to think about. It keeps me motivated."

Tara had the run of the Games until the Opening Ceremonies. The next day, despite mild protests, she agreed to fly to Osaka for two and a half days of intense practice sessions. During that time, Michelle flew in, and took over the Olympic practices.

Kwan's first chance to get onto the main ice in White Ring was

Wednesday, February 11, exactly one week before the short program. (Practice sessions were held in both rinks because of the demand for ice time with the men's and ice dancing practices and competitions.)

Tara was back from Osaka, so she was there too. Bobek still wasn't around. Rumors were flying that she had injured her hip. Carol Heiss Jenkins had received a phone call even before she came to Nagano to inform Tonia Kwiatkowski, the fourth-place finisher at the nationals, to keep practicing. Bobek was Bobek. Ms. January was facing February. Anything was possible.

In White Ring, for the first time, Kwan practiced her short program. When she moved down the ice as her music built to her final triple jump, she picked with her left foot—the one that was injured— and rotated three times. The triple toe loop. It was back in the short program. Her toe was well enough to replace the triple flip with the toe loop, the safer jump, the one she felt more comfortable with. Kwan and Carroll knew they didn't have to match the triple flip Lipinski had in her short program; Kwan would get the higher artistic marks, and her technical difficulty in other elements, including her inside-edge-to-outside-edge spiral, was higher than Lipinski's.

They learned this lesson from the 1995 world championships, when fourteen-year-old Michelle Kwan showed up with the toughest programs, skated perfectly, and finished fourth. That sent one simple message: Artistry wins.

Carroll and Kwan asked themselves: Why risk the triple flip when the triple toe loop would do just fine? Kwan felt more at ease with the toe loop. It was smart skating strategy. After all, the goal in the short program was simply to place in the top three.

But by no means were the two of them pulling their punches in either the short or long program. Nancy Kerrigan landed five triples in her long program at the 1994 Olympics; Kwan had seven triple jumps in her long program, the same number as Lipinski, although Lipinski did one triple–triple combination and one triple–triple sequence, and Kwan did neither. Doing two triples in a row is hard work; it requires the skater to land one triple, then immediately muster enough power and energy to launch and land a second one. A triple–double is easier.

Kwan had a triple toe loop–triple toe loop at times the previous season, and was working on a triple loop–triple loop earlier in the 1997–98 year. But she stopped doing the toe loop combination when she found out her toe was injured. Kwan's loop–loop combination, Lipinski's forte, was not consistent enough to throw into a big event.

From every signal the Kwan camp received, though, a triple–triple didn't matter. She didn't need to risk it. This was the lesson of the 1995 worlds. It also was the lesson of the 1994 Olympics. Nancy Kerrigan landed a stunning triple–triple—and still lost to Oksana Baiul, who landed a shaky double–double at the end of her program. In those Games, Baiul won the gold medal with three clean triple jumps. Skating wanted the artist to win the Olympic gold medal, just as Carol Heiss Jenkins always said. This was the message Carroll and Kwan heard over and over again, loud and clear. It was what they were being told with the marks at every competition Kwan entered in 1997–98: Skate America, Skate Canada, the U.S. nationals: "You're so good, you don't need anything more."

Kwan and Carroll said, however, that had she not injured her toe, she still would have had a triple toe loop–triple toe loop in her program. It just helped them breathe easier knowing she didn't need it.

In her initial press conference that Wednesday, sitting on a stage at the Main Press Center beside Carroll, both in their new red, white, and blue U.S. Olympic gear, Kwan made sure everyone knew she had no intention of wimping out. Saying she relished the role of the gold medal favorite, she said that a winning program, for her, would be to "skate well . . . if I don't skate very well and still win, it wouldn't mean as much."

She wanted to win the gold medal like her childhood idol and present-day buddy, Brian Boitano, with a perfect program. (Boitano wasn't in Japan to cheer her on, but he did give her two letters to open the night before the short and long programs.)

"Winning doesn't mean perfect," Carroll interjected. "I want her to be the best here, but that doesn't necessarily mean perfect."

"But I can be better," Kwan replied immediately, turning to look into Carroll's eyes as if they were holding a private conversation rather than a very public press conference.

The next day, Michelle and Tara both practiced their long programs in their late morning session in the practice rink. Benches were set up along the sides of the rink for reporters to watch; Robin Cousins, the 1980 Olympic gold medalist and a BBC commentator, sat and watched the two American teenagers.

Kwan came first, then Lipinski. They both skated well.

Cousins, one of those true artists who won the Olympic gold medal, was asked whom he liked better.

"I like that one," he said. "I like the speed, the spontaneity."

He was pointing at Lipinski.

Cousins got up and left.

The American journalists surrounding him had never heard a skating expert say he liked Lipinski's skating more than Kwan's. Never.

"Did you hear that?" one reporter said to another.

"He's not a judge," the journalist replied. "Forget it."

As the days in Japan wore on and the women's short program drew closer, interest in the two American girls grew more intense. CBS's ratings were down, Americans were not winning as many medals as U.S. officials had hoped, and interest in the Games in the United States appeared to be waning. At White Ring, in the nation's favorite Olympic sport, Americans had been shut out. Russians won the first three figure skating gold medals—the pairs, the men, and dance. The stories were uplifting, controversial (Pasha) and inspiring, but Americans love winners. And, to that point, there had not been anything higher than two fourth-place finishes by U.S. skaters.

A Michelle–Tara rivalry could save the Games.

The rivalry was trumped up by reporters wishing for another Tonya–Nancy saga, but they knew this was way too much to expect. Those two infamous stars of the last Olympics had met again, prior to the 1998 Games, for a headline-grabbing Fox television special that paid each a significant sum. Harding's appearance was not shocking; she needed the publicity and the money. But Kerrigan always said she hated having her name tied to Harding's when she, of course, was the victim of the 1994 knee-clubbing.

Kerrigan spent four years trying to distance herself from the attack. And then she stunningly agreed to appear on the same TV set with Harding, reemphasizing the very link she was forever trying to break.

"I would like to apologize again for being in the wrong place at the wrong time and with the wrong people," Harding told Kerrigan on the show.

Later in the show, Kerrigan said, "I am glad you moved on and I hope that you can find happiness and maybe children can learn from these mistakes."

Compared to that crass world of pay-for-controversy television, Michelle Kwan and Tara Lipinski were a breath of fresh air.

In reality, though, the rivalry in skating was not Tara vs. Michelle; it was Michelle vs. Michelle. The question after Philadelphia was how high she could raise the bar. If she made a mistake, or somehow beat herself, she could open the door for Tara. In eight head-to-head meetings, that's what happened. Kwan won five, Lipinski, three (the three in a row from early 1997). Otherwise, Tara was fighting for the silver medal. That was the message of Skate America and of Philadelphia. Michelle was in complete control.

Nonetheless, the two girls' lives, words, and triple jumps were examined in excruciating detail in hundreds of newspaper, radio, and television reports around the nation in the days leading to the short program, February 18.

There was an ironic twist to the stories. Tara Lipinski, the child who was obsessed by her sport, was enjoying a happy-go-lucky existence in the Village. Meanwhile, Michelle Kwan, whose entire season had been marked by a sense of freedom and joy on the ice, was living a serious, focused routine away from the Village.

The Kwan way sounded extremely smart when a nasty flu bug swept the village, taking out dozens of athletes, including Elvis Stojko, Alexei Yagudin, and Tanja Szewczenko, the stylish German who had overcome nearly two years of illness and injury to become a favorite for a bronze medal at the Games. She couldn't have had worse luck; she came to the Olympics, caught the flu, spent several days in bed, tried to practice, looked like she was sleepwalking, and withdrew before the women's competition began.

At least Stojko and Yagudin had a chance to compete; after going through so much to get herself back to the top of her sport, Szewczenko left Japan before the women's short program began. She couldn't bear to watch it.

The Lipinskis and Burg were concerned about Tara's health, but hoped that a bout with the flu after the nationals meant she wouldn't catch anything at the Games. Plus, the kid wanted to stay in the Village. She said so, and that was that.

"I wouldn't want to just come to this competition like a worlds, stay in a hotel and not go to Opening Ceremonies," Lipinski said.

That's exactly what Kwan was doing.

While Lipinski took a delightful joyride through the Games, Kwan was her usual introspective, intriguing self.

Sometimes she sounded nervous:

"I tell myself not to think that this is my life and the Olympics," she said. "If this doesn't work out, I've got other chances."

Other times, she sounded like a fun-loving kid:

"Have you noticed the strawberries here?" she asked reporters gathered in the mixed zone two days before the short program.

"They're so big and perfect. Did you know they were grown under artificial light?"

Twenty-five reporters gave Kwan a collective blank stare.

"I just had to tell you that," she said, shrugging.

The journalists broke into warm laughter.

A moment later, a crackling noise, the sound of someone talking, came from Frank Carroll's jacket pocket.

Carroll pulled out a walkie-talkie.

"The car's here!" It was Danny Kwan's voice coming out of the speaker. "The car's here!"

Carroll held down a button and talked into the speaker.

"Soon, soon," he said. "We know. Relax. Over."

Agent Shep Goldberg had brought walkie-talkies from home so the Kwan team could communicate around town.

That was only one of the ways Goldberg and the Kwans planned ahead. The Hollywood studios gave them videos of the year's hottest movies, including *Titanic,* and *As Good as It Gets.* To pass the time at night, the Kwans and Goldberg gathered in one of their hotel rooms to have their own private screening.

During one of their visits to the mixed zone, reporters asked Kwan and Carroll if they had heard the news about Peggy Fleming.

"What news?"

"She has breast cancer," one of them said.

Kwan and Carroll's jaws dropped in shock. They had not heard.

They were quickly told that Fleming was expected to be fine after having surgery.

"She's okay?" Kwan asked the reporters. She looked at Carroll. Her eyes searched his. She looked scared. Fleming was a good friend.

"We were just talking about life being short and enjoying the experience," Carroll said.

Within a day, Kwan called Fleming back in California to wish her well. In many ways, the news reminded Kwan of the moment she heard that Scott Hamilton had cancer the previous March, while she was at the world championships. For a skater trying to survive in the world's biggest pressure-cooker, such news was an instant reality check.

In the spring of 1997, Hamilton underwent four rounds of chemotherapy, followed by surgery June 24, and his cancer was in remission. He was skating and touring again, and spending hours on end in White Ring, attending the Olympics as a commentator for CBS.

As the women's short program approached, Hamilton was cornered by reporters. He didn't have to talk about cancer anymore. He was once again talking about his sport.

"The tough thing is that every four years, you're in this position," he said of Kwan and Lipinski. "The question is: Will you ever be in this position again?"

As Michelle Kwan came onto the ice in White Ring arena to warm up for the women's short program at the Olympic Games, Lori Nichol stood in her living room near Toronto with a portable phone pressed to her ear, pacing.

"I can't believe this is it," Nichol said into the phone. "All these years working toward the Olympic Games, and here it is."

It was seven on a snowy, dark Wednesday morning in Canada. A reporter sitting in the press seats behind the row of judges in White Ring at nine Wednesday evening was calling Nichol so she could listen to Kwan's music over the phone and find out instantaneously how her skater was doing.

Nichol was the one member of Kwan's inner circle who did not go to Japan. She considered it, but because she spent so much time away from her husband and three-year-old son during the rest of the year, she decided it was just too far to go for such a length of time. As Kwan's choreographer, her work on the Olympic programs was finished. There was nothing more for her to do except send cards and gifts to Frank Carroll and Michelle Kwan, rack up the phone bill, and pray.

In the arena, Kwan's name was announced and she was taking her starting position, the one Nichol had helped her create the previous July.

At the same time, Nichol was taking her listening position. She climbed the staircase in her home, sat on the top step in darkness, clutched the phone, and waited to hear the play-by-play of Kwan's short program. Canadian television was supposed to show the event live, but a men's hockey game was still going on. So Nichol had to rely on the voice on the phone, 6,000 miles away.

Kwan's music, the two beautiful piano pieces by Rachmaninoff, filled the arena. Nichol heard the music through the telephone and knew exactly what Kwan was doing on the ice. She knew she was gliding into the triple lutz combination, the do-or-die element of the short program, twenty-seven seconds into the performance.

Nichol held her breath and closed her eyes.

She listened for a particular musical note, the one on which Kwan usually landed the triple lutz.

She heard the note.

She didn't hear any response from the reporter.

For a split second, she panicked.

"Yes!" came the word from Japan.

Kwan was back safely to earth.

Nichol exhaled, but said nothing.

Fifteen seconds later came the double axel.

"Yes!"

When Kwan landed her final triple jump, the triple toe loop, Nichol bounced up and dashed down the stairs back to the living room.

She began talking into the phone.

"Is she on the music?"

"Is her spin centered?"

"How does she look?"

"Lori," the reporter said, "she's smiling."

When the music built to the spiral, Kwan's difficult and exquisite move in which she raises her left leg high and glides on the blade of her right skate, Nichol found herself doing the exact same steps at the exact same time on her living room carpet. In bare feet, wearing a sweatshirt and shorts, Nichol leaned on the inside of her right foot, then the outside, shifting her balance in Canada at the exact moment that Kwan made the switch from one edge to the other in Japan.

"I can't believe I just did that," Nichol chuckled.

Kwan spun to her conclusion. Nichol heard the music end, and knew Kwan had been flawless. Standing nearby, on another phone, was Lenore Kay, Nichol's music consultant who had driven twenty minutes from her home to hear events unfold in Japan. Kay edited the music that was coming through the phone line.

Nichol looked at Kay.

She was crying.

Nichol hugged her.

Nichol's son Austin came over to see what was happening.

"What's wrong?" he asked Nichol. "Are you sad, Mommy?"

"No, honey."

"Are you happy?"

Still cradling the telephone, Nichol knelt down to give him a hug.

"Oh, yes."

When the short program was over, and all twenty-eight women had somehow lived through the most stressful two minutes and forty seconds of their careers with varying degrees of success, Kwan was in first place, carrying eight of the nine judges' top placements with her standard nine 5.9s on the bottom row of marks. Lipinski, who also was perfect, was second, with that last first-place vote (from France) and a long row of "2s" for placement.

Russian veteran Maria Butyrskaia was a flawless third, and China's Lu Chen, back after her difficult 1997 season, was fourth, with just the slightest glitch on a jump and a spin.

Nicole Bobek, however, was seventeenth.

She came to Nagano less than a week before the short program, suffering from a sore hip and bronchitis. She fell on her triple lutz. She doubled her triple toe loop. And she stepped out of her double axel. It was a clean sweep: three jumps, three bad mistakes.

Several Americans wondered what Tonia Kwiatkowski, the fourth-place finisher at nationals, would have been able to do in that Olympic short program. She was back at home, working for Cleveland's CBS affiliate WOIO as a skating analyst for the Olympics. While she still was getting good at the art of live television, there was no doubt she was a demon when it came to clean short programs.

But it was Bobek representing the United States at the Olympics, not Kwiatkowski.

And Bobek was history.

Her countrywomen, however, were on top of the world.

As she began skating, Kwan looked at the U.S. flags waving in the audience, heard the cheers, and said to herself, "I'm in heaven.

"People are clapping, millions of people are watching on TV, and I'm skating. It's just me and the ice. When I'm on the ice, I don't think anybody can stop me."

It may have been heaven. Or perhaps it was Philadelphia. That's the feeling she had at the nationals, and she came close to recreating it at the Games. But not quite. Kwan was more deliberate in her skating, a smart strategy for getting through the Olympic short program without a mistake. She wasn't quite as carefree as she had been at the nationals, but she was good enough. It was a bit of a shock that she lost the French judge to Lipinski (Kwan 5.6, 5.9; Lipinski 5.7, 5.9), but she dominated the others. The Hungarian judge gave Kwan 5.7, 5.9 and Lipinski 5.6, 5.6. Just as at Skate America, more than a dozen skaters mathematically could have been placed between Michelle and Tara on that judge's scorecard.

But Lipinski was second no matter how anyone looked at it, and that meant she was in striking position. She was ecstatic. After she landed her triple flip, the jump she crashed on at the nationals, she burst into a big smile. When her music ended, she wanted to keep going. She wished the program had been four minutes long. It was like a practice day in Delaware, or Detroit. She didn't want it to end.

"It seems so hard and when you do it, it's like a miracle," she gushed as she sat beside Kwan in the press conference. "This was the most happiest time of my life."

Richard Callaghan, Tara's coach, also was encouraged by something that didn't always happen for Lipinski. Five judges gave her a higher artistic mark than technical mark. They were saying that they liked her presentation, not just her jumping. Much of that had to do with the speed with which she skated, which was noticeably better than Kwan. Kwan was much more exquisite and refined, and her "inbetweens," the elements between the jumps, were richer and purer. But Lipinski was not just a whirling dervish on the ice anymore. She was landing jumps and selling them. She was bold and aggressive. She was going for everything. It was nothing like her tentative Philadelphia performance. She was skating the way she was living life in the Olympic Village. She was having fun, and she was unencumbered.

Kwan performed the way she was living in Japan, too. She was cautious, intelligent, and not particularly spontaneous. It was smart. It was logical. And it appeared to be working.

By the time they met with reporters, Kwan and Lipinski had drawn their skating positions for Friday's long program. Kwan was first, just as Ilia Kulik had been in the men's long program, when none of his strongest challengers skated well after him. Irina Slutskaia, who was in fifth place, was second. Chen was third, Surya Bonaly (sixth place after the short program) was fourth, Lipinski was fifth, and Butyrskaia was last.

Mike Burg was anxious about the draw. He wanted to know what position Tara had selected. When he saw it scribbled on a page of a reporter's notebook, his eyes shot to the names.

"Michelle's first," he said, searching, searching.

"Tara's fifth. That's great! Perfect."

Kwan said she thought going first was fine. She knew it would cut into her warm-up time; instead of going all out the full six minutes, she would jump and skate for about four minutes, then come back to Frank Carroll and slowly relax and get her heart rate down to begin her performance when the others left the ice. Many thought the second skating position was best because it allowed the full warm-up time, but also let the skater stay in his or her skates and get ready to go right back onto the ice. Every other spot required strategic waiting; there were pros and cons to any slot in the final group.

The first spot was a strange one. On one hand, because Kwan was Kwan, if she skated cleanly, she would get good marks, probably 5.8, 5.9. A judge could not afford to go much higher, for to do so would be to prejudge the competition. A 5.8, 5.9 could win the gold medal; a judge would know simply to go lower with his or her marks for all the other skaters. But if a judge gave Kwan 5.9, 5.9, or 5.9, 6.0, that would ostensibly shut out anyone else. With the sport under the gun for controversial ice dancing judging, it was unlikely any judge would do that.

When she picked the plastic disk that gave her the first spot in the last group, Kwan ensured Nagano would not be Philadelphia. There would be no 6.0s, no matter how well she skated.

And she also ensured that Lipinski would at least be in the ballgame. The kid would have a chance. Her youthful exuberance could have an impact on the judges after a long night of skating. Sometimes the best impression was the last. The judges were human beings, after all.

There was another issue, the who-was-following-whom factor. Kwan followed no one, of course. But Lipinski came after Bonaly. Of the six skaters in the last group, Bonaly was the least artistic. Compared to her, even the slightest bit of artistic flair would look like it belonged in the Louvre. Lipinski's artistry was developing daily, and was quite good. But it would look even better to judges who had just sat through four minutes of Surya—and were a good half hour removed from watching the subtle beauty of Michelle Kwan.

The luck of the draw. All skaters deal with it, and anyone can rationalize it, but on Wednesday night after the short program, it looked like it all belonged to Tara Lipinski.

"If I skate my best," Lipinski said, "anything can happen."

The kid had lost the short program, but was amazingly pleased with herself. On her way out of the press conference, after lingering longer than Kwan, she looked into the faces of the reporters she had seen every day in the mixed zone and asked, "Do I still have the gold medal for the media?"

Even though those reporters adored Kwan, they were getting to know Lipinski in a way they never had.

They quickly assured Tara that the mixed-zone gold medal was one Olympic medal she was not going to lose.

The day in-between the short and the long program was not a day of excruciating tension. That would come Friday afternoon.

But Thursday, February 19, was a day of analysis in Japan. And both coaches were talking about speed.

"To win," Callaghan said, "Tara would have to skate her very best, with the speed she had last night."

"I think Michelle was probably a little bit conservative last night," Carroll said, "I think she needs to skate with a little bit more energy. I think she was holding back a little tiny bit to do everything right. For the long program, I'd like to see the entire picture, not little vignettes all the way through."

Carroll later talked to Michelle about skating a little freer, about "going for it."

But could that happen? She was a smart girl. She knew what was on the line. Once again, she was the hunted, not the hunter. It was like Nashville. Kwan had the most to lose. The night of the short program, Callaghan had said that as a rule, the skater in first place was not going to be as loose as the skater chasing her.

"When you're in second, you think, 'I want that.' When you're in first," Callaghan said, "you sort of look back."

It poured Friday at the Winter Olympics. A dreary, steady winter rain pounded Nagano. Traffic was terrible leading to White Ring that night. The emperor and empress of Japan were arriving. Michelle Kwan and her parents and agent were stuck in the line of cars, and, finally, Michelle jumped out and ran two blocks through the rain to White Ring. But security personnel stopped her until the emperor's wife looked out the window of her car, recognized Kwan and waved. Only then did they let her in to make her run for the Olympic gold medal.

At the time the Kwans were sitting in traffic, Nicole Bobek was finishing her disastrous Olympic experience on a stunningly dreadful note. Little more than a month earlier, Bobek had been touted as a strong medal hope. By the Olympic long program, she was simply trying to survive for four minutes on the ice.

The day before, she fell at least a dozen times in her practice session. It was an amazing number of falls for a woman who was on the ice only thirty-eight minutes. She sobbed as she skated off.

"Tell them I'm sorry," she asked a U.S. Figure Skating Association spokeswoman to relay to reporters. "I am here and I am still fighting."

In the long program, she landed just one triple jump, fell on three others, and stepped out of a double axel. It was embarrassing.

But Bobek was delightfully philosophical afterward. She knew that she had held it together for just about as long as she could. Injuries, illness, all those years of moving and changing coaches—it was amazing she made it to the Olympics at all.

"Hopefully, this Olympics, people will remember me for how hard I tried and not how bad I did."

Bobek was gone, headed to an ice show or made-for-TV competition. A career of promise had dissolved into a terrible seventeenth-place finish, the worst Olympic finish for an American singles skater since 1936.

At 9:30 P.M. in Nagano, Michelle Kwan popped out from behind the blue curtains separating the backstage hallway from the entry way to the ice. Frank Carroll was with her. One minute later, she set foot on the white Olympic ice for her warm-up. She wouldn't leave the ice for ten minutes. In that amount of time, she almost certainly would know whether she was the Olympic gold medalist. That's what the experts said. Kwan was in control of her destiny. No falls, and she wins.

She pumped her fist as she went to the spot where she started, in the corner of the rink, arms by her side, just like Janet Lynn. Kwan wasn't a fist-pumper by nature. She was trying to get herself going.

She did not smile as she did in Philadelphia. She was focused, and she was thinking, and everyone could tell. What Kwan had discovered with Lori Nichol in the Kwans' TV room after Thanksgiving—how Janet Lynn was able to concentrate without looking like it—was not coming through at that moment on the ice. Her mind was working. And that wasn't the idea of this long program.

It was not going to be an easy four minutes for Michelle Kwan.

Slowly but beautifully, she went about her work. She hung onto a triple flip seventy-five seconds into the program, and, eleven seconds later, somehow dug out the landing of a double axel that was launched with a deliberate takeoff.

She ebbed and flowed with her music. She showed how strong she was when her second triple lutz, the most difficult jump any woman attempts, was higher and more certain than her first. The first one came half a minute into the program. The second one lifted off at three minutes and thirty seconds. Olympic gold medals were won on such jumps.

Kwan moved down the ice and picked in for her triple toe loop, then came back toward the middle of the ice, to the multicolored flower painted in the center of the rink, the symbol of the Nagano Games. She was slightly behind her music, so her finishing pose—the "wing it" move, her "Olympic moment," as Nichol called it—came one second too late, and not quite at center ice.

But no one in the arena noticed. Kwan threw her arms into the air. She was finished. The Americans in the audience were standing.

"I think she's done it," Carroll said to Jim Disbrow, the U.S. figure skating team leader standing nearby.

"I think she has," Disbrow said.

Kwan was spent. It was over. All the pressure, the four years of building to that ending—and she was done. She came off the ice—it had been a good ten minutes, all in all—and was swallowed up by Frank Carroll's waiting arms.

They went to Kiss and Cry, holding onto each other.

There, tears welled in her eyes and fell onto her cheeks. She was crying out of happiness, and out of relief.

Kwan put her arm around Carroll.

They were expecting those 5.8s and 5.9s.

Everyone was.

The first set of marks popped up:

"5.7, 5.7, 5.8, 5.7, 5.8, 5.8, 5.7, 5.7, 5.8."

Lori Nichol was watching the live television broadcast on the CBC.

"Oh-oh," she said in her living room.

The exchange with Jim Disbrow was ringing in Carroll's ears.

"Maybe she *hasn't* done it," Carroll said to himself, feeling a little bit sick.

The presentation marks popped up: all 5.9s. As spectacular as ever. But Carroll couldn't get it out of his head: There were five 5.7s staring him in the face. All it took was five judges to win the gold medal.

What was with the 5.7s? The girl lands seven triple jumps, fights for the landing of just one of those jumps, spins in two directions, and she gets 5.7s?

Carroll and Kwan left the TV cameras and walked to the men's dressing room, one of their favorite hideaways in skating venues around the world. Michelle took off her skates.

"This is going to be a long haul," Carroll said.

They sat around for a few moments.

"I'd like to go and sit with my Mom," Michelle said. Estella Kwan was backstage, just down the hallway.

Michelle left. Carroll stayed behind in the dressing room.

All those years waiting to coach a gold medalist, and now he had to wait some more.

Irina Slutskaia skated after Kwan. She put a hand down to break a near-fall on one jump and finished the same place she started, fifth.

Elegant Lu Chen came next. Her only goal at the Olympics was to prove to the skating world that she was not yet finished, that her troubles with her federation (officials still made her speak Chinese when her English was impeccable) and a foot injury could not ruin her. Her spirit had been broken a year earlier, but she had slowly rebuilt her life and her career, reminding herself that if she could get into shape, her love for the sport would shine once again. She shuddered at the thought that she would be remembered for her dismal performance in Lausanne. She wanted a different ending to a brilliant Olympic division career.

And she got it. Sandra Bezic created a beautiful program, skated to "Butterfly Lovers," a Chinese *Romeo and Juliet*–style fable, and Lu-Lu, as the skating world calls her, put everything together one last time. She landed five triple jumps and sobbed on the ice, bowing humbly. For presentation, she received all but one 5.8. The memory of the awful 3.0 from Lausanne faded quickly; Chen's name moved into the standings behind Kwan's as the skaters kept coming.

Bonaly was next. Much of what she did was forgettable: she fell on a triple salchow early in the program and held onto numerous bad landings of other jumps.

But she said a most memorable good-bye to the Olympics. With thirty seconds remaining in her program, Bonaly performed a back-flip, a move that has been illegal for years, but one that she loves doing in shows (and the occasional Olympic practice, as she did in Albertville in 1992).

She sped by the judges, just so they all would know what was about to happen, and then threw herself backward into the air.

It was an in-your-face message to the judges: I'm outta here. Au revoir. Drop dead.

The judges sent a message back: Okay, fine. Here's tenth place.

"It was sad to see her do that," said Sally Stapleford, the referee of the women's competition. "She lost between .2 and .4 of a point, for what? It was done to be rude to the judges. That's sad."

The skating world had turned upside down.

It was a perfect time for Tara Lipinski to step onto the ice.

Mike Burg, the man who had never given up hope of winning the gold medal—from Skate America to Paris and the loss to "The Human Zamboni," then on to nationals—loved the position his little client was in.

"She skates like Germany [the Champions Series final], she's a player," he said to himself.

She skated like Germany, the one time in her career where she won a title without having a chief rival make a mistake. From the moment her music began playing and she began skating, Lipinski grabbed the judges by the throat and all but yelled, "Look at me!"

Her double axel was the low line drive it always is. Her triple lutzes were flutzes, although there were no required deductions in the long program, so her marks didn't drop. She hung on slightly to the precarious landings of two jumps in the final minute. But her historical triple loop–triple loop was better than nationals. She smiled and tore around the ice and had a ball. She took the judges along for quite a ride.

When she hit her finishing pose—as close to the end of the music as she had been all season—she couldn't contain her joy. Tara began running, taking four big steps in her skates until she pumped her fists and drank up the crowd's applause.

She breathlessly joined Callaghan and Megan Faulkner, her coach from Houston, in Kiss and Cry. They had less than a minute to wait before the scores came up.

Callaghan and Faulkner each grabbed one of Tara's hands.

What would the judges do?

Backstage, Frank Carroll waited to hear the scores in the men's dressing room. Michelle Kwan was down the hall with her mother. They hadn't watched Tara skate; they would wait to hear the marks, and they would know.

Although the skating marketplace certainly had changed over the years, and the difference between a gold and silver medal wasn't as great as it once was, when those numbers popped onto the scoreboard in a few seconds, they would forever change the lives of two American teenagers.

Who was going to be Dorothy Hamill?

And who was going to become Janet Lynn?

The first row of scores shot up, the ones for technical merit:

"5.9, 5.9, 5.9, 5.8, 5.8, 5.9, 5.9, 5.8, 5.9."

Megan Faulkner's expression changed dramatically. Her face

brightened as if she had just been let in on the world's best secret. All of a sudden, it was Christmas morning in Kiss and Cry. Tara's coach from Houston saw that the little girl who skated around the Christmas tree in the Galleria Mall as recently as 1993 was about to do the unthinkable. The marks were that good.

The presentation marks jumped onto the television screen within moments.

Tara didn't look at the scores. She looked for the number of first-place ordinals that she won.

Six.

Out of nine.

She screeched.

The 1998 Olympic gold medalist leaped to her feet in joy.

In the stands, Mike Burg stared at the right-hand corner of the big scoreboard at the end of the rink above Kiss and Cry. Nothing appeared in that spot until the second set of marks was posted. The space was blank. He stared and stared.

The marks came up.

Two numbers and one letter popped into the corner:

6X1.

Six first-places.

The Olympic gold medal.

"Holy shit!" Burg screamed. "She did it."

Sitting on her couch at home, Lori Nichol didn't look for any numbers. She simply watched Tara, and saw her scream.

Immediately, Nichol knew.

She pictured two things.

Michelle Kwan at that exact moment.

And Frank Carroll's face.

Nichol wanted to cry.

A few moments later, she did.

Frank Carroll never saw the scores. He heard them come over the arena's public address system. He knew what Michelle had received, and he knew what he heard was better.

"Oh well," he said to no one, crestfallen. "Been there, done that."

He kept talking to himself.

"I guess I've got to go tell Michelle, find her and let her know."

He trudged down the hallway. It was one of the longest walks in his life.

He found Michelle. She was with her mother. She was crying.

Carroll didn't have to tell her anything.

After the sultry and unsmiling Maria Butyrskaia skated, and did her best to keep up with the teenagers at the advanced age of twenty-five, the order was set: Lipinski, Kwan, and Chen, winning her second consecutive Olympic bronze medal. Butyrskaia finished fourth.

Tara Lipinski soon climbed the medal podium, just as she had imagined she would when she played with the Tupperware bowls as a two-year-old in 1984, and was given a real gold medal. Michelle Kwan, her eyes red and her makeup gone from crying backstage, remained composed and bowed her head to receive her silver medal. The two U.S. flags were raised, and both girls stood still for the national anthem. Lipinski was giddy. Kwan, standing below and behind her, was dazed, but she was surviving.

Just how well she was coping became evident in the packed press conference room minutes later.

"I knew this competition wasn't going to be a piece of cake," she said. "I came here looking for a good performance, and I skated my best. I trained hard. There was nothing more I could have done. This might not be the color medal that I wanted, but I'll take it."

Kwan soon was talking about competing in the sport's Olympic side until 2002, about continuing to skate until the Salt Lake City Olympics. Lipinski was in a dream world, barely thinking of February 21.

"I'm happy," Kwan said. "C'est la vie, right? It's life, right? You never know what you're going to get."

A reporter asked the two girls to talk about the other. Ah-ha. The "rivalry" question.

Lipinski went first—Kwan deferred to her throughout the news conference—and talked about what a fabulous night it was and blurted out that Kwan had "skated great," even though she had not watched.

It was Kwan's turn. She took the microphone in her hand.

She looked to her right, directly into Lipinski's eyes.

"I like you, Tara."

The comment caught dozens of tired, cynical reporters completely off guard. They had always known Kwan was a class act. They had

watched her survive—and even thrive—through other disappoint-
ments, but this was something quite amazing. Not even an hour after
the most crushing defeat of her life, Michelle Kwan was already carrying on. And, in the process, she carried her sport to a new and
delightful level of sportsmanship.

Four years earlier, there was a whack on the knee.

Now, "I like you, Tara."

Lipinski smiled. She looked a little uncomfortable and didn't know
quite what to do, so she said nothing in return.

For all their outward displays of normalcy, Kwan was confused, and
Frank Carroll was too.

While Tara went to the Olympic Village and slept with her gold
medal, Michelle went to her hotel and cried some more.

What in the world had just happened to her? Kwan had been cautious, but what great skater wasn't careful at the Olympic Games?
Peggy Fleming and Scott Hamilton had not skated their best, but they
still won. In 1992, gold medalist Kristi Yamaguchi put her hand down
on one jump and doubled another. Her winning performance in 1992
would have earned her only the bronze medal in Nagano. Or, perhaps, fourth place.

Kwan's performance was so good, it would have won her every
other women's Olympic gold medal in history. She would have
defeated Oksana Baiul in 1994, Yamaguchi in 1992, Katarina Witt in
1988 and 1984, and on and on.

It was just her luck to run into Tara on the night of Tara's life. The
two girls participated in the most perfectly skated battle in the history
of Olympic figure skating. The Battle of the Brians (Boitano and
Orser) was sublime, but Orser made a mistake. The Witt–Debi
Thomas rivalry was wonderful, but neither had landed seven triple
jumps, and Thomas made several errors at the 1988 Games.

But Tara and Michelle stood up to the incredible pressure of being
the Games' most discussed athletes and did not flinch.

All kinds of coaches and judges and other skating experts believed
that if that kind of flawless battle occurred, Kwan would win it.
That's what judges for years had been saying to her through their
marks. Artistry breaks the tie in the long program, especially at the
Olympics. You're the artist, Michelle. You win.

What Michelle had—deep edges and gliding spirals and smooth,
seamless skating—was thought to be what the judges wanted. The
6.0s in Philadelphia told everyone this. No one mentioned anything

about triple–triple combinations. No one said a decision might come down to speed and smiles.

And yet, in the biggest upset in Olympic skating history, it did. The Kwan camp wondered about what might have been. If she only had skated faster, with more joy. If only the girl known for skating from her soul had not gotten so nervous that she covered up the very thing that made her so great. If she only had had the triple–triple. If, if, if . . .

But Kwan, Carroll, and Nichol weren't complaining. They were realists. They knew that, just like Nashville, Hamilton, and Lausanne, Kwan had opened the door just far enough to let Lipinski come charging through one more time.

"I didn't really let go," Kwan said. "In my mind, I was thinking I had to land every jump. I didn't want to make a mistake. This teaches me a lesson, that I need to become free and really enjoy the music and the performance and let myself go."

"That look in the eye," Frank Carroll said. " 'Going for the gold' is a good expression. It's not caution. It's abandonment."

It all came down to the delightful exuberance of a tiny teenager, and the understandable caution of a girl who has lived a little longer.

It's the difference between being fifteen and being seventeen, between having no fear, and knowing exactly what fear is. Two years earlier, Kwan won the world championships over Lu Chen by skating after her and going for every jump (she also had one of the most majestic artistic programs ever, "Salome").

Perhaps fifteen was becoming the perfect age to win in women's skating.

Isn't that almost exactly what the late Carlo Fassi predicted when the sport dumped compulsory school figures in 1990?

As he said in 1987, "If we cancel figures, it will be like gymnastics, with young girls who can do all the jumps at age thirteen and quit at age fifteen. I don't like gymnastics anymore. It's little muppets just tumbling around. Where is the beauty of that?"

The sport was changing dramatically, and Kwan was caught right in the middle of it. The poor kid; when the judges wanted an artist in 1995, she was a jumper. When they wanted a jumper in 1998, she was an artist. The rug was yanked out from underneath her in Nagano. Figure skating pulled a fast one on a young lady who could not have been a more loyal servant, a better role model, or a more worthy legend-in-waiting.

Skating's fascination with Tara Lipinski was, however, completely understandable. She took the judges' breath away. She was not the total package Kwan was, but she could jump, and she could tear across the ice, and she could remind everyone of just how great it was to be fifteen. She was having too much fun to be denied. Kwan, Carroll, and Nichol knew that, and respected it.

Over and over during the days leading up to the competition, both Tara and Michelle said they simply wanted to skate their best and see where that got them. They said that because they knew a figure skating decision always is a strange thing. It comes so quickly—the judges take no more than ten or fifteen seconds to punch in their marks—but it lasts forever. Lipinski won because six people she doesn't know thought she was better, while only three people thought Kwan was. Lipinski will forever be the Olympic gold medalist—mentioned in the same breath as Peggy Fleming and Dorothy Hamill—because of those judges' split-second decisions.

Nancy Kerrigan lives with a controversial 5–4 decision every day of her life. Now Kwan would have to do the same thing. If two judges had given Lipinski 5.8s instead of 5.9s for presentation, Kwan would have been the gold medalist. In the minds of Susan Johnson from the United States, Jan Hoffman of Germany, and Maria Miller from Poland, she was. It's significant that Johnson, asked to pick between her country's two girls, went with Kwan. And Hoffman's choice was rather predictable: He chose Baiul's artistry in the split decision with Kerrigan four years earlier.

The quandary the judges were in—whether to go with the better overall skater, or the one who came on like gangbusters that night—was noticeable a full day after the event ended.

"It's a pity you couldn't really have two gold medals," referee Sally Stapleford said after meeting with the judges.

"I wish there were two gold medals," Kwan said when she heard about Stapleford's comment, "but it wouldn't mean as much if there were two gold medals."

While the decision was a shock to skating's tradition-laden system, it was a godsend for those who had to try to defend figure skating as a mainstream sport. Never again could some guy holding a beer dismiss skating in the usual manner. He could never again say the sport was rigged. The ultimate upset had occurred. It wasn't a matter of resumés; skating had become like any other sport, where the winner was determined, based on what happened in one competition, on one night.

Lipinski pulled off the victory because everything went her way.

For more than two years, every move she and her parents and Mike Burg made turned out to be the right one. There wasn't an accidental step made by the Lipinskis; everything was planned perfectly. They desperately wanted the gold medal. And, with a little luck, they got it.

It began with their decision to move to Detroit to train with Richard Callaghan, whose serious, driven ways were perfect for the little jumping bean. But there was luck involved. Had Nicole Bobek not left Detroit weeks earlier for her next stop on the road, Tara certainly would not have come. No coach would take on a second contender in the same event a few weeks before the nationals.

There was another coincidence that made it possible for Tara to win in Nagano. It also involved Bobek.

Faced with the decision about whom to send to the 1996 world championships after Bobek withdrew from the San Jose nationals with an ankle injury, the U.S. Figure Skating Association's international committee almost replaced Lipinski with Bobek. By a 13–12 vote, it sent Tara. Had the committee not sent Lipinski to Edmonton—had just one person changed their vote—she would not have been "grandfathered" into the 1997 world championships in Lausanne, which she won. Had Tara not attended the 1996 and 1997 world championships, and had she not had the world title attached to her name, she would not have been taken as seriously by international judges at the 1998 Winter Olympics, and it's doubtful she would have won. But she did, and it all started with that 13–12 vote in a room in San Jose Arena twenty-five months before the Olympics.

Then there was the blind faith of Mike Burg. Despite withering criticism of his skater in the media, he pressed on, maintaining time and again that international judges loved Tara and would treat her more kindly than U.S. judges ever did. Munich showed him that; judges who were believed to be looking for artistry loved her jumping and her pizzazz. They were smitten.

As recently as two days before the women's short program in Nagano, he was chastising reporters for "not giving Tara a chance." He would browbeat anyone in sight to defend Tara.

Burg had predicted in 1995 that the third spot in the women's event at the 1996 nationals was "wide open." He was alone against the world in his belief that Tara could win that spot. Most skating people told him he was nuts. Tara couldn't come into the senior division and finish third her first year, they said.

Of course, Tara came into the senior division and immediately finished third.

Among the entire Lipinski gang, Burg was the only one who came out of Philadelphia with a smile on his face. He knew second place was fine at the 1998 nationals. He knew the pressure was off Tara. He knew Michelle would be the one in the spotlight. Tara was better as an underdog; both of them, Burg and Tara, loved creating havoc in their own worlds. Let Michelle be the favorite, Burg said. We'll see what happens on February 20.

Burg was right. He didn't know skating all that well, but he knew sports, and he knew human nature. Oksana Baiul taught him all he needed to know about where skating was headed. When she won the Olympic title at sixteen, Burg saw a whole new world open to him. Little girls as superstars. Prepubescent jumpers winning big titles, just as they did in gymnastics. He jumped into skating with both feet.

At fifteen, Tara became the youngest Olympic figure skating champion ever. It didn't hurt that she hit the Olympic Games before she reached puberty. For Burg, having a little girl win in women's skating was all part of the master plan.

Burg knew, as did most skating people, that Lipinski had some built-in advantages in 1998 that she would never have again. Without her eye-popping triple loop–triple loop combination, Tara likely would not have won the gold. But how long after the Games would Tara have that combination jump in her repertoire? What would happen when Tara went through puberty? With a few extra pounds on her hips and thighs, would the loop–loop come as easily?

"It's tough on the body and tough on the mind," Burg said of Olympic division skating. "Do you want that lifestyle or do you want a performing, entertaining lifestyle?"

The question was the same one that was put to Baiul four years earlier. She chose the entertaining lifestyle. Her life became a "mess," she said.

Burg vowed that would never happen to Lipinski.

"If she was the queen of England," he said, "she'd probably skate four hours a day."

He said that when they made their inevitable post-Olympic trip to New York for a tour of the morning shows, he had already been warned to schedule ice time.

Nonetheless, when a child reaches the ultimate goal in her life before she becomes a junior in high school, problems can be very difficult to avoid. What's the new goal? How can you get excited about Skate America or Nations Cup? What's left to prove?

"We said, 'Let's do the right thing,' " Burg said. "We've seen some bad moves made by some big-name skaters. Tara has seen those mistakes. She knows them. She's not going to make them."

Burg didn't mention Baiul by name, but the reporters who had him surrounded knew who he meant.

Burg was walking a tightrope. He was preaching care and caution, yet he had never lived a careful or cautious day in his life. Before the Games, he had broken new endorsement ground for Lipinski: Her face was on the back of the "skating Barbie" box. She was on Minute Maid cartons. She had a clothing deal with DKNY. She was tied into Chevrolet, and she couldn't even drive.

With the gold medal, the sky was the limit. Ten million dollars, maybe fifteen.

Why not bigger endorsements? Why not Hollywood?

As for Baiul, it turned out that one of the most unfortunate decisions she made was signing a $1.5 million deal with a promoter to skate in ten made-for-TV events in the eighteen months following the 1994 Games. She dislocated her kneecap prior to the first event, yet she kept on skating.

She never was the same again.

Who was that promoter?

Mike Burg.

Sally Stapleford was hoping not to lose either Tara or Michelle from the Olympic division of skating.

"It would be sad for them and sad for the sport if they walk away prematurely," she said. "They have so much potential and they are so young. It would be sad if they looked back in ten years in regret and said, 'What if I had stayed in?'"

The day after the competition, there were hints of what the two girls wanted to do. Kwan sounded definite about the 2002 Olympics moments after she won the silver medal, but, by the next day, she said she would take her future "one thing at a time." She did say she would attend the 1998 world championships in Minneapolis in little more than a month to try to regain the title she lost in Lausanne to Lipinski. She was excited about that.

Lipinski said she couldn't commit to anything. It was doubtful she would head into the strange world of professional skating at such a young age. Then again, Lipinski was breaking all the old rules. The girl who was the ultimate skating competitor was pressed on the subject of attending the 1998 worlds. She didn't have an answer. She said she hadn't given it any thought.

One day later, she said she would be there.

But there was a risk involved in showing up to face Kwan, just as there would be in anything Lipinski did the rest of her skating career. What if she lost to Michelle? The contest had been very close in Nagano. Even American fans who sided with Lipinski knew two things: that Kwan was the more complete skater, and that they adored the way she handled the disappointment of coming in second.

Kwan would be a sentimental favorite in Minneapolis. Would it tarnish the gold medal, even a little bit, if Lipinski lost to her there?

On the other hand, if Lipinski beat her again, she could claim that the Olympic gold medal certainly was no fluke.

These were the interesting decisions a fifteen-year-old Olympic gold medalist would have to make.

Kwan, too, was in an unusual position. Beloved, but the runner-up. Better all year, but second on one night. The one most people wanted to watch, but the one without the title.

This sounded extremely familiar. Kwan had heard many stories about someone like that.

Janet Lynn was back in her life.

Like Kwan, Lynn went to the Olympic Games in Japan and didn't win. She finished third, forever endearing herself to skating fans by smiling when she fell on a sit spin.

Kwan didn't fall, but she reacted to her troubles the same way Lynn did.

Michelle Kwan and Janet Lynn: two of the most revered skaters ever, and not a gold medal between them.

So they pushed on, the two American teenagers, heading to a lifetime of fame and fortune and enchanting decisions. As for the 2002 Olympics, who could know? When a sixteen-year-old and fifteen-year-old were the two most recent Olympic champions, it wasn't very encouraging. Four years before the '94 and '98 Games, no one had heard of Oksana Baiul or Tara Lipinski. Wasn't it likely that the Olympic gold medalist in 2002 was just another little nobody in 1998, a delightful eleven-year-old like Elizabeth Kwon from Fairfax Ice Arena, only beginning to find her way?

Why would Kwan and Lipinski have any reason to believe figure skating would allow a nineteen-year-old and twenty-one-year-old to battle for the gold in four years' time?

Nonetheless, Kwan was intrigued.

"I have my chance in 2002," she said. "If I want it bad enough, I'm going to go and try again."

Six days after Kwan won the silver medal, Lori Nichol flew to California to begin working with Michelle and Frank Carroll on Michelle's program for the spring tour, as well as to start discussing the upcoming 1998–99 season.

There were 1,442 days until the Opening Ceremonies in Salt Lake City. It was a long time: time enough for one particular teenager to stay in skating, or to go to college, or to turn pro, or to try something new.

But Carroll and Nichol knew that if Kwan was even remotely considering the next Olympic Games, they might as well start working.

There was no time to waste.

1998 Olympic Results

WOMEN

1. Tara Lipinski, United States
2. Michelle Kwan, United States
3. Lu Chen, China
4. Maria Butyrskaia, Russia
5. Irina Slutskaia, Russia
6. Vanessa Gusmeroli, France
7. Elena Sokolova, Russia
8. Tatiana Malinina, Uzbekistan
9. Elena Liashenko, Ukraine
10. Surya Bonaly, France
    Others
17. Nicole Bobek, United States

MEN

1. Ilia Kulik, Russia
2. Elvis Stojko, Canada
3. Philippe Candeloro, France
4. Todd Eldredge, United States
5. Alexei Yagudin, Russia
6. Steven Cousins, Great Britain
7. Michael Weiss, United States
8. Zhengxin Guo, China
9. Michael Tyllesen, Denmark
10. Viacheslav Zagorodniuk, Ukraine

PAIRS

1. Oksana Kazakova and Artur Dmitriev, Russia
2. Elena Berezhnaia and Anton Sikharulidze, Russia
3. Mandy Woetzel and Ingo Steuer, Germany
4. Kyoko Ina and Jason Dungjen, United States
5. Xue Shen and Hongbo Zhao, China
6. Sarah Abitbol and Stephane Bernadis, France
7. Marina Eltsova and Andrei Bushkov, Russia
8. Jenni Meno and Todd Sand, United States
9. Peggy Schwarz and Mirko Muller, Germany
10. Dorota Zagorska and Mariusz Siudek, Poland

DANCE

1. Pasha Grishuk and Evgeni Platov, Russia
2. Anjelika Krilova and Oleg Ovsiannikov, Russia
3. Marina Anissina and Gwedel Peizerat, France
4. Shae-Lynn Bourne and Victor Kraatz, Canada
5. Irina Lobacheva and Ilia Averbukh, Russia
6. Barbara Fusar-Poli and Maurizio Margaglio, Italy
7. Elizabeth Punsalan and Jerod Swallow, United States
8. Margarita Drobiazko and Povilas Vanagas, Lithuania
9. Irina Romanova and Igor Yaroshenko, Ukraine
10. Kati Winkler and Rene Lohse, Germany
    Others
21. Jessica Joseph and Charles Butler, United States

ACKNOWLEDGMENTS

Dozens of skaters, coaches, choreographers, judges, agents, and officials allowed me unprecedented access to their work and their thoughts during one of the most important years of their lives. Without their kindness and help, I could not have written this book.

I especially want to acknowledge the following people: Lori Nichol, Audrey Weisiger, Joe Inman, Tamara Moskvina, Frank Carroll, Tonia Kwiatkowski and her family, Carol Heiss Jenkins, Brian Wright, Mike Burg, Shep Goldberg, Michael Weiss and his family, Michelle Kwan and her family, Brian Boitano, Linda Leaver, Janet Lynn Salomon, Jirina Ribbens, Caroline Silby, Michael Rosenberg, Alexei Urmanov, Alexei Mishin, Rudy and Laura Galindo, Scott Davis, Nancy Kerrigan, Jerry Solomon, Peggy Fleming, Jean Hall, the Tew family, Heather Linhart, Kristin Matta, Lynn Plage, Sally Stapleford, Cindy Lang, Stuart Ridgway, Linda Reynolds, Michael Cunningham, Sandra Bezic, Susie Wynne, Tom George, Leah Adams, Henri and Anna King, Carrie Bunzendahl, and Lenore Kay.

Friends who took on the role of editor/advisor/critic include Tracy Kerdyk, Victoria Churchville, Michelle Kaufman, Jeff Barker, Tony Reid, Steve Woodward, and Marty Aronoff. They came through for me when I needed them the most. Thanks also to Sandy Evans, Steve Hoffman, Chris Spolar, Sandy Davis, Bobbye Pratt, Craig Miller, Craig Fenech, Meredith Geisler, Leslie King, Jill Schuker, Susan Reed, Laurie Saxton, and David Hansen.

From the press room, I want to acknowledge my colleagues and friends who went out of their way to help make this book better: Philip Hersh, Jo-Ann Barnas, Penny Dain, Debbie Becker, Jere Longman, Diane Pucin, Terry Foster, Johnette Howard, Filip Bondy, Amy Rosewater, Lesley Visser, Bonnie DeSimone, Randy Starkman, Mark Starr, Jody Meacham, Mark McDonald, John Powers, Ed Swift, Ann Killion, Nancy Armour, Barry Wilner, Chris Carmody, Kathie Farrell, Jeff Greenholtz, Mike Penner, Tatjana Flade, Meg Streeter Lauck, Lana Sherman, Yvonne Gomez, Lois Elfman, Mark Lund, Steve Milton, Steve Buffery, David Winner, and Mike Moran.

Many thanks to the editors and staff of *USA Today,* for whom I wrote during the Olympic season. Monte Lorell, Janice Lloyd, Joan Murphy, and Porter Binks were especially helpful throughout the year.

Thank you to my friends at the *Washington Post,* particularly Assistant Managing Editor/Sports George Solomon. Some of the events described in this book, including quotes from the Lipinski family, first appeared in my stories in the *Post.*

I also wish to thank ABC News, particularly the people at *Good Morning America Sunday,* for my various sports assignments. Bret Marcus deserves special mention for his unwavering encouragement.

Every step of the way, I was supported by my terrific editor, Lisa Drew, whose calm, reasoned manner made writing this book a joy. I can't imagine a better person to work with on a project such as this. Lisa's assistant, Blythe Grossberg, came through in dozens of ways as well. And Pat Eisemann, skating expert that she is, gave me several top-notch ideas. Thanks also to Jay Schweitzer and Phyllis Heller. The people at Scribner are a delight; it once again was an honor for me to work with them.

And then there's Chris Calhoun, my agent and my friend. By taking care of business with his usual flair, Chris made my job very easy. And he made me laugh at all the right times.

Finally, I want to acknowledge my family. Thanks to my two sisters, Kate and Amy, and my brother, Jim, for their unconditional love and support. Amy is a great editor, and Kate's wonderful common sense usually keeps me out of trouble. Jim still thinks hockey is the better sport on ice, but we're working on him.

Thanks also to Tom and Angela for their interest, support, and kindness.

And a special thank you goes to my mom and dad. Years ago, they bought me my first pair of skates.

Now, they do a fantastic job videotaping skating broadcasts.

Among other things.

INDEX